PELICAN BOOKS

A 204

THE SYMPHONY

EDITED BY RALPH HILL

Ex Libris

Ann Smallbone

The Symphony

EDITED BY RALPH HILL

PENGUIN BOOKS

Penguin Books Ltd, Harmondsworth, Middlesex
U.S.A.: Penguin Books Inc., 3300 Clipper Mill Road, Baltimore 11, Md
AUSTRALIA: Penguin Books Pty Ltd, 762 Whitehorse Road,
Mitcham, Victoria

—

First published 1949
Reprinted 1950, 1951, 1954, 1956, 1958, 1961

—

Made and printed in Great Britain
by C. Nicholls & Company Ltd

CONTENTS

INTRODUCTION

THIS book on *The Symphony* is not intended to appeal to the musicologist nor yet to the untrained listener who is not prepared to do some thinking about his music. The listener who knows what he likes and likes what he knows and considers that technical knowledge is a handicap to the true appreciation of music may well turn away from this volume. It is not for him (nor her).

It is generally acknowledged by modern critics that formal analysis as practised by the pedants of the nineteenth century was a worthless, inartistic study, which had no aesthetic value whatsoever. The dirty brown-covered tomes of Ebenezer Prout are monuments to the harm music has suffered at the hands of the pedantic analyst. Pity the many poor creatures who learned from the Prouts to hate music, as many learned to hate poetry from the Prouts of literature. I wonder what old Ebenezer (he ought to have been invented by Dickens) would have said had he lived to hear J. A. Westrup, Oxford Professor of Music, pronounce over the radio (during the B.B.C.'s Jubilee week) that 'Music is first and foremost something to be enjoyed. The object of "musical appreciation" is simply to help people to enjoy music more. But it may easily fall into the error of supposing that information about music is valuable for its own sake.' Walter Sickert also wrote: 'Pleasure, and pleasure alone, is the proper purpose of art.' I imagine that old Ebenezer would have considered Westrup and Sickert fit only for eternal damnation!

Now the enjoyment and pleasure of music is not only a matter of lovely tunes, stirring rhythms, and gorgeous orchestral colouring. There are subtleties of harmonic change and tonality, of structural detail and development of themes, and of instrumental treatment that are not necessarily apparent even after repeated hearings of a work. It is

not that these important details are made purposely
obscure; in fact they are sometimes extraordinarily obvious,
so obvious that the wood cannot be seen for the trees. Any-
how, a knowledge and understanding of these subtleties I
have mentioned will help people to enjoy music more, more
intensely and more completely.

It is to such people who think about music and want to
study the composers' thought and processes that this book
is addressed. In other words, to intelligent listeners. A
knowledge of the elementary principles upon which the art
of music is based is of course necessary. Most intelligent
listeners have already acquired such knowledge. Those who
have not can easily do so.

The chief purpose of this book is to provide a guide to the
repertoire of the symphony – the standard repertoire of
symphonies that you are likely to hear most frequently
in the concert hall, over the air, or on the gramophone
record.

The fact that there was a limit to the space at my disposal
meant that I had to be selective. First, I ruled out the
symphonies of those eminent dead composers which are
rarely performed. I refer to such composers as Bizet,
Balakirev, Chausson, Rimsky-Korsakov, Roussel, Saint-
Saens. Why, then, you might ask, did you include the
symphonies of Liszt? The answer is that it is an Editor's
privilege to give the casting vote on borderland cases, and
although Liszt's symphonies are neglected I consider them
to be of greater historical importance than those of the
above-excluded composers. Secondly, I ruled out the
symphonies of living composers under the age of sixty,
whose symphonic work was incomplete and perhaps not
yet established. Thirdly, it was obviously impossible to
include all the symphonies of Haydn and Mozart, and
unnecessary to include the early symphonies of Schubert,
Mendelssohn, and Dvořák. The biggest difficulty was to
include a fair and adequate representation of Bruckner,
Mahler, and Bax, whose long and elaborately conceived
symphonies have earned an important place in the development of the late-Romantic Symphony, but are too rarely

performed. Some readers may consider that less than justice has been done to these three composers. If so it is I who must take the blame, rather than my contributors.

Each contributor was assigned a composer, whose symphonies were in both his head and his heart. He was briefed to go his own way in the handling of his task, keeping merely to a skeleton plan of reference. The result is interesting because each contributor has brought an individuality of treatment to his commentary on the general plan and outstanding details of a composer's symphonies, and has thus given great variety to the book as a whole. With the exception of two or three chapters where the assistance of a score is essential if you are to understand the full significance of the text, these comment-aries could be studied with profit during a gramophone performance without the printed music. The use of the latter, however, is in all cases preferable and desirable. It may be mentioned that each set of commentaries is pre-ceded by an Introduction summing up the main character-istics of the composer's symphonic style, and at the end of each chapter there is a selection of music-type illustrations, which are referred to in the text.

I should like to thank the following publishers for kindly giving me permission to reproduce certain extracts from their copyright publications:

Boosey & Hawkes Ltd. (Mahler, Symphonies Nos. 4 and 9).

Breitkopf & Härtel, Leipzig. (Sibelius, Symphonies Nos. 1, 2, and 4).

Chappell & Company, Ltd. (Bax, Symphonies Nos. 3 and 6).

J. Curwen & Sons, Ltd. (Vaughan Williams, Symphony No. 3).

Wilhelm Hansen, Copenhagen. (Sibelius, Symphonies Nos. 5, 6, and 7).

Alfred Lengnick & Company, Ltd. (Dvořák, Symphonies Nos. 1, 2, 3, and 5).

Novello & Company, Ltd. (Elgar, Symphonies Nos. 1 and 2, and Dvořák, Symphony No. 4, Op. 88).

Oxford University Press. (Vaughan Williams, Symphonies Nos. 4, 5, and 6, and Sibelius, Symphony No. 3).

Schott & Company, Ltd. (Rachmaninov, Symphonies Nos. 2 and 3).

Stainer & Bell, Ltd. (Vaughan Williams, Symphonies Nos. 1 and 2).

I also take this opportunity of offering my sincere thanks to my contributors for their willing, friendly, and authoritative co-operation.

London, S.W. 15   RALPH HILL

I

The Symphony and Its Development

RALPH HILL

SYMPHONY, like most words we use in every-day conversation, has enlarged and changed its meaning through the ages. Carlyle used it in its poetic sense when he wrote that 'their domestic symphony was liable to furious flaws'. Some musically illiterate people still use the word in its now obsolete and archaic connotation of music that is concordant or euphonious – euphonious, of course, to *their* ears.

However, the word symphony was first used in music to describe a passage or passages for instruments alone that served either as an introduction to or an interlude in a vocal work. For example, the introductory *sinfonia* for three flutes to Peri's opera *Eurydice* (1600) and the interlude for orchestra entitled 'Pastoral Symphony' in Handel's *Messiah*.

When the orchestral introduction to Italian opera was extended and became an important instrumental piece of music in its own right the word *symphony* gave way to *overture*. Composers also worked out a formal scheme for these overtures consisting of three clearly defined and melodically varied sections: A (fast) – B (slow) – C (fast). This formula became the distinguishing feature of what was called the *Italian Overture* in contradistinction to the *French Overture* of which the formal scheme consisted of two well defined sections: A (slow) – B (fast in fugal style) that was sometimes amplified by a return to A, or the addition of a new section C (slow) or of one or more independent pieces in dance forms.

If some of these Italian overtures, which were imbued with the gay spirit of *opera buffa,* became popular (despite the chatter of the audiences) they were often performed as separate items in the concert room. Thus the formal scheme of the Italian overture was eventually adopted for a distinctive

type of composition written specifically for the concert
room, and sinfonia or symphony was the title given to such
music. It is worth noting in passing that the Symphony and
the solo (which derived from the Italian operatic aria) both
originated in Italian opera, but after their inception were
developed and perfected by the German school of composers.

During the second half of the 18th Century when the
homophonic (or harmonic) instrumental style had become
firmly established, it brought about a new conception
of music, a conception based on the aristocratic and
bourgeois idea of amusement and entertainment – that
is to say, a style of instrumental music conceived for
performance in the courtyard, garden, concert room, and
private chamber. At first these varied intentions were by no
means clear in the actual style of the music, which were
often interchangeable. It was therefore inevitable that there
should also be a certain amount of confusion over the use of
the terms applied to the variety of forms of instrumental
music that were being evolved. There were the Sonata,
Suite, Overture, Symphony, Cassation, Serenade, Nocturne
(Notturno), Divertimento, and the chamber Trios, Quartets, Quintets, etc. Although these terms were often used
indiscriminately two basic formal types emerge – the suite-
type and the sonata-type. The suite-type consisting chiefly
of a string of dance movements (perhaps opening or closing
with a march) is represented by the Serenade, Nocturne,
Divertimento, and Cassation; while the sonata-type consisting usually of three or four movements of a non-dance-
like character (with the exception of a minuet movement)
embraced the Overture, Symphony and the various chamber music combinations. At first there is little to differentiate between the respective styles of orchestral music
written for the concert room and music written for chamber
ensembles – the chief difference was the number of instru-
mentalists employed.

For example, Haydn's early string quartets could be
performed equally well and effectively by a small ensemble
as by four solo players. In 1755 Haydn was invited by a

wealthy Viennese music-lover to take charge of his private orchestra at his country residence, and for this orchestra Haydn wrote a series of eighteen works for strings with *ad libitum* parts for oboes and horns, and called them notturni, divertimenti, or cassations, all of which are now published as string quartets in three sets of six, forming the Opp. 1 – 3. The first set was introduced at Paris in 1764 as 'Six Symphonies or Quartets for two violins, alto viola, and bass'. Haydn's instrumental treatment is very simple: the themes are given to the first and second violins, the 'cello plays groups of reiterated notes which provide the basis of the harmony and the viola doubles the 'cello at appropriate harmonic intervals. The result is virtually a violin duet with a bare viola and 'cello harmonic background. Opp. 1 – 2 contain five movements: Allegro-Minuet No. 1 – Andante – Minuet No. 2 – Allegro; but in Op. 3 the second minuet is dropped.

Music in the open air was a popular form of entertainment in Austria. The occasion might be a garden party, a public festival or function, or a serenade. A Viennese almanac dated 1794 describes the atmosphere of the last-mentioned nocturnal entertainment: 'On fine summer nights you may come upon serenades in the streets at all hours. They are not, as in Italy, a mere matter of a singer and a guitar. Here serenades are not meant for declarations of love, for which the Viennese have better opportunities. Such night music may be given by a trio or quartet of string instruments or a wind ensemble, frequently by an entire orchestra, and the most ambitious serenades are performed. The evening before the name-day of some fair lady will produce a lot of this kind of entertainment. It is just these nocturnal musicales that demonstrate the universality and the greatness of the love of music; for no matter how late at night they may take place one soon sees people at their open windows, and within a few minutes the musicians are surrounded by a crowd of listeners who rarely depart until the serenade has come to an end.'

Mozart's Notturno (Serenade No. 8), which consists of three dance-like movements, was written for some such occasion, and was originally scored for four orchestras each consisting of two violins, double bass, and two horns. The work exploits a cleverly devised triple echo effect. The first orchestra plays a complete tune, the second orchestra repeats, or rather echoes, the latter half of the tune, the third orchestra echoes the last quarter, while the fourth orchestra repeats the last eighth. The same process is then repeated with a fresh tune. In his *Serenata Notturno* Mozart employs two orchestras, of which one consists of two violins, violas, and double bass, while the other has two violins, viola, 'cello, and drums.

There were two kinds of Serenade: one for performance out of doors, the other for indoors. The first, which was usually scored for wind instruments, was essentially light in style, the second was more serious and elaborate, in keeping with its chief purpose of celebrating an important marriage ceremony or adding distinction and diversion to the solemn proceedings of prize-giving day at a university. The Serenade seems to have had no fixed number of movements, but one of them often took the form of a miniature concerto for one solo instrument or a concertante for several solo instruments. During the last quarter of the 18th century the concertante style became very popular, particularly in Paris, and the *Sinfonia Concertante* was specially favoured. The *Sinfonia Concertante* combined certain characteristics of both the symphony and the concerto and was designed to show off the virtuosity of one or more brilliant players. In 1770 when Mozart visited Paris he was asked to write for the four wind virtuosi of the famous Mannheim orchestra a 'symphonie concertante pour la flute de Wendling, le haut-bois de Ramm, le cor de Punto et le bassoon de Ritter'. Mozart, however, substituted a clarinet for the flute.

The origin of the term Cassation is obscure and uncertain, but it belongs to the serenade or divertimento class. It comprises seven or eight movements and was intended to be played at banquets. It was also known to lighten occasionally the solemnities of a university gathering. Occasionally it was featured at open-air functions.

I have tried to describe the musical soil in which the

symphony was nurtured, so now let us examine the symphony itself in its early and later manifestations. The development of the symphony runs parallel with the development of the sonata and is intimately and essentially connected with the foundation, expansion, and perfection of the modern orchestra. Perhaps the most gifted and outstanding pioneer in the early development of the piano sonata, symphony, and concerto was C. P. E. Bach (1714–88), son of Johann Sebastian, who for the greater part of his life worked in Berlin and Hamburg, and whose harpsichord sonatas Haydn carefully analysed and studied when a youth.

In the sonata and symphony C. P. E. Bach adopted the three movement plan of the Italian Overture, but in matters of construction and formal symmetry he added importance and interest to the first movement, which became the pattern for the most vital and highly organized movement (usually the first) or movements in the sonata, symphony, and the kindred forms of chamber music. Reduced to a mechanical formula the procedure of early sonata-form was as follows:* (A) *Exposition:* Theme in tonic key, subsidiary passage-work, modulation to the key of the dominant or that of relative major or minor; (B) *Digression:* allusion to the opening theme in the new contrasting key, and then a series of passages modulating freely; (C) *Recapitulation:* restatement of the theme with some slight changes all within the confines of the tonic key. The foregoing is no more than a 'mechanical formula' as the infinite variation of detail and of personal method of composers, varying even from work to work, constituted the actual living and continuous process of the development of sonata-form.

At this stage the appearance of the contrasting key in the *Exposition* did not mean the introduction of new thematic material, the material used was either a mere extension of the opening theme or a string of fragmentary melodic phrases. But composers soon began to introduce either a

* Some critics, and rightly I think, define Symphony and Sonata as styles rather than as forms, which suggest a set pattern or design, such as the sonnet or the parallelogram.

definite second theme or a series of melodic phrases or sentences of a more definite character, which gave greater emphasis to the change of key. What I have called the *Digression* was turned into a primitive *Development* section, which often started off with an allusion to the first theme in the contrasting key followed by its expansion, and then free modulation. The *Recapitulation* was entirely concerned with the re-establishment of the tonic key, and the first and second themes are restated in that order, both in that key.

The exploitation of key contrast or colour has been aptly described by Professor Gerald Abraham as the "mainspring" of instrumental music during the great classical period, which is summed up in the work of Haydn, Mozart, Beethoven, and Schubert. The principle of key as opposed to mode was firmly and finally established by Bach, and henceforth it dominated the whole conception of music. It has continued to persist up to the present day, although the encroachment and extension of chromaticism during the 19th century and the rival claims to the dictatorship of the major and minor scale system by whole-tonality, polytonality, and atonality during the 20th century have somewhat dulled, if not in some cases destroyed, our feeling for and perception of key. The contrast and complex development of themes and subjects*, coupled with an equally complex scheme of key relationship characterized the methods of symphonists from Beethoven onwards.

In passing, it is interesting to note that in opera Mozart recognized the dramatic possibilities of well calculated key schemes worked out on symphonic lines. Discussing Mozart's operatic finales, Professor D. J. Grout says that 'each finale is a unique form, resulting from the translation of a dramatic action into symphonically conceived music by a master of that style. They are, consequently, invaluable

* Theme and subject are two very loosely-used terms. A theme is a single and complete melodic idea, while a subject in a sonata or symphony may consist of several themes or subsidiary ideas grouped together. The first movements of Brahms's symphonies are built on subjects rather than themes. The theme has been compared to the sentence and the subject to the paragraph.

sources for study of the principles (as distinct from the patterns) of symphonic form in the classical period.'*

Describing some of the problems that the early classical
composers had to solve Professor Abraham says: 'in the
early days of classical sonata-form the passages of transition
from one subject to another, one key to another, were apt
to be perfunctory: effected by scales and empty or at least
non-thematic, passage-work; it never occurred to the composers that joins were features to be concealed. It did occur
to later composers; they make their transitional passages
more and more from bits of actual thematic material; they
use all their technical craft to embroider over cadences –
the punctuation marks of music – and to produce at least
the semblance of continuously woven texture, not of pieces
of material sewn together.' Abraham goes on to warn us, I
am glad to say, not to assume that historical development
and technical progress necessarily heighten aesthetic value.
If the seams are clearly to be seen but are beautifully made
they can be as aesthetically justified as a join that has been
made by an invisible process.

Returning to C. P. E. Bach, it must not be thought for
one moment that he was without any gifted rivals working
and experimenting in the field of symphony and sonata.
There was, for example, his brother and pupil, J. C.
Bach, who worked most of his life in London and as a symphonist influenced the young Mozart. There were also a
group of composers in Paris, and a group in northern
Italy headed by G. B. Sammartini (c. 1704–74), whose
work had some influence in fixing the style and form of the
symphony. His symphonies thus provide a link with the
Italian 'Sinfonia avanti l'opera'. (Incidentally, there is too
great a tendency among musical historians to claim the
symphony as a German invention.) Then there were
Boccherini, Dittersdorf, Gossec and more than fifty other
composers of equal and lesser importance working in Germany and greater Austria. Among these was a group of composers who worked at the court of the Duke of Mannheim.

* Donald Jay Grout. *A Short History of Opera*, Vol. I (Oxford
University Press, 1947).

Duke Carl Theodor (1724–99) was an outstanding patron of the arts and he turned Mannheim into a centre of German culture. He spent a fabulous amount of money on artistic and scientific institutions, museums, and libraries, and at his court employed some of the finest musicians and artists in Europe. The Mannheim School of symphonic composers consisted of about a dozen highly skilled musicians, most, if not all, of whom were members of the orchestra. The two outstanding members were Johann Stamitz (1717–57) and his son Carl (1746–1801).

The Mannheim Orchestra, which in 1777 consisted of 10 first violins, 10 second violins, 4 violas, 4 'cellos, 4 basses, 2 flutes, 2 oboes, 2 clarinets, 4 bassoons, 2 horns, 2 trumpets, and drums, was famous throughout Europe. Its playing was characterized by its fiery spirit, excellence of ensemble, uniformity of bowing, and beautiful phrasing. In 1775 Dr Burney, the English musical historian and critic, wrote: 'Since the discovery which the genius of Stamitz first made, every effect has been tried which such an aggregate of sound can produce: it was here that the *Crescendo* and *Diminuendo* had birth: and the *Piano*, which before was chiefly used as an echo, with which it was generally synonymous, as well as the *Forte*, were found to be musical colours which had their shades, as much as red or blue in painting.'

Both the technical and artistic quality of the playing and the size of the Mannheim Orchestra were exceptional. The normal orchestra of the period consisted of strings, oboes, and horns supplemented by some other instruments, such as flutes, bassoons, trumpets (and later clarinets) if and when necessary or available. It took the greater part of the eighteenth century to establish a full and properly balanced wind ensemble: for a long time composers of symphony used wind instruments merely to reinforce the strings at moments of climax, to underline strong rhythmic pulsations, or sustain the harmony; only gradually were they given independence and allowed to become melodists in their own right. In a series of articles on *The Founders of the Symphony* A. E. F. Dickinson* draws attention to the fact that the orchestra

* *Monthly Musical Record*, 1947–8

of the Viennese composer Wagenseil (1715-1777) 'is usually strings with horns *ad lib* – no oboes – but a Symphony in D dated 1746 is for strings, oboes, horns or trumpets, and drums. Moreover, the *andante* is for strings and flutes. The alteration of wood-wind within a symphony was common. The oboes, the descant shawms, were the traditional *ripieno* instruments, in company with the strings, but the possibilities of the flute as a soloist were recognized and quickly led to whole symphony parts for oboes or flutes, the oboe having nothing particular to recommend it in ensemble except its penetrating quality. It is clear also that in Bach's time many players could play both instruments.'

The early symphonists favoured three-movement symphonies. However, about 1740, G. M. Monn, a Viennese composer, wrote a symphony consisting of an Allegro, a slow movement in the style of an aria, a minuet, and a final Allegro. The inclusion of a minuet was an innovation, and this four-movement scheme was later generally adopted.

It is obvious from all this intense activity that neither Haydn nor Mozart* had anything to do with creating the symphony and formulating its early principles of design as it was once commonly supposed. Like most other things the development of the symphony shows that it was the result of a slow and varied process of evolution, the beginnings of which, like the source of a great river, were fed from numerous small tributaries. As we have seen, Haydn's early symphonies were modelled on the works of his older

* Mozart was also directly influenced by the Italian and Viennese symphonists. Referring to Mozart's Symphony No. 27 in G (K. 199) composed at Salzburg in 1773 when he was 17 years of age, G. de Saint-Foix says in his book *The Symphonies of Mozart* (Dobson, 1947): 'Did Mozart, on reaching Vienna, intend to complete the set of Italian overtures written on his return from Milan? This is not unlikely, for a Sinfonia in G major (K. 199), with the *Andante grazioso* typical of this set, fits absolutely into the framework of these overtures. But at the same time this curious instrumental piece, brilliant and Italian in style at first, shows such peculiarly Viennese qualities that we have at times the impression of hearing echoes of the orchestra of Johann Strauss. Rhythms of Viennese dances follow each other in all three movements and – a significant point – the finale opens with a sort of fugato that soon takes on a waltz rhythm; decidedly we are in Vienna.'

contemporaries, particularly C. P. E. Bach, while Mozart began by following in the footsteps of J. C. Bach. Once the two great composers had mastered the principles of sonata-form and realized its possibilities, to say nothing of the possibilities of orchestral treatment, both turned out a more or less continuous stream of symphonies which for invention, imagination, and expressiveness easily surpassed anything that had been produced by the most gifted of their contemporaries. Indeed, Mozart's last three symphonies and most of Haydn's last series of twelve (London) symphonies remain within the technical limitations of their period unsurpassed masterpieces.

Haydn and Mozart gave considerable musical and dramatic significance to the Introduction and Coda, and both used their imaginative genius to make the *Development* a real test of intellectual power pursued to an aesthetic end. It was not until the nineteenth century that the symphony was released from the bondage of the keyboard continuo part which was a relic of another age and conception of music. In polyphonic vocal music the bass 'thread' was vital to the whole texture, and the harmonic conception in homophonic music also demanded the use of the continuo as a prop for the harmony, which was distributed over the whole ensemble, or rather texture, of the music. Directly composers of the early classical symphony realized that the simple harmonies could be built up and sustained not only by the strings, but even more effectively by wind instruments, the harpsichord with its figured bass accompaniments became redundant.

The development of the Symphony from the time of Beethoven, who brought the classical style of symphonic writing to its most perfect and highly organized state, up to the tonal monsters of Mahler shows the gradual change from homogeneity to heterogeneity, of increasing elaboration and complexity and deviation from the essential purities of the classical style. Furthermore, the ever increasing range of colouristic effect made possible by the development of harmony and the mechanical perfection of wind instruments, and the subsequently increased technical

proficiency of every kind of instrumentalist, offered to the
composer new resources of virtuosity and expression, which
were the touchstones of the romantic *Zeitgeist* that so dominated 19th century thought and feeling. But as the orchestra
grew in size, so the symphony also grew in length, and the
internal structure changed and paid only lip-service to the fundamental principles of sonata-form, as you can see by com-
paring the analyses in this book of the symphonies of Liszt,
Mahler, and Sibelius with those of Beethoven and Brahms.

C. P. E. Bach, the Mannheim School of composers,
Haydn, and Mozart were the chief instigators in the final
formation of the properly balanced classical symphonic
orchestra, which ideally consisted of 8 or 10 1st violins, 8 or
10 2nd violins, 4 violas, 4 'cellos, 4 basses, 2 flutes, 2 oboes,
2 clarinets, 2 bassoons, 2 horns, 2 trumpets, and drums.*
Beethoven wrote for such an orchestra and for special
occasions (Ninth Symphony) added double bassoon, piccolo,
two more horns, and trombones. From then onwards four
horns and three trombones were added permanently. Except
for an increasing number of strings, the Beethoven orchestra
continued to be the standard orchestra even up to the
present day. Berlioz, Wagner, Mahler, Strauss, and many
other composers of our own time pursued the path of
Gargantua and created a fashion for the *colossal,* which has
now declined and has been placed in its proper perspective.
After all, size in itself is no criterion of aesthetic and intellectual values. If it were so then Beethoven's Fifth Symphony would be an inferior work of musical art to Mahler's
Sixth Symphony, which demands an orchestra of 16 1st
violins, 16 2nd violins, 12 violas, 12 'cellos, 12 basses, 4
flutes, 4 oboes, 1 clarinet in E flat, 3 clarinets in B flat, 1
bass clarinet in B flat, 3 bassoons, 1 double bassoon, 8
horns, 4 trumpets, 3 trombones, 1 bass tuba, 2 harps, 1
celesta, timpani, cymbals, and tambourine.

* Of course, there never has been any unanimity over the number
of players in the string section of an orchestra. The first consideration has
always been finance, although an even balance between strings and wind
was also a desirable necessity. However, a full quota of strings reaching
the limits of good balance may produce an enviable richness of tone, but
it is a luxury nevertheless.

2

Joseph Haydn (1732-1809)

CECIL GRAY

INTRODUCTION

DURING the course of the nineteenth century, largely as the result of the influence exercised by current evolutionary theories and dogmas, music came to be regarded as a more or less impersonal and collective activity in which each successive great master stood on the shoulders of his predecessor, and summed up in himself all previous knowledge and experience, adding something of his own to the common stock which was then taken over by his successor, and so on.

In accordance with this conception, Haydn was the precursor of Mozart, and Mozart of Beethoven – the bud, blossom and fruit respectively, of one genealogical tree – and the prominent and honourable place assigned to Haydn in the annals of musical history has been due, not so much to his actual individual achievement as to the part played by him in the evolution of symphonic form, of which he was popularly, but erroneously, supposed to be the inventor. Hence the familiar and endearing appellation of 'Papa' Haydn which has been bestowed upon him by former generations of musicians. In so far as he was appreciated for what he was in himself, and not merely for his part in the work of others, it was on account of the attribution to his music of the secondary qualities implied in the paternal designation – a mellow benignity and imperturbable cheerfulness, coupled with a touching suggestion of senility, or second childhood.

Such, in brief, was the general conception of musical history, and such the particular place in it ascribed to Haydn, which prevailed until quite recently. To-day, fortunately, this naive and mechanistic view is largely discredited, though it is still to be encountered in text-books and orthodox histories of music, and is consequently still inculcated at academies and conservatoires. The first decade or so of the present century witnessed the emergence and liberation of Mozart from the humble role of a mere forerunner to Beethoven which had previously been assigned to him, and the recognition of the fact that his art is not only utterly different in kind from that of his great successor, but also in no way inferior to it – many people today, in fact, would go further, and maintain that Mozart was by far the greater of the two. For some time longer, however, it was customary to regard Haydn as little more than a kind of embryonic Mozart, and it is only within quite recent times that his independent greatness and absolute equality has come to be recognized and appreciated by the musical public in general. Haydn, in short, is no more contained in Mozart than Mozart in Beethoven. Mozart was no more capable of excelling Haydn in his most individual and characteristic achievements than Haydn was of surpassing Mozart in his. It may be true that there are certain works here and there, and particularly isolated movements, which one might hesitate to ascribe definitely to one or the other, but such cases are those in which neither composer is at his most personal and distinctive. The collective impression that their respective outputs convey is one of complete and profound dissimilarity.

The first step towards the just appraisal of the genius of Haydn is to rid oneself entirely of all the associations of ideas evoked by the sobriquet of 'Papa' Haydn. In the first place, it is not even justified in the primary, historical sense in which it was originally applied to him – i.e., in his alleged capacity of being the 'father' of the symphony. As Ralph Hill shows in the first chapter of this book, recent research has proved abundantly that, even apart from C. P. E. Bach, many of the composers of the Mannheim and Viennese *Vorklassikern* schools were in the field before him – Karl Friedrich Abel, Georg Matthias, Monn, Johann Stamitz, Georg Christoph Wagenseil, the Italian Giovanni Battista Sammartini, and many others too numerous to mention. It is impossible to say for certain who is the authentic and un-questionable father of the symphony; the list of putative parents is long and impressive. The only certain thing is that it was *not* Joseph Haydn. That he was the first great master to practise the form, and to make it his own, is another matter. None of the examples produced by his many pre-decessors survives to-day in the concert-hall, but more than a score of Haydn's fabulous total of one hundred and four will live as long as the art of music itself.

The symphony, in the hands of Haydn's predecessors, developed from the Italian overture, consisting of three movements; an initial *allegro,* followed by a slow movement and a final *allegro.* With Haydn, of course, the form is en-larged to four movements, with a minuet and trio con-stituting (almost invariably) the third movement. It still remains to be decided whether Haydn was, or was not, the first symphonist to make this revolutionary innovation. Some authorities claim the honour to be that of the Belgian composer Gossec, others that it belongs to Monn, while still others attribute it to various members of the Mannheim school; but here again, whoever was the 'father' of the minuet, there can be no question but that Haydn gave this movement its distinctive character and place in symphonic form. The minuet, as it had formerly existed as a movement in the form of the suite, was a slow stately dance of an aristo-cratic character. Haydn makes of it something entirely different, completely new. He takes the dance form out of the eighteenth century court *salon* in which it was languishing, into the open air of the village green, and makes of it a robust virile type of movement unlike anything which had gone before.

But this was not the only respect in which Haydn was an innovator in symphonic form; each of the three traditional movements was basically transformed and revolutionized by the daring and originality of his genius. With regard to his treatment of first movement form, Tovey rightly observes that 'the orthodox theory of a sonata form with a first sub-ject in the main key and a second subject in a complemen-tary key will do fairly well for Mozart and Beethoven as

long as we understand by "subject" no single theme but a
large group of heterogeneous material. And it is fairly true
for Mozart and Beethoven that, after the "exposition" of
these two groups, there will be a "development" which
develops whatever it chooses from these themes by grouping
their fragments into changing combinations in various
shifting keys; and that, with a return to the main key, there
will be a "recapitulation" which recapitulates the first and
second subject, both in the tonic ... But with most of the
mature works of Haydn this account simply will not do' –
and indeed, of all the great masters of the symphony Haydn
is the most daringly unorthodox and unconventional in his
procedure, and the most protean in form, especially in his
first movements.

In his slow movements also, however, he was a revolutionary innovator, and would appear to be the first composer to introduce here the monothematic principle of a
subject with variations in place of the two-part form which
had previously prevailed – most of his slow movements are
so constructed. Apart from that, the emotional content is
frequently of a poignance and · intensity which has no
parallel in the work of his immediate predecessors. But it is
perhaps above all in his finales that Haydn's supreme genius
and originality are most clearly apparent, and his invariable
felicity, in both senses of the word – spontaneous gaiety and
absolute rightness and sureness of touch. Even in his happiest
moments Mozart is never far from tears; with him one is
always conscious of the Vergilian *lacrimae rerum* – with
Haydn never. As for the Horatian *curiosa felicitas* with which
Haydn chooses exactly the right vein in which to conclude
and round off his symphonies, I am reminded of the remark
once made to me by one of our most talented composers
when assailed by doubts and difficulties in the course of
writing the final movement of one of his works: 'there is only
one composer whose last movements are always absolutely and
invariably right,' to which I replied 'of course – you do not
need to mention his name; we all know it.' Every one, surely,
will agree with Alan Rawsthorne's dictum and my endorse-
ment of it; he could have been thinking only of Haydn.

Lastly, and perhaps most important of all, is the revolutionary nature of the innovations which Haydn introduced in the orchestration of his symphonies. He was the first composer to make a complete break between chamber music and that of the concert-hall. So far as can be ascertained the orchestra for which his latest and greatest symphonies were composed consisted of about forty players – no fewer; and, considering the far smaller dimensions of concert-rooms in his time compared with those of to-day, the sonority of his orchestration must have been a veritable revelation in its period. He was, indeed, regarded by his contemporaries as a scandalously noisy composer. Equally important in this connection is the banishment from his mature scores of the old principle of the *continuo* part, according to which the harmonies were filled in or amplified by the composer at the *cembalo* or harpsichord. The scores of Haydn are absolutely self-sufficient. Finally, his writing for the wood-wind was of epoch-making significance and novelty; nothing like it had ever been known before and it still holds its own in comparison with that of any subsequent composer. Particularly original and personal is his writing for the bassoon – an instrument for which he seems to have entertained a particularly warm affection.

The primary characteristic of Haydn's symphonies, however, consists in the amazing range of thought, variety of form, and breadth of style which they exhibit, viewed as a whole; and this makes it particularly difficult in his case to choose examples for the purposes of critical comment and analysis. Never was there such an *embarras de richesse* to confront a commentator. It would be easy to choose another equal number of specimens in no way inferior to those selected. While all his symphonies conform outwardly to the conventional formula of first and last quick movements with a slow one and a minuet between, Haydn invariably succeeds in imparting to each work a distinctive character and personality of its own, and in investing each constituent movement of them with an unparalleled variety of resource and wealth of invention.

SYMPHONY NO. 85 IN B FLAT MAJOR (*La Reine*)

THERE are two main outstanding landmarks in the course of Haydn's prodigious symphonic output – the first represented by the series of so-called *Paris Symphonies*, the second by the *London Symphonies*. Both sets were the outcome of definite commissions from impresarios or concert agents in these respective art centres, and it would seem that the incentive provided by these foreign displays of interest in his art stimulated Haydn to his most ambitious efforts and highest achievements.

In the year 1784 the Parisian society named *Concerts Spirituels*, of which one Le Gros was the director, invited Haydn to compose six symphonies for performance by them, of which the present example is probably the best – certainly the best known. Its sub-title is due to the fact that it is said to have greatly pleased Queen Marie Antoinette when it was played in the Galerie Henri III of the Tuileries in her presence. Her expressed appreciation may have been due partly to the nationality of the composer, which she shared, or partly to the fact that the French *chanson* of the period entitled 'La gentille et jeune Lisette' is introduced – possibly to a combination of the two factors – or it may simply have been due to a fondness for good music.

It is scored for the usual strings with two oboes, bassoons, horns, and solo flute – this latter feature, by the way, being of frequent occurrence in the symphonies of Haydn. More often than not, in fact, he seems to feel and to write for the flute as a solo, celibate instrument – an attitude which its innocent, virginal tone-quality justifies.

First Movement. *Adagio – Vivace*. Nearly all the first movements in Haydn's symphonies begin with a slow introduction, and this is no exception to the general rule. It opens with a powerful unison passage which, despite the emphatic initial enunciation of the tonic (B flat), and the absence of harmony, suggests rather the relative key of G minor.

One of the most distinctive features of Haydn's melodic style, incidentally, and one which sharply differentiates him from Mozart, consists in the fact that whereas the latter

almost invariably builds up his themes in symmetrical four
eight, and sixteen bar phrases, Haydn shows a marked predilection for irregular periods of three, five or seven bars.
This little introduction is a case in point, and consists in two
phrases of three bars each, followed by one of four.

The first movement proper *(vivace)* is chiefly built upon
the bipartite subject announced by the strings at the outset,
Ex. 1, characterized by long held notes for the violins with
a descending staccato bass for the lower strings. Rhythmically it constitutes a complete inversion of the introduction, consisting in two groups of four bars followed by one of
three. This with subsidiary material is developed at some
length before the appearance of the second subject (bar 78)
for oboe solo which, however, strikes one as being a continuation of the original thought rather than a new and
contrasted one, and this is emphasized by the closely related
descending figure of accompaniment for the strings, Ex. 2.
The interdependence of the two thematic units is brought
out in the subsequent brief and concise development section.

The recapitulation is accomplished with an originality
which is the hall-mark of Haydn's genius. A powerful
episode in G minor subsides into a cadential passage in the
dominant of this relative minor (D major) and then with a
sudden abrupt modulation the original subject steals back in
the tonic key (bar 212). The effect is as magical as it is unexpected. With most symphonic composers one knows only
too well beforehand the precise moment of the recapitulation
which, moreover, when it comes, is generally emphatic and
decisive. But Haydn seldom does the expected – and when
he does it is for that reason all the more unexpected.

Second Movement. *Romanze: Allegretto*. The slow movement in E flat consists of variations on a theme which, as
already observed, has been identified as a French *chanson* –
La gentille et jeune Lisette. The theme is introduced and
developed by strings alone at the outset, Ex. 3. The mild
and even tenor of the proceedings is then suddenly interrupted by a *fortissimo* passage in striking contrast to what
has gone before (bar 27), a noteworthy feature of which
consists in the separation and independence of the 'cellos and

double basses – probably the first example in musical history of this daring innovation.

In subsequent episodes the theme is developed with infinite subtlety and resource, particularly in that in which it appears on the second violins in the minor (bar 116) with contrapuntal embellishments. The whole of this section is again for strings alone, but when it has run its course the virginal flute coyly introduces itself with a staccato counterpoint to the restatement of the subject by the oboes in sixths, but after two bars they suddenly suspend operations and leave matters in the hands of the violins, in the form of a florid chromatic development of the subject doubled in the octave below by a solo bassoon. (It is interesting to note, incidentally, how often in this work, and in other works of the same period, Haydn has recourse to this odd form of doubling. In his middle period, in fact, he tends constantly to use the bassoon as a reinforcement of the upper parts, rather than as the harmonic foundation of the wind ensemble. Even in the very last works, it will be noted, the bassoon is written for as a tenor or alto instrument, and the lower octave of its compass is almost entirely neglected. Haydn, in fact, in his treatment of the bassoon, for which he had obviously a great affection, neglects entirely its tragic possibilities of expression, which are immense, and tends rather to emphasize its gay, lovable and laughable characteristics.) In compensation for their summary ejection from the foregoing proceedings the oboes are graciously allowed to have the last word – a privilege which they nobly justify.

Third Movement. *Menuetto: Allegretto.* This boisterous, rumbustious example of what is erroneously described by the composer as a minuet is a very good illustration of what was said earlier in these notes concerning Haydn's unceremonious treatment of this *ancien régime* dance form – cavalier, in fact, rather than chivalrous. One cannot easily imagine the courtiers of Marie Antoinette capering to these strains, which are more fitted to the emotional expression of the *sansculottes* who were already gathering hungrily outside the gates of the Tuileries, where the symphony was first performed.

The formal developments of the movement are crystal-clear, and stand in no need of critical comment or analysis. A noteworthy feature of the trio section consists in a tiny dialogue between the two oboes over a held octave pedal for horns, accompanied by strings *pizzicati* – an exquisitely imaginative little touch, supremely characteristic of Haydn.

Fourth Movement. *Finale: Presto.* This is one of the hundreds of examples to be found in Haydn of his mastery in constructing a movement of this kind. To be able to do the same thing so often, and yet always differently – what greater genius is there than this?

It is, of course, as usual with Haydn in his last movements, in rondo form, with a perpetually recurring main theme, Ex. 4, alternating with secondary material, in this case cognate rather than contrasted. The final return to the main theme, as in the first movement, is exquisitely effected in the same way – a boisterous episode fades out gradually into a finely moulded, wistful little lament for the first violins with a simple chordal accompaniment for the other strings; whereupon the subject returns, unobtrusively (with the characteristic octave doubling of violins and bassoon) *piano*, and works up to a gay conclusion.

SYMPHONY NO. 92 IN G MAJOR (*The Oxford*)

TOVEY in his *Essays in Musical Analysis*, says of this work that this typical product of Haydn's hilarious maturity was written for the occasion of his receiving the Doctorate of Music at Oxford. It proved too difficult for the available resources, and so an earlier work was substituted. On the other hand a later commentator, who is also the editor of the most recent available edition of the full score, Dr Ernst Praetorius, says that this particular symphony belongs to the Paris series, and was written before 1788 – the Oxford Doctorate was in 1791. This is a typical example of the confusion and uncertainty which still surrounds the work of Haydn. The greatest scholars and experts stand frequently in flagrant contradiction to each other in many essential respects. The sad truth of the matter is that as yet there is no authoritative, definite edition available of the complete works of one of the greatest masters of music of all time. The *Gesamtausgabe* of his works which was begun about half a century ago has been catastrophically interrupted by two world wars, and its resumption and completion seem to be as far off to-day as ever, if not further.

However that may be, it is a minor and comparatively unimportant point in question. What is much more important, and a point on which there can be no question of disagreement, even between the most eminent authorities, is the greatness of this so-called *Oxford Symphony* – it stands high among Haydn's many masterpieces.

The orchestration is the same as in the foregoing symphony, with the addition of trumpets and drums.

First Movement. *Adagio – Allegro spiritoso*. To revert to Tovey. He says, in his notes on this symphony in his *Essays in Musical Analysis* that 'the forms of the *Oxford Symphony* are, with every appearance of sonata style and symmetry, so free that adequate analysis would involve describing almost every individual phrase. There is hardly any long passage in the first movement that could be disposed of by a technical term, least of all by such terms as *second subject* and *recapitulation*.' The difficulties involved are here intensified by the condition of being precluded from having recourse to sufficient musical examples.

Tovey goes on to say that 'the introduction was undoubtedly in some former incarnation a saintly tabby cat whom Thoth or Ra (or whatever deity is in charge of cats) has elevated to the heavens of Haydn's imagination'. The deity in question (speaking as a fellow cat-lover) was the goddess Bast, but subject to this pedantic correction the statement is unexceptionable.

The *allegro* begins with a four bar phrase built upon the melodic and harmonic basis of the dominant seventh, the last bar of which gives rise to a succeeding clause in the tonic, Ex. 5. These constitute what, subject to Tovey's qualifications, may be called the first subject. After a short pendant it is restated with different scoring and subjected to some development, to say nothing of the introduction of fresh subsidiary material.

A dainty, tripping melody announced by the first violins, Ex. 6, then lays claim to the title of second subject (bar 72) – a claim which, however questionable, is not disputed by any rival aspirant to the honour. The frontiers between the exposition and the development sections are then artfully obscured by the device of beginning the latter with a continuation and discussion of this second subject. This development section, however, is characterized chiefly by the introduction of important fresh thematic material which first appears as a kind of counterpoint to the second subject, and gives rise to considerable developments (bar 95). Finally the recapitulation, when it duly appears, is merged into a coda of such dimensions and importance as entirely to displace the conventional centre of formal symphonic gravity. Altogether this is one of Haydn's most original and daringly unconventional movements in the matter of form.

Second Movement. *Adagio cantabile*. The slow movement is built chiefly upon repetitions and variants of the broad, grave, symmetrical eight-bar D major melody announced at the outset, Ex. 7. After they have run their course for some time there comes a sudden abrupt change, with a *fortissimo* outburst for the full orchestra in the minor, which alternates with a new, quiet, lyrical theme in F major which gives rise to considerable developments.

After this stormy interlude in the minor key with its attendant satellite in the relative major, the original theme returns with fresh variants and embellishments. The movement concludes with a lovely unexpected coda in which the F major subject of the middle section recurs, magically transformed.

Third Movement. *Menuetto: allegretto*. This movement is another example of Haydn's vigorous and boisterous treatment of the stately, courtly dance form of the minuet. Particularly original and attractive is the trio with its syncopated horn motive (doubled by bassoons), punctuated by *pizzicati* strings, and alternating with *arco* passages.

Fourth Movement. *Presto*. This final movement provides

a particularly telling exemplification of the dictum expressed earlier in these notes: namely, that Haydn is the unequalled and unapproachable master of the symphonic *finale*. The theme on which it is built, Ex. 8, is one of his gayest and loveliest, and the developments and variations, melodic and instrumental, to which it is subjected are infinite in number and protean in versatility. Other themes appear, reappear, but finally disappear in order to make way for the triumphant apotheosis of the chief subject. The solo flute, incidentally, plays a leading role throughout.

SYMPHONY NO. 94 IN G MAJOR (*The Surprise*)

THIS symphony was written in 1792, and was first performed, as far as can be ascertained, in London during the same year. Why this particular symphony should have been given this particular sub-title is a mystery, and should be allowed to remain so. Let us always respect, revere and preserve mysteries – they are the salt of life, and of art. The accepted explanation is the sudden *fortissimo* chord for full orchestra which occurs in the course of the slow movement. But this explanation is more surprising than the cause of it, seeing that one can hardly think of a single work of Haydn in which he does not have recourse to this most characteristic feature of his art – sudden, abrupt, violent transitions from one mood to another. Haydn, in fact, surprises us all the time. His entire work is a surprise – the greatest surprise in music, when you compare it with what had gone before – it is a new world.

First Movement. *Adagio cantabile – vivace assai*. Much more surprising than the chord which has given the sub-title to this symphony is the introduction to the first movement, with its lovely initial dialogue between wind and strings, merging into a delightful ensemble in which the wood-wind murmurs melodic fragments against a *sostenuto* string background. No better example could be found, by the way, of Haydn's nonchalant indifference to questions of key relationship than the fact that already, by bar 10, he has strayed so far from his point of tonal departure that he is writing F natural and G flat in an unidentifiable key. In this brief compass of – characteristically – seventeen bars, a whole world of enchantment is traversed in miniature.

The beginning of the first movement proper, as apart from the introduction, is equally surprising, and starts out as remotely from the original key, though in the opposite direction, as that to which the introduction modulates in the course of its brief career, with a G sharp in the accompaniment to the subject, Ex. 9 – a symphony in the key of G natural which, within a few bars, is pivoting around G flat and G sharp – where are we? What could be more surprising, and how much more so than a single *fortissimo* chord?

After this highly unconventional and eccentric behaviour the music subsides into an orthodox tonal episode. Note, however, the interesting disposition of the wood-wind at bars 31–35, Ex. 10, in which oboes and flutes dispute ascendancy.

In this symphony, by the way, we note a greater freedom and independence of the treatment of the wood-wind as compared with the foregoing examples with which we have already dealt, in which its utterances are generally doubled by the strings, either in unison or octave.

An extended development of the subject, together with the introduction of subsidiary cognate material, precedes the introduction of the second subject – if indeed it can be so called, for there is a more than suspicious resemblance between some of its features and those of the first subject. As so often with Haydn, in fact, the second subject appears to be a derivate from, rather than a contrast to, the first (bar 67), or perhaps one is wrong in saying that this is the second subject – a term more appropriately to be ascribed to the pastoral-like theme which follows, richly scored for strings alone on its first appearance (bar 80). With Haydn, in fact, as already observed, you never know where you are in the matter of thematic analysis. This is perhaps his greatest virtue – that he makes pedantic analysts look even more silly than they actually are – which is saying a lot. In order finally to confound the race he merges the recapitulation into a coda embodying fresh material all the time. In short, one of Haydn's most original and most unorthodox creations.

Second Movement. *Andante*. The slow movement is based upon a subject which, when one first hears it, seems as though one had always known it. Like all the best tunes ever written, past or present – and there is no reason to suppose that in this respect the future will be any different – it is based upon the alternation of tonic and dominant harmonies and melodic progressions, Ex. 11.

The melody, incidentally, was a favourite of the composer himself, in witness of which is the fact that he made use of it again in his oratorio *The Seasons*, in which, however, the *tempo* is sensibly quickened.

After its first (repeated) presentation by the strings alone, there comes the violent *fortissimo* explosion for full orchestra which gives the symphony its designation. The delightful continuation, or after-thought, initiated by strings alone, in which the wood-wind eventually participates, is succeeded by a series of resourceful and imaginative variations, embellished by counterpoints. An unsuspected latent grandeur in the theme is revealed in a minor episode, enhanced by magnificent flourishes for the strings. The return to the major tonality, initiated by a version of the theme in repeated notes, confided to a solo oboe, constitutes one of the most genial, in both senses of the word (the combination of genius with happiness), passages in the music of Haydn, who is, of all composers, the one in whom the two aspects of the word are most closely conjoined.

Third Movement. *Menuetto: allegro molto*. This is a very grand and richly scored example of Haydn's cavalier treatment of the decorous dance form of the minuet. The intervening trio, delicately and lightly scored in comparison, is based upon a very beautiful and highly original subject confided throughout to the first violins with occasional reinforcement in the lower octave by a solo bassoon – a favourite colouristic device of the composer which obtains an underlining, without a darkening, of the melodic line.

Fourth Movement. *Allegro di molto*. The last movement begins as a characteristically Haydnesque *rondo*, but gradually develops into a kind of first movement sonata form with a definite second subject (bar 75) which shares equally in the subsequent honours of the proceedings which demonstrate, in the words of Tovey, 'the height of Haydn's power in the unexpected – inevitable'.

SYMPHONY NO. 100 IN G MAJOR (*The Military*)

HAYDN is the only composer who has ever lived, so far as one can discover, to have written a hundred and more symphonies. In modern times the difficulty of surpassing the magical Beethovenian Nine has caused many psychological disturbances among modern symphonic composers. Most stop short before they get so far; Bruckner equalled the total but got no further; Mahler, overcome by holy awe of the mystical number, superstitiously evaded it by omitting to give a number to what was properly his Ninth Symphony, namely *Das Lied von der Erde,* and eventually overcame his superstition to the extent of writing what should properly be designated as his 10th, since when the Russian composer Miaskovsky, alone, has far out-distanced Beethoven and is now well on in his twenties, according to the latest statistics – but since none of them known to us is worth performing, the prestige of the accomplishment seems doubtful. Even Mozart himself progressed no further than the forties; but a hundred and more – only Haydn has achieved such a miracle and, what is more, all of them are worth performing.*

The achievement of his century undoubtedly prompted the composer to a celebration of the event, with an appropriate firework display. The fact that this symphony No. 100, should be the only one he wrote in which a large force of percussion instruments is demanded suggests that this festive gesture is no mere coincidence, any more than is the fact that it is the longest and perhaps the most formally ambitious of all his symphonies.† At the same time, it is interesting to note, in spite of this enlargement of structure

---

* It is perhaps worth recording that Johann Gottlieb Graun (1703–1773) is said to have composed 96 or 100 symphonies. – Editor.

† According to Haydn's own catalogue of 1805 this symphony is listed as his 112th! – Editor.

and instrumental resource, the composer maintains his predilection for a solo flute opposed to the duality of the other wind instruments.

This symphony belongs to the series of the so-called *London Symphonies*, and was first performed in London on 12th May, 1794, at one of the Salomon Concerts. As with the foregoing example *(The Surprise)*, the sub-title derives from the second movement, in which the percussion battery is unleashed for the first time – a very much greater surprise than anything in the symphony which bears this appellation. It should be added that some commentators profess to find militaristic suggestions in the first movement, and point to the fact that its second subject bears a resemblance to the *Radetsky March;* but such themes are by no means of rare occurrence in the music of Haydn.

First Movement. *Adagio – Allegro.* The habitual slow introduction is one of more than usual beauty, originality, and subtlety. Particular attention should be paid to the solo bassoon part in the first twelve bars, generally obscured by insensitive and impercipient conductors. Beginning with a mere doubling of the viola part, it assumes an independent role at bar 9 with interjections uttered against a continuation of the theme confided to the strings. A *sforzando,* chromatic passage for the latter leads to an abrupt modulation to an episode in G minor and cognate keys, which concludes with a singularly daring and, for its time, unparalleled harmonic clash, in which a pedal D for double basses and 'cellos sounds against a C sharp for flute and first violins, while a C natural occurs simultaneously in the oboes and other strings (bars 19–20).

The *allegro* begins in a fashion unique in classical symphonic literature, with the main subject delivered by the solo flute accompanied by the oboes only, Ex. 12. This consists in a regular eight-bar theme which, on its continuation for strings alone, has its last bar characteristically lopped off in order to make way for a closely related episode. We are now in the key of the dominant and are in consequence naturally led to expect here the appearance of the second subject; instead of which Haydn abruptly reverts to the first, which he proceeds to develop and discuss, beginning with the original instrumental disposition of flute and oboes; at bar 94 he presents us with the second subject which Tovey has rightly described as 'one of the gayest tunes in the world', Ex. 13.

After this has run its course, the working-out section begins, after a long, dramatic pause, with a development of this second subject, starting abruptly in the remote key of B flat, and leading to one of the most powerful and imaginative passages in all Haydn's symphonic writings – which is saying a lot – the study of which in the smallest details will more than amply repay the student.

The recapitulation is very free and on a very grand scale, with a *coda* in which considerable fresh developments take place.

Second Movement. *Allegretto.* The principal subject of the second movement of this symphony, Ex. 14, has been said by some commentators to be borrowed from the earlier symphony *La Reine* and to be based upon the old French melody called *La gentille et jeune Lisette;* but personally I cannot see that they are the same theme at all. That there is a certain resemblance between them is true enough, but nothing more. Which of them, if either, is the old French tune, I have been unable to discover. It matters little – nothing could be more authentically Haydnesque than each of them.

The movement opens in placid and unassuming fashion. Then, after a *piano* passage for wind instruments alone, the full orchestra complete with the hitherto unheard percussion instruments, bursts out with a minor version of the subject. Another minor 'surprise' consists in the unexpected introduction, towards the close, of a trumpet-call. Otherwise the movement consists exclusively of variations and developments of the one and only theme, sometimes with, and sometimes without, percussion effects.

Third Movement. *Menuetto: Moderato.* This minuet is unusual in Haydn's mature work in being a genuine minuet of the orthodox old-fashioned type rather than, as is usual with him, a reaching-out to, or prophetic anticipation of, the *scherzo* type of symphonic movement. It is solemn, stately, and decorous throughout, notwithstanding a considerable degree of vigour in the second section of the minuet proper. The *trio*, though strongly contrasted in character, similarly consists of an initial graceful period followed by a more strenuous section. Neither minuet nor *trio*, however, call for any detailed analysis. All is simple and straightforward – surprisingly so for Haydn, who generally gives an unexpected twist to everything he touches.

Fourth Movement. *Finale: Presto*. The last movement starts in a disarmingly deceptive fashion, with a theme, Ex. 15, which would seem to announce the advent of one of Haydn's innumerable *rondo* finales which, however unexpected in details, yet conform to a comparatively orthodox pattern in broad outlines. And so the movement proceeds for the first part of its vertiginous course, with a characteristically unexpected detail consisting in the abrupt modulation from E minor to B flat major at bars 12–13 – a magical stroke. But as the movement progresses it gradually divests itself of the features of conventional *rondo* form – with its alternations of one main theme with various subsidiaries and satellites – and develops into a full-fledged first-movement sonata form, with pregnant thematic developments, and romantic adventurings into remote keys. A particularly arresting example of this is the passage beginning at bar 160 which, already in the exotic key of D flat, passes through C sharp minor, E major, E minor, and so on, in an unending kaleidoscopic tonal sequence enhanced by an exquisitely imaginative instrumental treatment. The whole of this section, consisting of almost exactly a hundred bars, is one of the high-water marks in the whole of Haydn's gigantic output. You will not find anything quite like it in any other music, earlier or later.

Up till this point the supernumerary percussion instruments, introduced in the second movement, have been silent; the composer would almost seem to have forgotten their existence. But now, with the long deferred return to the tonic key, they make a triumphant return in an episode which is succeeded by the restatement of the main theme, at first in its original disposition, but with a continuation in the form of an exquisite little canonic dialogue between the solo flute and the first oboe over an accompaniment for the two horns. The movement then comes to a final exultant discussion of the subject for full orchestra.

SYMPHONY NO. 101 IN D MAJOR (*The Clock*)

THIS symphony was written, so far as can be ascertained, in 1794, and is one of the twelve which Haydn wrote specially for his London concerts. The first performance of this particular example took place on 4th May, 1795, at the Haymarket Theatre, London. The title, as with *The Surprise* and *The Military*, derives from a minor and unimportant feature of the second movement – a regular ticking rhythm for the basses which recurs throughout.

First Movement. *Adagio – Presto*. The customary slow introduction is in the minor key, and is initiated by a rising scale which clearly foreshadows the leading theme of the succeeding *presto*. This by the way, is unusual in Haydn; his slow introductions and subsequent fast movements are generally unrelated thematically. But here the resemblance is too obvious to be mistaken, or ascribed to coincidence.

The theme of the *presto*, Ex. 16, is characteristically Haydnesque in that it consists in two clauses of five bars each, followed by one of three, one of eight, and finally one of four. Small wonder that conductors who conceive eighteenth-century music as being habitually written in groupings of four bars – as it generally is, and especially in Mozart – should so often make such a deplorable hash of Haydn.

This gay, bustling subject is worked out at considerable length after its presentation, before the appearance at bar 81 of the second subject, Ex. 17, for strings alone. Here again irregularity is the order of the day; a deceptively symmetrical initial four-bar phrase leads to one of seven, then to one of six. A strenuous episode characterized chiefly by a descending chromatic *sforzando* passage leads to the development section which, as so often in Haydn's later work, begins with a discussion of the second subject instead of a reversal to the first, with the result that the transition from the one section to the other is almost imperceptible. On this occasion it is effected by means of a charming dialogue between first and second violins, in which the violas and 'cellos subsequently take part.

The second subject dominates the development section to the exclusion of everything else. Even after the triumphant reassertion of the first subject, with the recapitulation, the balance of power tends once more to pass to the second subject – but the first has the last word.

Second Movement. *Andante*. This highly attractive and supremely original movement is in ternary form (A–B–A), with a first and second subject, the latter in the minor (bar 34). The transition passage which leads from it back to the re-statement of the chief subject has rightly been described by Tovey as being of an 'audacity and genius without parallel in earlier or later music'. These are indeed strong words, but the music which gives rise to them is even stronger, and calls for superlatives which do not exist in any language.

On its return the first subject is confided to the first violins accompanied, in most original fashion, by solo flute, oboe, and bassoon alone. It is then developed and varied at considerable length with increasingly rich and imaginative instrumental embellishments.

Third Movement. *Menuetto: Allegretto*. The seeming simplicity and straightforwardness of this minuet movement should not mislead the listener or analytical student into a failure to recognize the skill with which the melodic line is built up, rising as it does from D in the first bar to E in the second, F sharp in the third, G in the fourth, A in the fifth, B in the sixth; then the *reculer pour mieux sauter,* which carries the line up to C sharp and D in bar 13 and a final triumphant E in the next bar, initiating a rapid subsidence down to the very note from which we started – a masterly piece of melodic construction.

A strenuous and purposeful sequel leads to a sub-section which begins with a downward chromatic passage for first and second violins in thirds, which is a development of bar 7 of the leading theme. On the return and development of the latter, the rainbow curve of the melodic line is enhanced.

If this minuet section is among the most artful examples of Haydn's treatment of miniature form, the succeeding *trio* section is one of the most artless. Against an unvarying background of tonic common chord harmony for the strings, the solo flute gives out an unsophisticated little tune, abruptly interrupted, however, by a violent *tutti* outburst (bar 93). On the resumption of the flute tune the string accompaniment is modified. There then ensues an exquisite dialogue between solo flute and solo bassoon, over the same chordal string accompaniment. A new line of thought, characterized chiefly by brilliant string figurations, first for violins and then for 'cellos and basses, paves the way for the return to the minuet section, with a final dialogue for the flute and bassoon.

Fourth Movement. *Finale*: *Vivace*. This is one of the many symphonic movements of Haydn which obstinately refuses to fit into the procrustean bed of form as conceived by the pedants. It starts out as if it were destined to become a typical *rondo*, but develops into something quite other. The initial theme, so far from alternating with various contrasted subjects, undergoes considerable and extensive developments of a symphonic first-movement type and engenders its own chief counter-subject. At bar 62, for example, what may at first appear to be a new theme is only a sophistication of the original one. The strenuous D minor section, which succeeds, though strongly contrasted in character, is nevertheless in essence a continuation and development of what has gone before.

The recurrence of the principal subject (bar 189) is in a considerably modified version, and takes the form of a double fugue. From this moment onwards the chief theme, with protean developments, dominates the movement up to its exultant conclusion.

SYMPHONY NO. 102 IN B FLAT MAJOR

LIKE the foregoing and succeeding examples, this symphony is one of the series of so-called *London*, or *Salomon Symphonies*.

It would appear to have been written in London in 1794. If it is less popular and less frequently performed than others in the monumental series, this is perhaps to be ascribed partly to the fact that it does not enjoy the specious attraction of a literary sub-title attached to some quite unimportant feature of the work – generally the second movement. But it is in no way inferior to any of its companions in all essential respects. How seldom, indeed, does Haydn fall below the level of his best, particularly in his later work, where his consistent, unflagging excellence is almost without parallel in music. Of all the great masters Haydn is to-day still the least appreciated at his proper value, which is no less than that of Bach, Beethoven or Mozart.

First Movement. *Largo – Allegro vivace*. Writing about this symphony in his invaluable critical analyses, Tovey says that the first movement has 'a form of its own which constantly upsets the orthodoxies of the text-books', and that Haydn 'tends to write his largest movements on a single theme'. As generalizations these statements are unimpeachable, and their truth has already been repeated and emphasized in the foregoing pages; but, with a due sense of the danger attached to the audacity of differing from the greatest of classical music scholars of his time and country, I must confess myself unable to see how these observations are applicable to the particular example in question. In broad outline it seems to me that this first movement is comparatively orthodox, and is definitely based upon two strongly contrasted main subjects.

In nothing is Haydn's consummate genius more clearly revealed than in his slow introductions to his first movements. This particular example is a perfect gem in miniature. The long-held tonic unisons, *crescendo* and *diminuendo*, which usher in the two first four-bar clauses; the way in which the last bar of the second clause introduces the initial phrase by the 'cellos and basses; the subsequent rising chromatic figure for syncopated strings and flute solo, with an expressive counter-subject for oboes, doubled in the octave below by second violins and then by violas in addition; the

final little upward *arpeggio* for flute – every rift in this miniature masterpiece of formal construction is loaded with ore.

The first subject of the *allegro vivace*, Ex. 18, is one that
lends itself to infinite development and extension, and
Haydn amply avails himself of these latent potentialities.

Particular attention should be paid to an episode which
occurs in the course of the proceedings (bar 57 *et seq.*), for it
plays an important role in the formal construction of the
movement, providing a link between the first and second
subjects, with both of which it is on intimate terms, though
never identifying itself with either. Its chief feature consists
in an ascending conjunct phrase in one part, and a descending one in the other.

The second subject proper, heralded and punctuated by
fortissimo unisons for the full orchestra, appears at bar 83,
Ex. 19. Its presentation is succeeded by the reappearance,
in a new disposition, of the mediatory episode alluded to
above. Note, by the way, the piquant clash of the adjacent
semi-tones of B flat and B natural.

The development section exemplifies one of Haydn's
favourite formal devices, the first part being built up on a
working-out of the second subject, and the second part on a
development of the first subject, which leads naturally and
inevitably to the recapitulation. In consequence, all three
formal sections of the movement are welded into an indissoluble whole. Similarly the subsequent coda, which is on a
large, almost Beethovenian, scale, also merges imperceptibly into the recapitulation. The development section, incidentally, is one of Haydn's most resourceful and imaginative constructions.

Second Movement. *Adagio*. This lovely movement is
based, exceptionally with Haydn, on an easier work –
namely, a piano trio in F sharp. He must have felt that in
the smaller medium he had not done justice to the wealth of
possibilities revealed, and he was right. This is one of the
most richly, yet delicately, scored of all Haydn's slow movements. An additional noteworthy feature of the movement
consists in the extreme rhythmic subtlety of the melodic
articulations. People who prate glibly about the rhythmical

invention of certain modern composers, and are hypnotized
by frequent changes of time-signature attached to unvarying metrical formulas, would be well advised to study this
movement of Haydn. It is in three-four rhythm throughout,
but the intricate sub-divisions within each bar are of infinite
variety and complexity.

It consists of variations on a single theme, Ex. 20. Outstanding features of the instrumentation are, firstly, the
employment of a single flute instead of the two in the other
movements of the symphony (as observed earlier in these
notes, Haydn tends to favour celibacy for the flute); the
quite exceptional use of mutes for horns and trumpets; and
the employment of a solo 'cello.

Third Movement. *Menuetto: Allegro.* In sharp contrast to
the foregoing movement, and no doubt designedly so, is the
directness and simplicity, both of rhythm and orchestration
of the minuet. On the other hand, there are, particularly in
the *trio*, moments of unexpected harmonic pungency. See,
for example, bar 71, in which F sharp for solo oboe and
bassoon in octaves is sounded against a string accompaniment of E flat (violas, 'cellos and basses), A flat (second
violins) and B flat (first violins) – and this odd discord
resolves, if you can call it a resolution, on to another discord.
Truly, Haydn is the most incalculable of composers, and nowhere more so than when he is at his most deceptively simple.

Fourth Movement. *Finale: presto.* This final movement
conforms more closely to the conventional *rondo* form than
most of those in the examples chosen in the foregoing notes.
It is true that considerable thematic developments of the
melodic material take place, but the orthodox *rondo* principle of the alternation of one main theme with subsidiary
episodes is for the most part observed.

The chief key to the plot of the movement is one of
Haydn's characteristic subtleties. The initial three notes of
the main subject, enunciated at the outset, Ex. 21, correspond with the concluding bar, which presents the same
progression in inversion. This relationship is seized upon
and emphasized at the outset, after the first double bar,
when the flutes and bassoons, doubling each other in thirds

at two octaves' distance, repeat the last bar of the subject, and then repeat it in inversion, constituting a repetition of the initial phrase. In the course of the movement this unity in duality becomes the lynch-pin of the movement, in comparison with which the alternating episodes, and even the integral re-statements of the subject, are relatively unimportant. The imaginative resource and ingenuity lavished on this little insignificant three-note phrase are without parallel in music until Beethoven, and unexcelled even by him.

Once this leading principle of the movement has been indicated there is little to be profitably added, except that the final returns of the principal subject are altered or truncated (bars 232 *et seq*.). The movement ends with an emphatic four-bar reiteration of the descending form of the three-note figure.

SYMPHONY NO. 103 IN E FLAT MAJOR
(*The Drum-roll*)

FIRST Movement. *Adagio – Allegro con spirito*. This symphony owes its sub-title to the fact that it begins with a roll on the kettledrum – certainly a sufficiently unorthodox procedure to deserve attention and warrant the appellation. The succeeding theme, for 'cellos, basses, and bassoons, in unison and octaves, is of a grave beauty and majesty unsurpassed by any composer. It consists of two clauses of six bars each.

The exposition of the first movement proper is, for Haydn, comparatively orthodox, consisting in regular first and second subjects, both of which are symmetrically constructed in four-bar phrases. They are not thematically related, but neither are they sharply contrasted.

The development section is full of dramatic surprises and consummate invention. The texture is more contrapuntal and intricate than is usual with Haydn. Contrary to his custom, however, he begins it with a reversion to the first subject instead of with a continuation and development of the second. The subsequent extended discussion of the latter results in the development section being largely an extension and elaboration of the exposition. The recapitulation also follows a normal and orthodox course – suspiciously so; and our suspicions are amply justified. When Haydn is being unimpeachably orthodox in his procedure we expect the unexpected, and here we certainly get it. After the conventional restatement of the second subject in the tonic key an obstreperous outburst for the full orchestra fades out into a *diminuendo*, whereupon the opening *adagio* recurs, heralded by the drum-roll – an effect unique, not merely in the music of Haydn, but in that of any other music before Beethoven. The concluding bars of the movement consist in a hilarious development, in diminution, of this *adagio* subject, followed by fragmentary references to the two chief subjects of the movement, anticipating Sibelius in this procedure by more than a century.

There is probably nothing of importance in modern music that has not, in one way or another, been anticipated by Haydn.

Second Movement. *Andante.* The slow movement consists in a series of variations upon two alternating themes, the first in C minor, the second in C major. The first subject is given out by strings alone, at first in bare two-part writing, Ex. 22. The unusual melodic line is cunningly wrought. Note how it rises, almost imperceptibly, from G in the second bar to A in the fourth to B flat in the sixth, and C in the seventh, and then falls. Reflect incidentally, on the fact, here illustrated, that the majority of examples of sustained melodic writing (as opposed to brief, pregnant, incisive motives) are fundamentally based upon this formula of a gradual ascent to a point, and a subsequent declension from it.

The sequel to this theme constitutes an interesting example of one of Haydn's favourite methods of melodic construction, more frequently encountered in his string quartets than in his symphonies – namely, the way in which he takes the last phrase of a theme as the point of departure for a new line of thought. The B flat E flat cadence becomes the initial phrase of a new subject, though not unrelated to the first (the characteristic rhythm of bar 4 recurs), and develops into a counter-point to the return of the original theme for the lower strings. Similarly, with the second (major) subject, the characteristic trill and turn of the fourth and eighth bars becomes the starting point of fresh developments.

There is a certain relationship, by the way, between the two subjects; not a close one, but as of cousins, exemplified chiefly in the first phrase of each, with the interval of C F sharp common to both.

The return of the second theme brings with it an elaborately figured violin solo part. For the rest, it is impossible to do justice to the richness and variety of resource displayed in the subsequent developments of these two themes without the aid of more musical illustrations than I have at my disposal. It must suffice to say that the fertility of invention, instrumental, melodic, and harmonic, give this movement a high place in Haydn's achievement. The second subject, incidentally, gradually assumes the ascendancy, and the movement ends triumphantly in the major key.

Third Movement. *Menuetto*. The characteristic melodic feature of the chief theme of the minuet movement is the rhythmic formula commonly described as the 'Scottish snap' – quite wrongly, for it is as common a feature of Hungarian music with which Haydn was, of course, familiar. Note, by the way, how, as in the foregoing movement, the descending fifth of the last bar of the theme becomes the initial phrase of the succeeding sequel, in the minor. The rhythmic formula already alluded to also recurs, imparting a unity to the two sections. The subsequent trio section is of an artless and engaging simplicity which stands in no need of commentary.

Fourth Movement. *Finale: Allegro con spirito*. This last movement is unique in Haydn's output for being based throughout exclusively on one subject, and for a complete absence of repeats. The music drives along from start to finish in an unflagging torrent of inspiration. There is not a bar in the movement which cannot be shown to have a thematic derivation from the glorious, majestic subject, which is treated with an imaginative resource and invention that not even Bach himself has equalled. This

movement defies definition by any text-book formula. It is not
a *rondo*, neither is it in sonata form, or in any category of form
other than that of itself, which, as already observed, is
unique. It defies analysis, and even if sufficient musical
quotations were available they would be of no use – one
would have to quote the whole movement. It is one and
indissoluble from beginning to end.

SYMPHONY NO. 104 IN D MAJOR (*The London*)

ALTHOUGH no fewer than twelve of Haydn's last symphonies were written in or for London, the specific title of
London Symphony as such has been accorded to the present
number, the last of the series, and the last symphony Haydn
wrote. It was composed in 1795 and received its first performance at a benefit concert in London in the course of the
same year.

Before proceeding to a detailed consideration of each
movement it might be as well to deal here with a curious
technical problem which applies also to the foregoing Symphony No. 103 in E flat, namely, Haydn's use of the clarinets, which is of rare occurrence, and confined to some of the
latest works. In the preceding example the clarinets are
used in the first and last movements only. In the present example the autograph manuscript shows parts for
the clarinets in the first movement alone. The clarinet parts
in the succeeding movements are a later addition – whether
in accordance with the composer's directions or due to the
initiative of some editor or other it is difficult to decide. But
whichever the explanation, the shy, tentative, hesitant
approach to this new tone colour on his instrumental palette
is of great interest. One gets the impression that Haydn felt
he ought to make use of this instrument on account of its
beauty of tone and infinite resource, but that he found it
difficult to incorporate it into the method of orchestral
writing which he had cultivated over a period of so many
years. In the instrumental writing of Mozart the clarinet is
of primary significance; the mention of the name of the
instrument always conjures up Mozartian associations. But

in the music of Haydn one always feels the clarinet to be an unwelcome intruder into the family circle – the beautiful strange newcomer who brings trouble into the household. It does not seem to belong, and no distinctive role, such as it deserves, is assigned to it in his work.

First Movement. *Adagio – Allegro.* Of all Haydn's slow and solemn symphonic introductions this one, the last, is without question the grandest. The incisive initial, unison phrase is Beethovenian in character, as is also the dynamic contrast between *fortissimo* and *pianissimo* at the close.

The noble, stately, chief subject, Ex. 23, of the succeeding *allegro* dominates the movement throughout, to the virtual exclusion of any other thematic material. Tovey even goes so far as to say that the first theme does duty for the second subject as well, but in view of his recurrent strictures directed against the text-book pedants, where Haydn is concerned, one is surely right in assuming this utterance to be a leg-pull. It is not, however, strictly justified, for there is a clearly defined second subject at bar 80, Ex. 24. It is true, however, that apart from its orthodox return in the key of the tonic at the end of the movement, it plays no part whatever in the proceedings. The first subject dominates throughout.

Second Movement. *Andante.* The monothematic principle of the first movement is carried over into the second, which consists in variations and developments of a single subject, embellished by counterpoints and elaborate instrumental figuration. Dramatic developments and conflicts occur midway through the movement, but are resolved in a tranquil close.

Third Movement. *Menuetto: Allegro.* The minuet conforms to type, in that the first statement of the theme is succeeded by a sequel which is a development and extension of it. But this particular exemplification of the conventional formula is more symphonic in its developments than usual. The subsequent *trio* section is in the comparatively remote key of B flat, which is entered abruptly, without any preliminary modulation. It is characterized chiefly by one of these flowing quaver figurations which Haydn so often favours in this section of his minuet movements. But the initial rising minor third recurs throughout the *trio*.

Fourth Movement. *Finale: Spiritoso.* Over a long-held tonic pedal – a rare occurrence in the music of Haydn, one of whose most noteworthy stylistic features consists in clarity of texture, and rapid movement in the parts – the chief, and indeed the only important subject of the final movement is given out by the first violins without any other accompaniment, Ex. 35, except sustained horns and 'cellos. The form of the movement is no doubt technically a *rondo*, in that the chief theme alternates with occasional episodes, but these are so few and of such small dimensions that the movement, seen as a whole, resolves itself into a symphonic development of one subject which is treated with infinite resource and inexhaustible invention, as in the corresponding movement of the foregoing symphony, and the first two movements of the present example.

Adequate formal analysis would demand an amount of space and musical illustrations which are here precluded. It must suffice to draw attention to an exquisitely poetic and imaginative passage towards the close, at which the flare of the full orchestra gives place to a little trilogue between two oboes and a solo flute, which latter behaves very oddly at the outset, leaping down two octaves and back again. The scoring at bar 309 *et seq.* also merits close attention on account of its astonishing boldness and unorthodoxy, with its double pedal in thirds for horns doubled by bassoons in the lower octave, and the independence of 'cellos and basses. You will not easily find such a page of scoring until modern times.

With this astonishing instrumental gesture concludes his last symphony. Nothing could be more typically representative of his bold, forward-looking genius. Equally significant is the formal tendency, so clearly exemplified in this work and its immediate predecessor, towards a monothematic structural principle – a course which was not followed by Mozart or Beethoven, but constitutes an anticipation of the ideals of the Romantic composers. Both in his consummate achievement, and in his prophetic, premonitory role, Haydn takes rank with the greatest masters in the history of music. There may be others as great; there is assuredly none greater.

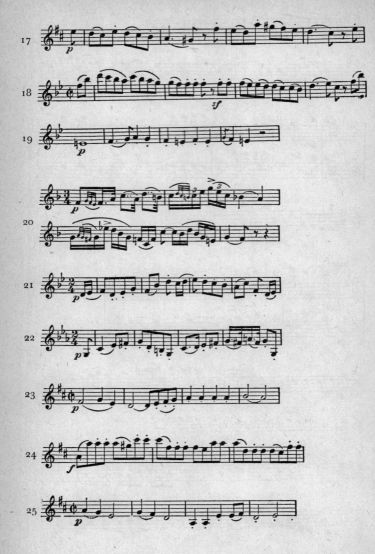

3

Wolfgang Amadeus Mozart (1756-1791)

ERIC BLOM

INTRODUCTION

IT is still sometimes asked by those who, for instance, regard Mozart as falling short of Wagner in 'range' or of Brahms in 'profundity' what the qualities may be that are supposed to make him one of the greatest composers. That question cannot be answered here, though, given adequate space, it is quite capable of being settled to the satisfaction of all but those who have no wish to be satisfied. But an essay on the best of his symphonies must begin with some attempt at accounting for his greatness particularly as a symphonist.

That greatness, it should be obvious, is not a matter of quantity, for, although he wrote over forty full-sized symphonies, Haydn wrote more than twice as many – and Beethoven only nine. Nor is it a matter of Mozart's doing anything to establish the symphonic form, as he established that of the piano concerto. That had been done before him, mainly by Haydn, and Mozart did not contribute nearly as much to its modification and expansion as Beethoven did after him, and Schubert too, if it comes to that – to mention no others.

Not that the mere shaping of musical forms, although great composers have often had a hand in it, is in itself an achievement making for greatness. Minor musicians all through history have often done most of the pioneering in that direction. 'Interesting historical figures', Tovey called them, the inverted commas indicating a certain amount of scorn, as a sweeping Toveyan remark to the effect that 'I.H.F.s cannot compose' unequivocally confirms. Be that as it may – and the I.H.F.s have at any rate written great quantities of music, whether we choose to call it composition or not – what concerns us here is to see what it is that a great master like Mozart does with a form like the symphony which he has neither invented nor greatly advanced for the benefit of later exponents. There must, we tell ourselves as we listen spellbound to a Mozart symphony, be something else than the contrivance and manipulation of structure about the creation of music in this or any other form.

There is indeed something else, and that something, hard as it is to define, is perhaps best called individuality. Mozart's handling of the symphony as a form differs from Haydn's only in the incidental details of procedure, and that does not mean a great deal if we consider that Haydn's own symphonies differ quite as much from each other in formal management. But no listener with any sort of ear trained to distinguish between styles – personal as distinct from mere period styles – could possibly for more than a moment mistake a symphony by Mozart for one by Haydn. The language may be the same, or nearly the same with some variants that amount merely to those of dialect; but what is expressed in that language belongs to different worlds of feeling, of spiritual attitude and of mental shape.

But if Mozart's individuality is easily enough apprehended by a listener with some kind of discrimination, it becomes tantalizingly elusive directly one tries to describe it on paper. Who is to say why exactly the opening of the great G minor Symphony gives a peculiar impression of just that apprehensive agitation, just that foreboding of tragedy? A technical explanation, that the movement is fast and the key is minor, does not help, for someone may remind us that the scherzo in Mendelssohn's *Midsummer Night's Dream* music is also fast and in a minor key (in fact the very same key, as it happens) without sounding in the least apprehensively agitated or tragic. When all is said, great inspiration remains a mystery, and formal analysis can help us only to see how that inspiration has been outwardly organized by the composer without accounting for its nature and quality.

Yet, though we may feel all sorts of things on hearing Mozart and respond to his music with an intuitive understanding that goes a long way towards meeting him in his own mental and emotional sphere, we are bound to fall back on technical discussion directly we try to write about his work. This cannot help to account for his artistic individuality, but it can at least show something of the ways and means by which that individuality communicates itself to others.

Mozart's way of reaching his listeners is to make use of a faultless technical equipment. His is so smooth and natural a technique as to be very easily overlooked. In fact we are not intended to be made aware of it or to admire it for its own sake: it is merely the means to an end, and in the case of one so supremely gifted a perfectly convenient and untroublesome means, even where it involves appalling difficulties. No parade is ever made of skill or learning. Sometimes, it is true, as in the finale of the *Jupiter Symphony,* sheer pleasure in the exercise of a staggering virtuosity takes hold of Mozart irresistibly; but even there the music remains clear, its surface undisturbed by the polyphonic problems he tackles, so that the hearer who remains unaware of them still enjoys the incomparable flow and polish of the music.

Mozart's sovereign ease in the handling of counterpoint is the very foundation of his style and one of the great differences between him and Beethoven, who happened to find counterpoint difficult – which is not to say that he eschewed it or that, when he faced it, he failed to do justice to his own peculiar genius. What distinguishes Mozart is the fact that he always applied this gift of his, whether he intended to write polyphonically or not, and that, considering how readily contrapuntal writing came to him, he made conscious use of polyphonic skill surprisingly rarely. But it was at the very root of his technique, even where he simply wrote accompanied melody. It is this which explains why his part-writing and his spacing are always, whatever the nature of the musical texture may be at the moment, superbly lucid and limpid. It is a mistake to suppose that great contrapuntists are at their greatest only where they use counterpoint ostentatiously. Even Bach by no means always did so. Besides, there have been very highly skilled masters of counterpoint who were dry and lifeless composers – who were in fact I.H.F.s and, in at any rate one sense of Tovey's dictum, could not compose. On the other hand Schubert was misguided when he thought, at the end of his short life, that he stood in need of lessons in academic counterpoint from Sechter, who is not much of an historical figure and certainly not an interesting one. A young genius who could write such a good continually moving bass against a vital theme as that in the finale of the Octet, or bring tunes that have any amount of value and character by themselves into such perfect combination as in the slow movement of the great C major Symphony, lacked nothing as a contrapuntist that a great composer of his sort could possibly require. And in this respect Schubert resembled Mozart, whose technique is that of a great symphonist because it is fundamentally that of a great contrapuntist. So much at least of his genius we can account for technically; but he would not have been the supreme personality he was if he had not also possessed gifts of imagination which it is beyond verbal analysis to expound.

SYMPHONY NO. 29 IN A MAJOR (K. 201)

AMONG Mozart's early symphonies this slender but extremely appealing work of 1774, scored for only the normal small Salzburg orchestra of two oboes, two horns, and strings, takes the foremost place in one's affections. The music of the years spent at the archiepiscopal court of Salzburg, where service imposed arduous duties without offering any of the pleasures of or compensations for creative work that are due to genius, is often merely ceremonial or merely entertaining. But ever and again the youthful musician took fire from his inspiration and wrote for his own satisfaction. If the Archbishop too was satisfied, so much the better, no doubt; but since he was clearly disposed to be pleased with smaller feats of skill than Mozart lavished on the present work, we may conclude that when the composer took such special pains as he did here, he had no thought of flattering his patron. As is the way of genius, the exercise of skill and the pleasure taken in it could not fail to kindle invention.

First Movement. *Allegro moderato*. There was no need whatever, once Mozart had hit on a very good first subject for a work in sonata form, to do anything more than use it as it came, as a thing of delightful shape. But when, as here, it was presently found to combine admirably in imitations, he could see no reason for not welcoming such a find. Whether such things happened by accident or design nobody knows. The answer to the mystery, one suspects, is that Mozart, when disposed to make use of contrapuntal feats, had a way of lighting instinctively on musical ideas capable of this kind of treatment, though we know that he would sometimes try out the trickiest passages on slips of paper. In the coda the first subject of the present movement makes a threefold imitative entry, at the three intervals of the common chord as in Ex. 1. That this can have been due to a happy chance is hard to believe, and, even if it was, it still took a born contrapuntist to become aware of its possibilities. On the other hand it is almost as difficult to imagine that such things came to so spontaneous a composer as Mozart was by a patient process of trial and error. The notion that complexities occurred to him by a kind of unconscious foresight is thus probably not so far-fetched as it may seem when first suggested. The second-subject group, in E major, is very sunny and gracious. One of its strains also makes use of imitative entries and another is a very enlivening bit of Italian comic-opera music that might have gone straight into *La finta giardiniera* written a few months after this Symphony.*

Second Movement. *Andante*. The slow movement, with muted violins, is in full sonata form, with a coda derived from the chief material. Its peaceful atmosphere is that of a sunlit garden and its finely balanced shape suggests that the garden is one with trimmed hedges and symmetrical vistas.

* The opera bears the K. number 196, but according to Alfred Einstein's revised edition of the Köchel catalogue it was written between September 1774 and January 1775, whereas the Symphony belongs to January 1774.

First and second violins are beautifully interlinked, and later the violas and the horns have melodic snatches made tactfully conspicuous.

Third Movement. *Minuetto*. An extraordinarily vigorous and original movement. The octave unisons for the oboes and horns on the rhythm of Ex. 2 at the end of each of the two parts of the main section are a daring innovation, and the immediate mocking imitation of it by the strings at the opening of the second part is irresistibly humorous. The trio section, in E major, is ingratiatingly gentle and produces some affecting chromatic harmony.

Fourth Movement. *Allegro con spirito*. The finale is pure *opera buffa*. The youth of eighteen betrays himself, not as inexperienced – one might almost say that Mozart was never inexperienced as an artist – but as cheerfully ready to grasp at an easy way of getting effects, and of carrying on, if it happens to occur to him and to suit his purpose. The many repeated bass quavers and the filling-up of inner parts with bowed tremolos are just the kind of least-resistance devices one may find in his early operas. But he soon remembers that he is writing a symphony, and there is artfulness as well as art in the linked sequential suspensions which continue the very pretty second subject; and this initial figure, Ex. 3, is used imitatively with great skill in the working-out. (The word 'pretty', by the way, though it happens to be the right one here, should not be taken to confirm the far too widespread view that Mozart is the 'dainty' composer, not only of the popular fancy, but even of the imagination of many musicians, especially of the nineteenth century, who ought to have known better and seen deeper. He could achieve prettiness incomparably well simply because he could express anything whatever that came within the range of the technical resources and the aesthetic conceptions of his time.)

SYMPHONY NO. 31 IN D MAJOR (K. 297)
(*'Paris' Symphony*)

THIS work, written for the Concert Spirituel in Paris during Mozart's long visit there in 1778, is not one to which many music-lovers, or even many Mozart-lovers, are greatly attached. It is very far from perfunctory in workmanship, but there is a certain cold brilliancy about the first movement and finale, several episodes in which, too, have a rather empty effectiveness. The truth is that Mozart was not very anxious to carry out this task, probably because he did not much relish complying with certain special requirements deemed indispensable by the conductor, Le Gros, if the work was to please a Parisian audience. He began it duly with the energetic downbeat (octaves for the violins) – the *premier coup d'archet* which the Paris orchestra proudly regarded as its speciality, but about which Mozart scornfully wrote home that the players merely started together, as orchestras did anywhere else. On the other hand he must have been delighted to find that he could use clarinets, for the first time in a symphony, though he had already met the newfangled instrument at Mannheim, so that this was not quite its first appearance in a score of his. What is curious about the *Paris Symphony*, and what makes it historically important, is that it is the only work by Mozart in that form which makes use of an orchestra complete with trumpets and drums in which clarinets appeared from the first together with oboes. It will be seen presently that the clarinet parts in two later symphonies containing oboes are afterthoughts.

First Movement. *Allegro assai.* Here is the *premier coup d'archet*, followed by a soft antithetical phrase in the manner of the Mannheim school and other early exponents of the symphony: Ex. 4. The formal procedure for this movement is peculiar and interesting. The first-subject group includes a graceful phrase which does not recur in the recapitulation at all, for there the music leads to the restatement of the second subject by way of further developments of Ex. 4, such as might more normally have found a place in the working-out section; and that section is made to emerge from the exposition almost imperceptibly, without the double bar with which Mozart usually makes a clear demarcation at this point.

Second Movement. *Andantino.* The slow movement begins

with the charming tune: Ex. 5. It is a lovely piece of placid music and is clearly more profoundly felt than the first movement and finale. But it did not please Le Gros, who was determined to persuade Mozart that it had not pleased the Concert Spirituel audience either at the first performance on 18th June. It was too long, apparently, and contained too many modulations! So a new and shorter movement was substituted by Mozart for the second performance of 15th August. To save possible confusion let its opening be quoted also in Ex. 6. For confusion there has been until quite recently. Even the third edition of Köchel's catalogue, until its editor brought out a corrected reprint, still stated that the *Andantino*, beginning as shown in Ex. 5, was the later piece, although it is quoted with the indication '98' bars, whereas the other is marked '58' bars. Let it be quite clear: the longer movement, which appears in all editions except the first one brought out in Paris, is the one representing Mozart's first intention, although it is fair to add that he said he liked both, each for its own peculiar qualities. It is quite possible that a modern audience might share his view; there is something to be said for an occasional performance with both the slow movements.

Third Movement. *Allegro*. The finale is very spirited, and Mozart had the courage to ration the *premiers coups d'archet* to one, for this movement begins stealthily with Ex. 7. It is in sonata form. The second-subject group begins with characteristic imitations, Ex. 8, of which rather more is made, briefly but with great polyphonic skill, in the working out. A cadence which appears to drive to a close in an alien key, but is jerked back into D major, is a witty feature of this finale, which ends with a fiery display for the full orchestra.

SYMPHONY NO. 34 IN C MAJOR (K. 338)

LIKE the *Paris Symphony*, this little but delightful work of 1780, the last composed at Salzburg, contains no minuet – an indication that we should not allow ourselves to be tempted into imagining either that Mozart followed a

French fashion in the earlier work or that the commission for K. 297 meant so little to him that he responded with as short a work as possible. (We have seen that one movement was found not short enough.)

There is no space, unfortunately, for an analysis of this little C major Symphony, but it must at least be mentioned as a particularly attractive example and as the work immediately preceding the last six great symphonies, which will be dealt with at greater length in a moment. First, however, the openings of each of the three movements of K. 338, at any rate, must be quoted:

I. *Allegro vivace:* Ex. 9. II. *Andante di molto:* Ex. 10. III. *Allegro vivace:* Ex. 11.

SYMPHONY NO. 35 IN D MAJOR (K. 385)
('*Haffner*' *Symphony*)

IN 1776 Mozart had written the D major Serenade (K. 250) for the wedding of the late Salzburg burgomaster Sigmund Haffner's daughter; in the summer of 1782 Leopold Mozart wrote to his son in Vienna asking for another work of the same kind to be sent to Salzburg for this family, apparently for some celebration connected with a title of nobility conferred on Sigmund Haffner, jun. Mozart complied, though he was overworked – so much so that only on pressure from his father did he send on a march as an opening movement (K. 408, No. 2) after the work had been dispatched. On the other hand it originally contained two minuets and was thus, so far as the disposition of its movements went, a serenade or cassation, the kind of work, in fact, required for a festivity at which we may be sure the movements were interspersed with conversation and refreshments and, we may at least surmise with fair certainty, a march was used for an opening procession, like a polonaise at a ball, and the minuets may have actually been danced. Mozart, however, called the work a 'Symphony' in his letters, and it is certainly symphonic in stature, though the form of the first movement and the nature of the middle ones show characteristic departures from the normal Mozartian symphony type.

First Movement. *Allegro con spirito*. It is usual to say that what distinguishes the first movement from all others in Mozart's symphonies is the fact that it is 'monothematic'. It is true that the first subject, Ex. 12, reappears in the place where the second is expected, and in the conventional key for such a subject (the dominant); but the fact is that there really is a second subject, and indeed one of the conspicuously melodic kind to be expected from Mozart, Ex. 13. All that happens is that the first subject remains present as a counterpoint, for the simple reason that it chances to combine ideally, either by a miraculous accident or by a still more miraculous contrivance, with the new theme. An attentive hearer will have noticed just before that it also goes smoothly with the bridge-passage leading from the first to the second subject and, earlier still (at the fifteenth bar from the opening), that it could be used in canon. Here, then, we have what is really distinctive about this movement: not that it is 'monothematic', but that it is, for a movement in sonata form, unusually polyphonic* – and polyphonic treatment presupposes the use of such a thematic tag as Ex. 12 in as many different ways as possible. Astonishing things happen in the working-out section, not only contrapuntally, but also harmonically. Within 34 bars Ex. 12 combines in all sorts of ways and the world of D major is turned topsy-turvy. After a half-close of D minor, for instance, there is a sudden plunge into the infinitely remote key of F sharp major, which in any case is almost unheard-of in Mozart.

Second Movement. *Andante*. The placid, friendly slow movement, in G major, is summer-garden music ideally fitted for a serenade. But there are depths of feeling below its calm surface, as so often in Mozart, who is a passionate composer, quite well enough brought up – musically speaking – to know how to behave in the eighteenth-century drawing-room, but often brooding on dark thoughts which become apparent to those who have learnt to know him

---

* Unusually, but not uniquely, for Mozart: the first movement of his piano Sonata in F major, K. 533, proceeds in a similar way and also makes a feature of contrapuntally combined first and second subjects.

well and to listen to him understandingly. The woodwind
sighs and the diminished-seventh inflection in this cadence
give a hint of such undercurrents, Ex. 14. Later on, as the
end of the first half of the movement and again the real close
are approached, Mozart uses a device that is peculiar to
him (there are many familiar instances of it in *Don Giovanni*,
for example): that of breaking off a cadence just where it is
about to reach its resolution and resuming it two or three
bars earlier, the concluding harmony being heard only the
second time. Here, however, this process is further complicated by a quite considerable extension of the cadence-
phrase at its second appearance, so that the resolution is
further delayed, with an effect that is at once tantalizing and
enchanting.

Third Movement. *Minuetto*. The one remaining minuet,
in D major, is energetic and festive. It alternates between
vigorous striding figures and gentle, graceful contrasts, as
though the music were alternately addressing male and
female partners in the dance. The trio is in A major
and has the happy songfulness to which that key so often
tempts Mozart. Trumpets and drums, which assert themselves in the main section of the minuet, are silent here. A
false note (D sharp) in the second-violin figures of
accompaniment is humorously emphasized by *sforzando*
markings.

Fourth Movement. *Presto*. Flutes and clarinets, which
were kept silent in the two middle movements, reappear
here. As a matter of fact they were afterthoughts even in the
first movement and finale: their parts were added by Mozart
at a later date. The conventional and obvious thing to say
about this finale is that it strikingly resembles Osmin's aria
in *The Seraglio* – the work which bears the catalogue number
(K. 384) immediately preceding that assigned to the *Haffner
Symphony*. Here is the main theme of the aria Ex. 15, and
here the first subject of the symphonic finale, Ex. 16. The
superficial resemblance is clear to the most unobservant –
which is perhaps why it has never failed to be noticed – and
it is, of course, quite possible that Mozart, being in a hurry
when he wrote the Symphony, found it convenient to fall

back on an idea that had occurred to him before, to set himself going. But the point is that other ideas immediately presented themselves to him which made the nature of the movement entirely different from that of the aria, though both pieces are wonderfully exhilarating. The aria is comically irascible; the symphonic movement has a second subject of a feathery lightness and grace which Mozart, whose sense of character in opera is faultless, could never have thought of in connection with Osmin, the fat, amorous, and bad-tempered keeper of the harem. It appears thus in its original form: Ex. 17; and later in this transformation, made even more captivating by the chromatic bass: Ex.18. This minor-key version is a genuine symphonic development, and it is quite in order to speak of a second subject, since it appears in true sonata-form fashion, first in the dominant and later in the tonic. Yet the first subject behaves like a rondo theme, for it recurs four times in the same shape. What is different is the way in which it is approached, each time more wittily than the last, in a movement that is perfect comedy from start to finish. The crowning comic touch comes at the last return of the main theme, when the concluding note A of Ex. 16 is unexpectedly stepped up to B, with the result that the closing pages are approached in a roundabout way.

SYMPHONY NO. 36 IN C MAJOR (K. 425)
('Linz' Symphony)

ON the way back to Vienna from Salzburg, where Mozart had gone in the summer of 1783 to present his wife to his father and sister, with no very satisfactory results, he and Constanze stayed at Linz late in October, on a visit to old Count Thun, who was a great music-lover and for whom Mozart composed this Symphony at very short notice. It was performed on 4th November in the Linz theatre. That its workmanship does not show a trace of haste anywhere might be accounted a miracle, were it not that Mozart's whole career shows that it meant no more trouble to him to write a perfect work than a perfunctory one, even when he was in a hurry. True, he could be shallow on occasion, but the only time he showed that he was capable of being clumsy was when he wrote *A Musical Joke* (K. 522), which is a deliberate parody of bad composition. His impeccable taste and technique saved him again and again when it came to carrying out a commission. In both respects the *Linz Symphony* is exemplary.

First Movement. *Adagio – Allegro spiritoso*. Slow introductions are rare in Mozart's symphonies. The fact that he did not shirk writing one here, as he could easily have done, is only another proof that if anything ever worried him in the process of composition, it was not lack of time. This introduction is brief but portentous and, as it turns out, deliberately ambiguous. With its pathetic melodies for interlaced first and second violins, its explosive accents and its sighing chromatics for oboe and bassoon, it might lead to some tragic set piece in an *opera seria;* knowing our Mozart, we might also expect it to preface a large serio-comic number like the great sextet in *Don Giovanni*. What it does introduce is a very cheerful and brilliant movement, in which we soon hear Handel's 'brave hallelujahs'. The first-subject group embraces at least eight separate ideas, every one a striking invention, but the whole long paragraph is so contrived as to achieve both contrast and relevance. Here is one of the inventions, apparently subsidiary, but important later on, Ex. 19. The second subject, very exceptionally in a classical sonata-form movement in a major key, begins in the relative minor of the dominant (E minor) and before it repents and goes on into the orthodox key of the dominant (G major) the wind parts try slyly to reassert the tonic (C major). This modulatory process is repeated, with different scoring, and G major is then firmly nailed down and not to be deflected even by chromatic allusions to No. 19, until the end of the exposition is almost reached. But here a passage of modulation that can lead equally well to C major, for the repeat of the exposition, and to A minor, for the working-out, appears thus, Ex. 20. If the repeat is not made the dual function of this passage fails to appear and an interesting point is lost.* The working-out begins, as will be seen, with an allusion to Ex. 19. It continues with extensions of Ex. 20 which turn it from a mere bridge-passage into a feature of thematic importance, and some fascinating transitory material then leads to the recapitulation. This, but for some new details, is perfectly regular, the transition between first and second subjects being so managed that the latter group now appears in A minor, F major and C major. Ex. 20 then provides a short coda, and to the last we have thematic references, the rhythm marked *a* in Ex. 19 appearing in the bass quite near the end.

Second Movement. *Poco adagio.* The slow movement, in F major, has the lovely Christmas serenity of Handel's and Bach's Pastoral Symphonies. No doubt the placid 6–8 motion partly accounts for this, but there is a spiritual rather than purely musical kinship. Also, there are some touches which for Bach and Handel would have been those of an alien, futurist style. One of these is the loud wind-and-drums unison answering a gentle violin phrase, Ex. 21, and another the curiously spiky figures which briefly become a feature of the musical development after the expository section, Ex. 22.

Third Movement. *Minuetto.* A very simple but, being Mozart's, by no means artless dance movement. Trumpets and drums, which are often dropped in the minuets of classical masters, here add a certain pomp to the proceedings. But they characteristically refrain from doing the obvious by joining into the whole of typically trumpet-and-drum figures such as these in Ex. 23 where the first five notes are given to violins, oboes, and horns alone, the trumpets and drums joining only into the cadential chords. The idyllic trio makes use of first oboe, first bassoon, and string only.

* There are numerous classical movements in which repeating the exposition serves no purpose beyond that of lengthening the music and making sure that the thematic material is impressed on the hearer's memory – the former not always desirable and the latter superfluous and often tiresome in the case of very familiar works. There are others, as here, when the repeat is vitally important if the composer's scheme is to be appreciated.

Fourth Movement. *Presto*. The finale, in full sonata form, is from first to last perfect *opera buffa* music. Its verve is irresistible, its wit inexhaustible. The selection of one or two specimens for quotation is embarrassing: one wants to quote the whole movement in full score, for the orchestration is as enchanting as the thematic invention. A point at which both these qualities appear in equal measure may be singled out from the endearingly gracious second-subject group, where the violas stand out for a moment with warmly sustained notes, Ex. 24. The working-out makes a great deal of play with a theme that had turned up in the exposition as a merely subsidiary incident, Ex. 25. Immediately after its appearance as quoted it ties itself into a comically ill-tempered harmonic knot, sounding like an anticipation of Beckmesser's chalking up an alleged mistake. Afterwards it is turned upside down and rhythmically distorted. A regular recapitulation is followed by a brief and fiery coda based on the opening theme.

SYMPHONY NO. 38 IN D MAJOR (K. 504)
(*'Prague' Symphony*)

THE accepted German label for this work is 'Mozart's Symphony without a Minuet'; but we have already come across two other Mozart symphonies without minuets in these notes, and there are at least a dozen earlier ones, even if we consider only the complete and unquestionably genuine works. It is like calling *Twelfth Night* 'Shakespeare's play without a murderer'. Instead of this meaningless label that of *Prague Symphony* will do quite well, for although the work may not have been written expressly for Prague, it was certainly performed there, on 19th January, 1787. Mozart had gone to the Bohemian capital to enjoy the success of his *Figaro,* which led to the commission of *Don Giovanni,* produced at the Prague Opera the following October. There are several incidents in this Symphony which look almost like sketches for *Don Giovanni.*

First Movement. *Adagio – Allegro*. At the very opening, for instance, we hear the figure afterwards used for the stone guest's heavy footsteps in the second finale of the opera; and much else in this slow introduction resembles the music associated with the avenging statue. Then we have the following transition to the *allegro:* Ex. 26, which is almost exactly like that in the second-act sextet in *Don Giovanni*, except that there the key is E flat major. The opening of the *allegro* itself, moreover, proceeds just like that of the *Don Giovanni* overture, and here even the key is the same. A similar type of theme is followed by an ejaculation from wind and drums, and the captivating additional woodwind phrase at the theme's second appearance, giving it a new harmonic colour, is another anticipation. Nothing could be more eventful than this opening, nothing more enticing to a composer to go on giving his invention free rein. But what Mozart does, with the supreme tact of genius, is to let the power to invent and the power to develop give way to each other by turns, or rather to become so intermingled that development itself amounts to invention. When, after a vigorous transition, his main theme returns in A major, with a subtle harmonic change, it begins to twist itself into polyphonic complexities that no longer call to mind the overture to *Don Giovanni*, but the elaborately fugal one to *The Magic Flute*. Everything having been smoothed out by another transition, the second subject appears in A major. It is built – or rather airily woven – from figures of this rhythmic type, Ex. 27, but nothing short of quotation to its full extent (which is impossible here) could give an idea of its ineffable grace and charm. Its turn into the minor, with bassoons cutting rhythmically across the strings, the heavenly cadence flowing back into the major (Schubert's speciality, but never more enchantingly indulged in by him) and the new counter-subject which at the same time acts as a link to further developments of an earlier transition – all this has scarcely been excelled anywhere in music, even by Mozart himself. The exposition closes brilliantly with some new energetic matter incorporating an allusion to the first subject. We are still in the dominant (A major). In that key the working-out begins surprisingly with what appears to be a new and irrelevant idea, and not a very interesting one –

merely one of those tags that come in handy for polyphonic purposes, the hearer who comes newly to this Symphony will probably say – Ex. 28. (But see bars 9-10 of Ex. 26). And polyphonic its treatment certainly is, for it appears at once closely intertwined with imitations of itself, and then with a new figure. And just as we wonder what this material is doing at a juncture where more familiar matter ought to come in for development, the first subject does make its re-entry, not to oust the satellite theme, but to be combined with it in a dizzy feat of counterpoint into which, as if these wonders were not enough, the now familiar transitional theme is also made to enter presently. Even this is not all. We again hear the cadence-theme of the end of the exposition and then the first subject in its plainest form, as at the opening, as though a recapitulation were beginning. But this is a false start, humorously made to hoodwink listeners who have not the gift of absolute pitch. Those who have will know that they are in the wrong key – still, or again, A major. And there, in a moment, is Ex. 28 once more, starting new combinations with the main subject. But it takes full possession of the music for a little while, to assume, with perfect blandness, the task of leading to the real recapitulation at last. This proceeds normally, except that the new and fascinating modulations are gone through by Ex. 26 in order to get back into the tonic key for the second subject and that the concluding pages make a somewhat broader reference to the main theme than the corresponding passage had done at the end of the exposition.

Second Movement. *Andante*. The slow movement is mainly an outpouring of exquisite melodies, one after another. Here is the opening tune, introduced by the first violins, shown with a variant to flute and bassoon a moment later: Ex. 29. But if Mozart the melodist is to the fore here, he is none the less the great contrapuntist for not displaying his skill in that direction as openly as he did in the first move-ment. None but a superb contrapuntist could devise such a passage as Ex. 30, which, with all its melodic loveliness, depends not so much on a single tune as on the perfect interlacing of three melodic strands not very remarkable in themselves. At the end of the first part of the movement we come upon a new, simple but very beautiful cadence-phrase which gives rise to a criticism – for once – of Mozart's management of form, though it has validity only in the light of modern taste, which will not tolerate repeats of even one section of an already lengthy slow movement. There is no doubt that this piece would be too long if such a repeat were made. Yet if it is not, we lose the point of the modulatory development of the cadence-phrase, which comes immediately at the opening of the second section, and comes undoubtedly too soon. The composer's idea was that all the first part should stand between the original appearance of that phrase and its development, and if that does not happen there seems to be something lopsided about this movement as a whole. But the repeat too puts the composer in the wrong before a modern audience. There is nothing for present-day taste to do but to pay for its idiosyncrasies and make a choice between two evils.

Third Movement. *Presto*. The finale, on the other hand, is very short if the first section is not repeated, and it is so exhilarating that one cannot help resenting its ending too soon, though it could hardly be made to flash by quickly enough. Still, since brevity is the soul of wit, and wit is undoubtedly the soul of this finale, mingled with both fire and grace, one must be content to let conductors do as they think fit. The syncopations in the first subject should be noticed, Ex. 31. They do more than anything to keep the amusing game going later on, especially when they become so displaced between treble and bass that the parts appear to do their best to put each other off the stroke. The two rhythms marked *a* and *b* in Ex. 31 keep the music going until the second subject is reached, an inspiration scarcely less captivating than the corresponding subject of the first movement. It consists of three distinct phrases, the first and third for strings, the second for wind. The first is quoted in Ex. 32, while the second follows on immediately at the next bar, Ex. 33. The discreet drollery of the bassoon here is delicious, and the score is so transparent (actually the whole of it is shown above) that this often too self-effacing instrument is distinctly heard. At the second appearance this phrase is made even more exquisite by the addition of a single sustained E on a horn, one of those long-drawn notes which seem to amount to nothing, but in Mozart's scoring for horns often give an entirely new colour to a passage and make the listener tingle with delight. Thus can genius capture us with a single stroke while talent vainly piles effect upon effect. The rhythm *a* of Ex. 31 is very economically used to the end of the exposition, even where new themes – one in triplets and one with trills – appear. The working-out is wholly occupied with the comic entanglements of rhythms *a* and *b*, and the recapitulation is handled in a most original way, for instead of resuming its former shape it continues to be affected by the happenings of the working-out, and the music is wrenched from one unexpected modulation into another. After the return of the second subject the end comes quickly: nothing new appears by way of a coda.

THE LAST THREE SYMPHONIES

THE miracle of Mozart's last three symphonies – all of them things of perfection and each quite different from the others – finished within seven weeks and three days has been thought by some to be altogether inexplicable unless it is taken with one or two grains of salt. True, we must remember that we know only the finishing dates, and we cannot tell how much preliminary work may have been done, not only on the first of them but on all three before the actual process of writing down was begun. Even so the wonder is great enough if we consider the bare facts, of which the following are vital.

The E flat major Symphony (K. 543) was completed on 26th June 1788; the G minor (K. 550) on 25th July; the C major (K. 551) on 10th August. Observe that the catalogue numbers are not consecutive, so that, if they may be trusted for strict chronology, Mozart wrote between the first and the second Symphony a little March for 5 instruments; the C major piano Sonata for beginners (now unfortunately known in a popular dance music perversion called *In an Eighteenth-Century Drawing-Room*); the wonderful Adagio for string quartet intended to preface the quartet arrangement of the C minor Fugue originally written for two pianos; the easy Sonata for piano with violin in F major; a piano Sonata in the same key, which shares its variation movement with the preceding work and the rondo with the 'drawing-room' Sonata – the only sign of hurry we perceive in the works of this period; the Trio in C major for violin, 'cello, and piano; and a Canzonetta for 3 voices and 3 basset horns; not to mention 31 bars of an unfinished violin and piano Sonata in G major. What must be mentioned is that the first three works cited above all appear in Mozart's own catalogue under the date of the E flat Symphony, which is thus obviously the date of entry, not of composition. They may therefore have been written before the Symphony. If so, however, they would have interfered with the actual work on it, and if we consider that the piano Trio in E major was finished four days before the Symphony, we must still marvel at Mozart's fertility and power of application. In the last resort the fact remains that there is no rational explanation for the dates of this symphonic triptych: we can only accept the view that the ways of genius are inexplicable.

The expression 'symphonic triptych' must not be taken to suggest that Mozart had any idea that the three works should be performed together. Nevertheless they have been known to make an admirable programme, for they are wonderfully contrasted. It is scarcely possible to imagine any three works by an artist who is a very distinctive stylist to show greater differences. The first is, we may say, lyrical, the second dramatic, the third ceremonial. But they vary not only in character: they do so also in mood. The first has a kind of autumnal but not melancholy mellowness; the second is tragic and idyllic by turns, and somehow the latter atmosphere poignantly intensifies the former; the third utters festive sounds but at the same time gives evidence of an intense concentration of thought, the kind of foresight and hindsight that distinguishes a great mathematician or chess player.

These differences are intensified, if only outwardly, by the antithetical schemes of orchestration. The E flat Symphony is scored for one flute (no oboes), two clarinets, two bassoons, two horns, two trumpets, drums and strings; the G minor was originally for one flute, two oboes, two bassoons, two horns (no trumpets and drums) and strings – Mozart added two clarinets later, so that they are an afterthought, like those in the *Haffner Symphony*, but certainly *his* thought and therefore worth considering as a rule; the C major is for the same orchestra as the E flat, with the important exception that it uses oboes instead of clarinets.

SYMPHONY NO. 39 IN E FLAT MAJOR (K. 543)

FIRST Movement. *Adagio – Allegro*. The weighty and solemn slow introduction is made mainly from rhythmic patterns of repeated notes and chords, shot here and there with rapid scales, descending in the upper strings and rising in the bass ones. A sharply dissonant clash (D flat against C) near the end is an audacity for the eighteenth century that must have made Mozart's contemporaries mistrust the evidence of their ears, and the diminished seventh and augmented fourth appearing thus in canon just before the cadence leading to the *allegro*, Ex. 34, are hardly less daring. As for this main movement, it is one singularly difficult to perform, as regards tempo, and indeed hardly ever satisfactorily done in that respect. The reason is that while one secret of Mozart's greatness, nowhere more clearly evidenced again and again than in his operas, is his ability to accommodate a great many emotional or dramatic contrasts within a single tempo, conductors brought up on romantic notions of expression, fostered, one suspects, by composer-conductors like Wagner, Mahler, and their disciples, established the idea that these contrasts should be emphasized by fluctuations in pace. To do this is to achieve exaggerated and often sentimentalized expression by sacrificing wholeness of conception and bigness of structure, and it should thus be regarded with suspicion wherever it is encountered, no matter how eminent the interpreter. But it has to be confessed that in the first movement of the E flat Symphony

Mozart makes it almost impossibly difficult to bring all the ideas into the same tempo. The opening of the first-subject group, Ex. 35, is apt to seem too fast if taken at the speed that suits the energetic sequel, Ex. 36, and the structurally important figure in Ex. 37 in the transition to the second subject; and that in turn should on no account sound too hurried, Ex. 38. Nevertheless, the contradictory material must be somehow fused into a single impression in this great Symphony, just as in a great novel a many-sided personage is presented as a consistent character by an author of genius. The difference is, of course, that a novelist makes his impression on the reader without an intermediary, whereas the composer, to reach his hearer, is dependent on an interpreter, who may possess no more than talent. A feature not shown here in music type is a figure of descending scales following on Ex. 36, which we are at liberty to regard as being derived from those heard in the introduction. Another is the extension of the second-subject group by two more phrases for strings even more breathtakingly lovely than that quoted as Ex. 38. It should be noticed that the first continues in the wind while the strings go on with the second. There is some new cadential matter near the end of the exposition, which, however, closes with Ex. 37 in B flat major. This is immediately made further use of for the very concise working-out, where it tentatively appears in G minor only to plunge at once into A flat major, where the extension of the second subject undergoes a brief but exquisite transformation and Ex. 37, followed by the cadence material just mentioned, leads to a sudden pause and an unexpected short link to the recapitulation. This makes the new transition to the tonic key for the second subject in the simplest possible way, but for compensation there is some special interest in the coda, which makes use of the descending scales as well as Ex. 37.

Second Movement. *Andante.* The slow movement is in A flat major, a key very rarely used by Mozart and never at all as the main tonality of any large-scale work. (But then it has remained rather rare, for some obscure reason: how many symphonies in A flat, for instance, can the reader name off hand, apart from Elgar's first?) About the chief theme of this movement, Ex. 39, there is a deceptive simplicity, but it is soon found to be used with amazing artfulness. Before long its second figure (*B*) is moved forward half a bar, so as to coincide with the end of (*A*), and it appears later in the bass, at first only in a new restatement of the theme, but a moment later in combination with a beautiful singing phrase presented in descending sequences. That is not all: what appears at first to be a merely transitional figure in F minor, Ex. 40, becomes later the occasion for one of Mozart's most miraculous polyphonic feats – miraculous not just because it is as smoothly and easily worked as any counterpoint could be, but because it achieves an incomparable, burning beauty at the same time. Here is the incident in its most complex form, with those little final phrases, which had not at first occurred, tucked in comfortably all over the texture, just to make things even a little more difficult – and a great deal more exquisite, Ex. 41. In its further course the music makes very wide modulatory excursions, going as far on the sharp side as B major.

Third Movement. *Allegretto*. The stately and quite straightforward minuet needs no detailed description, and quotation in music-type serves little purpose, since there is no sort of thematic development. But the ceremonious music makes an admirable point of repose between the highly charged emotions of what has gone before and the humorous eventfulness to come in the finale. The trio, which rather unusually remains in the tonic key (E flat major), presents another kind of simplicity: it has a kind of barrel-organ effect, gained by a plain-waltz accompaniment and arpeggios in the gurgling tones of the low clarinet register. It is the second clarinet which produced these, while the first has the tune. This device was a favourite one with Mozart, for he often used it with the pleasure of one enjoying the handling of a new toy.

Fourth Movement. *Allegro*. The finale comes as near to Haydn in character as anything in Mozart's music. The sprightly theme that opens it, Ex. 42, might easily be taken as Haydn's, and so could much of the treatment, which lets

this scrap of tune carry almost the whole of an extremely
spirited and entertaining musical discourse. It is here rather
than in connection with the *Haffner Symphony* that one might
be justified in using the term 'monothematic'. A place is
properly made in the key of the dominant for a second subject, but when it comes to the point it is Ex. 42 again
which governs such new matter as there is. After that the
music makes comically drastic modulations: it plunges from
B flat major into F sharp major, for instance, with scarcely
a pretence at preparation. At the working out we get B flat
major followed immediately by an assertive dominant-
seventh of C major; but this is abruptly cut off before it can
reach its tonic, and after an embarrassed pause the ubiquitous theme turns up softly and smilingly in A flat major.
The next thing we know is that we are in E major, E minor,
C major, C minor, and so on, until a recapitulation is
approached in a roundabout way. It is quite short, but there
is an extended coda, which, however, ends very suddenly
with Ex. 42 having the very last word – or rather two words.

SYMPHONY NO. 40 IN G MINOR (K. 550)

MINOR keys, not where they appear incidentally by way of
modulation, but where they are used as the tonalities for
complete works, were adventures for Mozart, not to be em-
barked on lightly. We notice again and again that compositions in such keys at various periods of his earlier career
stand out by a greater originality and profounder significance. There is, for instance, the E minor violin and piano
Sonata (K. 304) of 1778 and the A minor piano Sonata
(K. 310) of the same year, a much earlier D minor string
Quartet (K. 173, 1773) and the C minor Serenade for wind
instruments (K. 388, 1782), all very remarkable and striking
works. More relevantly, we have an earlier Symphony in G
minor (K. 183, 1773), which is not only conspicuous among
the surrounding symphonic works by a youth of seventeen –
among other things it exceptionally makes use of four horns
– but in some ways anticipates the Symphony to be discussed here. As for mature works, there is no need to enlarge

on the extraordinary profundity and often tragic, dramatic or solemn significance of such things as the G minor piano Quartet and string Quintet, the D minor and C minor piano Concertos, the later D minor string Quartet, the C minor Fugue for two pianos or the A minor Rondo for piano solo, not to mention some of the Masonic music (the favourite key for which is C minor) or such wonderful pieces in the operas as the great D minor duet for Anna and Octavio in *Don Giovanni* and Pamina's G minor lament in *The Magic Flute*. This last key may be said to be Mozart's vehicle for the most pathetic music, while D minor is that for the most dramatic and C minor for the most sombre, taking things generally.

The present Symphony's predominant characteristic is certainly pathos, not only where it is agitated, as in the first and last movements, but also where it assumes a kind of uneasy calm, as in the slow one, or a smiling, pastoral placidity, as in the trio of the minuet. We are in the presence of one of Mozart's most personal expressions – a commentator anxious to emphasize its 'romantic' nature might prefer to say confessions; but however poignant these expressions may become at this or that point, and indeed the second subjects of both the first and the last movement are almost unbearably beautiful, they are still presented with an incomparable classical poise and restraint; nor does the composer find it necessary to lay stress on distress by committing drastic breaches of form anywhere. He could always make subtle modifications of the normal sonata form – if there ever was such a thing in the practice of great composers as distinct from the text-books – but these were enough for him to go where he would with perfect ease and freedom.

First Movement. *Molto allegro*. We have had a good deal of formal analysis by this time, so that Mozart's management of symphonic structure may now be taken for granted. A few brief pointers will be enough to draw attention to artistic wonders to be expected from this movement and those which follow it. Let the first subject be quoted, for instance, not as it appears at the outset but as it returns after a vigorous cadence-phrase, with which its re-entry overlaps in the most fascinating way before that phrase has had its say, Ex. 43. The touching second subject appears, as is usual (but not invariable) in classical sonata-form movements in minor keys, not in the dominant, but in the relative major, in this case B flat, Ex. 44. The extended repetition of this is even more heartsearching, and most so is the harmonically more highly charged version in G minor in the recapitulation. Before that, in the working-out, Ex. 43 had become involved in very complicated modulatory and polyphonic convolutions.

Second Movement. *Andante*. The slow – only moderately slow – movement, in E flat major, begins by weaving its main theme into an intricate texture of imitative entries, Ex. 45, and later the music is often flecked all over with little detached figures of the type first arising at the seventh bar, Ex. 46. A cross-rhythm which appears to turn the time for a moment from 6–8 into 3–4 is noticeable as a feature rare in Mozart*, Ex. 47. The fervently lyrical second subject, first in B flat, later in E flat, continues to be haunted by the demi-semiquaver figure and takes a surprising and passionately eloquent turn of modulation.

Third Movement. *Allegretto*. The minuet, as this movement is expressly called, is actually as far from the conventional dance movement, and even dance motion, as any Beethovenian or Schubertian scherzo. At the same time it is entirely different from anything either of these later masters ever wrote, except the minuet in Schubert's little Symphony No. 5 in B flat major. That movement is also in G minor and is obviously an imitation of the present piece, whether deliberate or unconscious no one can say. Mozart's minuet is passionate and restless. The energetic opening theme, Ex. 48, transformed as Ex. 49 telescopes itself into close polyphonic workings, and the music then runs to its conclusion quietly, in a sorrowful chromatic cadence. The idyllic trio, in G major, has already been described as pastoral, but it must be added that the pastures can only be the Elysian fields. The horns have heavenly parts.

* But see note on the C major Symphony (K. 551), Ex. 54.

Fourth Movement. *Allegro assai*. Passion and pathos run high by turns in the finale. The opening gave a hint to Beethoven for his early F minor Piano Sonata, No. 1 in the current editions, though not the first he wrote: Ex. 50. Sonata-form on a grand scale develops with great vigour before the gentle and almost unbelievably beautiful but somehow strangely unquiet second subject is approached. It is here shown in its first form, as it appears in B flat major in the exposition, Ex. 51, and one cannot refrain from quoting the lovely drooping cadence, Ex. 52. If ever Keats's Grecian urn had its counterpart in 'heard melodies', surely it is here. This subject-group becomes even more intensely lovely in its minor version in the recapitulation, which is reached by way of a working-out section beginning with a strange, abrupt rhythmic distortion of Ex. 50 and involving it in modulations and polyphonic entanglements no less complex than those in the corresponding section of the first movement.

SYMPHONY NO. 41 IN C MAJOR (K. 551)
('*Jupiter*' *Symphony*)

THE nickname of this Symphony, the origin of which is as obscure as that of the equally unwarranted fancy name of Beethoven's *Emperor* Concerto, can at best be retained for convenience of identification. However, if Beethoven's Concerto is truly imperial, Mozart's last Symphony is certainly godlike, and if we remember that the Thunderer had his lighter moments and the planet named after him is, as musicians have learnt, the 'bringer of jollity', we may pass the sobriquet, since it has been forced on us and is not likely ever to be released by those for whom nothing without a name can smell sweet.

First Movement. *Allegro vivace*. The first-subject complex is shown here as it appears after 23 bars that are in a sense introductory, for they come to a standstill on a bare dominant: Ex. 53. At the outset the phrases *a* and *b* had been stated alone. There is a second subject in the orthodox key and position, as well as a cadence-phrase borrowed from a

comic opera by Paisiello – so much for Jupiter! This seems
at first inclined to shoulder the whole working-out, but
some development of Ex. 53 duly follows, and there is more
in the recapitulation, serving at the same time for the transition to the second subject. (It may here be remarked,
generally, that Mozart often uses independent though never
irrelevant material for his working-out sections and that he
always knows how to keep interest alive in the recapitulations by finding endless different ways and different places
for his transitions to the second subject in the tonic key, to
approach which he has to devise a manoeuvre not used in
the exposition.)

Second Movement. *Andante cantabile*. The slow movement, in F major, with muted strings, is at first perfectly
serene; but there are strangely disturbing syncopations and
passing 'wrong' notes in a new theme in C minor, which
presently seems to lose all control by suddenly producing the
effect of 2–4 motion within the 3–4 time, Ex. 54. This is
the kind of thing a modern composer would self-consciously
advertise by changing his time-signature. At its return the
first subject is considerably more ornate, and in this form,
together with a second subject of a kind of drooping loveliness, it furnishes the close of the movement.

Third Movement. *Allegretto*. If there is any exuberant
joviality in the Symphony, it is not in the minuet, which is
curiously subdued, smiling rather than rollicking music.
The chromatic woodwind descent towards the end is
exquisite, Ex. 55. The trio is simplicity itself: gentle calls
in C major, a vigorous answer on the dominant of A minor
which never reaches the tonic definitely, and a melting
cadence leading back to the first phrases.

Fourth Movement. *Allegro molto*. This is sometimes called
the 'final fugue'. It is nothing of the sort: what we have
here is not a fugue but a finale in regular sonata form with
its material treated in very elaborately polyphonic fashion
not at every point, but almost continuously. There is a
second subject in the proper key and place whose two inter-
locked phrases are capable of combining contrapuntally
with the three belonging to the first-subject material. Here

is a passage from the coda where all five themes come together as by a miraculous coincidence, for the process
sounds so natural and musical that the amazing mental concentration which made it possible is not apparent to the
ear, Ex. 56. Yet the ear catches everything that is going
on, so lucid and well-aired is the score, and it all flows by in
a stream of beautiful music that will satisfy even those who
have no notion of the incredible skill that went to its making.
The second-subject themes are those shown as Nos. 4 and 5.
This is only one of the many wonders: the attentive listener
will come across Nos. 1 and 3 turned upside down, tunes
combining in canon with themselves or fitting against their
own inversions, entries overlapping closely in fourfold imitation, and so on. Even these things are only what each theme
is capable of doing alone; to their various capabilities of
combination there seems to be no limit except that set by
Mozart's perfect sense of proportion and timing. He knows
exactly when to cease showing off those dizzy contrapuntal
feats, and not the least wonderful portions of this movement
are those where the music suddenly smoothes itself out into
a plain statement, as if nothing out of the way had happened
at all.

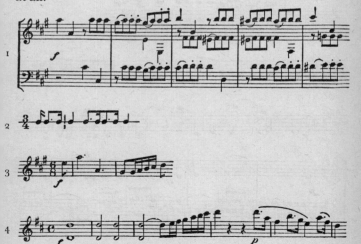

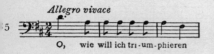

O, wie will ich tri-um-phieren

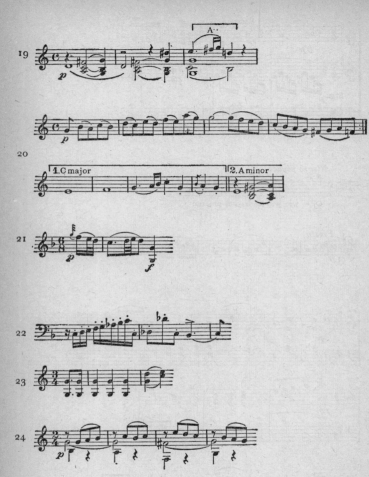

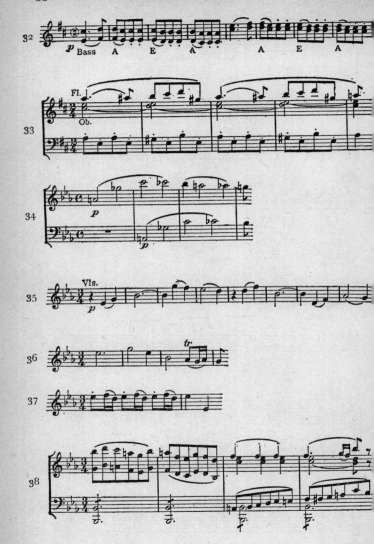

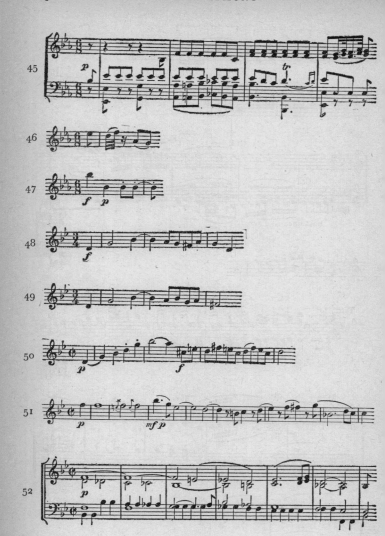

4

Ludwig van Beethoven (1770-1827)

A. K. HOLLAND

INTRODUCTION

BEETHOVEN's nine symphonies, with the exception of the first and the last, belong to his so-called second or middle period: that is to say, to the years between 1800 and 1815. The first of them was produced within five years of the last of Haydn's and scarcely twelve years after the last of Mozart's. That he should have been influenced in his early works by those masters, both of whom he met in his youth and from one of whom he had some lessons (though he afterwards declared that Haydn had taught him nothing) is natural enough. But his symphonies were not early works: even the first of them was not completed till his thirtieth year, and the great events of the revolutionary epoch stood between him and the spirit of his Viennese predecessors. And though outwardly he began by paying allegiance to the forms of the eighteenth century, he very early became conscious of his own evolutionary purpose. 'You yourself know,' he told the poet Matthisson in 1800, 'what change a few years make when one is always advancing. The greater one's progress in art, the less one is satisfied with one's earlier works.' When an English amateur offered him a sum of money to compose a symphony in his earlier manner, he indignantly repudiated the suggestion.

On the other hand, Beethoven was not greatly concerned with the characteristic tendencies of his own age. While he probably owed as much (and as little) to the composers of the French Revolution and to Cherubini and Clementi as to Haydn and Mozart, he jealously guarded his own independence of outlook and resolved never to write except in his own way. With the romanticism of Weber he felt small sympathy. Indeed, in art he was neither a classicist nor a romanticist, but a realist, and truth of expression was his constant aim. In the sense supposed by Wagner, he was not the prophet of the nineteenth century. Wagner's view that Beethoven's progress as a symphonist was from the absolutism of his earlier works to the moment in his last symphony when the human voice was called in to give precision to ideas which music no longer had it in its power to express, is almost the very antithesis of the truth. Apart from the fact that he himself expressed doubts as to the wisdom of the choral finale, it was certainly in the direction of increasing the expressive possibilities of purely instrumental music that his greatest contribution lay. The Eighteenth Century, despite its achievements in crystallizing the sonata forms, was on the whole the age of the transcendent human voice. It was Beethoven's mission to elevate the instrumental forms, and especially the symphony, into a position where they were capable of expressing the profoundest ideas and sentiments of which the human mind was capable. Whatever may be thought of his vocal works, there is never the smallest suggestion that he needed his music as such to be 'fertilized by poetry'. Nor were those ideas and sentiments (or what may be called the image of his creations) capable of being rendered in words, still less of forming the basis of a literal programme.

The inevitable accompaniment of Beethoven's search for an ever expanding spiritual content was an increase in the expressive range of his orchestral treatment, an enlargement of the formal architecture of the symphony. We are conscious of a bigger time-scale in the movements considered as a whole, a widening of key-relationships, a heightening and deepening of the tonal range. His introductions, when he resorts to them, assume a new significance and his codas are expanded to the proportions of a second development. In the co-ordination of the various sections of his movements, there is a continuous forward-striving logic, dispensing with the merely casual links which Wagner likened to the rattling of the dishes between the courses of a princely banquet. Above all, there is a sense of the work as a totality, a complete and unique expression. We have his own word for it that he always kept in mind the work as a whole. 'I alter a great deal, discard and try again until I am satisfied. And then inside my head I begin to work it out, broadening here and restricting there ... And since I am conscious of what I am trying to do, I never lose sight of the fundamental idea. It rises up higher and higher and grows before my eyes until I hear and see the image of it, moulded and complete, standing there before my mental vision.' It follows that each of the symphonies possesses a complete and separate individuality of its own.

Beethoven's orchestra begins by differing little in material particulars from that of Haydn, except that he uses clarinets from the outset. In the first two symphonies it comprises wood-wind, horns and trumpets in pairs, timpani and strings. In the *Eroica* he adds a third horn and in the finale of the Fifth a piccolo, contra-bassoon and three trombones. It is not until the Ninth Symphony that he employs four horns for the first time, together with 'Turkish' percussion (bass drum, cymbals, and triangle) in the finale, which also has the chorus and vocal quartet. But from the date of the First Symphony contemporary observers noticed that he used the wind section with a new emphasis (more like a wind-band than an orchestra, they complained) while from the Third Symphony onwards he gave a more independent life to his violas and double-basses. Beethoven associated with some of the greatest virtuosi of his day and his writing for the strings was always resourceful. (His meeting with Drogonetti, the famous bass-player, in 1799, no doubt accounted for the severe demands he made on this instrument in the Fifth Symphony and elsewhere.) In his use of horns and trumpets he was handicapped by the limitations of the instruments of his day, and it was not until his last symphony that he had a glimpse of new possibilities. Strikingly effective and original, on the other hand, is his use of the bassoon and the timpani.

SYMPHONY NO. I IN C MAJOR

BEETHOVEN'S First Symphony was produced in 1800, though it was probably begun some years earlier. Periods of music do not, as a rule, conveniently close at the turn of the century, so that when it is said that this work is 'a fitting farewell to the eighteenth century', there is no need to assume that Beethoven was either making a deliberate bow to his predecessors, Haydn and Mozart, or turning his back on them. Berlioz's remark that the symphony is not authentic Beethoven, inasmuch as 'the poetic idea is completely absent', is less than the truth. Beethoven had already produced a score of works in sonata-form for pianoforte, strings, and various wind-instruments, besides the Pianoforte Concertos in B flat and C major. He was not therefore in any sense an apprentice, even in his use of the orchestra. The stroke by which he leads off his slow Introduction of twelve bars, a dominant seventh chord pointing away from the main key and reaching the dominant at the fourth bar, was noted with disapproval by contemporary criticism, but was certainly not unprecedented. The scoring of the wind-band is both full and emphatic and lends a new independence to this section which is maintained throughout. The tension of the Introduction is released after some antiphonal chords in a quiet string scale which alights on the brisk first theme of the *Allegro con brio,* Ex. 1. This terse statement is lifted bodily to the next degree of the scale and thence mounts to the dominant. The rising sequences are developed to a climax and with the briefest of transitions the second subject appears, Ex. 2. The wood-winds exchange repartee with the strings. For a moment the scene is overcast as the bassoon descends into a minor key and the oboe adds a pathetic note, but the brisk atmosphere of the opening subject is restored. The development is built mainly on the terse figures of Ex. 1 with plenty of imitative passages. There is a straightforward recapitulation and a vigorous coda of 38 bars, with a rather pompously insistent close.

The Second Movement, *Andante,* opens with a theme, Ex. 3, which is demurely formal in its quasi-fugal treatment. The second strain, Ex. 4, preserves much the same features of repeated and dotted notes and the latter is continued in the drum-rhythm which accompanies a further theme in triplet semi-quavers and also appears in the short development section. Incidentally, the drums are tuned in C and G, while the main key of the movement is F. The so-called *Minuet* Movement Ex. 5, which Berlioz declared to be the one real novelty of the symphony, is actually the first of the characteristic Beethoven scherzos. It goes right away with a tremendous rush in the strings, punctuated by the wind and a single drum-tap. Here is the unmistakable note of the dynamic Beethoven. A tense and mysterious series of modulations brings back the first strain of the Scherzo in fuller scoring. The Trio is equally original with its blocks of wind-chords off-set by interpolated string passages. Of the Finale it may be said that while it glances over its shoulder at the eighteenth century, it contains one or two touches of the authentic Beethoven humour and wilfulness. The introduction of six bars with its series of false starts in the first violins, culminating in a complete scale which lets in the theme, is a typical whimsy, Ex. 6. The tunes are as delightfully child-like as any of Haydn's. See, for example, the dancing second subject, Ex. 7, and the syncopations at the close of the exposition. The coda is full of Beethoven's bluffing humour, disappointing expectations and solemnly introducing just before the end an entirely new notion in the shape of a few bars of prim little march-rhythm, Ex. 8, as if the characters in the comedy were preparing their formal exit.

SYMPHONY NO. 2 IN D MAJOR

THE Second Symphony was written in 1802 and appeared exactly three years after the first at a concert in which it had for companions the First Symphony, the C minor Piano Concerto and the oratorio *The Mount of Olives*. It was begun at Heiligenstadt, outside Vienna, in the intervals between the black depression which came with Beethoven's realization of his approaching deafness. There is nothing of that here, but rather the vision of 'pure joy' of which he wrote in the famous 'Testament'. The struggle for self-expression was no doubt severe: he is said to have re-written the symphony three times. But there is no trace of hesitancy in the finished work. It is on an altogether more spacious scale than the

First Symphony. Both the introduction and the slow movement are longer than anything of the kind written up to that
time. The scoring is richer, though the orchestral palette is
identical with that of No. 1.

The Introduction *(Adagio molto)* is remarkable for its
imposing unisons (with one descending arpeggio figure
curiously suggestive of the Ninth Symphony), the rich ornamental treatment of the strings and wood-wind, and its
modulatory freedom. It runs without a pause into the *Allegro
con brio*, of which the principal subject, Ex. 9, is no more than
an ornamented version of the notes of the common chord
of D swinging up and down. It is repeated at a higher level
and is joined by new figures, gradually pressing on with
greater urgency towards the key of the second subject in the
dominant, a broad rising theme, Ex. 10, of a more ceremonial character. Again the accompanying figures appear
in the violins. The whole of the exposition is based on the
simplest elements of scale and arpeggio, but the effect is one
of a series of brilliant surprises. The whole movement, with
its flourishing and upward striving has a fanfare-like
bravado.

The slow movement *(Larghetto)* is a long lyrical outpouring in which Beethoven unfolds one lovely melodic idea
after another. After the martial strains of the first movement, trumpets and drums are silent throughout. The
movement is in sonata-form. Ex. 11 shows the opening of
the first section. The second subject group, Ex. 12*a*, contains
several subsidiaries; particularly noticeable being the nonchalant little tune shown in Ex. 12*b*. By way of contrast to
the profusion of the *Larghetto* the scherzo is well-nigh laconic.
The subject, Ex. 13*a* is tossed in fragments from one instrument to another in a style of 'open-work', which Berlioz
likened to the gambols of fairy sprites. But these sprites are
imps of mischief. The Trio, Ex. 13*b,* is deliciously scored
with wind and strings playing a game of hide-and-seek.

The Rondo-Finale opens with an explosion – of laughter –
and out flies one of the wittiest of Beethoven's themes, Ex.
14. The secondary theme, Ex. 15, pretends to be a little
more serious in tone and even attempts a sort of canon. The

episodic theme, Ex. 16, is sedate enough but is punctuated with little gusts of derision from the violins. Ex. 14 returns but now it is developed at some length. There is then a round-up of all the themes and a fully developed coda which springs several new surprises. Altogether the movement is the most characteristic of the mature Beethoven in his more boisterous mood, that we have yet had.

SYMPHONY NO. 3 IN E FLAT

BEETHOVEN'S next symphony, the *Eroica* has been surrounded with more myth and fable than almost any of his works. We owe to his faithful, if somewhat stupid, friend and biographer, Anton Schindler (on whom Beethoven passed off a number of curious remarks as to the origin of his works) the story that the first idea for the symphony came from General Bernadotte, the French Ambassador in Vienna in 1798. The subject was to be Bonaparte. Czerny, on the other hand, quotes another friend of the composer, Dr Bertolini, as saying that the symphony was inspired by the death of the English general, Abercrombie, who led an expedition to Alexandria in 1801 and was killed there. The general in due course became the 'English Admiral' in the minds of certain German commentators, who were thus enabled to detect clear traces of the sea in the work. Another version has it that the original inspiration had to do with the death (falsely reported) of Nelson. That the symphony, whatever its origins, was to be dedicated to and actually entitled Bonaparte seems to be authenticated by the fact that a copy exists in which the words (in German) 'composed on the subject of Bonaparte' may still be read. And even after the well-testified incident in which Beethoven is supposed to have torn out the title in a rage on hearing that Napoleon had proclaimed himself Emperor, he is said to have told the publisher Breitkopf that the symphony was 'actually entitled Bonaparte'. When the latter died in 1821 Beethoven is reported to have remarked that he had already composed the music for that catastrophe. The name *Sinfonia Eroica* first appeared on the published parts two years after the famous incident and was elaborated by the words 'composed to celebrate the memory of a great man'.

Many attempts have been made to interpret the symphony in terms of biography, as if Beethoven intended to portray his hero's career, cut short apparently after the first movement. The position of the Funeral March has been declared to be a mistake, due to the convention that the slow movement should stand second in the order of the movements to a symphony. But the fact that Beethoven was not bound by that type of convention is proved by the Sonata Op. 26 of two years earlier in which the funeral march is placed after the scherzo. Berlioz disposed of the difficulty by supposing that the scherzo in the symphony represented the funeral games of Greek tradition after the heroes' death, while Parry read into this movement an effort to portray 'the fickle crowd who soon forget their hero and chatter and bustle about their business or pleasure as before'. But all these purely subjective interpretations tell us precisely nothing. Scarcely more illuminating is the suggestion that in choosing the theme of his *Prometheus* ballet (which occurs in the finale, the *Dances of the Men of Prometheus*) for this last movement, Beethoven wished to symbolize the idea of the Prometheus legend, the bringing of fire to mankind, in relation to his subject. It is simpler to suppose that Beethoven was fond of this theme (he used it in four places – for the ballet, a contredanse, the Variations Op. 35, and the *Eroica Symphony*) and considered it appropriate material for his purpose.

We shall do well, therefore, to dismiss all these wild surmises and concentrate on the music as it stands. It suffices that Beethoven clearly wished to give us his ideas on the subject of heroism and had no intention of retracting them when the idol turned out to have feet of clay. It has often been said that with the *Eroica* a new chapter was opened in the history of the symphony. Not only in physical scale but in spiritual content it surpasses all classical symphonies up to its time and most that have been written since. That Beethoven was conscious of its exceptional importance may be gathered from his preface in which he says that 'this symphony being purposely written at greater length than usual should be played nearer the beginning than the end of the concert', though his ideas on the subject of that position 'shortly after an overture, an aria, and a concerto' are not ours. But not only is it long, but it marks a new stage in Beethoven's power of organizing his material and shaping it to its predestined end. And this despite the fact that in the first movement particularly the thematic substance is exceptionally rich and abundant, that the development contains for the first time some entirely new matter and that the coda of 140 bars has the proportions of a new section. Paradoxically, it has been claimed that the movement has no principal subject, either first or second. In fact, however, the use of the term 'subject' to imply an extended theme rather than a group of subjects is quite unnecessary, and at any rate a principal subject appears, after two formidable chords, in the third bar, Ex. 17, though we are perhaps not in a position to appreciate that on hearing the work for the first time. Wagner possibly had this symphony chiefly in mind when he declared that, whereas in the ordinary course classical composers stated their principal themes and then proceeded to dissect and 'develop' them, Beethoven was the first to present his themes in a fragmentary form and then proceed to weld them into a gigantic whole.

In fact what is difficult in the opening movement is to differentiate between thematic and non-thematic material. A passage such as that quoted in Ex. 18 which occurs at the twenty-second bar might appear to be an ordinary piece of connective tissue, yet it forms the basis of one of the most momentous climaxes in the development. Various other figures, of which two are quoted, Exs. 19a and 19b, are of no less significance. The opening theme, Ex. 17, is stated three times in the exposition and each time with a different termination. Then Ex. 19a begins to prepare the way for the dominant B flat in which key the second subject-group appears. The definitive theme is shown in Ex. 20a. This is followed by a counter-statement in the minor, wood-wind and strings being used antiphonally. A climax is reached and then a cadence-passage brings the exposition to a close with a reference to the opening. The working-out is equally

well-knit and ranges over a wide area of distant keys. Its
most remarkable features are the episode in E minor introducing an entirely new subject, Ex. 20*b*, and the famous passage just before the recapitulation where the orchestra is
held in suspense and the strings hold dominant harmony
while the horn softly intones the opening theme in the tonic.
This was the passage that nearly secured for Beethoven's
pupil Ries a box on the ears for saying that 'the damned
horn had come in too soon'. The enormous coda of 140
bars includes a re-statement of the episode Ex. 20*b* in
the supertonic and the movement reaches its powerful
end with a total of 689 bars – a truly unprecedented achievement.

The well-known *Funeral March* may be dealt with more
briefly though it is on no less spacious a scale. The theme has
two limbs, Exs. 21*a* and 21*b*, each announced by the strings
and repeated by the wind. There are two episodes: the first
a trio in the tonic major (C) which is shown in Ex. 22*a*, and
the second, arising out of a return of the March theme, a
solemn fugato in F minor, Ex. 22*b*. After the reprise comes a
wonderful moment when the violins whisper a new theme
which sheds a momentary ray of hope on the mournful scene
(Ex. 23), but this passes and the movement ends with a sad
and halting reference to the main subject.

The Scherzo with its mysterious staccato mutterings in
the strings, the sudden burst into a full orchestral *fortissimo,*
the headlong syncopations, is also something new in symphonic music, and the first of a great line of 'daemonic'
Beethoven movements. The contrasting Trio is more jovial
with its horn fanfares but does not lose the impulsive energy
of the rest of the movement. The scherzo is repeated in a
varied form. The Coda is brief and ends with a dramatic
outburst in which the drums clinch matters. For the Finale,
as already mentioned, Beethoven had resort to the theme of
his *Prometheus Ballet.* It is a combination of variation and
fugue forms. The theme is stated *pizzicato* in the bass after a
short but spectacular introduction. In the third variation
the *Prometheus* tune appears in the bass, Ex. 24, and
in the fourth the bass theme is treated as the subject of a

fugato. The fifth variation introduces a new marchlike theme but the bass maintains in sketch form the original subject. This is in G minor. Then both tune and bass return for the next section in C major and a second fugue occurs based on an inversion of the original theme. Lastly, there is an *Andante* variation (surprising in its position at this point) which gives us the tune in rich harmony. This is developed on massive lines and followed by a *presto* coda which is not mere sound and fury, for it contains a suggestion of a new variation on the tune. These last two sections are indeed a 'fitting farewell' to the whole epic. We may conclude with the words of Berlioz: 'Beethoven has written works more striking perhaps than this symphony, and several of his other compositions impress the public in a more lively way. But it must be allowed that the *Eroica Symphony* possesses such strength of thought and execution, that its style is so emotional and consistently elevated, besides its form being so poetical, that it is entitled to rank as equal with the highest conceptions of its composer.' And it was, as we know, its composer's favourite symphony.

SYMPHONY NO. 4 IN B FLAT MAJOR

IT has been remarked by J. W. N. Sullivan that 'the greater importance the world has always attributed to the Third, Fifth, Seventh, and Ninth symphonies compared with the Fourth, Sixth, and Eighth, is not because of any purely musical superiority they possess, but because everyone is more or less clearly aware that greater issues are involved, that something more important for mankind is being expressed.' This is no doubt true, but it would be as unwise to suggest that the even-number symphonies are thereby out of the main stream of Beethoven's development or of smaller artistic significance as to hold that the comedies of Shakespeare are at their ripest of smaller value than the tragedies. All through his middle period Beethoven seems to have felt the need for relieving the intense concentration of his idealistic works by writing others of a more genial human character. And this alternation was not at all conditioned by the outward circumstances of his life, for such was his grasp of the purpose and character of each of his creations that he was able to work, as his sketch-books and actual words prove, simultaneously on compositions of widely different tone and inspiration. It is known that Beethoven was already at work on the C minor Symphony when he turned aside to complete the Symphony in B flat in 1806. There is no doubt that this period was on the whole one of comparative happiness, and the compositions contemporary with the symphony, such as the G major Piano Concerto and the Violin Concerto, belong to the more serene aspects of Beethoven's art. But all attempts to read into the symphony a reference to any specific emotional experience are mere guess-work.

Apart from the Seventh Symphony, the Fourth contains the most imposing introduction of any in the series. It consists of thirty-eight bars of tense groping figures held together by sustained octaves, the whole passage having a curiously remote and shadowy effect. It is remarkable as being the only instance in which the theme of the *Allegro* is actually born out of the figures of the introduction. The stroke by which Beethoven brings in the *Allegro* may be compared with the 'false starts' in the finale of No. 1. But here the ascending scale-passages, instead of lengthening, get shorter: the pulse, as it were, quickens and the emotional effect is one of almost breathless eagerness to plunge into the new atmosphere. The principal subject, Ex. 25, is a full-blown tune made up of broken chords followed by a quiet *legato* scale passage. This impetuous subject figures predominantly in the working-out. The second subject, Ex. 26a, continues in the same happy vein and is followed by a sequential passage in minims working to a *crescendo* and giving way to a delightful little canon between clarinet and bassoon, Ex. 26b. A feature of the development to be noted is the new counter-theme which is added to the working of the principal subject. The transition of the recapitulation is heralded by a striking passage accompanied by drum-rolls, the latter being maintained at one point for twenty-five bars.

The *Adagio* for sheer beauty of sound and texture is

unsurpassed in the whole series. The throbbing accompaniment in the second violins is a feature almost throughout, and its initial figure recurs just before the close of the movement as an unaccompanied drum solo. The *cantabile* theme, Ex. 27, is re-stated by the wood-wind with elaborations. The second theme, Ex. 28, is introduced by the clarinet with an entrancing accompaniment which prolongs the mood of the first part. This middle section moves to a passionate climax and then the first theme returns in a more florid version. There is a wonderfully significant passage for the first and second violins alone which leads to the final reprise of both the subjects.

The third movement, though labelled *minuet*, is actually a scherzo and the first example in the series in which the Trio is also repeated in alternation with the minuet section. The theme of the scherzo, like that of the opening movement, is built on broken chords and is of great rhythmic ingenuity, being a combination of two- and three-pulse groupings. The finale is full of innocent humour and high spirits, with its swirling first subject, Ex. 29, and almost Haydnish second subject, Ex. 30*a*, but the whole treatment and temper of the movement are pure Beethoven. There are one or two incomparable little touches, such as the bassoon solo just before the reprise, the gay lilt of the violins (beginning at bar 248) and the augmentation of the main theme, Ex. 30*b*, eked out with pauses, a few bars before the end – a naive but still effective joke.

SYMPHONY NO. 5 IN C MINOR

THE Fifth Symphony owes its popularity to a variety of causes, not the least being the fact that it is a work that combines a powerful emotional appeal with the utmost force and directness of expression. The legends surrounding it are harmless enough. Berlioz relates that the famous singer Malibran on hearing it for the first time was seized with convulsions and had to be carried from the hall, and another story says that a veteran of Napoleon's Old Guard on hearing the famous C major entry of the finale sprang to his feet exclaiming '*C'est l'Empereur!*' That Beethoven did actually use the words attributed to him by Schindler ('Thus Fate knocks at the door') about the opening notes, there seems no reason to doubt. Their only drawback as an explanation is that they do not explain anything that matters. The point to bear in mind is that, while the four-note rhythm certainly does dominate the first movement as a whole, the significance of its first statement is no greater than that of a chapter heading. We do not even know for the moment what key the notes are in. And it is only as the movement develops that we realise that we are in the presence of a tragic conflict. Nor is it as obvious as it has seemed to some writers that the opening motive (as it is considered) reappears in the third movement, for the rhythm is entirely different. Only by the most unmistakable formal means can such parallels be established as significant. When Beethoven wishes to make such allusions, as in fact he does in the finale where he recalls the theme of the third movement, his intentions are made clear beyond a doubt.

What we have in the opening statement, therefore, is not a mere tag or motto but an extensive theme which stands out in all its completeness and the melodic contour of which is actually underlined when it is distributed over the wood-wind at the end of the movement, see Ex. 31. The movement is certainly one of the most concentrated that Beethoven ever wrote, for even the second subject, Ex. 32, has for its accompaniment the same inescapable rhythm. The transition to it is as terse as it could be. Even when the tension is for a moment relaxed, as in the passage at bar 197, there is an almost unbearable suspense before the fury breaks out with renewed clamour. Even the poignant little oboe cadenza is linked melodically with the outline of the preceding passage.

The slow movement (*Andante con moto*) is a set of continuous variations, linked by an alternating theme. The principal subject, Ex. 33, is given out by violas and 'cellos in unison over a pizzicato bass. The secondary theme, Ex. 34, begins quietly in the same key (A flat) but after a moment's hesitation suddenly breaks out triumphantly into C major. Psychologically this is much more significant than any remote thematic resemblances or 'germinal themes', for this is destined to be the mood and key of the last movement. The variations are rather formal, but the drama of the movement is kept alive by the mysterious modulating bridge-passages. The variations proceed in the style of 'divisions', i.e., with the note-values halved. The next transition is by way of a passage in contrary motion for the wood-winds and then the C major episode bursts forth again. Towards the end the tempo quickens with a wonderfully expressive little passage in which the bassoon utters a minor mode version of the opening phrase and the oboe interjects plaintive cries. The coda is consolatory in tone with one surprising 'lift' in the melody and the movement closes in full splendour and confidence.

The third movement is unique in its plan. The introduction, Ex. 35, is mysterious and elusive, climbing out of the basses. Then a relentless march-like theme is introduced by the horns. This procedure is repeated in a more elaborate form, with full scoring. This section reaches a climax and dies away. The Trio, Ex. 36, beginning with fugal scurryings in the basses, is often classed as grotesque if not humorous, but it is grim humour at the best. Beethoven originally intended to make a double repeat of the scherzo and trio, as in the Fourth Symphony, but changed his mind and invented instead one of his supreme strokes of drama: the long passage of suspense in which for fifteen bars the drums softly tap out a rhythm while the strings sustain a bare third out of which the violins emerge with wisps of the scherzo motive. This continues for 28 bars when with a rising excitement the whole orchestra (with trombones and double-bassoon making their first appearance in a symphony) blazes forth into the finale, Ex. 37. When the second theme arrives, Ex. 38, it is with an important counter-phrase in the 'cellos which comes in for good use in the development. There is a subsidiary subject, Ex. 39, which later forms the basis of the *presto* coda. But the stroke which has been universally admired is the reappearance of the scherzo theme just before the recapitulation. Yet there is a subtle difference in the atmosphere. This reminder of the sombre past is no more than a shadow cast by memory on the radiant present.

SYMPHONY NO. 6 IN F MAJOR

BEETHOVEN seems to have fully anticipated most of the objections which were likely to be raised to his next symphony, the *Pastoral*, whether by the literally or the romantically minded. To poor Schindler he explained that the realistic suggestions of the nightingale, quail, and cuckoo in the second movement were put in by way of a joke, and then proceeded to pull the wool over his ears by declaring that a certain arpeggio figure represented the yellow-hammer. Beethoven's attitude to the country was that of a person who really did love it, without being in the least sentimental or romantic about it. He went to considerable pains to set down what he was after in this symphony. Anyone, he said, who has received an impression of life in the country will be able to imagine without a lot of superscriptions what the composer intended to convey. And, in the famous phrase which he prefixed to the manuscript, the symphony was 'more the expression of feeling than painting'. For the rest 'the audience must discover for itself what the situations are', for mere pictorialism, if carried too far, defeats itself. Even without the chapter headings which Beethoven put over his movements, we should have been able to discover that this was an impression of country sights and sounds. It is not therefore as programme-music in the narrower sense that we must regard the symphony, although the descriptive titles were taken almost literally from an earlier work by one J. H. Knecht *Musical Portrait of Nature*, whose pitfalls it is clear Beethoven knew how to avoid. The realism resides not in the very slight allusions to natural phenomena but in the simple acceptance of a common emotional experience.

The first movement ('Awakening of happy feelings on arriving in the country') is evolved almost entirely from the figures which constitute the first subject, Exs. 40*a* and 40*b*, with a sort of roundelay which forms the nominal second subject, Exs. 41*a* and 41*b*. It is all as seemingly artless as bird-song, yet the movement is a perfectly organized whole. The second movement ('By the Brook') is likewise in sonata-form. The sketch-books prove that Beethoven ruminated attentively in just such a scene and he has reproduced in this gently flowing 12/8 movement a perfect symbol of the mood engendered in him. Ex. 42*a* shows the opening phrase and 42*b* the cadence-theme which constantly recurs. The scoring is remarkable for its use throughout of two solo 'cellos as a permanent undertone. The bird-calls, so marked lest there should be any mistaking the nightingale, quail and cuckoo (flute, oboe, and clarinet), are the merest cadenzas of a moment, just before the close of the movement.

The third section ('Peasant's Merrymaking'), though not so marked, is a scherzo and trio. It is thoroughly rustic in character and there is much more true realism than in either of the preceding movements. Beethoven has some mild fun at the expense of the local musicians. The mechanical repetition of the same few notes on the bassoon suggests that he is more asleep than awake, while the oboe misses his count and comes in on the wrong beat, Ex. 43. A change to 2/4 time brings in a tune which may possibly have some folk-associations. After this there is a shortened reprise and a *presto* coda which heralds the approach of the thunderstorm. This, we must allow, is a superb piece of impressionistic tone-painting, but it is not without its formal logic. The pattering quavers which have ushered in the storm, Ex. 44*a*, are transformed at the end into minims as the last mutterings die away and the atmosphere begins to clear. The finale (Shepherd's Song – 'Happy and thankful feelings after the storm') opens with a Ranz des Vaches, played first on the clarinet and then on the horn, out of which springs the naively happy rondo theme, Ex. 45. Simply as a score the *Pastoral* is in many ways the most entrancing of the symphonies. Right at the end Beethoven adds an inspired touch: a muted horn softly echoes the yodelling notes with which the movement opened.

SYMPHONY NO. 7 IN A MAJOR

BEETHOVEN in his later years is said to have discussed with
Schindler the idea of giving poetic titles to his sonatas. On
the whole it is just as well that he refrained, though it is
doubtful whether in the case of the symphonies those which
do possess titles have given rise to greater irrelevancies than
those which do not. The Seventh Symphony has not escaped
the attentions of the poetic interpreters. With Wagner's
generalized verdict that the symphony represents the
'apotheosis of the dance' there need be little cause for
quarrel, until people begin to interpret the phrase as an
encouragement to translate the symphony into terms of
ballet. (There is a curious story that Wagner himself on one
occasion attempted to 'dance' the symphony to the piano
accompaniment of Liszt.) Berlioz attempted to be more
specific when he described the first movement as a country
dance *(Ronde des Paysans)* and thereby brought down on
himself the wrath of Grove. Now the odd thing is that about
the time that Beethoven conceived this symphony he was
engaged in making some arrangements of Irish folk-songs
for the publisher George Thomson of Edinburgh and in one
of these *(Nora Creina)* there is a very curious resemblance to
the theme of Beethoven's finale, Ex. 53. This discovery has
led other investigators to pursue the matter further, with the
result that certain parallels with other Irish folk-tunes have
been traced in each of the remaining movements. But it is
hardly sufficient justification for labelling the symphony
Celtic. Whatever Beethoven absorbed he made his own, and
the Rasoumovsky quartets are not Russian, for all that Beethoven used some scraps of Russian melody.

What is as plain as a pikestaff is that the symphony in all
its four movements is controlled by persistent rhythmic ideas,
while at the same time it is organized on the most spacious
symphonic principles. The Introduction *(Poco sostenuto)* is
the longest that Beethoven wrote. Berlioz dilated on the
originality of the opening with its oboe solo punctuated by
full chords, Ex. 46a, and the soaring scale passages in the
strings. Obviously something on the biggest scale is in train.

There is a second theme, also in the oboe, Ex. 46*b*, and both are worked over. The transition to the *Vivace* is by way of a series of reiterated E's which hold us in suspense until with a gathering momentum the rhythm which is to play so large a part in the movement becomes established and the principal subject, a fully-fledged tune, is presented, Ex. 47. Beethoven in this work reverts to the orchestra which he used for his earliest symphonies, but the treatment, especially of the wind, is full and at times massive. The pulsating rhythm scarcely ever relaxes, though it undergoes some modifications in the second subject group, Exs. 48 and 49. In its most emphatic form of repeated dactyls it occupies long stretches of the development and only in the coda, in the extraordinary passage where a pedal-point is sustained for twenty-two measures (causing Weber's alleged remark that Beethoven was now ripe for the madhouse), is there a change of pulse.

The *Allegretto* is one of Beethoven's most famous movements and perhaps the one that had most influence on the romantic composers (e.g. Schubert in his great C major symphony). It is perfectly straightforward in its quasi-rondo-cum-variation form and is again coloured by a persistent, though less drastic, rhythm, rather march-like in character. The chief theme in A minor is enriched with a haunting counter-subject, Ex. 50. The lovely episode in the major, Ex. 51, has a double accompaniment of triplet figures and beneath it the solemn rhythm of the opening section, which is now repeated. Then follows a short fugal episode based on the first theme. Both subjects, Exs. 50 and 51, are repeated and there is a short but poetic coda.

It will suffice to quote the principal figures of the impetuous scherzo, Ex. 52*a* and contrasting Trio, Ex. 52*b*, said to be based on an old pilgrim's hymn. Each section comes round twice and after the scherzo has been finally repeated the Trio attempts to return once more but is cut short by a few abrupt chords. The finale bursts in after two thunder-claps, with delirious abandon, as of some wild Bacchanale, Ex. 53. There is a subsidiary theme, Ex. 54*a*, and a graceful second subject, Ex. 54*b*, which is a welcome foil to the more tumultuous rhythm of the rest of the movement.

SYMPHONY NO. 8 IN F MAJOR

AFTER this rhythmic orgy Beethoven turned, as so often
after producing a work of great tension and stress, to a composition of a totally different character. The 'little' symphony in F, as he called it in distinction from the 'grand'
symphony in A, is neither so little nor so light as we may
imagine from its length, the shortest of all except the First.
It is characterized by its good nature and, one or two
explosions apart, its urbanity. On more than one occasion
Beethoven declared the seventh to be among his most
important compositions but, perhaps because he was piqued
at the reception of the new work, which, so far from being a
throw-back to his earlier manner, is actually one of his most
mature masterpieces, he declared that its lack of success
meant that it was so much better than its predecessor.

This, be it noted, is Beethoven's second symphony in F
major. That he had certain ideas as to the quality and
character of keys (such as that F minor was a 'barbarous'
key) we know. But this work is as far removed in spirit from
the *Pastoral* as is the town from the country. Even the trio of
the minuet movement is not really bucolic. It is the urbane
wit and (for Beethoven) the unusually polished manners of
the work that in the main distinguish it. Throughout, it
moves with perfect assurance and ease. Take the opening
theme, Ex. 55. It has the pith of an epigram. And it actually
serves in that capacity to round off the movement at the end.
But instead of being a 'germinal motive' in the narrower
sense it is merely the tag on which the discourse is hung.
It is part of a fully-formed subject which expands in the
most genial fashion. So too the second subject, Ex. 56, is an
equally expansive and unconcerned melody. Yet that this
is no mere airy persiflage we soon realize from the vigorous
punctuation that appears from time to time and the emphatic octaves which bridge the close of the exposition and
the beginning of the development. Beethoven very rarely
employs the triple *forte* marking, but twice in this movement
he prescribes it, once to signalize the return of the first subject in a much weightier statement and once at the climax

of the powerful coda of over 70 bars. This passage is the most dramatic in a movement that promised to be merely urbane and charming. Suddenly the climax is hushed; there is a bar's silence, a few bars in which the strings and wind alternate with 'mark-time' chords; then the terse comment of the opening phrase, Ex. 55*a*, and the movement is over.

In place of a slow movement Beethoven writes an *Allegretto scherzando*. This exquisitely playful movement needs no description. Whether we choose to hear in the accompaniment the ticking of Maelzel's Chronometer (fore-runner of the metronome) or not, the delicacy and humour of the music are sufficient in themselves. There is a whole procession of themes, Exs. 57, 58*a* and 58*b*, and the movement would appear inconsequential if it were not so wittily welded together. Berlioz confessed that he had never been able to explain the comically sudden ending, in the vein of Rossinian opera. But perhaps it does not need explaining.

Having had a scherzando, we do not need another, so Beethoven writes a classical minuet and trio of the old order. As elsewhere in the symphony the bassoon enjoys special favours, and in the trio horns and clarinet come prominently into the picture. The finale is full of Beethovenish humour and surprise. The first theme, Ex. 59, chatters gaily away, dying down to a rare *ppp*, only to be rudely awakened by an excruciating C sharp *fortissimo*. This is at once quitted and the theme repeated by the *tutti* as if nothing in the world had happened. There is a touch of Rossinian burlesque in this chattering opening. The second theme, Ex. 60, wears a more serious face, but the undercurrent of laughter is never far below the surface. The development wanders off into a remote tonal by-path only to be jerked back arbitrarily by a comical stroke of the drums and bassoon which perform an octave-dance on the tonic. The coda begins with some detached allusions to the first theme against which a new figure in minims is presented leading to a brilliant delivery of the theme in D major. This is cut short by the bassoon-drum joke and once more the theme is in the tonic. We now see the purpose of that monstrous C sharp. Beethoven pivots on a D flat, calls it by its enharmonic name of

C sharp, drives it home and immediately out comes the theme in F sharp minor. However, with another of his semitonal shifts he manages to get back home and now at last we can have the second subject in its lawful key of F and all is set for the final outburst of high spirits.

SYMPHONY NO. 9 IN D MINOR

A PERIOD of eleven years elapsed before Beethoven completed his next and last symphony. He had conceived the idea of setting Schiller's *Ode to Freedom* (later altered to *Joy*) * as early as 1793. There was originally no connection in the composer's mind between this project and the instrumental symphony in D minor, which began to occupy his thoughts in 1817. Sketches for an instrumental finale, dating from the year 1823, exist, and these subsequently became embodied in the finale of the A minor quartet. On the other hand he seems to have made some progress with the Schiller Ode before the idea of the Choral finale occurred to him. That he had also conceived an idea for a Choral symphony is clear from some sketches he made in 1818. It was to be based partly on the ancient modes and the voices were to be used in the finale 'or as early as the Adagio', the text of which was to be taken from Greek mythology. The *Allegro* was to be a 'festival of Bacchus'. Beethoven, as we have seen, frequently worked on more than one symphony at a time and in this case a whole complex of ideas seems to have become fused into the work we now know as the *Choral Symphony*.

Wagner, in an elaborate interpretation of the work which sees the whole of the first three movements in the light of the choral ending, believed that the introduction of voices was

---

* Some years ago in a *Radio Times* article Professor Abraham pointed out that Schiller's ode was written in 1785, on the eve of the French Revolution, and at a time when liberal ideas were beginning to make themselves felt. The ode was really addressed not 'An die Freude' ('To Joy'), but 'An die Freiheit' ('To Freedom'). Owing to political necessity Schiller was forced to substitute 'Freude' for 'Freiheit', somewhat to the detriment of the poem. It is clear, however, that Beethoven, and probably numerous other people, were perfectly aware that 'Joy' was merely a thin disguise for 'Freedom'. – Editor.

the logical and inevitable outcome of Beethoven's art. 'We cannot but admire (he says) the manner in which the Master prepares the way for the human voice and for speech as absolutely necessary, by this everpowering recitative for the bass instruments which, almost passing the limits of absolute music, comes prominently forward as though it were urging on the others to explicitness ...' But there was more than a touch of special pleading in Wagner's argument which clearly pointed to the conclusion that Wagner carried on where Beethoven left off. As we know, Beethoven himself came to doubt the wisdom of the choral finale and the other symphony was never completed. But whatever Beethoven may have said in a moment of doubt we have no cause to assume that he made an artistic mistake. Equally we have no reason to read into the first three movements interpretations based on the unhistorical assumption that they were written with the choral finale, as we now know it, in mind.

A year before its completion the London Philharmonic Society had commissioned a symphony from Beethoven and duly sent him the fee for it. Notwithstanding this, the actual first performance took place on 7th May 1824, in Vienna. The reception was overwhelming, though the symphony was under-rehearsed. The story is well-known which tells how Beethoven was present in the orchestra and so deaf that one of the soloists had to turn him round as he stood with his back to the audience, in order that he might *see* the applause which he could not hear.

That the Ninth Symphony is, even by comparison with such mighty works as the *Eroica* and Fifth Symphonies, on a totally different psychological plane, that it raises vaster issues than anything in Beethoven's previous symphonic writing, has been generally agreed. Each of its movements is unparalleled in constructive power and in the span and magnitude of its musical ideas. The opening is one of sustained mystery and intensity. From a region in which all seems nebulous and ill-defined (a bare fifth on A in the second violins and 'cellos supported by horns) emerge the first faint foreshadowings of a theme which is presently hurled at us, with the force of Jove's thunderbolts, by the

whole orchestra in unison, Ex. 61. This portentous opening
is next re-stated in the tonic D minor and the full subject
transferred, still fortissimo, to the key of B flat. For the
moment it is with the termination of this gigantic theme
that we have to do, and this in rising sequences marches
remorselessly onwards till we reach the transition to the
second subject-group, Ex. 62a, which has been supposed to
bear some faint resemblance to the 'Joy' theme of the finale.
The key of B flat is now established and the second subject,
Ex. 62b, begins, distributed over the wind against rising
staccato figures in the strings. Out of this a climax develops
in the emphatic punctuations of a new motive, Ex. 63,
followed by one of Beethoven's most melting modulations to
a remote key. The closing section of the exposition contains
several new figures and ends with a remarkable passage in
which the whole orchestra thunders out in vast unisons a
tremendous affirmation. The development carries us back
to the shadowy atmosphere of the opening but is largely
concerned with the terminal figure of Ex. 61 and the subject
of Ex. 62b. The start of the recapitulation is signalized by a
return to the opening but now, instead of the shadows, it is
presented *fortissimo* in the blinding light of the tonic major.
This, however, changes to the minor when the full subject,
Ex. 61, appears. We need not follow the recapitulation in
detail. The enormous coda of 120 bars is tantamount to a
new development and reaches out to one of the most terrify-
ingly dramatic endings in the whole of music. Toward the
close an entirely new phrase is heard in the wood-winds over a
sinister ostinato figure in the strings and then comes a final but
expanded version of the first subject, an uprushing scale,
and the terminal figure, Ex. 61, which clinches the whole
movement.

The second movement (*molto vivace*) is not actually labelled
a Scherzo but it is the mightiest of all Scherzos. It opens with
a terrific octave descent over the chord of D minor, in the
rhythm shown in the first bar of the principal subject, Ex. 64,
the drums, tuned in octaves, having the third note of the
scale. Then the theme sets off pianissimo and is worked in
fugue. It is repeated fortissimo and moves toward the

dominant in which key the second subject, Ex. 65, appears but still punctuated by the opening figure, with a sequel from the second bar of Ex. 64. This exposition is then repeated. In the development the rhythm is compressed into three-bar periods and then again expanded to four beats, and finally in the briefest of codas goes into duple time. The Trio in D major, Ex. 66, is a more flowing section treated in double counterpoint. The scherzo is repeated with a short coda and a passing reference to the Trio.

The scheme of the slow movement consists of two alternating themes (*a* and *b*) the first of which is treated in two variations between which occur two interludes. Two bars of introduction lead to the first theme in B flat, Ex. 67, *adagio*, a melody of wonderful depth and pathos. The second theme, Ex. 68, is in D major, *andante*. Then comes the first variation of *a* and a new treatment of *b* in G major. The Adagio returns and is treated discursively as an interlude followed by its second variation. There is a long and beautiful coda.

Now comes the famous link in which Beethoven solved the problem of introducing voices into his finale. First the orchestra (minus the strings) breaks out into a confused clamour. This is rebuked by the string basses in a short recitative. Again the tumult breaks out and again the basses reply. Then the main themes of the first three movements are tried over, only to be rejected by the recitative, though in the case of the *Adagio* with evident regret. Parry believed that the earlier movements all had reference to the finale. If so, it is difficult to see why they should be so categorically rejected. For rejected they are. A new theme is tentatively propounded by the wood-wind and immediately greeted with acclamation. So we hear at last the great melody which is to form the basis of the choral variations, Ex. 69. But first it is played by the orchestra and expounded in three instrumental variations. For the last time the clamour breaks out and now it is answered by the human voice in recitative: 'O friends, no more these sounds continue, Let us raise a song of sympathy, of gladness, O Joy, let us praise thee!'

These are Beethoven's own words. He did not set the whole of Schiller's Ode but chose about a third of the stanzas, arranging them in his own order. The chorus takes up the baritone solo's exhortation and joins in the second strain of the theme. There is a short orchestral *ritornello* and then the quartet sings the tune and proceeds with two variations on it. This time the chorus joins in the exultant coda. The next section (for tenor solo and chorus) is a complete change of atmosphere. It is in the form of a march accompanied, among other things, by the 'Turkish' delights of bass drum, cymbals, and triangle.

Next comes an orchestral interlude in the form of a double fugue, at the end of which the chorus breaks out joyfully with a repetition of the opening stanza. At this point Beethoven introduces an entirely new theme, Ex. 70. It is sung first by the male voices and then the full chorus to the words: 'O ye millions, I embrace ye! Here's a joyful kiss for all.'

This is followed by a wonderful *adagio* passage in which Beethoven touches mystic heights. After this the chorus breaks out into a double fugue based on a version of the 'Joy' (or Freedom) theme Ex. 71 combined with that of Ex. 70, culminating in the notorious passage in which the sopranos sustain a high A for twelve bars. The final section or coda begins with the soloists singing antiphonally a new strain, Ex. 72, which develops as the chorus enters into a sort of universal 'round'. There is a magical moment where the pace halts and the soloists have eleven bars of florid polyphony and then the chorus dash into the final stretto which is based on a diminished version of Ex. 70. But just before the end the chorus is pulled up with a *maestoso* passage on the words 'Daughter of Elysium, Joy, O Joy, the God-descended', in a last lingering farewell. So the orchestra is left to add a few bars *prestissimo* and to finish, as did the chorus, with a final drop from A to D.

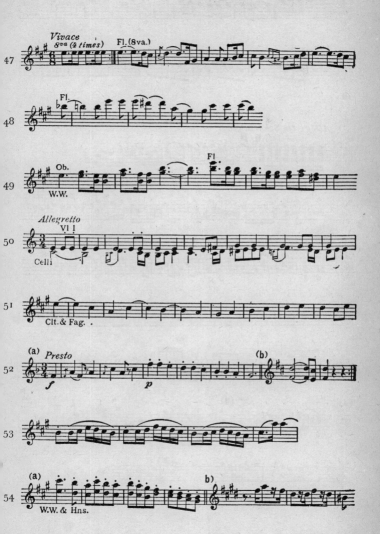

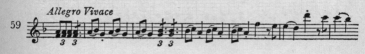

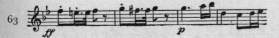

O —— ye mil -lions I —— em-brace ye!

Franz Schubert (1797-1828)

WILLIAM MCNAUGHT

INTRODUCTION

THE usual numbering of Schubert's symphonies is in the order of their composition.

1. in D	1813	
2. in B flat	1814–15	
3. in D	1815	
4. in C minor	1816	The *Tragic*.
5. in B flat	1816	
6. in C	1817–18	
7. in E minor and major	1821	Unfinished and unpublished.
8. in B minor	1822	The *Unfinished*.

(A problematical *Gastein* Symphony, 1825, the score of which is lost.)

9. in C	1828	(Often called 'the great C major symphony to distinguish it from the lesser one in the same key.)

Only a small part of the seventh symphony was fully written for orchestra, the remainder consisting of sketches or mere jottings. Completed scores by J. F. Barnett (1883) and Weingartner (1934) have been performed; but the music has not proved of sufficient value to secure a permanent place for the work.

As regards the *Gastein Symphony*, evidence of a lost score exists only in a few contemporary letters and reminiscences that refer to it as completed at Gastein during a holiday journey in 1825. They leave little doubt that a now unknown symphony did exist. It has been conjectured (by Schumann and others) that the Grand Duo for piano, Op.

140, which is more like orchestral than piano music, is the lost *Gastein Symphony*.*

With these works omitted, the list falls into two divisions: first, the six symphonies that Schubert wrote before he was of age; second, the two masterpieces in B minor and C major that are the perpetual wonder of the musical world. The early symphonies arrived at a time when Vienna was under the impact of Beethoven's works of the middle period. It was too soon for the full nature of these revolutionary works to be grasped; certainly too soon for a juvenile composer to emulate their richness of language and dramatic power. Schubert's first six symphonies belonged to the eighteenth-century order that had reached its highest point in the late symphonies by Mozart and Haydn; and, being immature works of a type that had been brought to maturity by two great masters, they occupy but little place in the history of the symphony and its current repertory. What they had of their own was Schubert's cast of mind and turn of speech and all the little things that made them Schubert's music and nobody else's. But before Schubert's self could realize its full power it had to cast off the over-riding protection of the classical masters and work out a course of its own. In this winning of independence there is a contrast between the symphonist and the writer of songs. Schubert did not compose a great symphony until he was twenty-five – a late stage for him – whereas he had been writing songs in the grand manner since his nineteenth year. The reason lies partly in the inconsistency of genius, but more in the fact that the two arts were widely different in nature and in the time of their growth. In romantic song Schubert had no predecessors. He created the type and had no rules to learn; each lyric and miniature drama prompted its own form and procedure and the gifted young musician had only to follow his instincts. But to write a symphony at all meant learning a craft that Haydn and Mozart had evolved only by half a century of masterly insight and experiment. In this path the gifted young musician had a long way to catch up. And even

* Or *Gmunden-Gastein,* since it must have been in progress at Gmunden before the holiday party reached Gastein.

then there was that more distant goal, the nineteenth-century symphony inaugurated by Beethoven.

When Schubert did come to write nineteenth-century symphonies they matched themselves with Beethoven's in one important aspect. From the *Eroica* onwards each of Beethoven's symphonies inhabits a separate world of its own creation and lives its own special life throughout the length of four contrasted movements. To some extent this distinction of temper and grain had shown itself in the late symphonies of Mozart and Haydn. But in Beethoven the contrast between one symphonic character and another showed itself in the whole fabric and personality of the music – think of the *Eroica* and the seventh symphony, of the fourth and the fifth. Such works belonged entirely to the age of romantic art which was then beginning, and to the age of individualism of which Beethoven's life and works were the symbols. They set up a new order of artistic responsibility to which nineteenth-century symphonists paid tribute with such diverse works as Mendelssohn's *Italian Symphony*, Brahms's C minor, Dvořák's *New World* and Tchaikovsky's *Pathetic*. To this category, which is not wholly one of merit, Schubert's B minor and C major symphonies belong in full status. The B minor is among symphonies a work apart, living in its own habitation, obeying only its own code of feeling and expression. That unique quality does not liken it to a Beethoven symphony, for it belongs to a romantic region that scarcely fringes on Beethoven's country. Can we say the same of the C major? There are analogies between it and Beethoven's seventh, from the slow introduction to the furious jig for finale. But one batch of parcels may be like another, till you open them.

There is one pleasant ingredient that Schubert introduced into high-class instrumental music. It came from the streets and cafés and homes of Vienna: not directly from the songs of the people (though these are known to echo from some of Schubert's scores), but rather from the spontaneous gaiety and care-free, pleasure-loving spirit of the old city. Translate this into the language of melody, and a good deal of Schubert is likely to join in the tune. You will find little of it

in Beethoven or Brahms, for they were not Viennese by
birth; but you will find it in Strauss's waltzes and his opera
Die Fledermaus.

The classical methods of procedure in symphonies and
kindred works were never, as they are often represented, a
set of rules imposed on composers by a higher power. To
Haydn and Mozart they were expedients which they saw
reason to keep in practice; to Beethoven they were prescrip-
tions to be ignored at need. Though Schubert, in his youth
and inexperience, was largely bound to conform to the code,
he treated one of its ordinances with considerable freedom.
An early adventurer in key-colour and key-changes, he took
his own line with regard to the key-system within a movement. A few technical words and a diagram may serve to
explain a manoeuvre that he often employed. Taking a
movement in the key of A for illustration, a classical form
would have its two main sections contrasted as follows:

Exposition   Recapitulation

              2nd subject   1st subject   2nd subject

1st subject

              In E

   In A   In A   In A

The part on the right covered much the same ground as that
on the left, but with adaptations to bring the music round
to the key of the beginning; and it had to sound just as
natural. This was a test of skill to which the great composers,
Mozart above all, responded with conscientiousness and
subtle art. But Schubert had a habit of re-introducing his
first subject in the key a fifth lower:

Exposition

            2nd subject

1st subject

           In E   Recapitulation

  In A   2nd subject

                  1st subject

                               In A

               In D

so that all he had to do was to transpose his exposition bodily
with some slight re-arrangement of the scoring, and nothing
fresh to compose. Actually he did introduce small changes,

as will be seen in the fourth and fifth symphonies; but in general his recapitulations of this kind give a sense of going over old ground instead of the renewal and forward progress that is typical of the orthodox form.* But Schubert's manipulations of key were not all of this trouble-saving order. In the last two symphonies his treatment of keys and key-changes increased and enriched the harmonic territory of the time.

Schubert learnt to orchestrate by playing in an orchestra; not a body of high-class professionals who could play any notes set before them, but a band of young players in whose hands any unsuitable or unpractical writing for instruments would betray itself. It was this orchestra, at the Imperial Seminary in Vienna, that played his first symphony when he was seventeen. From this tuition he emerged fully competent at an early age. His scores always show a strong feeling for instrumental character, and they invariably sound well. His only notable innovation was a less formal and more lyrical use of the trombones; remarkable instances will be pointed out in the notes on the ninth symphony. In writing for the horns Schubert had to accept the limitations of the natural-note instrument, which are described in any text-book; the opening horn solo of the ninth symphony is a good index of the possible departures from the written chord of C. In spite of this close confinement Schubert could produce magical beauty with a horn solo; two such memorable moments occur at the return to the first theme in the Andante of the Unfinished Symphony (bars 135–141) and at a similar return in the Andante of the ninth (bars 248–259). A strange intrusion of the trombone will be seen at bars 286–290 in the Andante of the *Unfinished*, Ex. 1. Any modern composer would give these *ppp* notes to the horn; but in Schubert's time a horn in E could not assist in the key of A flat.

In the early symphonies Schubert was writing for the orchestras of moderate scale that were likely to perform the music of an unknown young man. The score of the *Unfinished*

---

* The most thorough-going example known to the writer occurs in the last movement of Schumann's piano concerto.

Symphony, with the Graz Philharmonic in view, was more elaborate; and the whole conception of the Ninth Symphony was in scale with the finest orchestral resources of the time. In each of the four scores to be considered the foundation was normal: Strings, 2 flutes, 2 oboes, 2 clarinets and 2 bassoons. Other instruments were as follows: Fourth symphony: 4 horns, 2 trumpets, 2 drums; Fifth symphony: 2 horns; the *Unfinished* and the Ninth: 2 horns, 2 trumpets, 3 trombones, 2 drums.

SYMPHONY NO. 4 IN C MINOR (*The Tragic*)

THE title was given by Schubert himself, who was evidently more impressed than we are by the weight of his elegiac thoughts. To an age brought up on the deep and tremendous epics of the nineteenth century young Schubert's fit of seriousness comes no nearer to tragedy than the postures and frowning countenance of an actor – the frown in this case being the key of C minor. Since all the other symphonies of the early group were light-hearted works this temporary change of mien is discussed as if it were an aberration that needed explaining. But it was not the first time Schubert had turned his note to tragedy, pathos, and dark matters. During the twelve months that preceded the composition of the fourth symphony he had set thirty poems by Goethe, including *Erlkönig;* and in that branch of composition he was a fully-fledged artist and a master. It is not strange that some of this tragic inspiration should have sought an outlet in instrumental music. That the result was only moderately successful is a symptom of his immaturity in the more highly-organized art of the symphony. In point of fact, an analytical note on the fourth symphony has to take the line that it is not a very good work.

First Movement. *Adagio molto – Allegro vivace.* The Introduction is an excellent page, and though it may last but a minute and a half it deserves inspection. The principal idea, in its two forms, Ex. 2, occurs nineteen times at nine different pitches; thus while the music dwells on a single point every bar brings something new.

It is in the *Allegro vivace*, from bar 30, that critical deroga-
tion begins to find its scope. The first tune (bars 30–38)
could have occurred to any Kapellmeister*; the arpeggio
figure (bars 39–42) means to be stern but is only stiff and
stolid; the quavers of bars 43–50 are a common formula.
That the second subject (bars 67 onwards) should arrive in
the wrong key – A flat instead of E flat – is a mild piece of
unorthodoxy. Far more noticeable is the fact that nowhere
in this exposition do we meet any sign that Schubert was
one of the world's best melody-makers. A page later we do
meet a sign of his fondness for sudden and picturesque
changes of key. But there is something mechanical in the way
he goes about it (bars 85–108): first a passage leading to a
plunge from A flat into E; then the same passage leading to
a plunge from E into C; then the same passage leading to a
plunge from C into A flat. Eight bars each time: and three
major thirds add up to an octave, bringing us back to where
we started. One almost adds Q.E.D.

The development begins with a promising thought (bars
135–142); but soon the Kapellmeister enters, not develop-
ing but reiterating himself (bars 141–161). Then for a
moment the genuine Schubert shows his hand with another
surprise key-change, this time one of rare beauty; the
harmony of bars 169–175 is shown in Ex. 3, which will bear
many repetitions at the piano. In the next few bars we see
why this piquant twist of harmony came about. Schubert
intends to play that labour-saving game of his in the choice
of keys. Hence this sudden slip into G minor for the return
of the first subject (bar 177); from this point he has only to
transpose bars 30–84 (with adjustments in the scoring), and
there is his recapitulation ready-made, with the second
subject turning up in E flat (bars 214–232). But the movement has to end in C – how to get there? Schubert has recourse to that passage with the sudden leap from key to key
that he used three times in the earlier part; only this time
twice is enough, with a clever piece of adaptation at bar 236.
Is all this 'too technical'? The manipulation of keys was a

* An ordinary professional conductor-composer with a band
(Kapelle) at his disposal.

study to which Schubert gave close and sustained attention. To him it was a profoundly artistic matter before it was a technical matter; and in his maturity he was to develop it into a subtle and powerful art. It is interesting and worth anybody's while to watch this preoccupation of his in its early stages.

Second Movement. *Andante*. This is one of Schubert's country-walk movements. That is not an idle or a facetious description; it is an attempt to fix a label to a familiar type that is almost a form – for it makes tolerable a lingering repetitiveness that would be a fault in a different mood. The danger of the label lies in its being read as a 'programme': it is music itself that goes for a walk, not a person. The darker episode that disturbs the peace of this movement from bar 53 and again from bar 162 is there as a musical need. It brings contrast; it gives point to the resumption of the original walk; and it brings a little repertory of its own to mingle with that walk at a late stage. See Ex. 4. This is one example among many of Schubert's way of keeping repetitive music free from staleness. There are wisps of novelty, small unmomentous surprises (in speaking of the Fifth Symphony we shall find a name for them) and by them the music is kept demurely alive.

Third Movement. *Menuetto: Allegretto vivace*. This being a tragic symphony it is time to resume the serious note. It takes the form of a fast minuet full of stern chromatics and modulations towards the darker side (G flat at bar 20. C flat at bar 68). On the whole the movement is a concentrated instance of Schubert's free and mobile use of harmony. Ex. 5 and Ex. 6 (bars 26–28 and 39–42) show two little articles of harmonic usage that Schubert did not pick from the air around him. The Trio of the movement (bars 54–86) begins with a tune that he might have picked up from the wind-band in a Vienna pleasure garden.

Fourth Movement. *Allegro*. Again the Kapellmeister shows his hand: the first tunes of this and the other *Allegro* movement surely came from the same factory. But anything can be forgiven for the sake of bars 33–36, a gem of melody that is quoted as Ex. 7. The figure at bar 63 provokes one more use of the word Kapellmeister. But it is the last, for the movement gathers an impetus which removes it from the range of that class. The second subject (bar 85, typically in the wrong key) is not a notable invention in itself; but it has the power to lead on and on, and is continually given fresh starts by changes of key. During the closing passage of the exposition (bars 129 to 194) Schubert hits on an unusual way of shifting the key a semitone higher, and gets so taken with it that he does it three times more, which is about twice too often (bars 143–158).

The development begins with a plunge to the depths of tragedy and to a series of low notes that become convenient pivots for more modulation; you would be hard put to it, during the next thirty bars or so, to guess what chord is coming next. At the end of the development (bar 293) the first subject turns up in the major, a thing which is not done by minor-key subjects at this point. One quickly sees why, for Schubert uses the key of C as a stepping stone to A minor, and from that position gives a flagrant exhibition of his favourite labour-saving method. Apart from orchestral adjustments, bars 309–481 are a transposition of bars 21–193. Nothing fresh to think of for 173 bars of music – is this a record?

But there remains a final impression. It does not put these cavillings out of court; but it mounts beside them and reduces their proportion. The work has impetus, it moves confidently and has a property not shared by some works of higher inspiration, for it always knows where it is going and why.

SYMPHONY NO. 5 IN B FLAT

THIS is, with good cause, the favourite among the early symphonies. Yet when we come to examine that cause we may have some difficulty in discovering the whole of it. As a rule, when a musical work holds a permanent place in the world's regard we can size up and more or less describe the properties that give it vitality and long life. We can point to inspired and original melodies, passages of deep feeling, dramatic effects, ingenuities of one kind and another, and all those incidents where the symphonic plan makes the situation and the composer has used it imaginatively. But if we look into Schubert's fifth symphony with an eye for such things the yield is small. It is not enough to account for the work's having cheerfully survived while so many meritorious symphonies like those of Gyrowetz, Spohr, Raff and Rubinstein, have passed away. Schubert's is a small-scale work, however you measure it; it throws no new light upon the conventions which it obeys; its melodies and figures scarcely emerge from the vocabulary of the period; its little vivacities are not of the kind that carry you away; generally speaking it enters but a little way into the region of musical thought where the landmarks include the *London*, *Jupiter*, and *Eroica* symphonies. Yet people who set their standards by great works such as these have a particular liking for Schubert's little 'prentice effort. How does it get past their defences? To account for this we have to bring in a word that occupies a peculiar place in the vocabulary of music: Schubertian. It is not a parallel to other adjectives of the kind such as Chopinesque or Brahmsian, for it is little concerned with a personal idiom. It stands among other things for the way in which small and curiously engaging effects keep on cropping up from nowhere; they have an element of surprise, but with it an air of naturalness. It may not sound like a particularly penetrating criticism to say that Schubert's Fifth Symphony succeeds because it is so full of Schubertisms. Yet it is a real statement of the case. Since this is the important part it will be better to annotate the work by Schubertian than by symphonic points. But there is one of these that cannot be overlooked; let it be dealt with at once. It is an example of what was shown in the diagram a few pages back. At bar 172 of the first movement Schubert introduces the first subject in E flat, and twenty or thirty bars may pass before it dawns on the listener that this is the formal recapitulation; which is a matter for reproach, since these sonata-form regulations are designed to let every listener know where he is. The change introduced at bars 215–230 (a case of conscience?) is not enough to remedy the effect of going over old ground instead of forward into new. Of course if we know what Schubert is up to we can enter into the spirit of his little game and enjoy it with him: we are not university examiners. And there need be no doubt that Schubert used this device because he liked it. It is an early example of that freedom in the use of keys and key changes that was his chief contribution to instrumental music.

We come to the Schubertian moments; they are too many for a list, and no one list will be the same as any other. The following notes indicate a few places where that character may be recognized.

First Movement. *Allegro*. Bars 1–4. Could the sending up of the curtain be more happily or more aptly done? There is nothing quite like this in the classics of the time. Bars 5–12. The music could get along with only the harmonic bass, and be rather dull. These imitations of the violin part make all the difference. Bar 10. The little run-down of the violins comes just where it is needed to relieve the sameness. Bar 80. There is humour in this picking up of a mere cadence-phrase in another key. Bars 118–134. A delightful expansion of the four introductory bars, with a scrap of newly-discovered melody thrown in. Bars 118–171. The whole of the development is taut and pointed, and it goes on springs.

Second Movement. *Andante con moto*. Bars 1–23. One of the shapeliest melodic strains in existence. The type of phrase is such as Haydn used, and not a half-bar emerges from that familiar idiom. Yet the whole is entirely self-made and has the air of something that has not happened before. The riddle is how it comes to possess that individual arresting beauty with so little striving, and so little that is either individual or arresting in its detail. Three times this melody is played through. The second time (bars 71–89) it is adorned in the violin part and carried into its minor key. The third time (bars 118–128): further embellishment and change? No; for his culminating effect Schubert goes back to original simplicity and even a shortened version; for this is a lyric, not a theme for treatment, and it rises highest by being its genuine self again. That emotionally expanded last bar (127) does not come under the head of 'treatment'.

Third Movement. *Menuetto: Allegro molto*. This movement so teems with Schubertisms that it is better to abandon the catalogue. One, however, shall be mentioned: the descending bass in bars 69–74 is in the vein of Beethoven and the Mozart of *Die Zauberflöte*. Also, it is a six-bar phrase; it might throw an incidental light on this movement (and others in the four symphonies) to find out just where, and how often, Schubert breaks the succession of fours and eights with a six (or twos and fours with a three). See, for instance, the Trio of this movement.

Fourth Movement. *Allegro vivace*. Schubert was disposed to lower his standard a little on coming to the fourth movement of a symphony or chamber work. Here the drop is less noticeable than in certain works of greater import; but it does occur, and is registered by the feeling that less happens in this movement than in the other three. Perhaps there are fewer Schubertisms to enliven the mechanical course of the music. In the construction of the movement there are two chief points to note.

One is the repeat within a repeat: bars 17–46 repeated within bars 1–152; this means that the first sixteen-note phrase of the chief tune is heard at least seven times in the exposition alone. Thus the repetitiveness to which allusion will again be made shows itself at an early stage.

The other point is that this time Schubert does not have recourse to the diagram on p. 129. He brings the first subject back in its right key (and what a parade he makes of it – bars 209–236!); consequently he has to re-compose part of his exposition, which he does at bars 286–314. To that extent he acknowledges the rule. But it is not enough to redeem the movement of its repetitiveness. A composer with an enduring sense of responsibility would have introduced some variety into the preceding section (first subject, bars 237–283) and the following section (second subject, bars 321–394), instead of falling back, as Schubert does, on so much copying. But the shortcomings of the last part do not efface the endearing impression of this charming, Schubertian work.

SYMPHONY NO. 8, IN B MINOR
(*The 'Unfinished'*.)

IN 1823 the Styrian Musical Society at Graz made Schubert an honorary member. Writing his letter of acknowledgement, Schubert promised to send the score of a symphony. Later on he sent the score of the 'Unfinished' to Anselm Huttenbrenner, artistic director of the society, using Anselm's brother Josef as his messenger. No performance took place. Anselm kept the score until 1865, when he gave it to the conductor Johann Herbeck, and the work was given its first performance. Two years later it was played at the Crystal Palace under Manns.

Why was it left unfinished? Many thousands of words have been devoted to that unanswerable riddle. Attached to the two existing movements is the piano sketch of a Scherzo, complete as to its first part, but extending only a few bars into the Trio. The supposition is that Schubert became dissatisfied with the movement and put it aside. At least it establishes that Schubert did not intend his symphony to consist of a movement in B minor and a movement in E major.

'The only part of music that really matters is the part that you cannot write about.' No work in the classical repertory brings home the truth of this saying more surely than the Unfinished Symphony. One may discuss its melody, harmony, emotion and drama at a great expenditure of words and yet leave the essential part unrevealed. The only form of explanation that can do any service is that which concerns the work as a symphony, and therefore incurs the charge of being 'merely technical'; it is under that reservation that a few marginal notes are now to be offered. Yet such remarks belong to a branch of study to which the great symphonists from Haydn to Brahms gave unremitting care. Actually the technical business of the lay-out of a movement is everybody's concern, for the idlest listener can have his enjoyment enhanced by the way a composer plans the dialogue of his ideas.

First Movement. *Allegro moderato* (in B minor). Which is the 'main theme'? Formally it is the wood-wind tune from bar 13; but this serves only to start the exposition (bar 13) and the recapitulation (bar 223) and is nowhere quoted or developed. The ground-theme of the movement is the introductory one of bars 1–8; it supplies nearly the whole of the development (bars 111–218) and acts throughout as a recurring motto.

Bars 38–43. Haydn, Mozart, and Beethoven had made a fine art of the transition from first to second subject. Schubert makes a dramatic short-cut, not as a way of saving trouble, but as an alternative process that happens here to be strikingly effective.

Bar 62. The twice-told melody threatens to lead into itself once again: here, in fact, a great composer gets into a hole – perhaps deliberately, for the sake of his dramatic way of getting out of it.

Bars 71–104. Though this is still the exposition, the theme is treated in a manner that would normally be reserved for the development section. But Schubert can afford to be previous, for his development is to be chiefly occupied with the motto theme. Bar 151. When Schubert does recall the second subject it is only by its syncopated accompaniment – a telling stroke of allusiveness.

Bar 218. Since we have had so much of the motto theme Schubert does not need to re-state it at this point. The resumption is in its right key – the tonic; so here Schubert does not shirk the task of adapting and largely re-composing bars 9–61.

Bars 230–252. On the contrary he introduces well-planned key-changes, with the effect that the movement is always advancing.

Bar 258. The second subject is now in D, which is more suitable to its nature than the orthodox key of B. But Schubert wishes the section to end in B for the sake of that great re-entry of the motto theme at bars 324–335. So he makes his adaptation – where? Compare bars 274–280 with bars 60–63, and see how a flash of genius can spring from a 'mere technicality'.

Second Movement. *Andante con moto*. The music of this composition needs no tribute and leaves little to discuss.

The whole is as lucid as could be, and within its enclosure of emotional feeling and expressive colour everything is said with a leisure that is part of the mood. The course of the movement can be shown by one of those alphabetical schemes that incur the frequent reproach of being non-musical, or anti-musical:

Bars	A	B	A	P	Q
	1–32	32–44	45–60	60–95	96–111
	X	A	B*	A	*P
	111–141	142–173	173–185	186–201	201–236
	Q*	A	Coda		
	237–256	257–268	268–312		

For all its repellent appearance this schedule closely and vitally represents the pattern of the sensual and poetic effect of the music as it plays upon any sensitive mind; and as such it is used for reference here. It is largely a plan of key-changes. An asterisk means that somewhere in the section so marked Schubert has altered the previous key-course in order to display his tune in a new light. The first asterisk (bar 178) does this admirably, for it brings back the whole of the opening part in a new key. The asterisk before P (bar 201) shows where that section supervenes differently upon what precedes it; the result is to carry the section PQ into A minor and major, thereby prolonging the excursion towards the less sharp keys and giving it a balanced part in the shape of the movement as a whole. Thence Q has to have its adaptation (bars 252–256) in order to bring back the key of E.

Section X is interesting. Schubert has in view that passage of return (bars 135–142) which has been referred to as magical. But it needs to be done from the region of C or E minor, and now he is in D (bar 111). The next twenty bars show him working his way towards the requisite key, and not only doing it with perfect naturalness but making a fine passage of it.

The coda deserves a word. Music contains many famous last words; but rarely so inspired a farewell as this. It is the most romantic moment that had occurred in music down to 1822. In fact the whole movement (lying in its drawer for forty years) was a precursor of that age which was then to dawn over the world of music under the title of romance.

SYMPHONY NO. 9, IN C

SCHUBERT composed the symphony in the spring of 1828.
That year the Musikverein of Vienna tried it over, but
found it too difficult to play in public. Schubert died in
November, and for ten years the score lay undisturbed.
Schumann discovered it in 1838 and sent it to Mendelssohn,
who performed it at a Gewandhaus concert in Leipzig. In
1844 Mendelssohn put the work into rehearsal for a London
Philharmonic concert; but the string players laughed at the
music of the last movement, for which they have never been
forgiven. Mendelssohn withdrew the symphony in a huff.
The first performance in England was given in 1856 by
Manns at the Crystal Palace. Until the *Unfinished* arrived
in 1867 the C major was the only one of Schubert's nine
known in England.

Were they such base fellows, those Philharmonic players
of 1844? They knew only what was passing under their
eyes and their fingers; let us see what they found there
before agreeing to condemn them. Look through the violin
part: what do we find? Passage after passage of reiterated
rhythmic figures that are of no musical point in themselves;
in the first movement 150 bars of one pattern, 90 of another;
in the Scherzo 300 consecutive bars to a single pattern (if
the repeat is observed); in the finale 120 bars of one pattern,
110 bars of the same pattern upside-down, and 50 bars of
another pattern. So the wheels go round, while we enjoy
the journey. The players of 1844 could not know, as to-
day's players know, that this was the whirring and the
breathing of a new creation. Was not Mendelssohn himself the real culprit? Surely a few strong words from a man
in his position would have brought that meeting to order
and saved everybody's credit?

Of all the great symphonies this is the least argumentative.
It does not ask you to follow a train of thought or to sym-
pathize with a display of feeling. The music is simply
enjoying itself, and its logic is that of a cross-country run,
with now and then a change in the swing of the cantering,
and during the third movement a long halt in Arcady. The

symphony is a musical tonic, and is loved for its invigorating winds and its freedom from care. It has spontaneity of both kinds; for Schubert, we know, was quick to arrive at his final thoughts; yet the music gives that sense of ready self-growth and natural connection that most composers achieve with great labour or not at all. It has something more: a sense of the unpremeditated in the course which the music runs after it has given itself birth.

First Movement. *Andante* (*Introduction*) – *Allegro*. The very first tune shapes itself irresponsibly, as if it were trying itself over. Then it wanders on while the various instruments try it over among themselves, soft or loud; it wanders casually into A flat and back (bars 48–58); the violins find themselves engaged in a triplet accompaniment (bar 61); so they work it up and decide to lead straight into the *Allegro*.

The long exposition of this movement is really quite simple, for it is one dance measure after another (with standard form for the mere disposal of details). Ex. 8 (call it the heavy heels of men) keeps things going for 50 bars; then Ex. 9 (call it the light toes of women) takes charge for 120 bars. That little three-note polka motif (marked 1, 2, 3 in Ex. 9) is ubiquitous but never over-present, for its uses are varied. Its G major outcome in bar 174 is a pleasant surprise straight from the Schubertian quarter (these lilts from the Vienna cafés rarely echo in Haydn, Mozart, and Beethoven). A remarkable and justly famous passage begins at bar 196. The violins pick up the 1, 2, 3 theme and they and the basses go on repeating it like children who have just seen a joke; the middle strings bandy arpeggios on a middle terrace of sound; and amid this humming activity the trombones come out with one of the best epigrams in the whole *corpus* of trombone music (Ex. 10).*

* Compare this with the first two bars of the symphony and observe a correspondence of three notes. Contrary to general opinion the present writer denies that the later theme is 'derived' from the earlier one. The whole of the present passage gives the impression of spontaneous generation from its own surroundings; it is, so to speak, freshly minted, or arises from the foam fully-armed, and owing no parentage to some other tune that uses those three notes in a different sense.

From the dark key of C flat the trombones firmly elbow the
music into the brightness of G major, and the exposition
ends, with the polka rhythm still having its say (bar 240).

Schubert's novel and lavish art of key-change plays a
considerable part in this movement. It has done so in the
exposition, and will do so throughout the development,
with the trombones again as the chief driving force (see
especially bars 304–316). For the lead back to the opening
music – always a critical point in the design of a sonata
movement such as this – Schubert changes his manner for a
moment: instead of the urgency and the sense of flight, a
moment of lingering contemplation and subtle thematic
play (bars 326–355). When this sinks to a cadence in C the
first subject drops in almost unobserved, and the thing has
been done marvellously. For fifty bars the first subject,
formerly so boisterous, goes about its business on tip-toe:
a rare effect – where else is it matched?

In this recapitulation Schubert of course goes modulating
and finds that when his second subject is due it enters best in
C minor (bar 440). He accepts the position and makes the
tune itself modulate to where it ought to be – in A minor
(bars 453–460). When the movement has completed its
formal course (bar 569) it puts on a spurt, and throws away
all notions but those of flight and, even now, modulation.
On the post Schubert bethinks himself of the first tune
of the symphony, and displays it proudly as a coda (bars 662–
685).

Second Movement: *Andante con moto*. The *Andante* of the
Fourth Symphony was described as a 'country-walk' movement, the excuse being that the label almost denoted a
musical form. The theory is that the mood and the melodic
and rhythmic type plead for a leisureliness and prolonged
similarity that might come under reproach in music of a
different character. Schumann put it another way when he
spoke of 'heavenly length'. At any rate this gently peri-
patetic Andante is the longest, most leisurely and, in the
world's opinion, the best of its kind. It has a pattern that
can briefly be represented as an alternation between a
march-like strain and a song-like strain:

		Song		Song	
	March	in F.	March	in A	March
Bars	1–88	89–159	160–266	267–329	330–380

The plan serves for the pointing out of a few remarkable
episodes. In joining the first Song to the following March
(bars 148–160) Schubert makes a famous tip-toe effect of
horns and strings; it is shown as Ex. 11. In Schumann's
words, 'every other instrument seems to listen, as if aware
that a heavenly guest had glided into the orchestra'. The
March being resumed, the trumpet proposes a new
accompaniment (bar 160), and for page after page the little
summons echoes from the company of instruments. For
further variety the music is worked up in anger (bars
232–249); and from the sudden hush that follows the
'cellos seem to speak in remorse (bars 253–266). When the
Song returns it is worth while to study how the strings
accompany it; the scheme is set forth as Ex. 12. At the end
of this section we come again to the tip-toe passage, this time
with the trombones posing as heavenly guests. In the
concluding pages there are new rhythmic fancies and
unpremeditated thoughts. When the end comes, it might
have come two pages earlier, or later.

Third Movement: *Scherzo*. For a piece of playfulness this
movement is oddly thorough-going in its attention to form.
In fact the first portion, as far as the Trio, is a complete
sonata-form in itself. All the usual components are there:
first subject (bars 1–29), second subject (30–56), development (57–152), first subject (153–193), second subject (194–
220), coda (221–238); and everything in its right key. An
ambitious scheme for a scherzo: inspired, shall we say, by
the only extant model, the scherzo of Beethoven's ninth
symphony?

In the melodies and rhythms we hear something of the
Viennese Ländler; that is to say, waltz-time music when it
still belonged to the country and had not been taken into
the ballroom and made sophisticated. The long-drawn
Trio is much in the character of Ländler music; and so is
the scoring: fancy asking the strings and trombones of a
first-class orchestra to plug away at that empty stuff! (So

the Philharmonic players of 1844 might have thought.)
But we who listen at ease are aware only of the beauty of
the tune and the nostalgic pathos that gently colours it.

Fourth Movement. *Allegro vivace.* There are plenty of
rapid movements in the great classics; a number of them
are made of better music than this one, but there is none
that matches it as a poem of speed.

It begins without the formality of a tune; and when the
impulse of a melody is added to it at bar 37 it is not a
symphonic theme of great moment. But it is the very song
of pace; those violin triplets within the wood-wind crotchets
are a rare notion for suggesting pace without flurry. The
second subject (bar 170) comes like a change into top gear
(one's similes from locomotion have to be sought where they
can be found), and to an equable, level speed. Only the word
'inspiration' will do for this exhilarating tune; and it is
astonishing to learn, from the manuscript, that Schubert
did not think of it until after he had written something
quite different in those bars.

The great moment of the development is where the bass
instruments seize on the second subject and make great
play with its four pounding notes (bars 472–510). As the
music grows quiet this refrain holds its course. We move in
crotchets instead of quavers, but there is no sense that the
swiftness has gone out of the music; only the rattle of it is
out of hearing for a moment. When it breaks out again (bar
593) we may not realize for a moment that Schubert has
brought us round to his first subject in the key of E flat
instead of C, a most unconstitutional proceeding. But by
the time we have gone through four of his symphonies we
know what to expect of his high-handed ways; besides, in
this case we acknowledge a master-stroke; it initiates a
great game with the keys that continues right through to
bar 712, where Schubert rejoins the straight path. It is from
this movement above all that we discover what Schubert
had in view when he began, in an early symphony, to make
keys his playthings.

When musicians have, for the length of three movements,
questioned the real greatness of the Symphony in C, this

Finale gives a clinching answer. It is one of the biggest
feats in music – the way Schubert put symphonic traditions
to the rout. It has been done only once; and symphonic
traditions have had their own back since Schubert died.

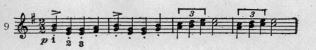

(Celli & Bassi pizz.)

6

Hector Berlioz (1803-1869)

J. H. ELLIOT

INTRODUCTION

IT is a commonplace that Berlioz holds a unique position in the history of music, and we have tended to regard him as standing rather aside from the main paths – a lonely phenomenon having little direct influence on musical development save as an apostle of programme music and compiler of a catalogue of novel orchestral effects. Thus his importance in the symphonic succession has often been overlooked.

This is due in part to a very common error. There are superstitions in music no less than in other spheres of life, and none is more potent than the belief – which has sometimes been held by composers as well as historians and critics – that the symphony is a stabilized, almost an objective form. Not of course that it is conceived as a rigid mould into which music is to be poured; on the contrary, a very high degree of elasticity, an indefinite stretching in almost any direction, is considered quite legitimate. But at the back of the orthodox believer's mind is the conviction that a symphony should be a development from, or should in some way be identifiable with, the classical conception of the form exemplified in its first perfection in the work of Haydn and Mozart.

Now, there is no adequate justification for this idea. It has arisen, one may suppose, from the fact that the early development of the symphony, a long and laborious growth, seemed to tend inevitably towards the particular kind of solution brilliantly and magnificently offered by Haydn as the first of the truly great symphonists. But it is too often forgotten that the work of Haydn and his army of co-workers represents only one of an infinite number of possible developments from the germ idea of the symphony. This, without retracing the threads through the old Italian and French overtures, may be stated simply enough as the basic principle of variety in unity, presented in a self-sufficing piece of ensemble music. The 'sounding together' which makes a symphony is not therefore infallibly and inextricably associated with sonata form or with any other specific form-principle, or even with any particular style – serious, philosophic, or what-not; nor of course does it exclude choral music or, in its instrumental guises, confine itself to the orchestra.

We may return to Berlioz, then, with the notion that his symphonies, so far from being isolated freaks lying beyond acknowledged boundaries, did in fact break new ground and sow the seeds of important new growths. Berlioz was hailed by some of his admiring contemporaries as the true successor of Beethoven. The judgement was not entirely grotesque. Beethoven, without completely bursting the bonds of the classical symphony, threw a flood of new light upon it and prepared the way for a hundred fresh adventures. The Haydnesque version of the symphony was not of course superseded: that it was still capable of being vitally adapted has been proved abundantly down to the present day, thanks largely to Beethoven's indication of the extent of its possibilities as an organism rather than as a mere framework. But the germs of entirely different developments were also implicit in Beethoven, and on some of these Berlioz fastened, though it is true enough that he lagged far behind the German master as a creative musician, and reflected the great man's personal methods only occasionally, and then in the most superficial way.

Berlioz wrote four symphonies. The first two, the *Fantastic Symphony* and *Harold in Italy*, are the ones most likely to be heard in the ordinary routine of concert-going and are the special subjects of this chapter. Each in its own way establishes a new genre of symphony, though neither makes an absolute break from the classical model. With the dramatic symphony with choruses, *Romeo and Juliet* – a sadly neglected work which contains some of Berlioz's most exquisite music, unequal though it is as a whole – he founded a new tradition which, though it has proved neither powerful nor widely popular, is undoubtedly important. Here Berlioz took the view expressed by Mahler to Sibelius during a discussion which took place between these two great opposites of recent times: 'the symphony should be like the world' – that is, it might embrace any-thing or everything instead of confining itself to a relatively narrow system of musical logic. In the work of Mahler himself, and in that of some of the latter-day Russians, this kind of symphony has been adopted. The last of Berlioz's symphonies, the *Symphonie funèbre et triomphale*, is held in low esteem by most critics, and it does perhaps too frequently balance on the edge of the banal. But it opened yet another symphonic channel: it was the first of the broadly popular, 'propaganda-poster' type of symphonies, colloquial in its mode of utterance and immediately arresting in its manner of presentation. Berlioz virtually employs a large wind-band, and adds a swinging choral part to the finale. Whether one likes the work or not seems to depend on how far one can enter into the spirit of proletarian musical enjoyment without, of course, throwing artistic standards entirely to the winds.

However, if we agree that Berlioz played a rôle of con-siderable importance in the development of the symphony and abandon generalities to come to the particular, as our special consideration of his first two symphonies demands, there are difficulties about this composer's actual music that have to be faced. Down to the present day there are musicians who will deny that Berlioz is a serious composer at all, just as there are others who will scarcely admit that he could take a false step. Of course it is easy to say that the truth lies somewhere between these two extremes, as indeed I believe it does; but we must try to delve a little further. On one point all must agree: that Berlioz's music is highly individual and that it is utterly unlike that of any other composer of the first importance. There are certain obvious reasons to contribute to this – the fact that he commonly

thought in terms of the orchestra, that his conception of
rhythm was often more pliant and fluid than that of his
fellow composers, that he conceived harmonic progressions
according to a personal scheme of logic that owed little
to the text-books, and so forth. But this does not dispose of the
problem: these are points that concern manner rather than
matter and they are all referable to one underlying cause.

Well, our aim should be neither to decry nor to defend
Berlioz but to try to understand him, and it may without
injustice be admitted – indeed, it seems fairly transparently
evident, as any but a partisan would probably agree – that
his wells of inspiration were not deep. The capacity for
evolving vital musical ideas that impress themselves on the
mind of the listener the moment they are heard was no part
of his normal equipment; the muse, with arms loaded with
gifts, visited him but rarely. He made shift time and again
with the most commonplace and even threadbare material.
'Berlioz certainly appreciated the value of common
chords,' wrote one of his whole-hearted admirers – and no
doubt this is one way of putting it, for your partisan may be
relied upon to deduce virtue from necessity. But nearer the
mark, perhaps, is the *mot* attributed to that mordant wit,
Heine (it was later reproduced by Bizet) to the effect that
Berlioz had not sufficient talent for his genius.

What, then, made Berlioz the great composer he unquestionably was, and to what may we account his arresting
originality? Surely we have a clue in his conception of the
symphony, which at times cuts clean away from the
accumulated traditions of the centuries. It was his extraordinary, his unique imaginativeness that led him to
conceive new worlds of music – and it was this peculiar
quality of creative energy that helped him to shape his
actual musical texture. This genius of imagination – for it
amounted to that – could not quite take the place of pure
inspiration plus the capacity to develop initial musical ideas
into inevitable mighty fabrics. Had he possessed these gifts
in addition it might well have been he, rather than Wagner,
who would have dominated the musical world of the
nineteenth century and changed the whole face of music; as

it was, his imagination led him at times to the conception of strange and compelling beauties – at other times, alas, into bathos and absurdity, for he sometimes overreached himself with disastrous results.

If we seek for a simple concrete example of the way in which Berlioz's singular creative talent worked we may well consider one of his common chords – one of those which punctuate the Hostias of his *Requiem*. There is nothing startling about the chord of F sharp major, least of all in root position; but give the bottom F sharp to the pedal notes of eight trombones, drive a three-octave wedge between the root and the third, and let three solo flutes have the third, fifth and the F sharp above – and a platitude of music has been turned into something exceedingly rich and strange. This remarkable experiment in orchestral sonority is an extreme instance, and no doubt a superficial one; but it does serve to illustrate the principle which I believe to be the most potent one in Berlioz's creative make-up – the capacity not to think in musical terms but to imagine music as an effect (often, of course, in the broadest way and on an imposing scale), even though his actual execution sometimes failed to carry him all the way to the goal.

There is another important point. We have heard much, far too much, about Berlioz the wild romantic, the composer who could write nothing that was not illustrative. The facts, as we shall see, simply do not bear out this contention. Certainly Berlioz plunged himself with enthusiasm into the French romantic movement and constantly referred his music to literary ideas. It is even possible that he began by mistaking the nature of his musical gifts; at any rate he manifestly evolved into a classicist at the end of his career, and from the outset his musical inspirations, such as they were, undeniably reflected a classical spirit – not in any conventional way, but because they were never 'fertilized by poetry' in the sense that Wagner's were. As far as they went, Berlioz's initial ideas were purely musical. But within limits music can be said to mean anything, and Berlioz said such things quite shamelessly – as indeed have many other writers of alleged programme music.

FANTASTIC SYMPHONY

THE *Fantastic Symphony* is an excellent illustration of this.
As is well-known, the work purports to be an 'episode in the
life of an artist'. To the Berlioz memoirs and biographies
one must go for the whole amazing story of how this
symphony is linked up with the composer's passion for
the Irish Shakespearean actress, Harriet Smithson – for some
obscure reason Berlioz always called her Henriette when he
did not, more understandably, allude to her as Ophelia –
who was actually present when the symphony was first
played in its revised and more or less final form in December
1832. The *Fantastic* has, of course, its programme: the young
artist, disappointed in love, has taken an overdose of
opium (Berlioz, it appears, had been reading a translation
of De Quincey that came out in France about this time) and
has dreams, some nightmarish in quality, and all centred
upon the beloved, who is represented by a leading theme,
or *idée fixe*, which recurs throughout the work in varying
shapes. The first movement is concerned with Reveries and
Passions – the vague longings, the ups and downs of the
emotional temperature. The second depicts a ball, at which
She-who-must-be-sought is among the dancers; he sees her
only in fleeting glimpses. In the third movement, In the
Fields, he wanders aimlessly; there are periods of serenity, but the dream begins and ends in profound melancholy. The fourth movement is a March to the Scaffold.
He has killed the beloved – or so runs the nightmare –
and must pay the penalty. The fifth and last movement
paints a Witches' Sabbath, macabre to the last degree;
his divinity, debased and wretched, is mocked in a horrible
orgy.

So far so good – and it is a typical romantic programme,
with its due quota of blood, skulls, and broomsticks. Moreover, Berlioz has actually brought back a certain symmetry
into the traditional symphonic groundplan – a shapeliness
destroyed by the insertion of a minuet and trio into a neat
triptych of quick-slow-quick. True, he has five movements
instead of the original three, but the slow movement is

again the pivot, with a balancing 'scherzo' and allegro
on either side. But the *Fantastic* is none the less a hotch-
potch, though undoubtedly one of genius. Berlioz had by
him an unfinished opera, *Les Francs Juges*, and from this he
lifted page after page – probably the whole of the fourth
movement and much of the slow movement as well. The
finale (possibly also the Ball Scene) was retrieved from a
Faust Ballet he had begun and abandoned. The opening of
the symphony was taken from a boyish work and the *idée
fixe* itself was previously used in a cantata written for the
Prix de Rome examination; it was called *Herminia* and was
based on Tasso's *Gerusalemme Liberata*.

Now, there is no need for us to be unduly affronted by
this re-hashing of old material. It is far more common than is
generally supposed – even in symphonic writing, from
Haydn onwards. Nor need we take too serious a view of
Berlioz's bland reference of his music to literary ideas totally
different from those with which it was originally associated.
Music is not, nor ever will be, an exact language, and
Berlioz's programme fits it as well as any other; moreover,
spatchcocked and dovetailed though it is, the symphony
holds together in an amazingly satisfying way. The composer's imaginative grasp of the total effect to be made has
performed the miracle. Nor is there really anything to
prevent our approaching the *Fantastic Symphony* as music
pure and simple, even in the finale, which is the most
extreme instance of Berlioz's consciously aiming at pictorialism on a large scale. And, by the way, it is worth
remembering that some of this music, which still sounds so
fresh, so original, and so 'modern' in spirit, was first
written before the death of Ludwig van Beethoven.

First Movement. 'Reveries and Passions': *Largo* leading
to *Allegro agitato*. Nothing could be more classical in
spirit than the opening of the symphony – quietly in the
wood-wind and horns, followed by a passage of gentle
melancholy in the strings. If it reminds us of anyone else,
that composer is Gluck – which is right and proper, for
Gluck was the musical idol to whom Berlioz paid his
earliest homage, and whom he worshipped throughout his

life. This opening largo – Berlioz was not above thus far following Haydn, whose finest symphonies commonly begin with a grave preamble – is an eloquent introduction. The *allegro* too is identifiable with the classical symphonic practice, if not with the traditional outline in all its detail. Here, at the outset, the violins in unison play the *idée fixe* and at once present it in varying shapes; the passage is forty bars long, but only the salient opening need be quoted, Ex. 1. Perhaps there are pages of dubious relevancy – there is some chromatic running up hill and down dale in the strings that does not appear to mean a great deal – but the movement as a whole is organically sound.

Second Movement. 'A Ball': *Valse allegro non troppo*. Opening with bustling strings (helped by harps) the music begins brilliantly in an atmosphere of excited expectancy, and Berlioz lets us hear, in the first violins, the tune of the waltz – a graceful if not very distinguished melody. At last flute and oboe sing the *idée fixe*, now ingeniously floating as it were above the waltz rhythm, Ex. 2, before the beloved is lost again among the whirling dancers. But we hear her again in a clarinet solo, this time in repose, before the movement rushes to its conclusion.

Third Movement. 'In the Fields': *Adagio*. The most original movement of the symphony. This begins and ends with some of those orchestral 'effects' which Berlioz, especially in his younger days, so dearly loved. English horn and oboe hold a dialogue by way of introduction: the scene is set in pastoral vein and a vague sadness hovers in the air. It is a long movement, but it is not only its length that creates the atmosphere of lonely vastness. Berlioz was a solitary soul – perhaps it was partly his own fault, but that is another story – and this *mal de l'isolement* is often to be sensed in his music: he could express to perfection despondency and weariness of spirit – 'the melancholy of existence', as a modern novelist has put it. Still, there are moments of happiness, or at any rate of tranquillity, in this fine movement. But the *idée fixe* returns to trouble the surface before the music dies away in profound sadness. The shepherds' piping is heard again; distant thunder rolls on four kettledrums (played with sponge-headed sticks) and the strings, with one horn, bring the movement to a quiet close.

Fourth Movement. 'March to the Scaffold': *Allegretto non troppo.* So far, at least, there has been no sign of the wild-eyed Berlioz of legend. Nor, perhaps, is the March, apart from its associations here, especially lurid. It may originally have been connected with some quite ordinary kind of march, though it accords well enough with the new programme if we are prepared to go some way to meet the author and accept his more or less normal grotesquerie as having a sinister import. It depends a good deal on the performance, and there is no doubt that a skilful orchestra under an imaginative conductor can make this music fairly blood-curdling, especially with some preliminary snarling from the muted horns and vigorous accentuation of the queer lurching theme that follows. The main tune of the march – not a very good tune, I fear – blazes out in brass and wood-wind a little later without causing any shudder – at least of terror. At the end is perhaps the only place in the symphony where the seams show too prominently – the point at which the clarinet wedges in part of the *idée fixe,* to be cut off by the crash of the guillotine knife and a noisy conclusion.

Fifth Movement. 'The Witches' Sabbath': *Larghetto,* leading to *Allegro.* The finale is rather another matter. This, as we have previously noted, is frankly pictorial. To say the truth, it is at moments positively ugly, though here again a sympathetic conductor and orchestra can give us plenty of extra-musical thrills by way of compensation. Nor is there any denying the extraordinary and brilliant ingenuity shewn by Berlioz throughout the whole movement. At the very beginning there are distant eldritch screams in the strings; the witches are broom-sticking all around us. Soon the *idée fixe* is heard in the clarinet, and it is now base metal indeed; then, after full orchestral shrieks of hideous delight it rushes off again (this time with deliberately vulgarized ornaments) in the tart and shrill tones of the little clarinet in E flat, Ex. 3. A reference to the fine old plain-chant, *Dies Irae,* is heard, Ex. 4, and this too is

debased into part of the wild orgy. At last comes the rondo
of the witches, skilfully and excitingly built up on fugal
lines. In short, it is fairly obvious ballet music of a peculiarly
pungent and realistic kind. The good Parisians would have
been astonished, no doubt, by Berlioz's Faust Ballet – but
they must have been utterly flabbergasted to hear such
music in the finale of a symphony. It is on this finale, almost
entirely, that the popular reputation of the *Fantastic Symphony* has been built; and it follows that the legend, which
tells us little about the fine music in at least three of the
preceding four movements, is unjust to the symphony and
its composer.

HAROLD IN ITALY SYMPHONY

TURNING to *Harold in Italy*, we may as well admit at once
that it cannot be compared with its forerunner as music,
though it holds together perhaps even more convincingly.
It is another pastiche, of course. Paganini asked Berlioz for
a viola concerto, but the great virtuoso rejected the preliminary sketches, which were apparently for orchestra,
chorus, and solo viola and were associated with the unhappy
end of Mary Stuart. So it all went into Berlioz's melting
pot, along with music from an abandoned overture on
Rob Roy, and the result was rather inconsequently referred
to Byron's *Childe Harold.* There is clearly some homage to
Beethoven in *Harold* – no doubt superficial enough. The
Pilgrims' March of the second movement is one of the crop of
pieces – Mendelssohn's *Italian Symphony* contains another –
inspired by the Allegretto of Beethoven's Seventh Symphony; and in the finale is a naïve copy of the retrospective
references to earlier movements heard in the last movement
of Beethoven's Ninth Symphony. It has also been noted
that the Harold theme itself, Ex. 5, is a sort of contrasted
treatment of the general idea behind the main subject of
the first movement of Beethoven's Seventh – an expurgated,
long-drawn-out echo, so to speak. But the general plan of the
symphony – especially the idea of long viola solos, a kind of
flirtation with the concerto – was pure Berlioz.

Tom Wotton, who was the most scholarly, if not perhaps the most impartial, of latter-day Berlioz critics in this country, has pointed out that in the *Fantastic* the leading theme was modified by its surroundings, whereas that of *Harold* displayed the opposite, 'a theme unaffected by its environment'. This is perhaps the outstanding formal feature of the *Harold in Italy Symphony*, the point that most clearly establishes its unity.

First Movement. 'Harold in the Mountains': *Adagio,* leading to *Allegro*. Harold in the Mountains is oppressed by the Berliozian-Byronic low spirits, and there is a depth of melancholy in the music. Presently the soloist enters to tell us that the dejection is indeed Harold's, and this is splendidly worked up by orchestra and solo viola until the atmosphere changes to something more happy in the second part of the movement, which is a stirring allegro. The late Professor Tovey, who was more than usually facetious on the subject of Berlioz – though his witticisms were levelled particularly at the out-and-out Berlioz fanatics – justly appreciated his skill as a composer, and he wrote with peculiar aptness of the first movement of *Harold in Italy*. 'Berlioz,' he says, 'cannot develop a theme; he can only submit it to a process aptly described by Dannreuther as "rabbeting". But this process leads to excellent climaxes, whatever it may be called.' In other words, Berlioz's imaginative genius conceived the broad arch of the movement and brick by brick he piled it up into a convincing structure. After this fine opening, however, there is a serious falling-off.

Second Movement. 'March of the Pilgrims': *Allegretto*. This is the pleasant Pilgrims' March, Ex. 6, with realistic touches in the monastery bells and strange mutterings like the intonation of prayers. The material is slight, and perhaps the movement outstays its welcome a little. It is pretty landscape painting of the Mendelssohnian order, though Berlioz's brush had neither the subtlety nor the finesse of that of his German contemporary. (In his *Memoirs,* however, the composer said that he improvised the movement in a couple of hours spent at the fireside, though he continued

to touch up the details during the following six years.)
The theme of the march itself is peculiarly haunting and the
bell effects – C and B alternating – play a not unimportant
harmonic rôle in the scheme. Harold, personified by the
solo viola, is present as an onlooker in this movement.

Third Movement. 'Serenade': *Allegro assai*. This Serenade
('of a mountaineer of the Abbruzes to his mistress' – Berlioz
omitted only to add the name of the lady!) begins with a
merry piping in oboe and piccolo over a drone bass – no
doubt a reminiscence of the Roman *pifferari*, who performed
on a crude sort of oboe to the accompaniment of a species
of bagpipes. There is a middle episode, in slower tempo,
after which the brisk melody is resumed. Harold intervenes
in the central part, pensively playing his own theme, but
at the end brightens up and gives us the second serenade
theme while the orchestra returns to the rhythm of the
opening.

Fourth Movement. 'Orgy of the Brigands': *Allegro
frenetico*. This vigorous movement evidently meant a good
deal to Berlioz. 'That furious orgy,' he called it, 'wherein
wine, blood, joy, rage, all combine and parade their
intoxication... the brass seems to vomit curses and answer
prayer with blasphemy... they laugh, drink, fight, destroy,
violate, utterly run riot!' Perhaps the listener sees this –
if indeed he sees it at all – through the wrong end of a
telescope. Berlioz in his earlier days was apt to confuse the
exuberance of his own pictorial conceptions with the actual
content of his music. Audiences may be pardoned if they do
not find all this frenzied detail in the finale of *Harold* and
enjoy it merely as a stormy and exciting conclusion, interrupted in its onward surge only by the reminiscences of
previous episodes in the symphony. But it is not to be compared with the Witches' Sabbath. All in all, *Harold in Italy*
is the weakest of the Berlioz symphonies, despite its originality and vigour of execution.

The Berlioz partisans have been loud in their complaints
of the shabby treatment accorded to their hero by critics
and historians. Well, the composer is still a difficult subject,
and for all his brilliance one cannot ignore his failings – the

frequent and palpable gaps between his intention and his execution, his extraordinary lapses of taste. But at least we can do him the justice of acknowledging that his symphonic work was not only legitimate but was also creative.

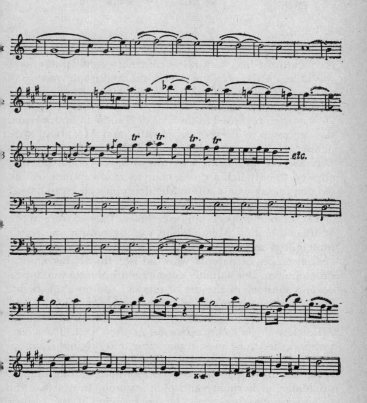

7

Felix Mendelssohn (1809-1847)

DYNELEY HUSSEY

INTRODUCTION

NOT even the bias, natural at centenary commemorations, was able, on the occasion of the hundredth anniversary of his death, to restore Mendelssohn to anything approaching the high position he held in public estimation when he died. He was then regarded as the heir of Handel in oratorio and the successor to Beethoven, Haydn, and Mozart in symphony. He was accorded by Sir George Grove in his *Dictionary of Music* an amount of space equal to that allowed to only half a dozen composers of supreme genius. No one to-day would allow Mendelssohn's claim to belong to that august company.

Yet in one respect our great-grandfathers were right. Without question Mendelssohn was by nature one of the most gifted musicians who ever lived. Born in fortunate circumstances of parents who did not thwart his musical development, but actually encouraged it, he showed a precocious mastery of the art of musical composition, beside which even Mozart's seems less significant. Mozart produced, at the age of seventeen, nothing comparable with the *Midsummer Night's Dream Overture* or the Octet. The Overture is, indeed, the most remarkable and original composition by any composer still in his teens. Apart from its perfection of form, what is even more astonishing than its originality of harmony and orchestration (things that can be appreciated now only by an exercise of the historic sense) is its mature imaginative comprehension of Shakespeare's poetry. As Grove remarked, the Overture brought the fairies into the orchestra and fixed them there. No other composer, before or since, has so successfully translated into music the gossamer world inhabited by Titania and her train. Perhaps only youth could do it; but youth must be armed with the technical equipment which only Mendelssohn possessed at the right age.

How was it, then, that this gifted youth failed in maturity to develop his exceptional talents to the level of great genius? It may have been due partly to his very facility in overcoming every technical obstacle, so that there is no sense of arduousness in his music; partly, too, to the felicity of his circumstances which made life exceptionally smooth for him. He was happy in his family, happy in marriage, happy in the multitude of his friends. Was not his name Felix and the charm of his personality famous? Not that he did not work hard; he worked himself, indeed, to death. But it was rather the amount of his labours than their intensity that killed him.

In addition to all this, there was something lacking in his character that prevented the full development of his artistic genius. Just as his hand-writing hardly changed from the neat calligraphy of his letters at the age of twelve to that of his last letters in 1847, so his music seems to stand still at the achievement, perfect within its scope, of the *Midsummer Night's Dream Overture*. He could – and it was one of the rarest feats in music – pick up the mood of the Overture nearly twenty years later and compose the incidental music, which is its perfect corollary and the best ever written for Shakespeare's play.

Mendelssohn's sole misfortune was to be born into a period when the only respectable objective for a serious composer was the symphony, with oratorio as a possible secondary objective. In 'symphony' I also comprise the piano sonata, the various forms of chamber music and the concerto. It was just in this sphere of absolute music that Mendelssohn was weakest – not, indeed, in what may be called the carpentry and joinery, in which he achieved a smoothness of finish comparable with the finest cabinet-making. He had not the ability to create the kind of germinal theme that grows and develops new form under the composer's hand, and generates conflict when brought into contact with the other themes of a like nature. His themes are essentially euphonious and blend peacefully with one another. His musical imagination was, moreover, essentially pictorial. He was rare among composers in that he not only showed a real appreciation of the graphic arts, but was himself a draughtsman of considerable accomplishment. So it is that, of all his music, the pictorial overtures and the incidental music and some of the *Songs without Words,* which are yet inspired by something more than a vague mood, have proved themselves most sure of survival. Even the two Symphonies which remain in the ordinary repertory, the *Italian* and the *Scotch* are musical records of his youthful 'Grand Tour' with definite topographical associations.

It is to be observed, too, that in all these works it is always the pleasant aspect of life or of the scene that Mendelssohn depicts. Though he suffered miserably from sea-sickness there is not a hint in his sea-music (the *Hebrides Overture,* for instance) of ocean in its more menacing and terrible moods. The charm that smoothed his path in social intercourse was sufficient, in his own eyes, for artistic creation. In this limited imagination lies the cardinal weakness of his genius. Great art calls for something more – a more inclusive vision embracing evil as well as good.

In addition to the two symphonies, which are described in detail below, Mendelssohn composed three others, excluding numerous juvenile essays. The First Symphony in C minor should, perhaps, be placed in the juvenile category, for it was composed when he was twelve. This student essay in the Mozartian manner need not detain us. The Second Symphony is *The Hymn of Praise* in which, following the precedent of Beethoven's Ninth Symphony, the last movement is a choral cantata. This once popular work, which was produced at Leipzig in 1840, has now fallen into desuetude. The Fifth Symphony in D minor was actually composed ten years earlier and was designed to celebrate the tercentenary of the Augsburg Conference in 1830. From this circumstance it obtained the name of *Reformation Symphony.* Its production at Augsburg was prevented by Roman Catholic opposition, and the symphony was first performed in Berlin in 1832. In it Mendelssohn makes use of some traditional Lutheran melodies, including the 'Dresden Amen', which Wagner later used in *Parsifal*. As a symphonic composition this is the least successful of Mendelssohn's mature works.

SYMPHONY NO. 3 IN A MINOR (*The Scotch*)

IN 1829, at the age of 20, Mendelssohn paid his first visit to England. After a successful stay of three months in London, where he conducted a performance of his Symphony No. 1 in C minor for the Royal Philharmonic Society who made him an honorary member, he went North in July, visiting York and Durham on his way to Edinburgh. In a letter to his family dated 30th July he gives an account of a visit to Holyrood Palace:

'In the evening twilight we went to-day to the palace where Queen Mary lived and loved; a little room is shown there with a winding staircase leading up to the door; up this way they came and found Rizzio in that little room ... and three rooms off there is a dark corner, where they murdered him. The chapel close to it is now roofless, grass and ivy grow there, and at that broken altar Mary was crowned Queen of Scotland. Everything is broken and mouldering and the bright sky shines in. I believe I found to-day in that old chapel the beginning of my Scotch Symphony.'

It is evident, therefore, that within a few days of his arrival in Scotland he had conceived the idea of a *Scottish* (or as it was called *Scotch*) *Symphony*. The romantic approach to his subject is evident in the terms of the letter just quoted and in his other letters describing the view from Arthur's Seat and his visit to the Hebrides, where he jotted down the subject of the famous Overture. So too, in Edinburgh, he made a note of the theme that appears in the Introduction to the first movement of the Symphony. But between conception and fruition many years intervened. The Symphony was not completed until January 1842, in which year

it was given its first performance in Leipzig on March 3rd
under the composer's direction. It was played at a London
Philharmonic concert two months later. The Symphony
was dedicated to Queen Victoria, one of Mendelssohn's
most whole-hearted admirers.

A peculiarity of the *Scotch Symphony* is that, though it has
four distinct movements, they follow one another without
a break and the Scherzo is actually linked to the first movement by a few modulatory chords. Mendelssohn adopted
this procedure again, even more completely, in his Violin
Concerto (1844), but, whether this was due to a dislike of
applause between the movements – he was annoyed when
the Philharmonic audience demanded an encore of the
Scherzo in his First Symphony – or was based upon the
precedent of certain works of Beethoven, it is impossible to
say. If the Beethovenian model is the explanation, however,
it must be said that in the *Scotch Symphony* at any rate
Mendelssohn hardly achieved the poetic effect which would
make the procedure seem inevitable, and not just a device
for securing continuity.

First Movement. *Andante con moto – Allegro un poco agitato*.
The movement opens with a long Introduction based upon
the theme which, as we have noted, came into Mendelssohn's
mind at the time of his visit to Holyrood, Ex. 1. The features
of this theme, of which the most conspicuous is the rising
fourth with which it opens, reappear in some form or other
in the other themes in the movement. In the first subject
Ex. 2 of the *Allegro*, for instance, the phrase marked *(b)* is a
variant of this introductory theme, while the second subject
also opens with an upward interval of a fourth.

The working-out of the movement follows the regular
lines of sonata-form. But, if Mendelssohn accepts the classical conventions, he does not lapse into mere formula. For
instance, he uses the little figure marked *(a)* in Ex. 2 as the
basis of an effective transitional passage *(Assai animato)*,
which leads to the entry of the second subject. This second
subject, again, appears not in the tonic major nor in the
dominant, as one would expect, but in B minor. Moreover,
it is stated by the clarinet as a counterpoint to a repetition

of the first subject on the violin, Ex. 3. Thus the whole material of the exposition is closely knit together *melodically*, such contrast as there is being obtained *harmonically*. But it must be said that in organizing his material in this way, Mendelssohn did deprive himself of the opportunity of creating a sense of tension in the development. All proceeds smoothly and gracefully but without any clash of opposing forces.

In the recapitulation the *assai animato* transition to the second subject is omitted, the composer reserving it as his last word in the lengthy coda, which it serves to bring to an exciting climax. The music then dies down and the movement ends with eight bars of the introductory *Andante* and the above-mentioned chords which serve as a link to the second movement.

Second Movement. *Vivace non troppo.* Although this movement may, for convenience, be called a Scherzo, its form is that of a sonata first-movement with two subjects stated, developed and recapitulated. After some preliminary scurrying by the strings and a crescendo from *pp*, the clarinet announces a melody which bears some resemblance to the tune of *Charlie is my darling*, Ex. 4. The second subject, a downward moving figure for the strings played *staccato*, also has rhythmic characteristics obviously derived from the composer's acquaintance with Scottish melody. There is a hint of the Scotch snap in the grace-notes. The working-out is gay and felicitous, and near the end of the movement the oboes and bassoons find a new and jaunty way of playing the first subject.

Third Movement. *Adagio.* Again Mendelssohn adopts the first-movement form, and again he astonishes us with the felicity of his invention. The opening bars contain the germ of the whole movement. The violins play the first bar of the first subject, Ex. 5, to which the horns reply with the rhythmic figure which is the chief feature of the second, Ex. 6. After nine introductory bars in this vein the violins play their *cantabile* subject in full. The second subject is given to the wood-winds and horns, with strings, trumpets, and drums added at the climax. While the themes are, as in the first movement, obviously designed for euphonious combination rather than for conflict with one another, Mendelssohn obtains effective contrasts of orchestral colour.

Fourth Movement. *Allegro vivacissimo – Allegro maestoso.* There is more contrast between the first and second subjects of the finale, which is exceptionally rich in material. The two themes of the first subject come as near to depicting the rugged scenery of the Highlands and the traditionally fierce and warlike character of their inhabitants as Mendelssohn's smooth Muse can manage. The themes of the second subject are broader and less emphatic, preparing our minds for the coda, which is, in fact, a peroration to the whole work based upon a new melody, Ex. 7, derived from the introductory theme of the first movement Ex. 1. By this means Mendelssohn contrives to solve the most difficult problems confronting the composer of symphonies: how to unify the four distinct movements into an artistic whole and, even more, how to make the finale the crown of the work without at the same time diminishing the importance of the first movement.

SYMPHONY NO. 4 IN A MAJOR (*The Italian*)

ALTHOUGH it is numbered 4 in the list of Mendelssohn's symphonies, the *Italian Symphony* was completed and performed before the *Scotch* (No. 3). It was the outcome of a request made by the Philharmonic Society of London in 1832 for 'a symphony, an overture, and a vocal piece' – a generous commission for a young composer in his 23rd year. In March of the following year Mendelssohn wrote to the Society offering them this Symphony in A major and two Overtures, one of them being *The Hebrides*. Like the *Scotch Symphony*, the work was inspired by recollections of his tour of 1829–31, which took him, after his visit to Scotland, to the chief cities of Italy. During its composition he complained that it was costing him the bitterest moments he had ever endured. There is not a trace of this bitterness in the music, which is as blithe, sunny and apparently effortless as anything in the whole catalogue of music. The score, which bears a dedication to the Philharmonic Society, was completed on 13th March, 1833, and the first performance was given at one of the Society's concerts exactly two months later.

First Movement. *Allegro vivace.* The movement begins after two bars of repeated chords for the wind, with an immediate statement of the first subject by the violins Ex. 8. It has a smiling air and the supple muscles of youth, moving fast but with an unhurried gait. This is spaciously treated to the extent of some 60 bars, after which a transitional passage occupying 50 more leads to the appearance in the dominant key of the second subject on clarinets and bassoons Ex. 9. This, too, is both athletic – its rhythm is much more subtle than its first two-bar phrases would suggest – and leisurely. After a climax has been reached the clarinet reintroduces the first subject in notes twice its original length – one of Mendelssohn's happiest strokes — and the exposition closes with its return in its original form.

The development opens with a lengthy fugato on a new theme derived from the transitional motive in the exposition Ex. 10. Again the rhythm is made more subtle than a bare statement of the theme will show, by the shifting of the accents as the fugal entries follow upon one another. Finally the music settles down to a regular march-rhythm and the first subject, Ex. 8, reappears on the wood-winds. Nothing displays Mendelssohn's mastery more clearly than his descent from the climax of this section – for, as in mountain-climbing, so in composition it is the descent from the peak that is the severest test of skill and nerve. From the valley so beautifully attained, another crescendo leads to the re-capitulation, in which the fugal subject, Ex. 10, replaces the clarinet's augmented version of the first subject in the exposition.

There is a coda (*piu animato*) beginning with a dialogue between wind and strings, which alternately play Ex. 8 and Ex. 10 respectively. Then with a rush of *staccato* triplets the energetic movement gathers impetus which carries it brilliantly to its end.

Second Movement. *Andante con moto.* The slow movement with its solemn march-like rhythm is said to have been inspired by the sight of a religious procession witnessed by Mendelssohn in Naples. The beauty of the melody, Ex. 11, is much enhanced by its orchestration, first in dark colours for oboes, bassoons, and violas, and then on the violins with a counterpoint for two flutes, and always over a steady *staccato* bass. The middle section of the movement in the dominant major key of A strikes a note of human pathos in contrast with the inexorable and passionless tread of the procession. Its theme Ex. 12 is first played by the clarinets – how often Mendelssohn uses this instrument to embody his most beautiful ideas! – accompanied by the horns over a steady (but not *staccato*) quaver-figure for the strings. The opening section is then recapitulated with some variations and enrichment of the orchestration.

Third Movement. *Con moto moderato.* The Minuet – for it is no Scherzo – is of a grace and simplicity that raise it above the level of mere prettiness. Such charm hardly lends itself to analysis and does not require thematic quotation. One might as well attempt to convey the effect of a butterfly by noting its shape and colour and printing a diagram of its flight. The Trio, in the dominant key, sounds quite a solemn note with its horn theme, without, however, becoming pompous. One might perceive in it an elfin-echo of the horns in Schubert's C major Symphony, were it not clear that Mendelssohn could not in 1833 have known that as yet undiscovered masterpiece, which he was to introduce to the world six years later. But there is closer precedent in his own juvenile masterpiece, the *Midsummer Night's Dream Overture.*

Fourth Movement. *Saltarello: Presto.* The finale carries a reminiscence of the composer's sojourn in Rome, which is the home of the *saltarello*, a dance with a quick hopping step. The movement is based upon two themes in this *saltarello* rhythm, of which the first is quoted as Ex. 13, and a third which has the continuous flow of even triplets characteristic of the Neapolitan *tarantella*, Ex. 14. From these ingredients Mendelssohn concocts a high-spirited and humorous movement, numbering among its other peculiarities, which differentiate it from anything written by anyone else, that it remains persistently in the minor key.

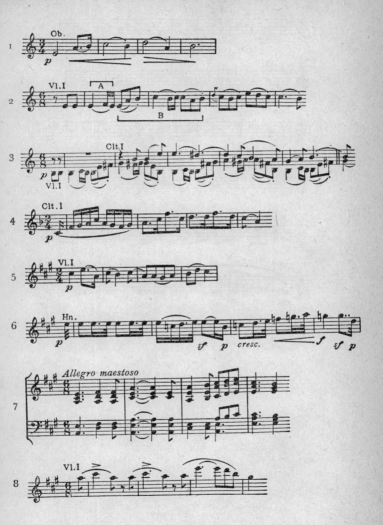

8

Robert Schumann (1810-1856)

STEPHEN WILLIAMS

INTRODUCTION

'SCHUMANN? My dear fellow, what are you talking about? He never wrote a symphony in his life. He just couldn't!' So pronounced a critical friend of mine, turning to me with raised eyebrows when I told him that I was writing on Schumann's symphonies. After which, of course, there was nothing to say. Poor Schumann just dropped dead on the spot.

Allowing for epigrammatic exaggeration, that is the kind of remark we hear far oftener than we hear Schumann's symphonies. Sometimes it is even more rudely expressed. Joseph Rubinstein, for instance, once wrote an article microscopically analysing the *Spring Symphony* and proving (to his own satisfaction at least) that Schumann could not compose at all; and it is a common enough opinion that Schumann wrote some masterly pianoforte pieces and some magnificent songs, and 'the rest is silence' – or if it isn't it ought to be.

Let us therefore take stock. What *is* all this talk about Schumann being unable to write a symphony? How much truth is there in it? The situation seems to be this: Schumann's critics maintain that he wrote good music but poor symphonies. They do not deny him genius (only people who were either deaf or daft could do that) but they deny him 'symphonism'. We all love Schumann's music. For myself, I love even his symphonies; but I know what his detractors are aiming at, and I am uneasily aware that they have some justice on their side. In general, they aim at two points: first, that Schumann's style was essentially lyric rather than epic; and, second, that he was a bad orchestrator.

On the first point, there is no doubt that when most of us hear the name Schumann we do not think of the symphonies; we immediately think of the *Carnaval* or the *Dichterliebe* – short poems, as flawless and shining as some of the Elizabethan love songs, the sonnets of Petrarch or those very lyrics of Heine of which the *Dichterliebe* is a setting. Epigrams, in fact. And here Tovey has, as always, something illuminating to say. Schumann, he points out, was a master of epigram. On the other hand, 'large forms imply the expansion of initial ideas by development; and development is the very thing that an epigram will not bear'. We take it, then, that Schumann's ideas were strong but his development of them was weak. Well, they have said similar things, and with even more justice, about that supreme lyricist Chopin: that he was short-winded, and that his larger works are merely bundles of smaller works with little or no relationship to one other. Yet who would on that account go through life without the F minor Concerto or the *Funeral March Sonata*? Schumann also was often short-winded; and we feel occasionally that his themes are too terse for anything so spacious and continuous as a symphony. Some of his shorter movements, too, can be enjoyed quite independently. We have no inevitable feeling that anything has gone before or that anything need come after. Yet I would rather listen to a bad symphony by Schumann than a good symphony by – but 'the task of filling up the blank I'd rather leave to you'.

When we consider Schumann's orchestration, however, I fear we must hang our heads and take what is coming to us. And *that* comes at times in such a questionable shape that we realize sadly why Schumann's symphonies are so generally unwept, unhonoured and unplayed. He was a poor conductor and he had only an imperfect knowledge of orchestral instruments. His scoring is often repellingly 'thick'; his themes wear so many clothes that their movements are impeded, and some of his *allegros* sound like a beautiful morning before the mists have cleared. Will the sun ever break through, or is the whole day going to be cloudy? In fact, if you wish to get the ultimate discomfort

out of a Schumann symphony, play an old recording on a
bad gramophone with a worn needle. We all know, I suppose, the history of the trumpet fanfare that opens the
Spring Symphony. Schumann originally wrote it for the horns
and pitched it a major third lower (beginning on the B flat);
but at the first rehearsal, owing to certain limitations of the
horns at that time, 'spring's clarion call', instead of rousing
the earth to action, only roused the world to laughter. And
we can imagine how discouraging this must have been to a
man as sensitive as Schumann; a blunder in the very first
bar! Even his efforts to improve things seem sometimes to
have been misguided; and his rescoring of the D Minor
Symphony was little more than a process of doubling – a
general thickening and underlining. Many people prefer the
original version, of which Brahms wrote: 'The original
scoring has always delighted me. It is a real pleasure to see
anything so bright and spontaneous expressed with corresponding ease and grace ... Everything is so absolutely natural
that you cannot imagine it different.'

By this time it begins to look as though my friend was
right when he said that Schumann couldn't write a symphony. But (and it is a very important but) we are not all as
fastidious as my friend. Some of us are content to forget all
about development, orchestration and the rest of it, and to
listen to a man pouring out his heart to us; and if occasionally
he stammers, or his voice is husky, or his speech hesitant,
then what his heart has to say is all the more appealing for
being inarticulate. So the most sensible thing is to forget all
I have written up to now and plunge into the symphonies
themselves. You may not admire them as symphonies, but
you will love them as music.

Just a few words about the order of composition. It is this:
    Symphony in B flat major (*Spring*): 1841
    Symphony in D Minor: 1841, revised 1851
    Symphony in C Major: 1845–6
    Symphony in E flat (*Rhenish*): 1850
So we see that the D Minor Symphony, published as No. 4,
was actually the second to be composed. Both this and
the *Spring Symphony* belong to what Schumann called 'the

Symphony Year'. Until 1840 Schumann had composed nothing but pianoforte music; and it is a rather quaint paradox that in the year of his marriage to a pianist he abandoned pianoforte music and burst into song. If his marriage had been an unhappy one this would not have been a paradox at all; but on the contrary, the marriage of Robert Schumann and Clara Wieck was almost comparable with that of the Brownings. The year 1840 was therefore the 'Song Year' and 1841 the 'Symphony Year'. And the first fruits of Robert's release into happiness was the *Spring Symphony*. His best symphony? I can't quite make up my mind; but undoubtedly the music of a man with spring in his heart, a poet in love with love and in love with life.

SYMPHONY NO. I IN B FLAT (*Spring*)

WHEN the Schumanns were living at Leipzig early in 1841 they kept a joint diary, writing in it each week in turn. About the middle of January Clara wrote out of her turn, and gave the reason: 'It is not my turn to keep the diary this week; but when a husband is composing a symphony he must be excused from other things. The symphony is nearly finished, and though I have not yet heard any of it I am infinitely delighted that Robert has at last found the sphere for which his great imagination fits him.'

The symphony was the *Spring Symphony*, inspired by a poem by Adolf Böttger, in which the poet calls on the spirit of the cloud to turn away, because 'spring has awakened in the valley'. In the following year Schumann gave Böttger his portrait, inscribed with the opening bars of the Symphony and the words 'Beginning of a symphony inspired by a poem of Adolf Böttger; to the poet, in remembrance of Robert Schumann.' The work was first performed from manuscript at the Gewandhaus concert, Leipzig, on 31st March, 1841. Mendelssohn conducted and showed his usual generous care when dealing with the music of a brother artist.

The *Spring Symphony* has, not perhaps a 'programme', but certainly a very different formula of moods, for Schumann thought of putting a title to each movement. The first was to be called *Spring's Coming*, the second *Evening*, the scherzo *Merry Playmates* and the last movement *Full Spring*. He abandoned this idea later, thinking that descriptions of the music might distract listeners from the music itself; and, indeed, when music speaks as eloquently as this, there is no need for the composer to explain it to us; just as when spring is here there is no need for the meteorologist to tell us so. We know it because we feel it.

First Movement. *Andante un poco maestoso – allegro molto vivace.* At once spring's clarion blows 'o'er the dreaming earth'. Schumann wrote to Taubert when he was about to perform the work: 'At the very beginning I should like the trumpets to sound as if from on high, like a call to awaken.' And it is, indeed, a veritable fanfare, a ringing challenge, that opens the introduction. But the earth has not quite shaken off winter's grasp. She shrinks back in fear; and her doubts and misgivings are expressed by modulations into various minor keys. At last, however, her courage returns, and she leaps up in answer to the challenge – to the proud, martial melody of the allegro, Ex. 1.

Spring has come – spring in fighting mood. In Meredith's words, 'The heavens are out in fleeces, And earth's green banner shakes'. The rhythmic opening sentence strikes out its sparks again and again, as if to dazzle all opponents. Then the energy slackens, and we hear the second subject in the clarinets and bassoons, Ex. 2, – a coy, reluctant withdrawal, which seems to suggest that the earth is a little awe-stricken at her own rashness. Spring's boisterous wooing has taken her breath away, and she must pause till it come back to her.

In the development section, Ex. 1 plays a dominating, not to say domineering, part. Schumann turns and twists it into an ingenious variety of shapes, and we shall particularly notice a tiny variant of it on a solo flute which pipes up like an exclamation of astonishment: 'Oh surely not!' it seems to say. But it is surely *so*! The music grows in power and exuberance, like an athlete rejoicing in his strength, and broadens to a majestic climax recalling the opening fanfare. Further development leads us to the coda, in which Ex. 1

prances along with eager self-importance, as though leading a victorious procession. Then comes a surprise: Schumann suddenly stops the ceremony and floats off absent-mindedly into a tender, romantic song, in whose later cadences we hear an intermittent A flat, the melody pleading to be allowed to sink into the subdominant. Then the trumpet call breaks in again, as though impatient to finish the movement.

Second Movement. *Larghetto*. Spring came in like a lion; but now the roaring rhetoric of the first movement has spent itself. The shrill clamour of the winds has died down and evening has fallen. This movement is an exquisite, sensuous lyric, beautifully shaped and so fully and warmly orchestrated that we might easily mistake the season for summer instead of spring. Perhaps there is always summer in the heart of a man as richly in love as Schumann was at this time. It is indeed a Schumann *Song Without Words* – but more in the mood of *Mondnacht* than of *Frühlingsnacht:* a meditation on the haunting melody, Ex. 3, which seems drowsy with the perfumes of the night. We hear it first in the violins, then the 'cellos drone it softly against the whispering voices of strings and wood-wind, and still later it is sung by the oboe and horn. The mood grows sombrely agitated – the night has danger as well as beauty – but peace finally returns. No – not finally: for just as the melody has closed for the last time, like a flower folding up its petals, the trombones enter with an impressive warning which takes us from E flat into G minor. And without a break we spring forward into the scherzo.

Third Movement. *Scherzo: Molto vivace*. This movement also surprises us: although it seems to begin in G minor, we find after a few bars that the tonality of the main subject is really D minor. It is a grim, hard-driving theme with a glow of anger in it, Ex. 4. Clarinet and bassoon then expostulate with it in a dialogue that seems to imply that there is no need to get angry and the storm will soon pass. But – 'No!' says the main subject, striding back; 'life is real, life is earnest!' It is more successfully appeased by the first trio, which translates us into the major, Ex. 5. Again the angry main subject blusters back; but this time it meets its match in a

second trio, which bounds impudently forward, making
boisterous fun of this earnestness, with a jocosity that reminds us of Beethoven in his 'unbuttoned' moods; and the
blusterer has hardly time to assert himself again when a
charming coda breaks in like a shaft of sunlight and –
another surprise – the scherzo fades quietly away in the
major.

Fourth Movement. *Allegro animato e grazioso*. 'Of the last
movement,' wrote Schumann to Taubert, 'I will tell you that
I like to think of it as Spring's Farewell, and that therefore
I should not like it to be rendered frivolously.' The orchestra strikes an attitude at once with a bold rhythmic figure
which seems to tower into the sky and sounds like a flourish
of chords announcing a star performer. We shall hear it
several times later in various forms, Ex. 6. Then the performer dances gaily in, to a tripping little melody in the first
violins (and invariably puts me in mind of a Sullivan patter
song), Ex. 7. This flutters about in various keys and is
finally driven home by a series of short, brusque barking
figures which seem to shut it in and bolt the door on it. Then
oboes and bassoons come trotting forward, Ex. 8. (I wonder
if Grieg had been listening to this when he wrote Anitra's
Dance.) It is promptly answered by the strings in a variant
of Ex. 6. But now that its captors seem to have vanished,
Ex. 7 comes mincing back, and all join in a riotous romp.
Then gradually 'the dancers weary of the waltz, the shadows
cease to wheel and whirl.' All is hushed while a soft horn call
is answered by a flute cadenza. Then off we start again with
the recapitulation. The coda blows and kindles this com-
bustible material, and the symphony that was born, as
Schumann said, 'in a fiery hour' ends in a brilliant con-
flagration. Spring departs as it came: with the heavens out
in fleeces, and transfigured by the music of a man whom a
great love had tuned to symphony-pitch.

SYMPHONY NO. 2 IN C MAJOR

I T is a tragically different Schumann we meet in the Second
Symphony. 'I sketched it,' he wrote, 'when I was still in a

state of physical suffering; nay, I may say it was, so to speak, the resistance of the spirit which exercised a visible influence here, and through which I sought to contend with my bodily state. The first movement is full of this struggle and is very capricious and refractory.' Spitta declared in the first edition of *Grove's Dictionary* that Schumann's symphonies were the most important 'since Beethoven's immortal nine'. When we think of Schubert's B Minor and C Major, and remember that Brahms's First and Second had been heard by that time (1879) such a statement sounds like the wildest nonsense. Yet, in this troubled, self-doubting work, Schumann *does* occasionally penetrate into the same world as Beethoven. It may be that sickness of body and soul had made the eyes of his mind unnaturally bright. On the other hand, it might just as easily have made them unnaturally dim. Until science has more lucidly explained the creative process – if it ever does – we must beware of 'the vanity of dogmatizing'.

First Movement. *Sostenuto assai – allegro ma non troppo*. We are not conscious at once of this unnatural brightness. It takes us some time to get into the composer's mind, and for a while we flounder in darkness, the brasses playing sustained chords while the strings grope about uneasily in the obscurity. Then the pace quickens and we struggle at last to the surface and strike out in the direction of the daylight, Ex. 9. We don't quite reach it; but we manage to keep harsh reality at a distance by constant movement and exercise. A second subject, in E flat, eases the tension a little: 'But the same restless pacing to and fro, and the same agitated heart was there.' Strange that one should so often find oneself quoting Matthew Arnold when writing about Schumann! Yet is it so strange after all? Was there not sometimes in both of them a stubborn discrepancy between the impulse and the form of expression?

This section leads to some woebegone chromatic descents, and we realize that the figure of the opening *allegro* was little more than a strenuous effort at escape. Or have we taken Schumann's own words too much to heart?

Second Movement. *Scherzo: allegro vivace*. Again we try to

stave off reality – running, running furiously until we are out of breath and the mind is as tired as the muscles. This time it is the first violins that do the work. They leap up in feverish, panting energy, Ex. 10. On, on they go, through page after page, filling every bar so as not to give us a second to think, picking and plucking at our exposed nerves. Will they never stop their insistent, maddening music? Yes, they do. Suddenly they are struck into silence, and the wood-wind seeks to comfort us with a trio, which begins with some arch triplets in thirds, Ex. 11. The strings give 'the retort courteous', gliding soon into a fragment of melody that always reminds me of a provocative little phrase in the *Figaro* duet, 'Crudel! Perche finora farmi languir cosi?' There is (again!) a foretaste of Sullivan in a figure with which the first violins carry on the wood-wind's triplets. But they soon weary of this delicate badinage and fly back into the persistent, pin-pricking animation of Ex. 10. A second trio – rather in the style of a chorale – awes them in-to silence for a few moments; but by and by they are fretting and murmuring again, eager to fill the approaching bars with a noise that will leave no time for reflexion. Which they do.

Third Movement. *Adagio espressivo.* Beethoven! Yes – but Beethoven with a difference: Beethoven with a heaviness that depresses the soul instead of a gravity that exalts it. Certainly, Beethoven 'wallows' occasionally in his slow movements; but other men, when they emulate him, lessen their own stature instead of his. Nevertheless, there *are* shreds of nobility – almost clouds of glory – about the first subject, which we hear in the violins, Ex. 12. There is a short interlude and then the broad melody returns, the movement relaxing into C major and slowly dying away. It is, no doubt, a relief to be rid of those dark, enervating flats; yet, once again, we feel that the problem has not been rewardingly solved.

Fourth Movement. *Allegro molto vivace.* Well, Schumann tries to solve it in the finale – and all but succeeds. 'It was only in the last movement,' he wrote, 'that I began to feel like myself again.' Yet the paradox is that, in the chief subject

at any rate, he began to feel like Mendelssohn, Ex. 13.
No one will fail to notice the resemblance between this and
the opening of the *Italian Symphony*. A second subject comes
out in an ingenious cross-rhythm – eight quavers keeping
time with a brace of triplets – and as we are nearing our
journey's end the oboes suddenly think of a fresh argument, Ex. 14. There is a fairly long coda; and now and then
we get that uncomfortable feeling we get at a play when the
last important word has been spoken and we keep glancing
up, expecting the curtain to fall. Schumann brings down his
curtain tardily – and perhaps a little doubtfully; as though
there are other things he could say if only he could cast them
into the proper form.

SYMPHONY NO. 3 IN E FLAT *(Rhenish)*

THE *Rhenish Symphony* was composed in 1850, and is thus
Schumann's last. Spitta wrote: 'The whole symphony is full
of vivid pictures of Rhineland life'; and one has only to
listen to the music to realize how apt this description is. In
spirit it is romantic, but the romance is by turns airy and
earthy. At times we watch in imagination the broadly flowing river through whose murmurous undersong comes the
voice of the Lorelei; we are knee-deep in its fragrant
meadows, wading through a sea of 'dark bluebells drenched
with dews of summer eves', and we turn our eyes to the
cloud-capped towers of its medieval castles. At other times
the meadows are filled with holiday-makers: blond youths
and buxom German fräuleins picnic under the trees or
dance to a rough rustic music – a village band perhaps –
which has just enough of the commonplace to chime in with
their mood. Good comfortable German romanticism; and
German romanticism, as one distinguished authority remarked, is like German beer – 'the more you have, the better
you feel.' Yet this Symphony is strangely neglected. Spitta
loyally asserts that 'although written in 1850, when Schumann's imagination was becoming exhausted, the work
bears no trace of any diminution of power.' Tovey, on

the other hand, thinks the neglect is due to the fact that
'Schumann's orchestration grew worse with the growth of his
experience as conductor at Dusseldorf.' For myself, I prefer
the first, fourth, and last movements. The 'homeliness' of the
scherzo has, for me, a slightly too comfortable, carpet-slip-
pered complacency, and in the slow movement Schumann
seems too easily satisfied with his musical ideas. Still, the
work as a whole has an undeniable, persuasive charm; and
I feel that with all composers we attach too much importance
to the circumstances in which the music was written. 'Ah
yes,' we say, nodding our heads wisely at a lugubrious
modulation into the minor; 'no doubt he had a headache
that morning; or perhaps the greengrocer was knocking on
the door with his bill; or perhaps his wife had left him – or
decided to stay with him.' The truth is that many a composer has written his lightest and brightest music in the face
of such disasters.

First Movement. *Lebhaft* (Lively). The orchestra sails off
at once into the main subject, Ex. 15. When I first heard
this symphony the figure in the fourth and fifth bars flashed
on my mind like a face one has seen before but cannot
remember where. Then I got it: of course! The opening of
Grieg's song, *The Last Spring*. There is no affinity of mood;
but to those who know the song the resemblance continually
nags – especially as that figure is the heart of the whole
movement. There is a kind of fierce joyousness in the subject
– joyousness rather than happiness – as if the composer were
deliberately forcing up his spirits. This determination to be
gay at all costs is gently reproved by the second subject, in
the doubtful, questioning key of G minor. 'Stay a moment,'
it seems to say; 'life may not be so easily conquered as you
think,' Ex. 16. These two subjects play off their arguments
against each other for the rest of the movement, the one
desperately confident, the other gravely dubious. Confidence eventually wins – with the help of a new theme in
the coda.

Second Movement. *Sehr mässig* (Moderate). Here we come
upon the holiday-makers – 'groups under the dreaming
garden trees' – the garden being definitely that of a rustic

tavern. They are dancing to a measured *ländler*, Ex. 17, the orchestra here irresistibly suggested (to me) the fat, comfortable drone of an accordion. It is a slow scherzo. The couples dance with leisurely steps, resolved not to injure their digestions by being too strenuous. A busy little semiquaver figure, strongly resembling Ex. 17, acts as accompaniment to the trio, a rather enigmatic melody in A Minor – at which the dancers seem to pause in dismay. Then the bandsmen come into the garden again (perhaps they have been refreshing themselves) and the couples revolve happily till the end of the movement.

Third Movement. *Nicht schnell* (Not fast). The slow movement is unusually short. It plays for only three or four minutes and might be described as a little poem; or if, like me, you remain unmoved by it, a piece of verse. The clarinets and bassoons begin a tranquil love song, the violas murmuring in the background, Ex. 18. This is gently led into the dominant and ambles on its slow deliberate way until the bassoons enter with the second subject, in which the lover grows more ardent – perhaps even a little resentful. Hitherto he has been speaking in set compliments, but now we feel that his heart is in his words, Ex. 19. But perhaps his beloved is rather like John Donne's mistress – 'Take my word she would not know a heart' – and so the set compliments return, and the serenade closes as calmly and formally as it opened, even the resentful theme being tamed and tranquillized.

Fourth Movement. *Feierlich* (Festive, solemn). This liturgical chant was inspired by a visit of the Schumanns to Cologne, where they were deeply impressed by the magnificent Cathedral. The tone of the movement is rather like that of the songs *Im Rhein, im Heiligen Strome* and *Stirb, Lieb' und Freud,* where also the music suggests a mighty stone structure which the voice of the organ fills, like lungs filling a breathing body. It is a tightly packed, closely concentrated piece of polyphony, the main theme beginning, Ex. 20. And towards the end 'the silver trumpets ring across the Dome'.

Fifth Movement. *Lebhaft* (Lively). The service is over and

we are out again in the glad sunlight and mingling with the bustle of the streets. But – something has happened to us: we have been released, a burden has been lifted, and we feel so light, so elated, that our feet scarcely seem to touch the ground as we skip along, Ex. 21. Gone is the strenuous pursuit of happiness we felt in the first movement. We *are* happy. We are free. As we dance along merrily towards the end we hear the 'Feierlich' theme again – but this time in the major. And perhaps we realize what has wrought this miracle.

SYMPHONY NO. 4 IN D MINOR

'HE has begun a new symphony,' wrote Clara Schumann in the diary of 31st May, 1841. 'As yet I have heard nothing about it, but, from Robert's way of going on, and D minor sounding wildly in the distance, I know that another work is being created in the depths of his soul.' This was, of course, the D Minor Symphony, which is therefore the second in order of composition but was published as No. 4 after Schumann had rescored it ten years later. On his wife's birthday, 13th September, 1841, he surprised her with the completed work, and it was performed shortly afterwards. Schumann was distressfully aware of those weaknesses in instrumentation which sometimes make his orchestral works sound like transcribed pianoforte pieces, just as Franck's Symphony sounds as if it had been orchestrated from the organ. He was not without hope, however. When he had finished this symphony he wrote in his diary: 'One thing I am glad of – the knowledge that I am still far from my goal and must strive to do better, and the feeling that I have the power to do so.' So ten years later he rescored the D Minor Symphony, making many parts of it 'fool-proof'. Whether he made them orchestra-proof or not, or really raised the value of the work is still matter for argument; and indeed some conductors have built their ideal version by fusing the earlier and later scores. Nevertheless the Symphony remains a noble document; and only pedants, asses, and others whose ears are long enough to detect clumsy orchestration and reject a work on that account will fail to be moved and charmed by it. It is true that Wagner called it 'banal', and Wagner was neither a pedant nor an ass; but it would not have been surprising if an excitable, voluble firework of a man like Wagner had found Schumann's whole personality banal. And the D Minor Symphony is a personal expression.

First Movement. *Ziemlich langsam – Lebhaft* (Rather slow – lively). We begin with an uneasy, ominous introduction, in which the first violins and other instruments hold the A, while bassoons, second violins, and violas wander restlessly about in D minor sequences underneath. The effect is that of vegetation swaying to and fro under the sea – a far-fetched simile, but it persistently haunts me. Then the pace gradually quickens, the first violins hint excitedly at the main subject and the *allegro* bursts forth, like Minerva, fully armed, Ex. 22. (We are reminded of the scherzo of the Second Symphony.) The figure in bars one and two is the key to the whole movement and appears again and again, commenting on every fresh emotional aspect. Schumann even uses it (slightly altered) as his second subject – if we admit that it *is* a second subject – after we have calmed down into the relative major. In the development, it passes through a bewildering sequence of keys and is presently used as a persistent retort to a new figure which may be summarized in Ex. 23, and which will be heard later in the work. Another new theme tries to bring peace, Ex. 24. Even this cannot console the key-phrase, which jumps up as if in contradiction each time it is repeated. But it is soon to be tamed: Ex. 24 suddenly blares out in commanding tones in D major and forces the key-phrase into the same tonality. The end is robust and cheerful. The Symphony is 'cyclic' in form, and Schumann intended it to be played without breaks; so we will please sit quite still and wait for the oboe to take us into A minor.

Second Movement. *Romanze* (Romance). Another tiny slow movement – and this time pure poetry: an exquisitely fragile, wistful little song, Ex. 25. But in the twelfth bar of the movement we hear those restlessly swaying figures that troubled the introduction, and for a while it seems that the oboe's little song has roused emotions too strong for it – like Siegfried when he tried to attract the wood-bird and wakened the dragon instead. We are soon in D major, however, with a solo violin weaving a pattern of beautiful arabesques. At the close the oboe repeats Ex. 25 in D minor, stealing back to the tonic only just in the nick of time.

Third Movement. *Lebhaft* (Lively). What a man Schumann was for surprises! The opening of the scherzo blows us bang into eighteenth-century England with a bumping, bumbling, bucolic tune that might have bounced straight out of *The Beggar's Opera*, Ex. 26. Leveridge or Shield could not have written a more typically English tune if they had tried. This the wood-wind punctuates with the crisp chords of Ex. 23. The trio is in quite a different world, the wood-wind slanting down in a limpid melody in B flat in which the chords seem to fall like feathery flakes of snow, and with violin arabesques that recall the second movement. By and by Ex. 26 comes stamping jovially back, only to be shamed into silence again by the trio; and the movement closes quietly in B flat.

Fourth Movement. *Langsam – Lebhaft* (Slow – lively). Schumann prepares us for the final *allegro* with a bridge section which has often been likened to the corresponding section in Beethoven's Fifth Symphony. Against solemn sustained chords the key-phrase of the first movement cries out beseechingly like a prisoner trying to grope his way out of darkness into light. The tone loudens, the pace quickens and at last the barriers are down and we spring forth into 'glad confident morning'. Are we perhaps a little disappointed? Is the sunlight weaker than we had hoped? Certainly the comparison with Beethoven dies on our lips: this is hardly the triumphant affirmation we were led to expect. And we cannot deny that there are one or two faintly embarrassing moments that recall Wagner's unpleasant adjective. Well, we console ourselves with the reflexion that even Beethoven could be 'banal' now and then – not to mention Wagner himself.

We at once recognize the main subject as Ex. 23 (with the key-phrase frisking about delightedly beneath it). Soon we are in A major with the second subject, Ex. 27. All goes 'according to plan'; but we pluck up our spirits at a new and rousing theme, Ex. 28, which leads us into the coda. An energetic *presto* hammers home the various nails, so to speak, and we are sent away rejoicing. A great symphony? Perhaps not; but the testament of a strong and gallant soul.

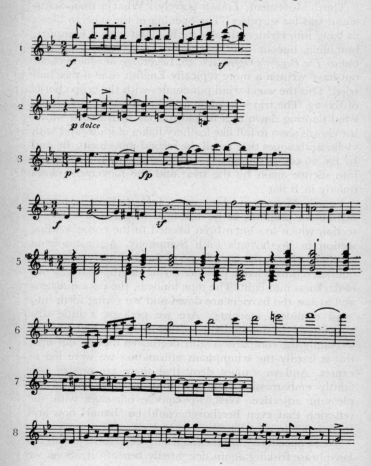

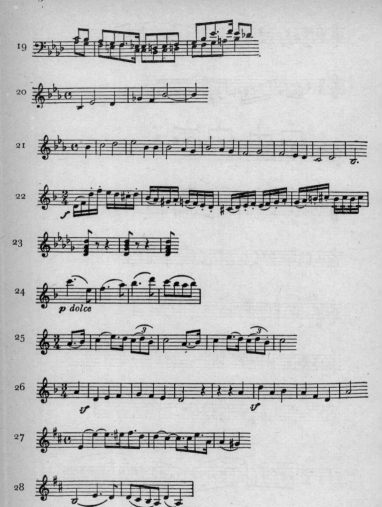

9

Franz Liszt (1811-1886)

HUMPHREY SEARLE

INTRODUCTION

IT is difficult to write any general introduction to the *Faust* and *Dante* Symphonies of Liszt. The two works are very different in character, and Liszt was not a symphonist in the ordinary sense – his achievements lay more in the direction of the symphonic poem. His only major 'abstract' work is the Piano Sonata in B minor, which is in any case a succession of mood pictures rather than a work constructed according to strict classical principles. Apart from the early *Revolutionary Symphony*, which he later recast as the symphonic poem *Héroïde Funèbre*, Liszt wrote only two symphonies, both inspired by literary models. But these are not simply musical portrayals of the books that inspired them, with pictorial effects and all, like Strauss's *Don Quixote*, for instance; they are more in the nature of a musical commentary on a literary work; they express, in fact, Liszt's reactions to Goethe and Dante.

Formally they are far removed from the symphonies of Beethoven or even Berlioz. Liszt applied to them the principles he developed in his symphonic poems; the form depending on the subject matter to be expressed and with much use of 'transformation of themes'. Liszt's themes are short and plastic, and vary their character according to the mood of the moment; and vast edifices are built up from simple phrases. Liszt's use of the orchestral palette is also original and daring, and is generally calculated to make the utmost dramatic effect; and those who appreciate drama in music really complain that the drama is overdone. Liszt showed great sensitivity in this direction, and his two works remain a remarkable, if unusual, contribution to the symphonic repertoire.

THE FAUST SYMPHONY

On 4th December, 1830, the day before the first performance of the *Fantastic Symphony*, Berlioz relates in his *Memoirs*: 'I received a visit from Liszt, whom I had never yet seen. I spoke to him of Goethe's *Faust*, which he was obliged to confess he had not read, but about which he soon became as enthusiastic as myself.' Gérard de Nerval's translation of *Faust* had appeared in 1827, and Berlioz had written his 'Eight Scenes from *Faust*' in the following year. In 1846 he produced his *Damnation of Faust*, which certainly influenced Liszt to write his own work; the *Faust Symphony* is in fact dedicated to Berlioz.

Liszt had some doubts about his task; shortly before embarking on the *Faust Symphony* he wrote to Princess Sayn-Wittgenstein: 'Anything to do with Goethe is dangerous for me to handle', and fifteen years later he wrote to a friend: 'in my youth Faust seemed to me a decidedly bourgeois character. For that reason he becomes more varied, more complete, richer, more evocative (than Manfred) ... Faust's personality scatters and dissipates itself; he takes no action, lets himself be driven, hesitates, experiments, loses his way, considers, bargains, and is only interested in his own little happiness.' But though Liszt's attitude to Goethe was certainly not one of unbounded admiration, the Faust legend did in fact inspire him to produce two of his finest works, the *Faust Symphony* and the *Two Episodes from Lenau's Faust* (of which the second is the well-known First *Mephisto Waltz*), and there is very little doubt that the first movement of the *Faust Symphony*, with its constant and remarkable changes of mood, is a portrait not so much of Faust as of the composer himself.

Liszt called his work A *Faust Symphony in three character studies (after Goethe)*: 1. *Faust*; 2. *Gretchen*; 3. *Mephistopheles*. It occupies over 300 pages of full score, lasts more than an hour in performance, and was composed in the remarkably short space of two months (August to October 1854). The final chorus was added three years later, and in the intervening time Liszt was able to try the work out with the Weimar orchestra, and make various alterations as a result. Up to that period, as a result of having to earn his living as a professional pianist, his study of orchestration had been somewhat sketchy, and a good deal of the scoring of the earlier symphonic poems had been carried out by Raff and Conradi. The *Faust Symphony* is one of the first works which Liszt completely scored himself, and no one can deny that the orchestration is, to say the least, extremely effective and striking.

The symphony was first performed on the 5th December, 1857, at Weimar, with the composer as conductor, in a concert in honour of the foundation of a memorial to Grand Duke Karl August (the patron of Goethe and Schiller) and also of the unveiling of monuments to Goethe, Schiller, and Wieland.

The *Faust Symphony* is scored for normal symphony orchestra, with the addition of piccolo, third trumpet, harp, and (in the last movement) tenor solo, male chorus, and organ. Apart from some passages in the second movement, Liszt does not attempt to portray Goethe's story in detail, and the first movement is a character study of Faust seen from many angles. Its form is difficult to analyse; it may roughly be described as consisting of a very long exposition followed by a short development section and a condensed recapitulation. It begins with a slow introduction which states two of the principal themes. The first, Ex. 1, with its whole-tone flavour, might be said to represent the mystical and magical element in Faust's nature. (Incidentally Wagner later made a considerable use of this theme in *Götterdämerung*.) It is immediately followed by the second, Ex. 2, a theme which assumes many aspects during the work, but generally represents Faust's emotional character, whether passionate, amorous or melancholy.

The *Allegro impetuoso* which follows has a feeling of passionate striving, and leads to a fortissimo statement of Ex. 1 on the trumpets and trombones, ending with sharp dramatic chords. The second theme, Ex. 2, on solo bassoon introduces a new theme, Ex. 3, of a stormy character. Beginning on the strings alone, it rises to a passionate climax, and is restated by the full orchestra. It leads straight into another emotional theme, Ex. 4, which plays an important part in the second movement. The excitement then subsides, and a passage marked *misterioso e molto tranquillo* introduces Ex. 1 on clarinets and pizzicato strings under an undulating violin figure. This leads through a short *plintivo* section based on Ex. 2a to an expressive statement of Ex. 2 on woodwind and horns, answered by solo viola phrases, which plainly portrays Faust's amorous nature. As the tension increases, the tempo quickens, and horn and trumpet calls herald the last of the Faust themes, Ex. 5, representing his heroic aspirations. Ex. 2 soon joins it, and the exposition ends with a *fff* restatement of Ex. 5 on the brass, accompanied by rushing string figures.

There is no break in the music, however, which dashes on into a restatement of Ex. 1 in canon between trombones and trumpets, followed by Ex. 3, which again rises to a powerful climax. Now at last the excitement dies down, and the whole of the slow introduction returns, followed by an *Andante mesto* section, in which Ex. 2 on clarinet and bassoon is combined with Ex. 1 on the lower strings, and Ex. 4 also makes a short reappearance. Now follows one of the most remarkable passages in the work; Ex. 1 is heard on clarinet and pizzicato violas under whole-tone chords for flutes and violins tremolando; all key-feeling disappears, and the effect is magical in the true sense of the word. Then a gradual crescendo, still based on Ex. 1, leads back to a violent restatement of Ex. 3, with which the reprise begins.

This section is much condensed; after Ex. 3 has reached its climax, Ex. 2 is heard again in its amorous form, and leads back to Ex. 5. This first appears quietly on solo trumpet, horns, and bassoon, but a *crescendo* passage based on Ex. 2 soon leads to a fortissimo restatement, followed, as before, by Ex. 1 in canon on the brass. Finally Ex. 5 rings out again on the trombones, and leads to a short coda, mainly based on Ex. 1. At the end Ex. 2 breaks in abruptly, the music seems to collapse into its main tonality of C, and it is Ex. 2 in its original form on the lower strings which has the last word.

After the storm and stress of the Faust movement, which seems to have been written at white heat throughout, the atmosphere of the second movement, Gretchen, is of a magical delicacy. A short introduction on flutes and clarinets leads to the main Gretchen theme, Ex. 6, on the oboe accompanied by solo viola – a characteristically original piece of scoring, and exactly right as a musical portrait of fresh and innocent youth. Soon a reference to Ex. 4 shows that Faust is not far from Gretchen's thoughts; it is followed by a short dialogue between clarinet and violins, depicting the scene where Gretchen plucks off the petals of a flower, murmuring to herself: 'He loves me – he loves me not – he loves me!' Then Ex. 6 returns with fuller scoring, and leads to the second main theme, Ex. 7, marked *dolce amoroso*.

As it dies away Ex. 2 on the horns (marked *patetico*) indicates the entrance of Faust on the scene, and the mood becomes more agitated. It is followed by Ex. 4 on the 'celli, *expressivo con intimo sentimento*, and finally the full orchestra enters with a quiet statement of Ex. 2 in its amorous form. The lovers have come together, and even the stormy theme, Ex. 3, can now be heard *soave con amore*. This leads to the reprise, which follows the exposition more or less exactly, except for the omission of the flower episode, and the insertion of Ex. 2 before the reappearance of Ex. 7. As the movement dies away a quiet reference to Ex. 5 seems to show that Faust's happiness is now complete.

Mephistopheles is the spirit of negation; and to represent him Liszt hit on the ingenious idea of only using parodies of the Faust themes, with (as we shall see later) one exception. After a short introduction, marked *ironico*, which sets the malevolent atmosphere, Ex. 2 appears in the abrupt form heard at the end of the first movement, and soon there is a hint at a new figure, Ex. 8, which Liszt borrowed from an earlier work, the so-called '*Malediction*' concerto for piano and strings, where it is marked *orgueil* (pride) in the original score. Next comes Ex. 1 on the clarinet accompanied by chromatic scales on the violas, followed by a rhythmically

altered version of Ex. 3. It runs its course much as in the
first movement, and works up to a powerful climax. Exs. 2
and 1 then reappear in their parodied forms, and a trill
passage in the strings and woodwind leads to the appearance
of Ex. 8 in the form quoted here.

After a false start Ex. 2 now starts up as a fugue on the
strings, and afterwards its 'abrupt' form leads to a fortissimo
statement of Ex. 5, which is parodied chiefly by the addition
of trills. It is interrupted by Ex. 3 (followed by Ex. 1 pizzicato under stopped horn chords), but Ex. 8 again builds up
a climax, at the crest of which Ex. 5 returns. Ex. 2 continues the savage and violent mood, till a sudden pianissimo
heralds the Gretchen theme, Ex. 6 – the only one which is
proof against parody.

But the respite is only momentary, and the diabolical
dance begins again with Ex. 1, followed by a full statement
of Ex. 3. Ex. 5 reappears, and the tempo increases; finally
Ex. 2 carries the music on to the ultimate climax, crowned
by Ex. 8. Twice Ex. 3 interrupts, followed by Ex. 1 and the
stopped horn chords; but the onward surge continues until
the crest is reached, and the music sinks down in exhaustion.
Then the entry of the Gretchen theme, Ex. 6, on horn and
solo 'cello leads to the final section of the movement.

This point was the original ending of the work, and it is
still played in this form when no chorus is available, but
there is no doubt that the final choral section sums up the
whole work and makes it complete. First the trombones hint
at the choral theme; then after a pause the male chorus
enters, singing the 'Chorus Mysticus' which ends the second
part of Goethe's *Faust*: adequate translation of it is quite
impossible.

Alles Vergängliche	All that is mortal
Ist nur ein Gleichnis;	Is but a semblance;
Das Unzulängliche	The incomplete
Hier wird's Ereignis,	Is here fulfilled;
Das Unbeschreibliche	The inexpressible
Hier ist es getan;	Is here attained;
Das Ewigweibliche	The ever-womanly
Zieht uns hinan.	Still leads us on.

At the words 'Das Ewigweibliche' the tenor soloist enters with the Gretchen theme, Ex. 6. Higher and higher he soars, till eventually the whole passage returns fortissimo with solemn fanfares. Again the tenor takes the Gretchen theme up to the heights; and finally Ex. 5 in the bass brings the whole work to a triumphant conclusion. With all its faults and longueurs, there is no doubt that in it Liszt wrote his masterpiece.

THE DANTE SYMPHONY

DANTE was one of Liszt's earliest loves; he had read him frequently in the 1830's with Marie d'Agoult, and in 1837 had written the first version of his *Après une Lecture du Dante* for piano (usually known as the *Dante Sonata*). By 1847 he had already sketched out the principal themes of the symphony, and intended at that time to get the painter Buonaventura Genelli to design lantern slides to be shown during the performance of the music. But he did not get to work seriously on it till the summer of 1855, and completed it in July of the following year. His original idea was to write three movements, Inferno, Purgatorio, Paradiso, corresponding to the three sections of Dante's *Divina Commedia*; but Wagner persuaded him that no human being could express in music the joys of Paradise, and the work now ends with a Magnificat for women's voices in place of a third movement. This is a pity, for the balance of the symphony is thereby destroyed; and though Liszt was certainly more at home in the infernal than the celestial regions, the task should not have been beyond his powers.

The work is dedicated to Wagner, and was first performed under the composer's direction at Dresden in November 1857. It was a failure, owing to lack of rehearsal, but on its repetition in Prague the following year it scored a great success. An introduction to the work by Richard Pohl was read out at the first performance, and is now printed in the full score; a good deal of it is the work of Princess Sayn-Wittgenstein.

It is shorter than the *Faust Symphony,* its two movements

lasting about three-quarters of an hour, but it needs a slightly larger orchestra, including cor anglais, bass clarinet, and two harps. The first movement, *Inferno*, (which incidentally was copied very faithfully by Tchaikovsky in his *Francesca da Rimini*) begins with a musical setting of the words written over the gates of hell:

Per me si va nella città dolente;
Per me si va nell' eterno dolore;
Per me si va tra la perduta gente ...
Lasciate ogni speranza, voi ch' entrate.

Through me is the way to the city of weeping;
Through me is the way to eternal torment;
Through me is the way among those that are lost ...
Abandon hope, all ye that enter here.

The Italian words are actually written in the trombone parts, and the last line is made into a musical theme, Ex. 9, which plays an important part in the movement. Then begins the musical representation of Dante's 'strange tongues, horrible cries, words of pain, tones of anger' which make up the whirlwind which ever rages in hell. A chromatic descending phrase, Ex. 10, is prominent at first, followed by hints of Ex. 11; the tempo gradually increases till Ex. 11 appears in an *Allegro frenetico,* and finally reaches *Presto molto,* with wild rushing passages for the strings. There is no abatement in the storm, Ex. 11 still remaining prominent, till a new theme, Ex. 12, also based on a descending phrase, bursts out on the full orchestra. It is answered by Ex. 10, which gradually works up to a climax and the return of Ex. 9 on all the brass in the slow tempo of the beginning. The storm now subsides, and drum beats in the rhythm of Ex. 9 lead to the central section of the movement.

Like Tchaikovsky after him, Liszt here portrays the unhappy Paolo and Francesca, whose punishment for their illicit love is to be incessantly driven about by violent winds in the second circle of hell. He begins with an introductory section presaging Ex. 13, first on violins in 5/4 time, followed by a bass clarinet solo answered by clarinets in thirds; then

after repeating this whole section he introduces a new
theme, Ex. 13, on the cor anglais to Francesca's words:

> Nessun maggior dolore
> Che ricordarsi del tempo felice
> Nella miseria.
>
> There is no greater pain
> Than to recall the happy days
> In time of misery.

The resemblance of this theme to Ex. 12 is obvious; it is
then repeated by bass clarinet and bassoon followed by flute
and oboe in canon. A 'cello passage leads to an *Andante
amoroso* section in 7/4 time; here Liszt portrays the lovers'
past happiness, and it is one of his most inspired passages.
Its theme, Ex. 14, is again based on a descending scale.

After the whole section has been repeated with richer
orchestration, Ex. 9 is heard sinisterly on the stopped horn
and a harp cadenza heralds the return of the tempest. This
begins with low horns and bassoons, and Ex. 11 soon appears,
embellished with trills. Low clarinets and bassoons create an
ironic atmosphere, and the storm soon reaches its height and
continues on its course much as before. Finally Ex. 10 used
as a ground bass works up to a last fortissimo restatement of
Ex. 9.

The second movement, *Purgatorio*, begins with an introductory passage, marked *Tranquillo assai*, which seems to
represent the scene where Dante, on leaving hell behind,
comes out into the light of the stars and sees the dawn rising
like the 'sapphire of the orient'; it is a passage of wonderful
beauty. After its repetition a semitone higher, we reach the
portrayal of the trials which souls in Purgatory must endure
in order to reach Heaven. A chorale-like theme on the
clarinets and bassoons, Ex. 15a, and its continuation on the
strings, Ex. 15b, indicate the yearning of these souls for ultimate happiness. Then a fugue on a subject, Ex. 16, akin to
Exs. 12 and 13, gradually builds up to an impassioned climax, ending in a *grandioso* section. An interlude for wood-
wind over violin arpeggios leads to a return of the chorale
theme, Ex. 15, in the same sad mood as before, but with its

continuation, Ex. 15b, the atmosphere begins to lighten, and soon the women's chorus enters with a delicate woodwind and string accompaniment to sing the Magnificat. In this final section Liszt uses diatonic harmonies with a modal flavour, and the general mood is joyful but tranquil, dying away at the end in ethereal chords. A second ending, which Liszt composed later at Princess Sayn-Wittgenstein's suggestion, brings the work to a fortissimo conclusion, but destroys the whole atmosphere of the final section, of Dante, having passed through Purgatory, gazing at the heights of Heaven above him and hearing its music from afar.

Though the *Dante Symphony* is not the equal of the *Faust* in sustained inspiration, its many fine passages certainly place it among Liszt's best works.

10

César Franck (1822-1890)

STANLEY BAYLISS

INTRODUCTION

CÉSAR FRANCK wrote only one symphony, but it is the only
non-programmatic symphony by a composer of the French
School to enter the accepted orchestral repertory of the rest
of the world. Saint-Saëns won wide popularity, but not one
of his symphonies had the success of his opera, *Samson and
Delilah*, not even his Third, which makes use of piano and
organ, in spite of the advocacy of Sir Thomas Beecham.
Even Bizet's sparkling early Symphony has now receded into the background, after a number of performances on its
recent revival from neglect. Debussy and Ravel wrote no
symphonies. The Third and Fourth Symphonies of Albert
Roussel are arresting, but have still to win general appreciation.

Yet, although this is the case, Franck's Symphony is by
no means an orthodox work. Tovey flatly says that it is just
as much a symphonic poem as are *Les Éolides* or *Le Chausseur
Maudit*. It is unusual in the number of its movements, having
three instead of the customary four. In this respect alone it
has affinity with the *Symphonie Fantastique*; but Berlioz, of
course, exceeded the usual four by writing five movements.

The first movement of Franck's Symphony is notable for
the alternating of slow and quick sections, and Tovey maintains that this practice will remind most listeners of Beethoven's String Quartet in B flat, Op. 130. But whether it
does or not, there can be little doubt that Franck was influenced by Beethoven. On the other hand, while there may
be formal likenesses between Franck and Beethoven, it is
debatable whether Franck's musical thought and expression
are akin to Beethoven's.

It has been usual to dwell upon the mystical aspect of Franck's art; yet is not the emotional content of the second movement of his Symphony something quite different to, and of a lower order than, that in the *Allegretto* of Beethoven's Seventh or the slow movement of the Ninth Symphony? Franck's music must be played with fervour, it is true, but it must also be played with restraint, otherwise the climaxes become blatant and vulgar and topple over into bathos.

Vincent D'Indy (pupil and biographer of Franck) set a very high evaluation upon Franck's contribution to musical method. It had better be stated as far as possible in D'Indy's own words. In Cobbett's *Cyclopedic Survey of Chamber Music* he argued that 'In the history of music there is a phenomenon which is almost periodically recurrent throughout the ages, and which is an important factor in the progressive development of our art ... An artist of genius, or even one of great talent, discovers – either in the domain of harmony or in that of form and construction – a path previously untrodden, some happy modification of the older symphonic scheme, in short, an innovation which revivifies and creates new resources for forms which seemed to be growing stereotyped through over-strict observance of conventional formulas. The artist's discovery, sometimes unwitting, is, strange to say, rarely followed up either by his contemporaries or by his immediate successors, and it is only after a slumber of forty or fifty years that the new idea finds a soil suitable for its development, and reaches its full growth in the works of another artist of creative genius.'

D'Indy instances Weber's system of dramatic composition based on significant keys in *Der Freischütz* and *Euryanthe*, which was taken up and carried to its fullest development forty years later by Wagner and led to the *Leitmotiv* system. D'Indy maintains that Franck took up the principle of cyclic composition found in Beethoven's Piano Sonata Op. 13, a principle characteristic of the sonatas and quartets of his third period, but one which was followed neither by Weber, Schubert nor Spohr.

This must be considered an exaggerated claim, since it

overlooks the influence that Liszt may have had on Franck's orchestral style and method – he dedicated an early piano trio 'à son ami Franz Liszt' – and (2) it places Franck's best work on a level with those of Beethoven's third period, and that is a claim that cannot be sustained. Nevertheless, the cyclic method by which themes are repeated in more than one movement to give a sense of added unity is a characteristic of Franck's method of composition.

Franck's Symphony was finished in 1888, two years before his death in 1890 at the age of sixty-eight. It is a curious fact that all the works by which he is now known – the Prelude, Choral, and Fugue for piano, the Violin Sonata, the String Quartet and Piano Quintet, for example – all date from his last twenty years. Did the Franco-Prussian War of 1870 release a spring in his mind? He had led a life of routine, teaching, and playing the organ at St Clothilde. He had made time daily for composition, but scarcely any of the music then written is known to-day. Nonetheless, the cyclic form or idea may be found in his first piano trio, written when he was twenty. Franck is a remarkable instance of retarded development.

He was a great organist and improviser, and both functions influenced his method of composing. D'Indy called him 'the genius of improvisation', while Colles speaks of his music as being at once 'reflective and impulsive'; and says that Franck, at the same time, exercised considerable thought upon matters of form and expression. He has been described as composing with a pencil in one hand and an india-rubber in the other. With the pencil he wrote down the ideas that came to him so readily; then, if he had second and better thoughts, he could easily erase with the rubber and write down the new ideas. These would come to him while he was doing other things. He would get up from teaching a pupil to note a theme, or find that ideas came while he was pounding away at, say, a Wagner score at the piano.

His orchestration, too, was affected by his having been so long an organist. He had not the instinct for mixing orchestral colours as master orchestrators like Wagner, Strauss or Elgar had. The effect of his scoring is that of an organist pulling out his stops. One wrathful critic even maintained that his Symphony would sound better if it were transcribed for a steam organ at a fair!

The score is remarkable for the use of a cor anglais. It is said that Gounod or one of the professors at the Paris Conservatoire exclaimed: 'That a symphony! Whoever heard of a cor anglais being used in a symphony?'

SYMPHONY IN D MINOR

FIRST Movement. *Lento – Allegro non troppo – Lento – Allegro non troppo – Lento – Allegro – Lento.* Although this movement may be divided into so many sections, unity is attained by the use made of the theme heard at the very beginning on violas, 'cellos, and basses, Ex. 1. At bar 6 the first violins answer, as it were, with Ex. 2. Franck's personal chromaticism is thus early in evidence.

These two themes undergo development until the twenty-ninth bar, when the first *Allegro non troppo* begins with a vigorous theme which is easily recognized to be a metamorphosis of the slow opening theme. The dynamics are now *fortissimo*, and the rhythm of Ex. 2 is slightly varied and more marked.

This continues for only twenty bars, at the end of which there is a slowing down of the time and a diminishing of the tone. The *Lento* recurs in F sharp minor, treated more or less as before, until the *Allegro non troppo* comes back, also in the same key. It has been suggested that this procedure holds up things, as it were, but it does so, on the other hand, only if the listener's mind is expecting or desiring something in orthodox sonata form.

The strings now introduce a new subject in F major, Ex. 3. The use of a rocking rhythm (bar 3 of Ex. 3) from the first subject should be noted. This leads to another theme which has been called the 'motive of faith', Ex. 4. It exhibits Franck's habit of making a theme revolve round a single note, giving an impression of constant or restless modulation. It is the rather blatant use made of this theme later on that has made Franck open to the charge of vulgarity. It is enunciated *fortissimo* and *sostenuto* in the higher strings and woodwind, the brass and basses joining in the triumphal march.

The main development section of the movement now begins with what Tovey has aptly described as a 'sudden gleam of D major' (Franck is rather fond of alternating major and minor). Scales passages based upon Ex. 2 are a prominent feature. The *Lento* recurs and then the *Allegro* until, nine bars before the conclusion of the movement, the opening theme is hammered home or forms the coping stone of the whole (whichever metaphor is preferred!).

Second Movement. *Allegretto*. If the first movement may be regarded as a species of development of the basic idea of an introduction and allegro, repeated three times, the second movement may be considered as combining the slow movement and the scherzo. Moreover, the scherzo may be said to have two contrasting sub-sections.

After sixteen bars of chords on plucked strings and harp, the cor anglais enunciates the celebrated theme Ex. 5, which revolves round F. To prevent the tone colour palling, this is continued by clarinet, horn, and flute.

The next landmark is a soft, sweet, song-like theme for the violins with a counter-theme in 'cellos and basses. The scherzo-like section comes with a fluttering theme in the violins (after a preliminary foreshadowing of the line it was to take). This is followed by yet another contrast on the clarinets, Ex. 6, also with a counter-theme in the lower strings. Before the end of the movement Ex. 5 and the fluttering theme are heard combined.

Third Movement. *Allegro non troppo*. Tovey describes this movement as 'festive, effective, and leisurely'. Few will dispute the cogency of those three epithets.

After six bars of preliminaries, the 'cellos and bassoons usher in, accompanied by violins and violas, a swinging theme which D'Indy described as 'joyous' and 'sanely vivacious'. It quite definitely does afford a healthy contrast to the morbid or sick-room atmosphere of much of the other movements.

This theme, Ex. 7, however, is not with us for long before

a new subject in the brass brings back the prevailing atmosphere of the symphony. The basic principle of sonata form is really one of dramatic contrasts, contrasts which are eventually reconciled. There are contrasts, of course, in Franck's symphony, but the motive force seems to be, not so much the drama of opposition, as the dominating of the whole work by a single mood.

Strings and wood-wind have a series of responses, the brass beginning a new subject, Ex. 8. The metre changes from two-two time to three-four time, and the cor anglais brings back the theme of the Allegretto, Ex. 5, with triplet figures accompanying it first on the violins and then on the violas. This re-introduction of a theme from a former movement well illustrates the principle of cyclic form; it is intensified by the occurrence again of the 'motive of faith' in the upper strings and the wood-wind. The movement now speedily moves on its own momentum to its conclusion with the recall of the first subject of the movement, Ex. 7. A notable feature of the construction is the use of an ostinato bass, that is the persistent repetition of a short phrase or figure. It begins at bar 350, page 134 of the miniature score.

II

Anton Bruckner (1824-1896)

RICHARD CAPELL

INTRODUCTION

LET us, for the moment, not peruse but merely cast a glance at the pages of a Bruckner score, thumbing them over for a first impression. Here, we begin by saying, is spaciousness. The eye catches, as likely as not, a glimpse of stately sequences sailing by; the chances are that it alights on a forest of murmuring or stormy string tremolandos. Horn-calls and horn-songs are everywhere; and if we happen to be near the end of the score the brass may be lifting up their voices in a hymn. The strings are perhaps persisting in a figuration that goes for page after page, and one may be reminded a little of the look of Schubert's C major symphony. Never does the page suggest Wagner – it is plainer – and never Beethoven, who is much more eventful and purposeful. Yet there may be moments when the look of the slow movement of the Choral Symphony comes to mind.

Brahms is never recalled. Everything here is broader and more expansive. If the score opens at a scherzo one may see the dancing of Fafner and Fasolt, with a tremendous pounding of clogged feet. Though Bruckner may give the direction *Fast* or *Very fast* these huge scherzos of his cannot, as is that of Beethoven's *Choral Symphony*, be fast in effect. *Ma non troppo* occurs again and again in the directions, and it is implicit when not expressed. The eye catches sight of plenty of counterpoints, but they are of the enriching and not of the dramatic sort. The voices of the woodwind enter, each according to its nature, a nature, which, according to Bruckner, is that of lesser kinsfolk of the virile horns. Still without actually perusing the score, we notice a naturalness in the utterance of each instrumental group. What each is required to say is well within the bounds of its possibilities; none is pressed to the periphery. A large music, then; symphonic movements that are like spacious landscapes; tremolandos that are like leaves of the forest, repeated figurations like cascades; with the calls of huntsmen sounding from near and far; with dances of hob-nailed peasants who look larger than life in the dusk of a holiday evening; a music filled with a sense of Natura Benigna, to whom it is all dedicated with unending wonder and thanksgiving.

What manner of man was its author? One of the great composers of the romantic century, Bruckner has, outside the German-speaking countries, obtained less of a hearing in the world than a whole host of his inferiors. The deeper reasons for the indifference his music has encountered in France, Italy, and England – as, for that matter, it formerly did in Germany – will be glanced at later. Among the secondary reasons has been the depiction of Bruckner (and not only by his enemies of the anti-Wagnerian faction) as a figure of fun. Bruckner admired Wagner devotedly; and this, in the quarrels between Wagnerians and Brahmsians, quarrels that were pursued in Germany to fantastic lengths of bad manners and spite, was an incitement to those who, like Hanslick, were unattracted by Bruckner's music, to personal attacks that were no less than ferocious. (In the other camp Hugo Wolf, an unbalanced critic, was as unmannerly.) On top of this came the first Life of Bruckner, which long held the field, by Rudolf Louis who, although one of his admiring pupils, made so much of the ingenuous side of Bruckner – the peasant who, already aged 44 when he went up from his province to live at Vienna, never became a man of the world – that this picture and a number of hoary anecdotes illustrating the simplicity of his nature and conduct have persuaded a world of cockneys that he was hardly more than a half-wit. Such chestnuts as the story of Bruckner's giving Richter, after a rehearsal, a thaler to buy himself a drink will be dispensed with here. After all, the most knowing of cockneys is just as apt to look a fool in the country.

Is it so very extraordinary that a peasant born and bred, a simple, God-fearing soul, should have written music of genius? It is. But the nineteenth century was one in which anything might happen, a century in which eminent men were eccentric and unique and not an intensification of types as they now tend to be. Bruckner's type is familiar, his eminence unique. In the Middle Ages he would have been an artist-craftsman, anonymous and contented. His uniqueness is this: that, in the century par excellence of individualism, he achieved a major work – major and original by the century's own standards – by simply applying himself, with no deliberate aim at originality, no conscious exploiting of his personality, to a job of work, the writing of symphonies to the glory of God, in the frame of mind of any honest craftsman.

Bruckner was not so intelligent as Berlioz, Liszt or Wagner, he was not so learned as Brahms; but he had all the instincts of a creative artist. Beethoven gave him the general idea of a symphony – four movements, including an Adagio and a Scherzo, an exposition with contrasted keys and subjects, then development and recapitulation – and it was enough. There is no evidence that he ever looked at all closely at a Beethoven symphony*; all the evidence, in fact, is that he was never interested in doing so, such is the gulf between his rapturous symphonic visions and the action, variety, and dramatic charge and release of the classical symphony. He must, in the years of his ecclesiastical service, have become familiar with quantities of old church music from Palestrina onwards, but no one was ever more devoid of archaic interests. His Masses naturally, but never self-consciously, carry on the tradition of the Viennese school. The 'historical imagination', indispensable to the critic and perhaps to the executive artist, is an incubus to creativeness, and Bruckner was creative. The past existed in him, as in all true creative artists, at a level rather lower than consciousness. His admiration and allegiance he gave to such creators of his own century – Schubert, Wagner, Dvořák – as he found expressing something of himself.

---

* It is said that not until he was 56 did he, when composing his solitary piece of chamber music, the F major quintet, make the acquaintance of Beethoven's later quartets.

He was, like all major poets, a man of his time. And, harshly though in some ways it treated him, he was fortunate in his time, which was, indeed, the making of him. At least, none other can be imagined as affording him such scope, such room for expression and expansion. A world of music in which the particular delight of the Schubert-Wagner age in beautiful sound for its own sake did not obtain – that delight which slowed down the whole motion of music, since to hasten then would have been like gulping down wine without savouring – a world, consequently, of music without the romantic grandeur and mystery which the new slow-moving time encouraged – how, we may ask, would Bruckner have fared therein, he who had had no wit or sparkle in him for an age that had first of all demanded such things, no drama or power of characterization, no lyric gift, nothing, in fact, but an outpouring of poetic sound which we have called a thanksgiving to Nature but which, in truth, sometimes seems like part of Nature herself, so majestic is the flow and ebb of its tides, its green depths of forest and admirable mountains.

He was nearly forty – the year was 1863 – when he made the acquaintance of *Tannhäuser*. He had never before heard a note of Wagner, and he was swept off his feet. The next few years abounded in such experiences and essays as are normally those of a lad of twenty. To 1863–4 belong two symphonies, in F minor and D minor (first performed in 1923 and 1924), which he rated as student-work, outside the canon of his Nine.* *Tristan and Isolde* swam into his ken, and thereafter for the rest of his life the score was always on his piano. He corresponded with Wagner; asked for a composition that the Linz Choral Society, which he conducted, might sing; and received the finale of the third act of *The Mastersingers*, which Linz thus heard before the Munich production of the opera.

It is convenient to give at this point a list of Bruckner's nine symphonies. The dates are from Kurth.

* But the D minor was revised and in part re-composed in 1869, i.e., between the composition of the First and Second Symphonies (see Ernst Kurth's *Bruckner* pp. 1120-1151).

No. 1 in C minor 1865-6. First performance Linz, 1866. Revised, 1890-1, and dedicated to Vienna University. First performance of revised version, Vienna, under Richter, 1891.

No. 2 in C minor, begun in London, 1871; finished, 1872. First performance, Vienna, under Bruckner, 1873. Revised, 1878, and after 1880.

No. 3 in D minor, 1873. First performance, Vienna, under Bruckner, 1877. First revision, 1876-7; second revision, 1889. Dedicated to Wagner.

No. 4 in E flat (*Romantic*), 1873-4. Revised, 1878-80. First performance, Vienna, under Richter, 1881.

No. 5 in B flat, 1875-77. Revised, 1878. First performance, Graz, under Fr. Schalk, 1894.

No. 6 in A, 1879-81. First complete performance, Vienna, under Göllerich, 1901.

No. 7 in E, 1881-83. First performance, Leipzig, under Nikisch, 1884. In London, under Richter, 1887. Dedicated to Ludwig II of Bavaria.

No. 8 in C minor, 1884-5. Revised 1886-7 and 1889-90. First performance, Vienna, under Richter, 1892. Dedicated to the Emperor Francis Joseph.

No. 9 in D minor (unfinished), 1889-94. First performance, Vienna, under Ferdinand Löwe, 1903.

Unavoidable even in the slightest sketch of Bruckner's work is the textual question. The position, unique in music, is this. There are large differences, differences not only of orchestration but also of form, between Bruckner's manuscripts and the published scores by which, down to 1934, the music was known. It will have been noticed (see the list of symphonies above) how Bruckner again and again revised his major works; and there is plenty of evidence to show that he gladly accepted instrumentational suggestions made during the preparation of performances, by Nikisch and other conductors who possessed a practical experience of the orchestra beyond his own. Löwe and the two Schalks, Josef and Franz, were the musicians principally associated with what we know as the *Universal Edition* (U.E.) versions.* These were the versions performed in the composer's

* The 1st, 2nd, 4th and 6th symphonies were originally published by Eberle & Haslinger, the 3rd by Rattig, the 5th and 7th by Guttmann, the 8th by Schlesinger-Lienau. All were by 1909-10 in the hands of U.E. See Egon Wellesz on *Bruckner and the Process of Musical Creation* (*Musical Quarterly*, July, 1938), for fuller details and for a judicious statement of the textual question.

lifetime, presumably with his acceptance. For all anyone
knows, the differences between the manuscripts and these
publications represent modifications sanctioned by Bruckner or even, in some cases, made by himself in proof (the
proofs have disappeared). But the posthumous symphony
presents a different case, one which supports the opinion
that the earlier modifications may be un-Brucknerian. Löwe
edited the work for performance and publication after
Bruckner's death; and to Löwe alone can be due the great
disparities which were exposed by the publication in 1934,
by the Musikwissenschaftliche Verlag (M.W.V.), of Bruckner's manuscript version. A vehement debate ensued, to
which fuel was added by M.W.V.'s publication of the
'original' version of other symphonies. That M.W.V.
represents Bruckner's original thought is clear enough; and
no less that U.E. is often a more effective, striking version
(Egon Wellesz has defended the elimination in U.E. of the
first subject in the recapitulation of the Fourth Symphony
finale as 'an improvement of the total effect'). To say more
would, for present purposes, be too much, unless one should
mention that, to add to the difficulties of the question, Hit-
lerian politics entered into the propagation of the M.W.V.
versions (Mahler, a Jew, having, not long before his death,
subsidized the U.E. publications).

Brahms, who was bitterly contemptuous of Bruckner,
would have been surprised to learn that in the twentieth
century Bruckner's reputation was to rival his own in the
German-speaking countries. England, on the other hand, a
country Brahms disliked but which has been the second
home of his art, has remained unresponsive to Bruckner*. A
no more than secondary reason for this is that our leading
conductors have not included one, like Furtwängler or
Bruno Walter, to whom this music happened to be particularly congenial. Dr Colles's criticism of Bruckner, in the
Oxford History of Music, is that he is not Beethovenian; he
was 'right outside symphony in the sense in which the

* One only of his symphonies – the 4th, in the M.W.V. version
(12th November, 1936) – has appeared in the programmes of the
Royal Philharmonic Society.

classics have defined the term for us'. True; but it may still
be asked whether what Bruckner has of his own to give is
not worth having. The answer depends upon the value one
happens to find in a music elemental rather than intellectual; and not so much serviceable (like Brahms's chamber
works, for instance) as hypnotic or incantatory. Do we submit to the spell of a characteristic Bruckner exordium, there
is richness in the experience; but it is a question of mood or
temperament. If the spell does not work and one 'accepts
with reserve' the opening of the Seventh Symphony, and
'awaits enlightenment from what follows' (Colles), disappointment is coming, what with the slow pulse of the motion,
the sagging or subsidence at the end of sections, sometimes
an inferiority in the secondary subject-matter and, generally,
a want of dramatic interest and progress.

Yes; it may be allowed that the experience is in the nature
of a ramble. But in what noble scenery! If there is not
development there is accumulation, that of repeated views
of prospects so grandly beautiful that only by gazing and
gazing can we take them in. Bruckner's notorious subsi-
dences – the halts for breath, as it were – come to seem
natural enough when the promise is known of the next
winding stretch of the mountain pass. The pace is slow, the
pilgrim lingers with many a backward look. But sooner or
later comes the climax of the Brucknerian finale – though
the delays have sometimes made this seem unattainable –
in the form not so much of a new scene or prospect as of the
pilgrim's accumulated appreciation of the old, which at last
calls forth all the enthusiasm his heart has to offer.

The greatest of Bruckner's music is in his Ninth Symphony, composed in the shadow of Beethoven's ninth. The
Eighth is a grand work, ending with the most magnificent
of the entries of Bruckner's gods into Valhalla*. The immense Seventh, which we shall look at a little more closely,
was the first to win for the composer a more than local

---

* Bruckner's gods, not Wagner's. The sound of Bruckner's music is
not Wagnerian, but his own. If we think of Wagner it is only because
of the majestically deliberate pace these two composers, and no others,
command.

reputation, particularly by the strength of the elegiac Adagio. The Sixth seems generally to have been reckoned as less interesting in its subject-matter, yet it remains a highly characteristic work. The Fifth wins through from a prevailing pensiveness, to tremendous jubilation in the fugal finale. The Fourth (*Romantic*) is the most familiar and popular of the nine; but the heroic Third is not so greatly its inferior. The first two symphonies, if of secondary interest, are already Bruckner's own in their breadth, the poetry of much of the subject-matter and often a romantic harmony which may have even a Schubertian magic.

SYMPHONY NO. 4 IN E FLAT

IN considering the Fourth Symphony we prefer to ignore the 'programme' which in a weak moment Bruckner attached to the work, only to pooh-pooh it later on. Commonplaces about knights and the Middle Ages are unworthy of the connexion. We need go no farther in that direction than to recognize the inspiration of the forest. The symphony begins *Con moto ma non troppo*, and out of the rustling of a low-lying E flat tremolando a horn-call sounds, first in the major, then in the minor, Ex. 1. Here is music that seems to spring from a primal element. The horns bring answers from the woodwind. Our Ex. 1 indicates the ranging modulations. The orchestra is aroused, and the first subject is continued with a figure whose germ we quote as Ex. 1*a*. Such motives do not lend themselves to symphonic exploitation in the classical way. It is their sequential and modulating recurrence, with varying weight of sound, which so often brings to mind the image of great mountain landscapes, remaining essentially the same though viewed from various approaches.

The second bar of Ex. 1*a* is matter for a climax; then, after one of Bruckner's at first disconcerting halts, with no bridge but F's held by the horns, the second subject begins in D flat (Ex. 2, where the principal motive is in the tenor). Now spreads before us a great expanse of music with two huge accumulations, chiefly of second-subject matter.

After the second of these the music, with some little play with the Schubertian accompaniment figure of Ex. 2, dies down to prepare for the development. This begins with the original horn-call, now in F, and proceeds with inversions, mounting sequences, and roaming modulations. The music falls into G major, and a passage of profound expressiveness – the most intense in the whole movement – leads back to E flat and a wonderfully beautiful version of the opening scene. After the recapitulation more is still to be said out of the author's fullness of heart, and there comes a broad coda of eleven pages, which begins with an inversion of the horn-call by horn and oboe.

After the wondering serenity of this movement the *Andante* comes in C minor with a darker pensiveness. The movement is funereal. It begins with our Ex. 3, and this melody returns twice in the course of the movement, each time with richer raiment. Between these appearances an episode occurs, first in G minor and the second time in D minor. Ex. 3 on its last return mounts to a mighty climax, then dies away in mournful phrases by horn, viola, and woodwind.

The famous scherzo in D flat, *Con moto*, again a piece designed on the largest scale, is music of huntsmen's horns with the poetry of the forest all around, and then, in the Trio (G flat, *Comodo*) a rustic dance monumental by force of an extreme naïvety. In spite of our resolve to do no more than touch upon the question of the rival versions, it must be said that in U.E. more than five pages of the scherzo are cut in the *da capo*, and that Tovey – writing before the publication of M.W.V. – which gives the *da capo* in full – admired the result.* In U.E. there is a similar cut in the finale.

Our Ex. 4 represents the two principal factors of the first subject of the finale. This is another piece of woodland music, but wilder and looser than the first movement – so

---

* 'The *da capo* of the scherzo violates Bruckner's precedents ... by taking an extremely effective short cut from the first stage of the exposition to the beginning of the development, the sudden hush being highly dramatic.' – *Essays in Musical Analysis*, vol. 2, page 77.

much we may say in spite of the homeliness into which
Bruckner drops in the second subject, Ex. 5*b*. But though
this is, like the episode in the *Andante*, a weakness of the
symphony, it becomes ennobled in the development. In
U.E. the recapitulation begins in D minor, and it may be
mentioned that in that version are several pages which do
not correspond exactly to anything in M.W.V. The coda
is a mighty crescendo of nine pages, which is at first pre-
sided over by Ex. 4*a*, but in which thematic shapes disappear as the flood rises and are at the end all merged in
elemental E flat chords. The symphony lasts about sixty-
four minutes.

SYMPHONY NO. 7 IN E

No less spacious is the celebrated Seventh Symphony, the
Adagio of which in itself lasts as long as many an entire
symphony of classical times. The opening, Ex. 6, a poetic
inspiration which came to the composer in a dream (he
dreamed that it was played to him on a viola), is again one
of those that proclaim Bruckner a great composer. Its
climbing arpeggio reveals a world like Shelley's 'crags and
silver towers of battlemented cloud'. Shapes here presented
will in the course of the movement be expanded in sequential writing of characteristic grandeur. After a climax the
second subject begins in B with the romantic strain of Ex.
7*a*. This, as was Bruckner's way, is soon inverted in a rich
context. The codetta begins *tranquillo* with Ex. 7*b*, with wind
counterpoints. Sequences of this motive rise to a climax,
then fall to the *molto tranquillo* of the development. This
begins with an inversion for clarinet of the first arpeggio
which, at the climax of the section, is presented grandly in
C minor. At the recapitulation the texture is enriched by an
inversion (flute and violin) above the original form (horn
and 'cello). The coda begins, *molto maestoso*, with the matter
of bars 12 and 13 of Ex. 6. Deeply solemn, it rises to a glowing climax.

Our Ex. 8 represents what seems to many to be the central point of Bruckner's creation. Here the composer uses

a quartet of Wagner tubas. Begun in the month before Wagner's death in February 1883, the wonderful elegy is known to have been conceived in anticipatory sorrow for that event. The form is a rondo, with two returns of Ex. 8, and an episode (Moderato, 3/4) which appears in F sharp and returns in A flat. The unforgettable C sharp minor subject, with its powerful continuation, may be left to speak for itself. The consolatory episode is of a beauty no less worthy of the whole. Ex. 8 on its second appearance expands in sequences like a mighty tide. The third time the magnificence is increased, and an immense crescendo culminates at last in C major, in glory. The splendour fades pathetically, C turns to D flat, and there comes an ineffable coda in which Ex. 8 is gradually merged into the chord of C sharp major.

The scherzo in A minor, *Vivace,* is one of the most imposing of its kind, with a wealth of themes and power of motion commensurate with its great length. The trumpet theme of the sixth bar was suggested to Bruckner by a cock's crowing. The Trio in F has a swaying motion in contrast to the pounding of the scherzo proper.

A certain relationship between the first subject, Ex. 9, of the finale and the arpeggio of Ex. 6 will be noticed; but what before was a free wandering is now tightened into a marching energy. The second subject, Ex. 10 – the E flat of which stands for G sharp – is hymn-like. Then by way of codetta comes another and more vigorous version of Ex. 10. This is to dominate the latter part of the development in a spirit of triumph. There is no recapitulation, but a sort of double coda (one feels the beginning of the end at Letter W of the score, but another beginning, and this time the real one, starts at Letter Z). We do not remember Bruckner's Seventh Symphony by its finale, consistent though it is in style. When the composer designed, as he did in his Eighth Symphony, that the finale should be all-important he reduced the proportions of the first movement. By instinct if not by reason he knew that, after the grandeur of the first three movements of the Seventh, no over-towering finale, even if possible, was appropriate.

Johannes Brahms (1833-1897)

HERBERT WISEMAN

INTRODUCTION

'TINTORET claimed the drawing of Michael Angelo and the colouring of Titian. Brahms, in like manner, may claim the counterpoint of Bach and the structure of Beethoven. And not only has he entered into the inheritance of these two composers; he has put their legacies to interest and has enriched the world with an augmentation of their wealth ... By his education, he learned to assimilate their separate methods; by his position in the latter days of Romance, he found a new emotional language in established use; by his own genius, he had made the forms wider and more flexible and has shewn once more that they are not artificial devices but the organic embodiment of artistic life.'

So wrote Sir Henry Hadow as long ago as 1894, while Brahms was still alive, and no writer since that time has made a truer evaluation of the composer. His style is founded on a deep love and reverence for his predecessors. In the first years which he spent in Vienna, the staple fare of his choir was the cantatas of Bach, and he welcomed with joy a present of the first five volumes of the Bach Gesellschaft, even though he afterwards found that he had to pay for these and the subsequent volumes himself. One cannot doubt that his wonderful mastery of counterpoint which, though ever-present, culminates in the great Passacaglia of the Fourth Symphony, was in no small measure due to his incessant study of these volumes.

He had, however, little sympathy with his contemporaries, for the 'new' music which they were producing or for the literary, pictorial, psychological or pathological bases on

which it was founded. The programme music of Liszt even
urged him to become one of four signatories of a rather ill-
judged protest. The story of his attitude towards Wagner is
one of a certain amount of frigidity concealed for the most
part under the exchange of polite courtesies. The only one
of whom he thoroughly approved was Dvořák, in whose
second symphony there are many traces of affectionate regard.

So far as form was concerned, Brahms was a classicist.
His most important works are in sonata form. When, as a
young man, he presented himself to Schumann with an
introduction from Joachim, he took with him the two early
pianoforte sonatas. Schumann hailed these as 'veiled symphonies'. His two Serenades for orchestra, written while he
was at Detmold, are delightfully Haydnesque. Tovey calls
them 'symphonies in every sense of the word, differing from
those known by the more dignified word not so much in
form and length as in style.' The D minor Pianoforte Concerto is, in Specht's words, 'more radically shaped into a
symphony with an outstanding piano part than even
Beethoven's concertos.' The trios and quartets which followed show his ever-growing mastery.

On another side, his power of extracting all that was
possible from his themes came from his love for writing
variations. The slow movement of the Piano Sonata, Op. 1,
is built on an old folk-tune, to which Brahms even appends
the words. This was followed by the great sets of variations
for piano solo on themes of Handel, Paganini, and
Schumann, and the touchingly beautiful set for piano duet
on a theme of Schumann which, at the end of his life,
Schumann believed had been communicated to him by
Schubert.

It was natural then that his final preparation for writing
a symphony should be the composition of the *Variations on a
Theme of Haydn*. Here we see not only the masterly treatment of the theme, but also a new feeling for orchestration
which, in some of the earlier works, notably the Piano Concerto, had not always been happy, and had provoked a good
deal of criticism. Indeed, critics of this aspect of Brahms's

art were not wanting either in his lifetime or since. It is true that he does not use the brilliant palette of a Berlioz, a Tchaikovsky or a Wagner, but he is not using the same sort of musical ideas. We know that to him the matter was always of more account than the manner of expression, as witness the fact that these very Variations appeared as a duet for two pianos as well as an orchestral essay, and that the great Piano Quintet – a symphony in all but dress – assumed three guises as a string quintet and as a sonata for two pianos in addition to its better-known form.

Brahms might not exploit the upper reaches of the strings; he might, in fact, use the strings more than the more showy composers would have him do – that was probably another outcome of his respect for the past; he might have a preference for grey tones, but he took great pains to indicate the exact amount of intensity required for each group (a fact which many conductors seem to overlook). There are many examples of masterly orchestration in the symphonies. Could anyone, for instance, improve on the introduction to the last movement of No. 1? The truth about his orchestration seems to be that he wrote what he wanted to be heard, and that, after all, is what matters.

He was a severe self-critic. One reads of many experimental works written and destroyed, and it is therefore not surprising to know that he was forty-three years of age before he produced his first symphony. 'A symphony is no joke,' he said; and he was always somewhat oppressed by what he felt to be the overwhelming greatness of Beethoven. He made several attempts to overcome this. Many of these were destroyed, though some of the ideas were used in, for instance, the *Requiem* and the D minor Concerto. He had actually written the first three movements of the first symphony ten years before he wrought out the finale. When it was ultimately performed it made at least one very good friend for him in Hans von Bülow, who wrote enthusiastically of the 'tenth symphony alias the *first* symphony of Johannes Brahms', and also said, 'I believe it is not without the intelligence of chance that Bach, Beethoven, and Brahms are in alliteration.'

SYMPHONY NO. I IN C MINOR

THIS had been for long in the mind of the composer and a
fairly complete sketch of the first three movements was in
existence by 1862. It was however, not produced until 4th
November, 1876, under Dessoff at Karlsruhe.

First Movement. *Un poco sostenuto – allegro*. The symphony
opens on a note of gloom and deep tragedy. The introduction section – *un poco sostenuto* – has a double theme. While
the strings, playing the top part in the following quotation,
strive upwards, the winds, playing the under theme, seem
to pull the music down to the depths of despair, Ex. 1.
These contrary tendencies are founded on a throbbing pedal
note C in the basses which seems to emphasize the relent-
lessness of fate.

A tragic dropping seventh followed by a sixth, played
legato by the winds and *pizzicato* by the strings, deepens the
gloom. A swaying figure on the strings built on the second
inversion of the tonic chord with the tonic itself omitted
leads to a repetition of the first outburst. A mournful phrase
on the oboe is echoed by the 'cellos and finishes this extra-
ordinarily pregnant introduction, which contains all the
germs which go to the making of the succeeding *Allegro*.
There is not a note in this unique movement which the
listener can afford to miss. Brahms has got far away from
the almost casual introductions of some of the earlier
masters. This is the text of the whole sermon.

The first four fiery bars of the *Allegro* are a quickened
version of Ex. 1, on which is immediately grafted a version
of the tonic chord theme mentioned above. Note again the
dual nature of this theme.

The dropping sevenths and sixths reappear, Ex. 2. There
is through all this first section a suggestion of immense
power. Nor is there any lifting of the clouds when the second
subject makes its appearance, for it has also been derived
from Ex. 1 with the 'tonic chord' figure in the bass. The key
has changed, but not the mood, Ex. 3. The continuation of
this is by means of another sad, drooping figure, Ex. 4. The
music grows quieter, the clarinets and the horns have a

pathetic duet. The calm, however, is not to last. An insistent *pizzicato* call from the violas is taken up by the rest of the strings, Ex. 5, and the great movement surges onward again.

Following the precedent of the earlier composers, Brahms asks that the whole of the exposition should be repeated. It is only in the Fourth Symphony that Brahms deprives himself and his listeners of the opportunity of hearing the main tunes twice before proceeding to their manipulation.

After the repeat, there comes the development, which is closely wrought but comparatively easy to follow. Here the tonic chord theme is first heard in canon in the remote key of B major. The wood-winds have some interesting solo passages, and then the figure in Ex. 3 is prominent. The only way to appreciate this section to the full is by repeated hearings. No amount of verbal description will enable anyone to hear the key-changes and the modifications of the themes.

Finally, after a period of preparation over a repeated G in the bass, the recapitulation is begun. This reappears mainly as it was in the beginning, with some changes in scoring and, of course, a new key for the second subject which appears first in D minor and then in C major. The Coda sums up with a gradual lessening of intensity and pace and the movement ends on the hopeful chord of C major.

Second Movement. *Andante sostenuto.* This is the work of Brahms the lyricist, the composer of the great songs, the romantic singer. After the gloom and strenuousness and nerve tension of the first movement, there comes a ray of light from heaven itself. The peaceful benignity of the opening E major tune on the violins is one of the great moments of music, Ex. 6. Its continuation on the oboe is equally lovely. Then the violins soar to great heights, making way for the oboe which, followed closely by the clarinet, then announces a new theme. A long held note is followed by an arabesque of semi-quavers which the strings accompany with syncopated chords. The movement proceeds upon its lovely way.

The addition of a violin solo still further enhances its

beauty, a specially noteworthy passage being that where the horns have the melody previously sung by the oboe and the solo violin adds a loving and graceful commentary. The movement ends on a note of deep philosophic calm and peace.

Third Movement. *Un poco allegretto e grazioso.* The peace is in no wise disturbed by the third movement. The mood, however, is less philosophic, less deep and more one of happy contentment.

A naïvely innocent tune is played by the clarinet. This consists of two five-bar phrases of which the second is an inversion of the first. It is continued by another light-hearted melody in a dotted rhythm and, after these two ideas have been discussed, the tune and the key change for the trio. This is in the key of B major in 6/8 time and starts with a dialogue between the wood-wind and the strings.

When the first themes are heard again, they are varied and slightly modified and the movement finishes with a tranquil reference to the rhythm of the trio.

Fourth Movement. *Adagio – piu andante – allegro non troppo ma con brio.* The introduction to the Finale harks back to the tragic mood that we had all but forgotten. It opens sombrely with the theme, Ex. 7. The strings try to brush the serious-ness aside with a curious *pizzicato* passage which gets ever louder and faster. These two passages are contrasted once more; there is a stormy rushing section and then, above a *tremolando* for muted strings, there is heard a wonderful tune for the horns. It is this passage which made such an impres-sion at the first performance of this symphony in England by the Cambridge University Musical Society on account of its resemblance to the chimes known as the 'Cambridge Quarters'. It is one of the most solemn and mysterious moments in the whole symphony. The flutes echo it, and the atmosphere of solemnity is still further deepened by a hymn-like theme played with soft majesty by the trombones and bassoons, the low tones of the double bassoon adding to it an organ-like depth. These four bars should be particularly noted, as they reappear at the climax of the succeeding *allegro*.

A further reference to the horn call leads to the appearance of the great C major tune with which the *allegro* starts – the tune which, because of its resemblance to that in the last movement of Beethoven's Ninth Symphony, prompted some critics to call this the Tenth Symphony, and others to accuse Brahms of plagiarism. Tovey dismisses this claim and says that the comparison has been made 'only because it is the solitary one among hundreds of the same type that is great enough to suggest the resemblance.' It is so well known that there is no need to quote it.

We now know what the violins were trying to play at the beginning of the introduction to this movement. They could then achieve only a short minor version of it, but now the tune strides on with great majesty and strength.

A passing reference to the melody for the horns leads to the second subject which adds to the general feeling of joyousness, Ex. 8. This is carried further by several subsidiary themes which all tend to pile up the excitement. All the previously-used material is reintroduced in varied guises that should intrigue the listeners' ears and test their memories.

At last a new theme appears, strongly rhythmical and incisive, the pace quickens and the music moves towards its climax. No one will miss the solemn entry of the four bars which were played in the introduction by the trombones and the double bassoon and which now appear more fully scored. Thereafter a few bars serve to bring the symphony to a close which is stupendous in its majesty and splendour.

SYMPHONY NO. 2 IN D MAJOR

No greater contrast can be imagined than that between the noble and profoundly tragic first movement of the First Symphony and the graceful beauty of the first movement of the Second Symphony. Yet, as has been indicated, the two symphonies were produced within a year of each other and Brahms was at least contemplating the second when he was engaged on the first.

After the gloom and nervous tension of the first symphony, Brahms must have found it a great relief to evolve the sunny grace and cheerful joy of the Second, just as Beethoven, after producing the great *Eroica,* found expression for his happiness in the charm and jollity of his Fourth Symphony. The Second Symphony of Brahms was first performed under Richter in Vienna.

First Movement. *Allegro non troppo*. The first movement, without any preliminaries, starts with a delightful, almost pastoral theme, Ex. 9.

The three features of this material should be carefully noted. The crotchets in the bass in the first bar are a sort of motto theme for the whole symphony and references to them can be traced throughout. The lovely melody on the horns and the calmly beautiful answer by the wood-winds are likewise essential to the further development.

The violins and violas soon enter with a dreamy phrase which is passed down the strings before being interrupted by a short drum-roll followed by three mysterious chords in the trombones and a phrase on the wood-winds which is an echo of the opening bar. After two repetitions of this figure a new tune appears in the violins, Ex. 10. This is worked up in a veritable blaze of sunlight, and thereafter a few *staccato* chords for the winds, with drooping octaves for the strings, carry through the necessary modulation and lead to the next main theme, which is sung by the 'cellos with the violas in the familiar phrase of everyday life, 'singing seconds' (which really means in musical terms playing mainly in thirds), Ex. 11. This delicious tune (with its drooping octave accompaniment) is developed and enriched, and then interrupted by a strongly-accented theme marked *quasi ritenente,* which in turn is succeeded by a forcible rhythm of quavers and semi-quavers, Ex. 12. Note here that the tune is derived from the opening 'cello and bass theme. The rhythm is exciting and plays a great part in the subsequent happenings, and here it helps to build up to a great burst of sound.

After this climax, the second subject steals in again on the violins, while the flute adds a charming embroidery. It is repeated with a change of colouring and some lovely harmonic changes, and a cadence of infinite tenderness. The whole of this first part is, in the manner of the older composers, repeated, and thereafter the development follows. This is concerned almost entirely with the materials of the first subject. It opens with the three bass crotchets and the horn tune, which is now continued by the oboe with a new melody. In the main this development is easy to follow, if the component parts of Ex. 9 and Ex. 10 are kept in mind. They are treated with the utmost freedom of development, cross rhythms, and colourings. One of the features of this section, and also of the recapitulation which follows, is the profusion of the counter-melodies with which Brahms enriches his first ideas.

Detailed description of the progress of the music is not needed. It is sufficient to say that the recapitulation is heralded by a climax in which the first two notes of the original horn melody are treated by the full orchestra in a most strenuous passage with strong cross-rhythms. After that there is a hint of more tender thoughts, with two references to Ex. 10, a long descending scale-passage for flute and clarinet, and the original horn tune appears in the oboes, with a varied accompaniment on the strings and horns. The second half of the tune is passed over to the second violins, and the firsts add a beautiful counterpoint. Along with the first part, the violas give out the theme of Ex. 10, so that it is heard here in combination with the first tune, and not following it. It is as if Brahms, after a long development section, had resolved to save a little time in the recapitulation.

The rest of the themes appear in due course, and they are summed up in a truly magical coda, which begins with a wonderful passage for solo horn and strings, and lingers lovingly on some of the beauties of the first theme.

Second Movement. *Adagio non troppo*. The second movement opens with the phrase, Ex. 13. It is quite characteristic of Brahms that in this he is really presenting two themes at one time, the first a downward phrase in the 'cellos and the second an upward phrase in the bassoons. These two phrases are both of great importance in the general scheme of the movement, but at their first presentation the 'cello tune is much the longer. It gives us 'linked sweetness, long drawn out' until it is taken up by the violins, while the 'cellos sing the counter-theme which originally belonged to the bassoons. The horn and wood-wind break in with a short section which starts with some imitative passages, and in due course the middle section, which is in quiet 12/8 rhythm, begins with a lovely tune. This is developed and followed by a quiet passage which leads to a more exciting section. The peace is disturbed by some rushing semi-quaver passages for the winds and strings, with chords for the brasses. The violins try to state the first 'cello theme, but are brushed aside. Then the oboes enter with the main theme, the violins have the one which was originally presented by the bassoons, and the bassoons embellish it all with another counterpoint in triplets. This is continued, and the complete theme is re-stated by the violins with some lovely variations. Another interruption occurs, and finally the movement comes to a close with references to No. 5 in the wood-winds. It is a complex movement and perhaps a little difficult to follow completely, but it has moments of rare beauty to which no mere verbal description can do anything like justice. Perhaps the best way for the listener is to allow the glorious music to come to him without too much effort to disentangle the various threads.

Third Movement. *Allegretto grazioso (quasi andantino)* – *presto ma non assai*. After the second movement, with its deep introspective mood, the *allegretto grazioso* comes like a glint of sunshine. Gone are all the psychological complexes, all the musings on the deep mysteries of life. We are now in the open air, untroubled by any such thoughts. The movement opens with a lovely tune for the oboe, accompanied by chords on the clarinets and bassoons with a *pizzicato* 'cello figure. It is all very happy, very dainty, and unsophisticated, Ex. 14*a*. Soon its tender minuet-like strains are interrupted by the whispering of the strings, Ex. 14*b*. This, as will, of course, be seen at once, is merely the main theme, Ex. 14*a*, stated in a different rhythm and at a different pace. The wood-winds and the strings chatter together excitedly for a few minutes, and then the whole of the comparatively small orchestra that Brahms uses in this movement shouts this tune, Ex. 15a. Note that it is derived from the motto theme contained in the opening bar of the first movement. The strings drop their voices and again start the whispered conversation, which goes on till Ex. 14a is resumed again, this time with a good deal of variation in colour and treatment. There is again a good deal of by-play when the next section begins with a downward rush in the strings followed by Ex. 15b which is a variant of Ex. 15a in the key of A.

These snippets of quotations have been given to show Brahms's ingenuity in presenting previously-used material in new guises by alterations of key, rhythm, and pace. Then there is a lovely attempt by the wood-winds to switch back to the original *tempo*. While the scurry is still going on, they suggest it quietly, and soon have their way. The first pace is resumed in F sharp major. Then the music gradually works back to the original key, and the whole movement ends in the same mood of happy contemplation in which it began.

Fourth Movement. *Allegro con spirito*. The last movement opens with a swinging tune played *sotto voce* by the strings, the first two bars in unison, and the second adopted as the bass of their continuation, Ex. 16. It is continued with the addition of bassoons, and afterwards of clarinets and flutes. After a few quiet bars, it rises to great heights in an extended version for the full orchestra, with the basses supplying a running commentary on the proceedings. Then the mood quietens. There is a clarinet solo echoed by flutes and oboes and the music settles down in the key of A major, the orthodox key, for the second subject. This proves to be a flowing tune enunciated *largamente* by the violins and violas and afterwards repeated by the wood-wind. This is continued by other branch themes, the most distinctive of which is started by the flutes and clarinets running about in thirds at an octave's distance and accompanied by *pizzicato* strings. A figure in which the 'Scots snap' is prominent leads to a repetition of the main theme.

Then comes a section marked *tranquillo*, in which

wood-winds and strings start a dialogue in triplet crotchets
(note again its derivation from the motto theme). The key
changes to B flat minor and there are lovely references to the
second part of the first subject. It is all quiet, remote and
somewhat mysterious, but soon the original key is resumed
and the recapitulation is begun in the full daylight of D major.
The first part is shortened and it is not long before the second
subject is heard in the main key. The coda is noteworthy for
the re-introduction of the trombones which have a very important part to play which no listener can miss. A reference
to the *tranquillo* theme temporarily quietens the music,
which soon builds up to a climax of great intensity and exciting brilliance.

SYMPHONY NO. 3 IN F MAJOR

THE Third Symphony was first performed, under Richter,
on 2nd December, 1883, at Vienna. It is the shortest of the
four and the work of one who is a complete master of all his
resources. It is terse, vivid and passionate. Its mood is in
complete contrast to the tragedy of the first and the pastoral
joy of the second. It is strong and heroic, and intensely alive.
Its vitality, indeed, is such that it is difficult to say why it is
performed more seldom than any of the others.

First Movement. *Allegro con brio*. The music opens with a
great theme, Ex. 17. Here we must note the introductory
chords for the wind and, in particular, the top notes of these,
F, A flat, F, which Brahms uses as a motto theme recurring throughout the symphony and serving to unify it. The
first main theme begins in the third bar, and afterwards
climbs through a middle part to the highest wood-winds,
while the strings proceed with the statement of the principal
tune. This comes to a quiet finish and is immediately continued by a subsidiary theme which is brightly scored for
strings and wood-winds. The motto theme in the brasses
leads to a modulation to D flat, in which key the subsidiary
theme is repeated.

Another statement of the motto theme ushers in the key
of A major, in which, after some quiet chords, the second

subject begins, Ex. 18. This takes the form of a happy dialogue between the oboes and the clarinets, with comments from the flute. Again we hear the motto theme, which this time leads to a further continuation of Ex. 18. At last, with some flashing unison passages in the wood-winds, and a change of key to A minor, the exposition comes to an energetic end. The development is very short. The most noteworthy section in it is one which begins with the horn singing the motto theme against a syncopated string accompaniment. But Brahms does not linger even over such a magically beautiful thought as this, and soon a re-statement of the motto theme, scored more fully, plunges straight into the recapitulation.

The great first subject glows with a wonderful incandescence. The second appears in D major, and then swings into F major, the principal key, and then there begins a most marvellous coda, in which Brahms, as if to make up for the shortness of the development section, releases the wealth of his imagination in a wonderful treatment of the first theme. The excitement passes, and 'a peace above all earthly dignities' ensues. The last few bars echo the first main theme, now shorn of its eager impetuosity, and in this mood of calm reflexion the movement ends.

Second Movement. *Andante*. The second movement opens with a quiet, restful theme played by the clarinets and bassoons, the last phrase being echoed by the lower strings, Ex. 19. The relationship of this echoed phrase to the motto theme will be clear to all. After it has been fully stated and enriched by a varied semi-quaver treatment, the second main theme is announced, like the first, by the clarinets and bassoons, with chords in the strings, Ex. 20. This section ends with some extraordinary harmonies, and immediately the composer starts a beautiful series of free variants on Ex. 19. These proceed on their leisurely way, and the composer's thoughts are comparatively easy to read. Towards the end of the movement, the extraordinary harmonies return, after which the clarinets and the bassoon muse over the opening bars of the main theme, and all ends in a mood of supreme ecstasy and wonderful beauty.

Third Movement. *Poco allegretto*. In the third movement, Brahms uses only a small orchestra of strings, wood-wind, and two horns. It opens with a suave, flowing tune for the 'cellos, Ex. 21, and its course is easy to follow. It modulates to C major, and then Ex. 21 returns in a more resplendent orchestral garb. The trio opens with the following series of chords played by the wood-wind, which the 'cellos punctuate with a broken utterance. A contrasted tune for strings follows this. The first idea reappears, and then the main section is repeated with a scoring entirely different from that employed in its first statement. A very short coda, which emerges from the opening chord of the trio, rounds off the movement.

Fourth Movement. *Allegro*. The last movement is an extraordinary patchwork quilt, compounded of many short themes, all most cunningly stitched together. In effect, it rounds off the whole symphony in the most noble manner, and is one of the finest movements which even Brahms ever wrote. It opens with an ominous theme in the strings and bassoons in a sombre unison, Ex. 22. One feels that almost anything may happen with such a theme. It is repeated with curious twistings of its original rhythm in the wood-winds, while the lower strings mutter in *arpeggios*. The trombones then announce a theme which is played *pianissimo* by woodwinds and strings, the double bassoon adding a note of solemnity, Ex. 23. The first theme recurs with wild outbursts of the energetic figure with which it closed, and soon we hear the real second subject, which is built on this triumphant tune, Ex. 24. This swells to a mighty climax, and then the development begins. It is concerned mainly with working out the various ideas contained in the first theme. The composer gives full play to his imagination, and every aspect of his subject is treated. At last the second subject reappears, and proceeds to a climax where the basses sing the opening phrase, accompanied by huge orchestral ejaculations. Then the music quietens, the muted violas give out a mysterious version of Ex. 22 in a new triplet rhythm in the key of B minor, the opening key is resumed, and suddenly the major key appears. The oboes have an augmented version of the main subject, and the motto theme of the first movement returns in unmistakable fashion. Ex. 23 is heard with a new significance. Now it might be a motive of beatific peace. There are more references to the motto theme, and finally the symphony closes with the violins repeating through two octaves the main theme of the first movement. The close has all the feeling of a beautiful, radiant sunset after a stormy day.

SYMPHONY NO. 4 IN E MINOR

Less than a year separated the first performance of the third symphony from that of the fourth, but the distance between the two in emotional inspiration is immeasurable. No. 3 is buoyant and heroic, picturesque and happy, and No. 4 is serious. The seriousness is not altogether the seriousness of tragedy, though there is tragedy in the work of a kind different from that of the first movement of No. 1. It is rather the contemplative seriousness of one who thinks deeply on the problems of life and of art. Even the last movement makes no concession to the human liking for a happy ending. On the contrary, it is the most serious movement of the four. There is nobility and grandeur in every page, and it is a remarkable reflexion of the personality of the composer and a perfect culmination of his work as a symphonic writer. In some ways it seems as if, in the three previous works, he had learned how to express his thoughts and emotions, to master all technical difficulties, and to make the intricacies of musical forms subservient to his will. Now all his energies are devoted to the one end – self revelation.

Because of this intense personal factor in the work, as well as of its unusual last movement, in which Brahms reverted to one of the older musical forms, the symphony was at first received coldly even by the composer's friends. Those who had had a chance of what may be called a 'pre-view' were doubtful about it and recommended changes, but the composer paid no heed. His enemies, and they were many, particularly in the Wagnerian camp, found it at its best 'Art without inspiration'.

Brahms, himself, conducted the first performance at Meiningen on 25th October, 1885, and immediately afterwards Hans von Bülow conducted performances at many towns in Germany and Holland. It was heard for the first time in this country at a Richter concert in London in May, 1886. A long period elapsed before it reached its present position of popular esteem, and one wonders what Brahms would have said had he known that it would ultimately be made the basis of a ballet – *Choreartium* – by Massine.

First Movement. *Allegro non troppo.* There are no preliminaries. The first movement starts with the announcement of the main theme by the violins. It is a fine long tune, nineteen bars in length, and I have not regretted so much until now the restriction which prevents my quoting the whole of it. As it is, I have quoted only two small sections, as these are the most fruitful in suggesting further ideas to the composer, Ex. 25*a* and Ex. 25*b*. Ex. 25*a* gives the first two bars. Note that the first three notes belong to the tonic chord – a characteristic of the composer. Note also the dropping third and the rising sixth. These are repeated in sequence a tone down. Then there is a dropping octave and a rising third also repeated in sequence, and then comes Ex. 25*b*. The whole is immediately repeated by the violins in broken octaves, while the wood-winds weave around it a delicate filigree of sound.

A new song-like phrase on the violins serves to pave the way for another important idea, Ex. 26. This, with its insistent rhythm, is given out emphatically by the wood-wind. Its rhythm, with its semi-quavers and triplet crotchets, should be noted and remembered, as it is put to much use subsequently. Here it leads directly to the first hint of the second subject, which is a tender tune for 'cellos and horns over a *staccato* bass, Ex. 27.

The violins now take up the thread and repeat the tune with some slight modifications. Ex. 26 obtrudes and gives some idea of the use to which it is afterwards to be put. There is a dialogue between *pizzicato* strings and *staccato* woodwinds rather reminiscent of the *pizzicato* passage in the introduction to the finale of the first symphony. Then, after a descending passage in the wood-winds, the flute, clarinet, and horn sing the lovely tune which you will find in Ex. 28.

Then there is a mysterious passage with shimmering *pianissimo* strings and the semi-quaver rhythm of Ex. 26 leading to a fine statement of it. This builds to a climax and then subsides on the dropping third of Ex. 25*a* and the exposition is at an end.

There is no repeat in this symphony and the development begins with a reference to the first theme. In its course, Brahms uses mainly Ex. 25*b*, Ex. 26, and the 'mysterious' passage to which reference is made above. Though short, it is very dramatic, and it ends with a beautiful meditation on Ex. 25*b* tailing off with a few bars marked *ppp* (an indication which Brahms very seldom allows himself) that leads to the recapitulation. This starts with the main theme in long-sustained semibreves and a reference to the 'mysterious' passage, but soon resumes its first rhythm and pursues a normal course. The coda opens with a majestic statement of the opening theme by 'cellos, double basses, and horns, answered in canon by the rest of the orchestra. It grows in intensity and in power until the final bars where four drum beats serve only to make the finish all the more impressive.

Second Movement. *Andante moderato.* The slow movement is sheer beauty. It opens with a call on the horns which sounds as though the movement were to be in C major, but at the fifth bar the clarinets, with the *pizzicato* strings, sing a wonderfully tender and wistful strain, Ex. 29. This is repeated with slight variations of colour, and afterwards expanded into a triplet passage, which leads to the appearance of the second subject – a broad cantabile tune for the 'cellos. After a very lovely series of developments, this tune reappears in the principal key, and leads to a beautiful coda in which the original horn melody recalls the curious alternation of C major and E major, which was a feature of the beginning of the movement.

Third Movement. *Allegro giocoso.* This is a real scherzo – the first that Brahms has permitted himself to write in his symphonies. It will be remembered that, in the previous three, he has given us quieter movements with a reduced orchestra in place of a scherzo. Here, he revels in a short and welcome bout of boisterousness and adds to his orchestra a piccolo, a double bassoon, and even a triangle.

The main theme is Ex. 30. Note the sudden drop in the fifth bar and its continuation, which foreshadows a tune which is to be heard in more complete form later. The second subject is given out by the strings with accompanying scale passages in the winds and has a more tender and graceful character, Ex. 31. After this, the first subject returns with some modifications. The middle section of this movement is marked *poco meno presto* and starts with a lovely phrase on the horns, which is really a growth from the main tune. Thereafter there is a free repetition of the first section, and a strenuous coda rounds off this bustling, vigorous movement.

Fourth Movement. *Allegro energico e passionato*. Gone now are the frivolous notes of the piccolo and triangle. In their place, for the first time in this symphony, we have the solemn voices of the trombones. Brahms discards all the forms usually accepted as suitable for last movements and writes a wonderful Passacaglia – or variations on a ground bass. He had on many occasions previously shown himself to be a master of the art of writing variations, and in this movement all his mastery is exerted to the full.

The short eight-bar theme is borrowed from Bach's Cantata 150 (*Nach dir, Herr, verlanget mich*) and is announced with the full strength of the wood-winds and brasses, Ex. 32. Thereafter it is repeated in thirty different variations, which culminate in a long and elaborate coda. The following notes may help you to sort out the variations. It should, however, be stressed that it is not necessary to attempt to follow the theme in all its guises. The total effect is colossally overwhelming.

1 *pizzicato* strings, horns, trombones and drums.
2 lower strings, winds in smooth flowing counterpoints.
3 full orchestra.
4 basses with descant on first violins.

5   basses with descending wood-wind figures.

6   basses with further development of the independent violin part.

7   a jerky rhythm in winds and strings with a broken version of the theme in the bass.

8   basses with semi-quavers in the upper strings which are further developed in

9   with wood-wind chromatic figures.

10   beautiful interchange of harmonies between strings and wood-winds.

11   the same idea further developed with some lovely triplets in winds and strings.

12   a change of time to 3/2 with one of the loveliest flute solos ever written. (It is enough to assimilate the serene beauty of this without worrying about the theme, which is wrapped up in the folds of the solo part.)

13   a change to the major key with a lovely interchange of courtesies between clarinet, oboe, and flute.

14   solemn chords in the trombones (*pp*) – a wonderful moment – a major version of the theme in the basses.

15   the same mood continued with the addition of wood-winds finishing on an incomplete harmony which leads to

16   a loud insistence on the original theme by the wood-winds, as if to call the attention of the composer to the fact that he has strayed from his text.

17   the beginning of a more agitated section with the theme in the 'cellos.

18   the theme, decorated, in the wood-winds, with brasses added.

19   a *staccato* variation, with the theme, decorated, in the first violins.

20   still *staccato*, with triplets working up to

21   the most exciting version, with full orchestra and wild string rushes.

22   – a sudden hush, triplets in the strings, and detached syncopated chords in the wood-winds.

23 an increase in tension, the triplets become more
    assertive and work up to

24 a climax in the full orchestra, with the theme over-
    riding it all in detached string triplets.

25 continues the mood with the theme transferred, still
    in triplets, to the horns.

26 sinks to a *piano* with the theme still on the horns.

27 resumes a quieter mood with the wood-wind ex-
    changing falling thirds.

28 continues the gracious mood of 27 with a singing
    descant in the wood-winds.

29 has a series of falling thirds in the strings, *pizzicato*.

30 builds up and expands to a *ritardando* after which the
    coda bursts in with the glare of the full orchestra.
    The pace quickens and the excitement becomes
    intense. The theme is present, of course, but Brahms
    feels himself free to modulate more freely than he
    could do during the variations. Seldom has there
    been so fine a peroration in music – a wonderful
    finish to a wonderful symphony.

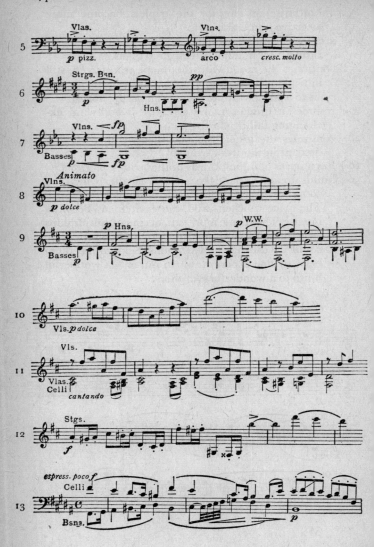

Alexander Borodin (1833-1887)

HUBERT FOSS

INTRODUCTION

As we look back, to-day, across the interval of some eighty years or so, at the Russian 'Five', as the nationalist group of composers called themselves, two men stand out with remarkable clarity as composers of exceptional power – Mussorgsky and Borodin. Of the other three, Balakirev, who was the centre of the group, has earned more of our respect than our affection, Rimsky-Korsakov has a handful of works that remain popular (especially *Shéhérazade*), and César Cui is largely forgotten.

They were an extraordinary group to cause so much attention and to create so much music that has not only survived but has deeply influenced the course of the musical movements that came after them. For they were all, in truth, amateurs, ill-equipped as composers and much of their lives absorbed in other affairs than musical composition. Thus Cui was an army officer who rose to general's rank and was an authority on sieges, Rimsky-Korsakov (who later attained the highest technical skill) was a serving naval officer, Balakirev started out as a mathematician, Mussorgsky, after some army service, became a civil servant, and Borodin was a medical and scientific professor at a University. It is not surprising to find in the lists of their works several that were never completed by the composers in their lifetimes.

Mussorgsky wrote no symphony, Balakirev only two which are not remembered to-day, and Rimsky-Korsakov's *Antar* is the only one of his three symphonies that is still performed. Borodin therefore may rightly be called the symphonist of the Russian Nationalist School, for his Second

Symphony is a familiar work, and his First is played not infrequently by Beecham, Lambert, and others.

But apart from this, what distinguishes both Borodin's and Mussorgsky's work from that of their colleagues is something that it is difficult to pin down on paper for analysis, for it is a combination of imaginative and musical qualities which one can describe (it is no definition!) only as 'meaning'. An extraordinary intensity of emotion, the direct utterance of the peasant and his folk-songs, a primitive sense of colour, all of these things, complicated by intellectual power and a high culture, are some of the ingredients that go to make up Borodin's 'meaning'. He had (and Mussorgsky had it, too) an unrivalled capacity for crowding an immense quantity of truth and significance into the shortest possible musical phrase: he does not seem to have arrived at that pregnancy of phrase by any process of whittling down a longer phrase, or by hammering out his ideas in sketch books as Beethoven did. Rather, Borodin would appear to speak naturally, like a prophet, in swift, short, and direct themes of few notes, which afterwards he set himself to expand by development. If we look for comparison to the music of Rimsky-Korsakov, we find no less of the Russian folk-idiom, of Russian colouring and Slavonic ways of thought. We find, instead, that he lacks this 'meaning', this pregnant intensity of utterance, so that his works seem in memory more pleasant than prophetic, more picturesque than deeply significant. Borodin and Mussorgsky stand isolated in musical history on this account: they spring from no apparent musical source, but come straight from the Russian soil. 'No composer,' Gerald Abraham has written of Borodin – 'no composer less derivative ever lived.' And no other has attained so secure a position in the hierarchy of genius with so slender a bouquet in his hands to offer us. Only, each stalk bears a flower: there is no filling of it up with mere foliage.

Born in 1833, Alexander Borodin was the natural son of Prince Luke Ghedeanov, whose estates lay in the Caucasus region (the point has its importance in explaining Borodin's sense of semi-oriental colouring). In early years he showed great scientific promise, but also a strong feeling for music. His education was directed towards medicine and chemistry, and it is interesting to observe that it was for his scientific and not his musical achievements that the Soviet government erected a statue in his honour. But he ardently pursued his hobby of music, composing works that are no longer extant, playing the flute, oboe, and violoncello, and early making a friendship with Mussorgsky, simultaneously with the writing of scientific papers.

It was only after his appointment to the Assistant Lecturership in Chemistry at the University of St. Petersburg (now Leningrad) that Mussorgsky brought him into contact with Balakirev, the 'father' of the Five. There is no doubt that already in Borodin there had grown up a passionate and quite conscious desire to write national music, but, Abraham tells us, Balakirev found that he 'regarded himself as an amateur, and ascribed no importance to the impulse that drove him towards musical composition.' After his first meetings with the 'father', Borodin set himself down to the task of writing a symphony: the first draft was completed by December, 1862, but owing to his constant application to scientific work, it was not completed and performed until five years later, 1867. In the way of that oddly sympathetic company of composers, the work as it was written was gone over note by note by Balakirev, and no doubt discussed with great frequency with the others. The second Symphony occupied one year longer in the writing (1871–7), and was interrupted not only by medical distractions but by his contributing Act IV to that curious, unfinished, composite work, *Mlada*.

It would require a volume of social history (even if one knew enough about it!) to recreate to-day the patriotic feelings that were bubbling over in the minds and souls of the new Russian composers of the 1850–70 period. Nothing similar has ever happened in England. The intensely felt consciousness of English nationality (so pleasingly covered by the word 'Englishry') that inspired equally Marlowe and Gibbons, Shakespeare and Byrd, Drake and Campion, Sidney and Dowland, in what we loosely call the 'Tudor'

period, was as unconscious as the Russian desire for national
expression was almost externally present in the Russian
mind. In actual fact, the music of four of the 'Five' gives the
best picture of that feeling, a far better picture than words
can. Throughout all the movement there was that age-old
feeling of Russia's holy purpose, as well as a desire for self-
realization in Slavonic terms. The new musical movement
was saturated with Russian history and legend: it was acutely
aware that the huge country spread from within hail
of European culture down to Georgia and, farther on, the
Himalayas, northward to the Arctic and eastward to the
primitive Mongolian tribes. It was the whole of Russia, in
all its various phases of development and savagery, that the
composers wanted to express; and if in Balakirev's *Russia*, in
Mussorgsky's *Boris* and *Night on the Bare Mountain*, and in
Borodin's *Steppes of Central Asia* and Symphonies they failed
to encompass, to net in as a captive for art the whole vast
territory, it was not for want of trying, with bare hands and
minds, to entrap the prey, but because of human frailty and
the shortness of life. Borodin in his Second Symphony comes
as near to the elemental in life as anyone ever had before
him. He tries (more freely than Balakirev, who had a
similar aim) to give us a picture of the Pan-Russia, its life
and character. The wonder is that he could put so much of
it on paper for instruments to play to others.

Partly because of the literary influence of their helper and
co-worker, Vladimir Stassov, the minds of Mussorgsky and
Borodin directed themselves into the channel of opera. Each
wanted to write a national epic of his own country. The
desire never left them. Borodin, despite his turning to the
symphony as a first vehicle of expression, yearned always
after the stage as his real medium for music. *Prince Igor* and
the Second Symphony stumbled along together, in their
progress of composition, hand in hand. Borodin told Stassov
(we are informed) that the music rejected from the *Prince
Igor* draft would not be wasted – 'it will all go into my
Second Symphony'! That symphony is almost as much a
natural epic as the opera; and Abraham has well said of the
more formal work that 'perhaps it was the *Igor* of his dreams'.

The extraordinary thing is that Borodin should have constructed his symphonies (two completed and one unfinished)
on so 'classical' a model – that is, so strictly according to the
accepted form. True, he puts his scherzo second in all three,
before the slow movement. In general, his procedure is as
orthodox as any one else's could be who lived later than
Berlioz and Liszt, to be influenced by one and personally
encouraged by the other. The final result is, of course,
anything but orthodox. The proper procedure led to an
entirely new result. It may be worth while, in a paragraph,
to examine some of the causes and effects.

Borodin's symphonies are essentially dramatic in content,
however formal in shape he thought he had made them
(and his formal control is admirable). But his operatic
hankerings led him to sudden bursts of orchestral sound, to
strange, almost primitive contrasts of orchestral colour, to
an heroic manner of a kind hitherto unadopted in symphonic works – for Beethoven's *Eroica* contains his most
carefully formulated and elaborately constructed first
movement. The high colour of Borodin's cheeks suggests, always, the theatre rather than the concert hall. The
musical elements that form this style are exotic to the accepted symphonic manner. Russian folk-music has, as
Borodin has shown, a power to express 'meaning' in a
short phrase; and that short phrase was usually repeated,
somewhat in the manner of all oriental patterns. The
rhythms of this music were unconventional, and capable of
exciting development. The tunes themselves were brittle,
and could break easily into complete fragments. They were
as old as primitive civilisation, as new as the peasant who
still sang them in the composer's time (and no doubt still
sings them in many parts of Russia to-day). They combined
Europe and Asia, and had much of the nomadic tribes in
their make-up.

All these elements Borodin, in his vivid national consciousness, absorbed into himself and re-expressed in symphonic style. The mosaic-like orchestration, the short
melody repeated, the use of a melody at half the speed or
double the speed, the sound of the primitive instruments

themselves, the continual discussion of small pieces snapped off from the main twig of the tune: all these, and much more, are central to Borodin's style. Yet, analytically, one can follow his symphonies in form as if they were worked out 'according to Cocker'. The important thing is, of course, that they do not sound like that: they sound personal, and dramatic, and highly individual.

Of the three symphonies, No. 2 has obviously a greater share of 'meaning' (in the sense that I have not defined above) than No. 1; No. 1 is none the less an important and exciting work. Of a certain part of No. 2 Abraham has made an interesting comment, which is highly relevant here, I think; 'like Vaughan Williams at times, Borodin seems to be trying to distil the essence of all that is truest and noblest in patriotism, and like the Englishman, he has wonderfully expressed this most soul-stirring of passions in music of profound tranquillity.'

Running commentaries on the two completed symphonies follow below. It remains to say a word about the third. Two movements were left, neither completed nor revised: they were finished and orchestrated by Glazounov, under Rimsky-Korsakov's direction. Here it should be remembered that what we have in print of Nos. 1 and 2 had been looked over after Borodin's death by Rimsky-Korsakov, and that we do not know how much he altered and edited. It is to be hoped that the reviser did not do what he did to *Boris Godunov*, the extent of alterations to which we *do* know! The Third Symphony, in A minor, opens with a simple folk-song-like tune, and works up to quite an extended movement. The Scherzo (2) is in 5/8 time, in D major – B minor, and is perhaps the best of the three Scherzi. It swings, in the Trio, into B flat major. Someone should make this fragment (or can a fragment last nearly sixteen minutes?) available not only for study but for enjoyment.

SYMPHONY NO. I IN E FLAT

FIRST Movement. *Adagio-Allegro*. Less heroic than its companion and less tautly constructed, Borodin's First

Symphony has a splendour of its own which, apart from its very real existence in our ears, is remarkable in the first extended work of an amateur composer. There is no fumbling; the effects 'come off'; and the construction is at once formal and original.

We open in E flat minor with a descending melody announced at low pitch by bassoons, 'celli, and basses, Ex. 1. Continuous though it is, Borodin treated it as a composite collection of elements, making much of the little semiquaver phrase and also of the rhythmic figure in bar 2, with which indeed he opens his vigorous *Allegro* section on the drums (the third bar is also used as a principal idea). We come to a broad and peaceful main statement of the first theme (in whole and in the major).

The second subject is really a group of new ideas, a rising tune very firmly played, down-bow, on the strings, a charming chromatic passage on the strings, and then a short and characteristic melody, Ex. 2. The clarinet opens the development proper with bar 2 of Ex. 1, followed by one of those threatening brass octaves so common in Borodin's operatic-symphony style. In the discussion that follows all the fragmentary ideas are skilfully mingled together, and lead us to what is apparently the usual formal restatement of the first idea. But, as often with Borodin, it is the beginning of a new development that leads to the coda. After a long, high, wood-wind chord, the first idea is started in long notes, and becomes a peaceful epilogue, very lovely in sound.

Second Movement. *Scherzo: Prestissimo.* The principal subject, which establishes at once E flat major (the key of the first movement) consists of two phrases – one rising in string figuration and mainly pentatonic, the other a direct descending scale on the flute. All the time there is a persistent rhythmical background. Two other phrases are important – a curious four-bar chromatic fragment on the oboe, quoted in Ex. 3, and a rhythmic phrase (also four bars long) of wood-wind chords. All contribute to the somewhat light and airy discussion that leads rather suddenly to the Trio (so called in the score), in the key of

B major. The long melody, Ex. 4, is played by one oboe, with another and the clarinets making up supporting harmony over a held note on the double basses. It is a particularly charming melody, with the freest possible rhythmic flow and continual time changes that make the bar-lines superfluous to good phrasing. Indeed the whole Trio is delightful in colouring and treatment, and of greater weight than the rest of the Scherzo. We return as expected to the opening section, to which is added a coda based upon a new phrase derived from the others.

Third Movement. *Andante.* Just as he adheres to one key for the first two movements, so in time-signature Borodin adopts for all these three movements a triple pulse. The *Andante* consists of decorative variations of a single long melody and all its component parts: Ex. 5 shows it to be one of the composer's most beautiful adaptations of his native folk-song idiom: it is given out by the 'celli over bare fifths which show the basic key to be D. The demi-semi-quaver figure at which the example gives a hint is much used for arabesque and figuration; the cor anglais has it first, then the high flute, in a conversation in which the clarinet joins. So we come to a very full statement of the tune in its original form, presented by the whole orchestra.

Fourth Movement. *Allegro molto vivo.* In both the completed symphonies, Borodin gives us a *Finale* of an importance equal to, if not greater than, that of the opening *allegro*: both are highly wrought, extended pieces. The first (again in E flat) is strongly dramatic in style, with a frequent recourse to the device of repeated warning notes on the brass. The first subject is a striking and vigorous nine-bar tune, really very simple but containing a drop of a whole tone, of which good use is later made, Ex. 6. There is also an important rising phrase in the bass. After some swift development, the second subject shows itself as a melody of conjunct intervals, announced in octaves against holding horns. The development makes play with all these ideas, especially the rising bass-phrase, and is at once discursive and logical. We reach a soft passage on the wood-wind and then follows a most interesting *stretto*, on what is technically known as an 'inverted harmonic pedal': that is to say, a certain note in the treble, with some harmony, is held against other musical matter below it. It is a striking orchestral effect. There is a big climax and the first idea returns, in notes of longer duration, in the bass. The bass tune also recurs. The recapitulation is fairly regular but not in the least orthodox; it is full, and includes the passage on the inverted pedal in suitable key.

As a whole, this symphony is a brilliantly coloured work, with high and low colours in juxtaposition as in a Byzantine mosaic. What if the Scherzo (incidentally the weakest part of the work) is indebted to Berlioz, what if the slow movement deserves the epithet once given to it of 'Schumann-esque'? There is, on the contrary, so much that is new, original in method, and entirely unhackneyed or conventional that it has won itself a permanent place in music denied to most youthful symphonies. A recording is not only deserved by its merits; it is also much needed.

SYMPHONY NO. 2, IN B MINOR

First Movement. *Allegro.* A bold and vigorous opening phrase, Ex. 7a, sounds like an introduction, but in reality is a plain statement of the first subject, unheralded by even a polite cough. It says that it is in B minor, but the chromatic nature of the tune (which is not harmonized) makes it equally explainable in D major. A second half of the first subject occurs immediately in the upper register, Ex. 7b. Both halves are equally important, and both are treated in fragments all through the movement. We find Ex. 7a developed in all manner of rhythms and pitches.

Borodin moves quickly in his statement of ideas, and so we come before long to a contrasted subject, Ex. 8, a charming and very typical Russian tune, the basis of which is the five-note scale common to both Eastern and Western folk-music. The accents are worth noticing, for the slur marks are rather those of the phrase than of the mere bow. The 'cellos announce this new tune, and after them the wood-wind two octaves higher. But very soon we are back in the vigour of Ex. 7a, here lengthened in note-values, and come to a soft nothing of long held notes.

Suddenly, the drums enter with an exciting rhythm, backed up by the wood-wind, and so we start the real development of these germs of music. The three important phrases are interchanged and interwoven with great effect. After reaching D flat major we return to B minor, where trombones and tuba have Ex. 7a, and lead us to a kind of stretto on a long held brass-note – a common device in Borodin. Back comes the first subject, as it should, first of all at half the original speed, and then at double: the second subject quickly enters: and we soon perceive that for Borodin the 'recapitulation' is again no more than the beginning of a sort of second development or extra long coda. He leads us to three brass chords (marked *fff*) and so to the longest-drawn statement of A we have yet had. He shows that his first excitement bears serious extension.

Second Movement. *Scherzo: Prestissimo – Allegretto.* A startling chord in the first bars leads us into F major, with the horns repeating the note C rapidly. The first subject is in the shape of a spread V : in Ex. 9 you will see the rising part of the phrase, which is in fact somewhat figurated. All this is much developed in Borodin's own way, and repeated intact, somewhat in the Rondo style. There is also a syncopated figure of which much use is made. We break suddenly into an allegretto section in 6/4 time and in D major; a kind of 'trio' in the accepted classical sense. The oboe gives us a melody, Ex. 10, which cannot help reminding one of *Prince Igor*. Clarinet and flute take it up, and after some free modulation we hear it very broadly announced on wood-wind and strings, till it dies down to a pleasant nothing. The Scherzo is then repeated, but Borodin does not merely say *da capo:* instead he makes new and longer developments of his ideas, again taking us to a moment of stillness. He ends the movement on a long chord for two clarinets and four horns, starting *p* and sinking to *ppp*.

Third Movement. *Andante.* It is no surprise when this wonderful rhapsodic movement moves from F major to

D flat major. There is a quiet and slow call, rather nostalgic, on the clarinet, and then a solo horn, accompanied by harp, plays the long melody quoted in part in Ex. 11. It is again pentatonic, and again irregular in beat. The colouring of this movement defies all description and analysis. There is a sudden event – a turn to E minor with an F natural, and a new single-bar phrase, which is tossed about the orchestra and developed in conjunction with parts of the main tune. A chromatic scale-fragment is also newly introduced. On all these thematic scraps Borodin muses lovingly and rather oddly, swinging us up suddenly (as only he can) into an orchestral climax. Then some more musing, and we are led into a splendid scene where our main tune is presented in full panoply, on the strings in octaves supported by the whole orchestra. But we are not to be satisfied with this; we must think back to the fragments again, and the movement ends with the same clarinet call with which it opened, this time echoed by a solo horn.

It is impossible to convey in cold words the extraordinary effect of this movement on the ear of the sympathetic listener – the vast outbursts of national feeling, the nostalgia of the quieter passages, the tender but inexorable logic of the argument.

Fourth Movement. *Allegro*. This, the most extended movement of the four in the symphony, returns us to B, this time B major. Once more, we are reminded of *Prince Igor* from the opening bar; the preluding matter must make one think of the Polovtsian dances. The first subject is announced with full orchestral brilliance. I have quoted it, in Ex. 12, with treble and bass lines alone, untrammelled with harmony, for both lines are of great importance in the design of the movement. As before, Borodin breaks up his tune into self-contained pieces, and plays with them, till we reach a climax. Thence we come to our second subject, Ex. 13, announced by solo clarinet, repeated by flute (a third higher) and then by oboe, and so to a broad *cantabile* statement by the orchestra itself. We return to the first subject. A point of importance here is the orchestral colouring. There is a solo flute, in high register, over low strings and *pianissimo* drums, which produces an extra-ordinarily luminous effect: the flute is followed by the clarinet and then the oboe, and it is interesting to observe, aurally, how remarkably the contrasts between these instruments are made by the simplest means. Then comes one of Borodin's long notes on the horns – threatening here, it seems. The passage that follows is both operatic and symphonic in style – a part of Borodin's hankering after the theatre and yet properly educated into its more solemn place. The low strings give us a lengthened version of the first subject with great effect, and then we are swung into an exciting *stretto*, with the second subject occurring in slow time and with very grave dignity on the low strings and bassoons. The *stretto* continues, and the music works itself up (almost without the composer's help) to B major and a recapitulation. Only, once again, Borodin is not content with a formal restatement, and begins soon a new kind of development which throws fresh light on all his previous material. We have seen it already in a glittering and a dun-coloured dress: here it is anew, in a kind of justification of its various kinds of garment. The movement (and the symphony, for this is indeed a *finale,* an integral part of a whole work) ends with a coda that is very compressed in musical style, yet manages to use both the main tunes, or fragments of them, with telling argumentative effect.

The closer one studies this Second Symphony, the more it is revealed that, while Borodin always felt that his proper outlet was the stage, he was intellectually capable of controlling his ideas so that they would fit in with the accepted scheme of symphonic form. One's final impression of this symphony is not so much that it is a successful achievement (which it indubitably is) but that it is magnificently courageous, in expression and no less in restraint.

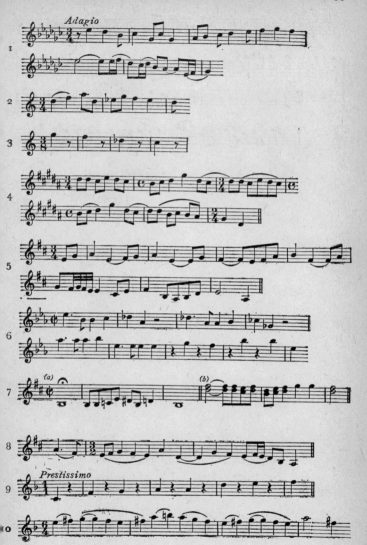

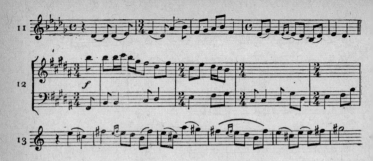

14

Peter Ilich Tchaikovsky (1840-1893)

MARTIN COOPER

INTRODUCTION

TCHAIKOVSKY was not a symphonist by nature. That is to say, it was not natural to him to express himself in sonata-form or to build a full-scale work on a strictly musical plan, without the assistance of those extraneous elements which have come to be loosely called a 'programme'. His melodies have scent, colour, glamour, and sometimes violent emotional expressiveness, but they are not seeds from which the composer can make a whole forest grow. They are not seeds for the very good reason that they are flowers: they appear in full blossom, one by one, and there is very little that Tchaikovsky can do with them except arrange them artistically into a bouquet. A ballet like the *Sleeping Beauty* is a large and exquisite bunch of these flowers: but so is the fifth symphony, and that is why it makes such a good ballet. Mozart, Beethoven and in his lesser way Brahms started a symphonic movement from what often seems very unpromising material. Think of the opening of the *Eroica Symphony* or Brahms's Third Symphony: the composer seems merely to be playing about with the notes of the common chord. But out of that extremely simple material he builds, one idea develops into different forms, takes on new meanings when seen in new lights and perspectives like a thought in a man's mind. For the symphony is thinking in music and to write a good symphony it is necessary to possess a good musical intelligence. Now Tchaikovsky does not think: he feels emotionally and he experiences with his senses and the result is often beautiful and pleasing to the ear, but it lacks the specifically symphonic character. He was quite aware of this himself. He wrote in a letter to a friend:

> 'All my life I have been much troubled by my inability to grasp and manipulate form in music ... What I write has always a mountain of padding: an experienced eye can detect the thread in my seams and I can do nothing about it.'

How much does this matter, if the result is pleasing? Is it merely an academic question, of interest to professors who themselves lack Tchaikovsky's creative power entirely? Not altogether, I think. Beauty of form – which really means organic growth – in music is essential in all the larger forms and in none of them more than the symphony. Like many of (though not by any means all) the best things in life it needs hard work and practice to appreciate it, and that is why we find Tchaikovsky's symphonies make an immediate appeal to the unreflecting, less musically educated section of the public, but meet with a good deal of criticism from trained musicians and people who have acquired a more discriminating taste in music. In Tchaikovsky's own lifetime the composer Taneiev complained to him that his Fourth Symphony 'gives the effect of a symphonic poem to which the composer has slapped on three more movements and called it a symphony'.

The first three of Tchaikovsky's symphonies are very seldom played, but they have many of the features which have made the last three so popular. The first (*Winter Dreams*) is a youthful work, and the first subject of the first movement, the adagio and the slow introduction to the finale are all folk-like themes, though only the last is an actual folk-song. The operatic influence is visible already in the scherzo (a transposed version of a scherzo written for a piano sonata) in the dramatic pauses which introduce the middle section, and in the brass fanfare which became almost a mannerism in later works and appears in the first movement. The second symphony (sometimes called the *Little Russian*) was written on Ukrainian folk-tunes, but Tchaikovsky found, as in the last movement of the first symphony, that he was not entirely at home with folk-music, and he used a folk-song only as an introduction, to a movement which was based on more conventional material. There were two versions of this second symphony, and as good a critic as Taneiev preferred the first (unpublished) version to the second. The second movement of the symphony was lifted bodily from Tchaikovsky's opera *Undine*, in which it appeared as a nuptial march, and this is significant in its suggestion that Tchaikovsky felt the distinction between symphonic and stage music as very tenuous, if at all existent. The third symphony (sometimes called the *Polish*) represented something like a reaction from the popular, folk-tune character of the second and shows the more eclectic, Western side of Tchaikovsky's character. Even so, side by side with obvious memories of Schumann, we find him automatically lapsing into his native Russian idiom and allowing what began as a conventional German theme to develop by the process of repetition and slight variation which is typical of Russian folk-song. (The last movement of No. 2 is a series of variations on a single theme which is repeated eighteen times in succession before it is varied.)

The break between the third and fourth symphonies is less artistic than personal. In none of the first three symphonies do we meet the unmistakable Tchaikovsky atmosphere – the almost painful emotional intensity alternating with aggressive gaiety, the hysterical climaxes succeeded by luxuriant self-pity, and, over each work the heavy atmosphere of Fatality, consciously represented by the motto fanfare in the fourth and all-pervading in the sixth.

SYMPHONY NO. 4 IN F MINOR

THE Fourth Symphony was written in 1877, immediately after Tchaikovsky's disastrous marriage and flight abroad, and during the warmest period of his strange relationship with the woman he never met, Nadejda von Meck, to whom the work is dedicated. It opens with the *Fatum* theme, Ex. 1, as Tchaikovsky called it – a sinister sounding fanfare in the brass which gives the atmosphere of the whole movement, hectic anxiety and fear of an unknown

Something (the *frei flottende Angst* of the psycho-analysts). The main body of the movement (*Andante sostenuto – Moderato con anima*) is marked by the composer as 'in valse time' and the rhythm of the first subject – dotted and syncopated – dominates the movement, Ex. 2. It is announced first by the strings, then the wood-wind, and after the first climax is over Tchaikovsky gives an inverted form of the theme to the basses while the horns play a sobbing figure which he was to use extensively in both his later symphonies. After a final fortissimo statement of the theme the clarinet and bassoon have a short bridge passage, dying away to a pianissimo before the clarinet introduces the second subject, in A flat minor instead of the conventional A flat major, Ex. 3. This is very lightly accompanied by the strings, but when the flutes and oboes take it up the 'cellos play a *cantabile* countersubject which finally develops on its own – rocking thirds in the violins (the key is now B major) answered by what is virtually a major version of the first subject *pianissimo* in the wood-wind. The dotted rhythm of this subject becomes more and more insistent and is finally hammered out in the brass as an accompaniment to a new B major theme in the strings. There are violent syncopations here too, at first in the wood-wind accompaniment and then in the main theme. After a big climax the movement dies down almost to a close at the end of the exposition.

The development section is heralded by a return of the Fatum fanfare in the trumpet, which reappears more and more insistently before the recapitulation. Much of the development is simply by means of the *inversion* – which we saw Tchaikovsky using in the exposition of the first subject, and by *sequences* – the playing of the same phrase in a succession of different (generally mounting) positions. The recapitulation is ushered in by the fanfare theme and a terrific climax in the whole orchestra. The first subject has virtually provided the whole material for the development and is therefore treated very shortly in the recapitulation. The key is the unorthodox D minor, in which the second subject too appears. There is a long coda, starting in F major, but interrupted again by the Fatum theme. A short interlude in D flat major, where the wood-wind have a theme in thirds marked *cantabile*, leads back to F minor and a quickening of the tempo and the last part of the coda is based on the material of the first subject, with the fanfare making a final appearance.

The second movement (*Andante in modo di canzone*) is in complete contrast. It opens with an oboe solo, accompanied by the strings pizzicato, playing a folk-like melody. This is taken up by the 'cellos and is followed by a less graceful interlude, in which the scoring is intentionally thick in a way that is rare in Tchaikovsky, Ex. 4. After a climax, bassoon and viola repeat the original melody ornamented by the strings. The *più mosso* middle section consists of a simple F major melody, Ex. 5 – also folk-like in character, though it resembles a dance rather than a song – and a postlude built on sequences, as described above. The return of the first melody is a remarkable instance of Tchaikovsky's scoring – the melody in the first violins, the rest of the strings accompanying *pizzicato* and the wood-wind contributing ornamental snippets. Ex. 4 follows again, rather abbreviated, and the movements end with the original theme in fragmentation, each phrase given to a different instrument until the bassoon plays it finally in toto and the first phrase, repeated four times, brings the music to a final standstill.

Tchaikovsky calls his third movement *Scherzo: pizzicato ostinato*, and whether it was suggested by the Pizzicato in Delibes' ballet *Sylvia* or Glinka's imitation of a balalaika chorus in *A Life for the Tsar* it is wholly effective. The main theme, in F major, is answered by a D minor section of equal length, which circles round the dominant of the key, with the off-beats accentuated. After a postlude built largely on intervals of the fourth the original tune returns with a short coda which leads to a new interlude. Hitherto only plucked strings have been used. Now the oboe announces an episode played entirely by the wood-wind and based on a naive tune such as a shepherd might play on a pipe, Ex. 6. Next it is the turn of the brass who play, in sharp *staccato* chords and very softly, a kind of puppets' march. The clarinet adds the shepherds' tune on top after a time and after several hints in the wood-wind the *pizzicato* theme returns in full and the movement ends with the whole orchestra contributing snatches of melody and rhythm from their original 'solo' episodes in a grand ensemble.

If the third movement suggested a vignette of everyday life in a Russian village, the last (*Allegro con fuoco*) is definitely a festival. After two introductory flourishes in the orchestra the wood-wind announce the folk-song *In the field there stands a birch-tree*, Ex. 7, forlorn and deliberately clumsy with the peasant clumsiness which marked the second episode of the slow movement. The introductory flourish appears again and then the whole orchestra announces a broad and jolly tune, well punctuated by percussion, a near relation of the *più mosso* of the slow movement, Ex. 8. This is followed by a series of variations on the folk-song – two sets divided by the reappearance of the second theme, which forms the material of the coda after the Fatum fanfare has made a rather unexpected appearance – the spectre at the feast. The whole movement is typical of Tchaikovsky at his best – in its ingenious and varied orchestration and the unfailing charm and effectiveness of his melody and colour – and at his worst, in its complete shapelessness. It is perfect music for a ballet scene, poor stuff as the finale of a symphony.

SYMPHONY NO. 5 IN E MINOR

THERE was a gap of eleven years between Tchaikovsky's Fourth and Fifth Symphonies, years which saw the composer rise to European fame. But public acclamation could do nothing to solve the personal problems of Tchaikovsky's private life, and we find the same introspective melancholy and self-pity in his next symphony: in fact, it is the unifying principle of the whole work, informing the middle and last movements as well as the first. As in the fourth, the introduction gives the emotional atmosphere of the whole work – a gloomy theme in the lowest register of the clarinet, Ex. 9, the main body of the movement (*allegro con anima*) starts with the first subject in the woodwind above short chords in the strings and when they take it over and the roles are

reversed the wood-wind have running semi-quaver figures
which lead eventually to a strongly-marked subsidiary idea
with a dotted rhythm. Before the second subject appears
two more short episodes – both of which play a large part
in the development – are introduced: the first, a short
melodic phrase growing outwards from a unison F sharp
in the wood-wind and sinking back again almost at once,
the second strongly rhythmical and answered by a desperate
sigh in the strings. This introduces the second subject (D
major in an E minor movement), one of the most haunting
and expressive of all Tchaikovsky's melodies, Ex. 10, and
mounting to an agonized climax which brings the exposition
to a close – a bouquet of some of Tchaikovsky's most
beautiful flowers which he proceeds to rearrange skilfully,
for there is nothing else he can do with them. The dotted
rhythm from the group of first subject themes is used as a
dramatic *ostinato* and leads back eventually to the recapitulation and a long coda, based on the first subject with
staccato chords in the brass marking the rhythm. After a
climax the movement dies away to nothing, ending with
the same dark orchestral colouring as the introduction.

The second movement (*Andante cantabile, con alcuna licenza*)
opens with solo passages – first for the horn, joined later
by the clarinet and then for the oboe with horn counterpoint, Ex. 11 and Ex. 12, and these melodies form the main
material of the movement. After the 'cellos have played
Ex. 11 with punctuating sobs in the horns and wood-wind,
Ex. 12 returns *con noblezza* in the strings against a repeated
throbbing accompaniment in the horns, and is carried
forward to a great emotional climax. The middle section
of the ternary movement starts again as a solo, or more
properly a duet, as the bassoon answers the clarinet solo.
Suddenly the atmosphere grows dark and tense and the
theme of the introduction makes a sudden appearance,
completely disturbing the tranquil melancholy of the movement. After a pause and pizzicato chords in the strings the
violin solo – at its most plangent, playing on the G string –
reintroduces Ex. 11 and this is gradually taken up by the
whole orchestra until Ex. 12 reappears at full strength –

con desiderio e passione, with desire and passion – in the strings, and rises quickly to one of Tchaikovsky's almost hysterical climaxes, in which he seems to be beating his head against the wall and collapsing in a storm of tears. At the height of the scene the sinister introductory theme, Ex. 9, appears again, followed by three unmistakable sobs, and the movement ends tranquilly with Ex. 12 played by the strings *dolcissimo*.

The third movement (*Allegro moderato*) is one of Tchaikovsky's most elegant valses and contains some beautiful ornamental writing of the sort in which the composer excels. The main theme is introduced by the strings, Ex. 13, and is answered by the wood-wind who then play Ex. 13 with a counterpoint in the first violins and violas. The middle section (corresponding to the trio) is based on a *spiccato* figure in the violins and then tossed from instrument to instrument, broken into fragments, and finally reappears as an ornament when the valse tune proper, Ex. 13, returns. Only in the coda does the introductory theme, Ex. 9, for a moment darken the atmosphere of a movement which represents a momentary escape from the profound melancholy of the rest of the symphony.

Like the first movement, the Fourth Movement (*Andante maestoso, Allegro vivace*) opens with an introduction in which the same material, Ex. 9, appears in a slightly different light, still gloomy but more solemn and march-like, with heavily-moving triplets in the strings and liberal use of the brass. This theme plays so large a part in the development section of the movement that it must be considered as an integral part of the thematic material and not, as in the first movement, simply as an introduction. The *Allegro vivace* opens with a short violent subject in the strings (double stopping) and taken up by the orchestra, Ex. 14. A second idea is introduced by the oboe and the pendant to this, played in imitation by different sections of the orchestra over a *crescendo* pedal leads to the second subject, Ex. 15. This too has a solemn march-like character which is emphasized by the *ostinato* bass over which it appears. The development is opened by Ex. 9 played in the brass

and punctuated by scale passages in the strings and wood-
wind. This is followed by rather academic development of
Ex. 14 and Ex. 15 in which Tchaikovsky tries his hand for
a short time at a formal contrapuntal passage but soon
gives it up in favour of the more loosely-knit dramatic
style which is natural to him. The recapitulation is
dwarfed by the intensely dramatic coda, starting in E
minor, with a series of fanfares in the brass and finally
issuing, with great pomp and circumstance, in a final E
major section, slower in tempo and *molto maestoso*, in which
the introduction to the movement appears in its richest
and most splendid form. At the very end there is a reminiscence of the first movement, and the symphony ends in
a blaze of splendour.

SYMPHONY NO. 6 IN B MINOR (*The Pathetic*)

ONCE again, as in the Third and Fourth Symphonies,
Tchaikovsky sets the mood of the whole work in an introductory passage (*Adagio*) to the First Movement – the
bassoons in their lowest register, supported by the double
basses only, only just stirring in the depths of their profound misery and climbing painfully, with a setback at
each step, the interval of a fifth, Ex. 16. When the *Allegro
non troppo* starts, it is with a subject based on the introductory material, but with the well-known atmosphere
of tense anxiety accentuated by restless movement,
Ex. 17. The whole of the first group of subject matter
is dominated by a rhythmic pattern typical of the
strings; but the brass soon appears with a warning fanfare, which later becomes a form of the opening phrase
of the movement. There is a long preparation for the second
subject which is finally ushered in by a solo passage in the
'cellos. (I have shown elsewhere* that, just as it is possible
to find traces of Bizet's *Carmen* in Tchaikovsky's Fourth
Symphony, so I believe traces of Verdi's *Otello* are to be
found in the Sixth. This solo passage is a parallel to Verdi's

* *Tchaikovsky*. A symposium edited by Gerald Abraham. Lindsay
Drummond: 1946.

introduction to the love duet in Act 1.) The main theme of the second subject group has neither the rhythmic interest nor the élan of the corresponding theme in No. 5, but it concentrates entirely on emotional expressiveness (muted strings, *teneramente, molto cantabile, con espansione*, Ex. 18). The countersubject to this starts as a duet between flute and bassoon, with the strings providing a *saltando* accompaniment. Ex. 18 returns in the full orchestra, with a new and solemn postlude and the exposition ends with a *pppppp* in the wood-wind. The development section starts with three rockets sent up (an S.O.S. as usual with Tchaikovsky) and a *feroce* fugato in the strings, which, to continue the metaphor, represents a sort of hectic bustle with all hands on deck. The fugato soon becomes an *ostinato* figure in the strings against which the trumpets' *fff* stands out like a desperate siren. After a moment's lull the brass start a *crescendo*, punctuated by agonized sobs from the strings, and a relentless, trampling march leading back to the opening phrase of Ex. 17, which is repeated against a typically 'anxious' rhythm in the horns. In the middle of the climax which inevitably follows the recapitulation proper starts; but before Ex. 18 appears again the siren-phrase of the trumpets builds up another climax over a dominant pedal, with answering groans from the brass. After an *ffff*, a quick decrescendo and a dramatic pause; and then Ex. 18 descends *con dolcezza*, with a rich counterpoint and every imaginable mark of expression, and the movement ends with 20 bars of a short funeral cortège in the brass, over a descending pizzicato scale in the strings.

The Second Movement (*Allegro con grazia*) is a kind of *valse macabre*, the regular triple rhythm replaced by the limping 5/4 with great dramatic effect. As in the waltz movement of No. 5, Tchaikovsky introduces some brilliant ornamental writing for the strings; but the more emotional mood returns in the trio section, with its sinister pedal and the sobbing of the horns, Ex. 19. Tchaikovsky makes a most unconventional rearrangement of movements, introducing a brilliant and extended march as his third movement, and ending, for dramatic and emotional effect, with an *Adagio lamentoso*.

The marchlike Third Movement (*Allegro molto vivace*) is the perfect example of Tchaikovsky's ability to create a whole movement by the endless repetition of a few melodic snatches which are given meaning and interest simply by the skilful variation of orchestral colour and setting. The first of these snatches to appear is the opening bar and a half of Ex. 21, which stands out in the oboe above the chattering staccato triplets of the strings. After playing ingeniously with this idea and Ex. 20 Tchaikovsky introduces a two-bar phrase from the first movement and this precipitates the growing climax from which Ex. 21 finally emerges in its complete form. This is answered by a more solid theme, soon to be taken up by the brass, Ex. 22. The introduction is then repeated with slight variations of orchestration and a carefully-prepared climax culminating in rushing scale passages in the wood-wind and strings brings back Ex. 21 and a long and brilliantly effective coda. The whole movement is a symphonic march, not military in character but related to the long, spectacular cortèges common in Russian opera and in Tchaikovsky's own ballet *The Sleeping Princess*. It has no organic connection with the rest of the symphony, apart from the affinity of a single melodic phrase with material in the first movement, but is rather in the nature of a *divertissement*.

The Fourth Movement (*Adagio lamentoso*) is the emotional counterpart to the first. There – whatever the details of Tchaikovsky's 'programme' may have been – the idea of death arouses horror and revolt and whips the music to perpetual hectic activity. Here, at the end of the grim ballet danced between Death and the Neurotic, active resistance is almost at an end, and the predominant mood is one of luxurious abandonment, with only one last hysterical protest against the inevitable. The double cry of Ex. 23 is twice repeated, each time with its calmer answer: and then a bassoon solo passage carries the listener back to the tone colour of the introduction to the first movement. After a moment's pause a syncopated variation of the 'anxious' rhythm already noted in the first movement appears in the horns, and over this the strings breathe their lament, Ex. 24, *con devozione*. Soon the whole orchestra takes it up and the syncopated rhythm becomes more urgent, until a climax is reached and a descending semiquaver passage in the strings, followed by a fortissimo chord and a pause, brings the music to a complete stop. This is nervous exhaustion, not death; and after the most speaking sobs the music starts again. This time Ex. 23 rises quickly, by means of repeated sequences, to another hysterical climax: and though the conclusion of this *crise de nerfs* is less dramatic and the music only gradually peters out, with renewed attempts to start Ex. 23 again, this time it is the end. Trombones and the bass drum gradually sink to a *ppppp* and the movement closes with Ex. 24, in the minor, disappearing into silence. There is no denying the enormous dramatic effect of the whole finale. Like the rest of the work it partakes of the nature of opera or ballet rather than symphony (the first and last movements are more operatic, the middle movements ballet *divertissements*). The immense popularity of the symphony as a whole is an eloquent commentary on what the general public in all countries look for in music – a reflection, magnified and dramatized, of its own unhappiness and frustration, combined with a purely emotional message of vague 'comfort'. In his own misery and his strong sense of self-pity Tchaikovsky discovered a language for the spiritual hunger and bewilderment of the modern man: and as long as that hunger and bewilderment last the sixth symphony is sure of passionate devotion from concert audiences and a response, even though unavowed or shamefaced, from many of those who find its shameless emotionalism distasteful.

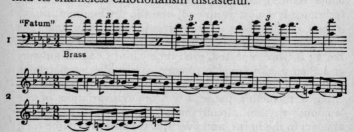

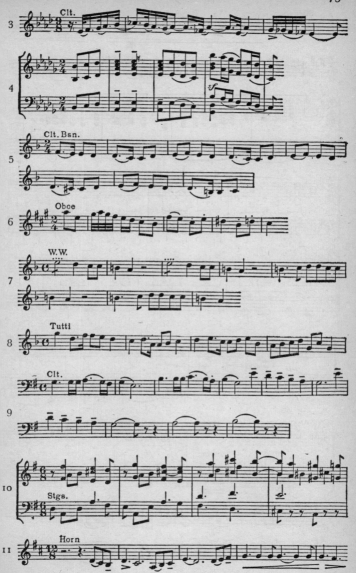

15

Antonin Dvořák (1841-1904)

ALEC ROBERTSON

INTRODUCTION

IT is unwise to put your trust in the numbers attached to
the symphonies of Schubert or Dvořák. Friendships of long
standing are apt to be threatened by a wrangle as to
whether Schubert's great C major symphony is his Seventh or
his Ninth. In point of fact if the so-called *Gastein Symphony*,
reported lost, has any real existence Schubert will have
to be credited with ten and not nine symphonies, of
which the great C major is, at present, indubitably the
ninth.

It will similarly come as a surprise, I imagine, to many
people who find the number five attached to Dvořák's last
symphony, popularly known by its sub-title, *From the New
World,* to be told that, like Beethoven and, with the reservation above, Schubert, he wrote nine symphonies. In
Dvořák's case one symphony, long missing, was discovered
in the Prague archives in 1923, and performed for the
first time by the State Radio Orchestra of Czecho-
slovakia, thirty-two and a half years after the composer's
death. This work, in C minor, with the sub-title *The
Bells of Zlonice,* is, as far as we know, the first one Dvořák
composed.

It may be as well, therefore, before proceeding any
further, to set out the correct order of Dvořák's symphonies.

No. 1. C minor (*The Bells of Zlonice*) (1865).
No. 2. B flat major (1865).
No. 3. E flat major (1873).
No. 4. D minor (1874).
No. 5. F major (known as No. 3) (1875, revised in 1887).
No. 6. D major (known as No. 1) (1880).

No. 7. D minor (known as No. 2) (1884–5).

No. 8. G major (known as No. 4) (1889).

No. 9. E minor ('*From the New World*', and known as
  No. 5) (1893).

The ordinary concert-goer is likely to hear only the 'big
five' amongst these symphonies, although the second and
third of them are occasionally broadcast by the B.B.C.
The deprivation is not a severe one, for even the first of the
'big five', the F major symphony, is an unequal work, and the
mature symphonic writer does not come into view until the
year of the D major symphony, composed five years later.

Both Dvořák and Tchaikovsky began to write symphonies
in their middle twenties, unlike Brahms who, abandoning,
with native caution, earlier attempts, waited until his
forty-fourth year before launching his first completed
symphony: but Dvořák shared with Brahms a passion for
the destruction of his musical first-born and it is doubtful
whether he meant *The Bells of Zlonice*, his first symphony –
if it is actually his first – to survive. Zlonice is a small
coal-mining town, not far from Dvořák's birthplace at
Nelahozeves, to which the family moved in 1855, preceded
by Antonin three years before, and the symphony may be
a tribute to the memory of Antonin Liehmann, the school-
master organist whose portrait Dvořák painted so lovably
in one of his operas, *The Jacobin*. As Dvořák revised the
orchestration of his Second Symphony, in B flat, twenty-
three years after it was written and gave it an opus number
it seems that he did not intend to destroy it, and would
have been glad to see it in print. Both in this symphony and
in the next one in E flat, composed eight years later, the
influence of Wagner makes itself felt, particularly in the
orchestration; and this second symphony sounds entirely
uncharacteristic of the composer, although he himself professed great affection for it. It is in the next symphony, the
early D minor, composed in the following year, when
Dvořák was convalescing after his Wagnerian fever, that
the lineaments of the born symphonic writer began clearly
to appear. The composer does not live up to the impressive
start of the work, and, though his ideas are good and he keeps

the music moving, the symphony is rhythmically monotonous and melodically diffuse. The best things in it are
the theme for the variations in the slow movement and a
typical pastoral tune in the last movement.

The following year, 1875, Dvořák composed the earliest
of his symphonies to retain its place in the repertoire
and, incidentally, to be recorded for the gramophone, the
Symphony in F major, the fifth in chronological order.

This symphony, written three years before the appearance
of the first set of Slavonic Dances, or indeed before any of the
music by which most of us know Dvořák, was dedicated to
the famous conductor Hans von Bülow and acknowledged
by him, in a generously phrased letter to Dvořák, as coming
from 'the most God-gifted composer of the present day,
next to Brahms'. Before looking over this symphony something must be said about the kind of music we shall find in
the five remaining symphonies and the characteristic
qualities of Dvořák's orchestration.

He had learnt the art of orchestration in the best possible
school, by playing, for a number of years, the viola in the
Czech National Theatre Orchestra, and, with six or more
string quartets to his credit, he had a thorough understanding of independent string writing, the fundamental
basis of orchestral tone; but we must take a skilled conductor's word for it that there are miscalculations in his
orchestration (due, he thinks, mainly to Dvořák's early
acquaintance with the raucous tone and rough style of
village bands playing his native music) which set 'many a
hard nut for the conductor to crack'.*

The ordinary listener, who is not engaged in nut-
cracking, is unlikely to notice Dvořák's village-band effects
unless they are forced on his attention as, for example, in
the slow movement of the G major symphony. Gerald
Abraham (in Fischl's symposium) finds this movement
'blush-making' – and I, it must be confessed, find it enchanting. The ordinary listener will notice these effects the less

---

*From the chapter on Dvořák's Orchestra by Julius Harrison in
Antonin Dvořák, a symposium edited by Viktor Fischl (Lindsay
Drummond).

because, possessed of the great secret of being able to keep his music moving, Dvořák irresistibly carries us along with him. The listener, however, can hardly fail to appreciate the composer's exquisite use of the wood-wind and of the horns, to which he allots some of his loveliest melodies: and in this connection Dvořák's love of his garden and of birds may well have been a determining factor. Of all this there will be occasion to speak later. To play in a Dvořák symphony, an instrumentalist will tell you, is a joy, because Dvořák distributes good things all round and does not think only of the players at the first desks: the second flute or oboe, or the second violins, are brought into prominence as well. Dvořák also always provides a liberal allowance of counter melodies, and these, with his rhythmic genius and wide range of dynamics, give his music heartening vitality.

Dvořák's individual orchestration colours music that, like Schubert's, which it so often resembles, is above all exquisitely lyrical and sensuous. One can be sure that the second subjects of his first and last movements, his slow movements, the trios of his scherzos will, almost invariably, sing their way straight into our hearts, just as his lively dance rhythms set our toes twitching. It was Dvořák's ambition to show the world that a Brahms could come out of Bohemia. If that ambition, and his affection for Brahms, his very good friend, led him to look not, as Smetana always did, only at his own country for inspiration, but also at the great cosmopolitan city of Vienna, his symphonies never proceeded very far before he relapsed into his native dialect. The least national of them is the great symphony in D minor, which he said 'must be so as to shake the world', the most national, the G major, an altogether more modest affair. Now that all these five symphonies have been recorded, four of them by the Czech Philharmonic Orchestra, and the last four, at least, can be heard regularly in the concert hall and on the air, it is to be hoped that the listening public will come to appreciate the fine music of the D major, D minor, and G major symphonies, as well as finding in them a good measure of the qualities that have so much endeared *From the New World* to them.

SYMPHONY IN F MAJOR.
(known as No. 3)

FIRST Movement. *Allegro ma non troppo.* The movement begins with a simple theme on two clarinets, Ex. 1, mostly spun out of the notes of the chord of F major, accompanied by the same chord *tremolando* on the violas, and held on horns and 'cellos; the whole thing sounding the pastoral note one finds again in the F major String Quartet of 1893, mis-called *The Nigger.* The next theme, Ex. 2, of this first-subject group, loud and lively, carries the direction *grandioso*, which is as personal to Dvořák as *nobilmente* is to Elgar.

To this succeeds the charming second subject, Ex. 3, Slav in character, and allotted, to begin with, to the first violins. Before the oboes and bassoons play it the full orchestra burst out with a sudden loud chord, an effect Dvořák repeats three times, but omits in the recapitulation.

The development section begins with the first violins obviously referring to the common chord theme of Ex. 1, but – an ingenious idea – using the well-marked cadence chords of this theme (*a*) with a triplet figure on flutes, clarinets, and horns to accompany it, and so leading to a poetic presentation of Ex. 1 in its original form on the flute over a very soft string *tremolando*. After much play with this chord on one instrument or another, or group of instruments, Dvořák brings in reminders of both his other themes (Ex. 2 and 3), and then quietly introduces the recapitulation, emphasizing the pastoral note of the movement by giving Ex. 1 to the third and fourth horns (not to the first and second). This time the second subject, Ex. 3, played by flute and clarinet, is enriched by one of Dvořák's charming little counter-melodies on the first violins' fourth, or G, string. In the quiet coda, Ex. 1 on clarinets unites with Ex. 3 on bassoons and string basses, after which flute and horn make the farewells of Ex. 1.

Second Movement. *Andante con moto.* The slow movement corresponds with Dvořák's definition of the Russian term,

Dumka, a piece grave and melancholy and occasionally gay, and is regarded by the composer's chief biographer as a forerunner of some fine examples, such as the *Dumky Trio*, which he wrote in later life. 'Cellos, first violins, flute and bassoon, successively play the nostalgic tune with which the movement opens, Ex. 4, violas and 'cellos accompanying its third appearance with the pattern of the four opening notes at double the speed, Ex. 5.

This note pattern is introduced into the brighter middle section in the major key (the tune given at first to oboe, clarinet, and horn), and is thereafter seldom absent from the score, Dvořák thus securing an all-over unity in the texture of the movement.

Another of Dvořák's typical counter-melodies, on the violins in octaves, accompanies the recapitulation of the first tune (flute and oboe). There is no break, but only a slight pause, between this and the next movement: and the transition is made by the 'cellos continuing to refer to the first tune of the slow movement, and five bars for string quartet with the horn poised, ready, at the pause, to lead the orchestra into the new key of B flat major.

Third Movement. *Allegro scherzando.* This scherzo, except for one outburst for full orchestra, is of rather a delicate character, in keeping with the mood of the previous movements; and the characteristic feature of the Trio is an antiphonal use of wood-wind and horns, and strings.

Fourth Movement. *Finale: Allegro molto.* A large and well-planned movement which begins with a vigorous theme in A minor, Ex. 6, the key of the slow movement; the choice of tonality gives the composer the opportunity of keeping the basic key of the symphony, F major, up his sleeve for a dramatic entry, in this key, of the theme when A minor is finally driven from the field. He chooses D flat for his lyrical second theme (violins in octaves) and adds further interest by a threefold reiteration of a common chord, at different points, which eventually leads to a beautifully ethereal reminiscence of Ex. 1 from the first movement, just before the full-blooded conclusion of the symphony.

SYMPHONY NO. 6 IN D MAJOR
(known as No. 1)

THE D major symphony, which Dvořák conducted, on his first visit to England, at a concert of the London Philharmonic Society, in 1884, was a great favourite with the English public at a time when the symphonies of Brahms were considered difficult of comprehension and the very name of Tchaikovsky was unknown. The enormous popularity of Tchaikovsky's last three symphonies and, in these later years, of Brahms's four symphonies have caused the public to give this, and the next two of Dvořák's symphonies, less than their due.

During the five years that had elapsed since the composition of the F major symphony, Dvořák's first set of *Slavonic Dances*, composed as piano duets in 1878 and orchestrated the same year, had been a huge success in Europe, and when it reached England three years later this fresh uninhibited music delighted the public in equal measure.

Dvořák's only large-scale work composed in the same year as the D major symphony, had been the rather unequal Violin Concerto; but in the D major symphony we find him at the height of his powers.

The village boy is able now to move amongst the great of the symphonic world with ease and assurance, and, one may perhaps assume, to pay gracefully, but not obsequiously, a compliment to Brahms's Second Symphony in the same key, composed three years before, by modelling the open bars of the first movement on the pattern of those with which his friend began his work.

First Movement. *Allegro ma non tanto*. As in the F major symphony, Dvořák begins with a strong affirmation of his chosen key, Ex. 7, and follows Brahms in modulating to E minor, but by means peculiarly his own. There are other superficial resemblances to the older master's layout which the interested listener can discover before we come to the characteristic direction *grandioso*, the playing by the full orchestra of the opening theme. Before the second theme comes in Dvořák quickens the notes of the final bar of Ex. 7

and then that of the one preceding it and adds a little scherzo-like figure (strings) which will make a bridge over to the second subject group and also be used as a counter-melody to it, Ex. 8. Dvořák adds to this lyrical tune on the 'cellos and horns a pendant theme of spring-like freshness for oboe, Ex. 9, and falls so much in love with it that he keeps it going right up to the end of the exposition. The bare and mysterious opening of the development, oddly reminiscent of Mendelssohn's *Hebrides* Overture, 'from the depths of which fragments of the first theme arise', has few parallels in Dvořák's music, but the whole of the development section is richly imaginative. We hear only the counter-melody of Ex. 8, but to the quickened notes of Ex. 7 is added, by the clarinets, a cadence of great charm. Another unexpected thing is a dramatic series of chromatic chords for the full string choir, which lead directly into the recapitulation.

In this new features are provided by the introduction of the quickened notes of bar (*a*) in Ex. 7 after Ex. 9 (the lyrical pendant to the second theme) has been worked up, as before, to a climax; and by the choral passage being diatonic, not chromatic, leaving the movement in a blaze of D major, but with the last word given, with delightful humour, to Ex. 9.

Second Movement. *Adagio*. One has only to compare this lovely movement with the similar one in the F major symphony to realize what strides Dvořák had made as a symphonic writer. The middle section of the slow movement in the earlier work was an obviously devised contrast: but in this work the music develops spontaneously. Wood-wind and horns sketch in the romantic background against which Dvořák's first violins sing the lovely lyrical tune. The time quickens for a hint of gipsy-band music and then violins, followed by clarinets, sigh out another romantically lovely tune, or rather phrase. Dark-toned violas now take up the opening tune, with the texture enriched by counter-phrases on oboe, first violins, bassoons, and double basses.

The short gipsy-band section is repeated, but now leads to a sudden storm in a tea-cup, after which the violins, in octaves, with flute, oboe, and clarinet counter-melodies, resume their enchanted singing. A short cadenza for the flute introduces the poetic coda, in which the various elements of the movement are summed up.

Third Movement. *Scherzo (Furiant): Presto.* The opening section of the movement fulfils the definition of the dance measure called Riant by giving us three (syncopated) measures of two beats followed by two measures of three beats within the framework of the time-signature ($\frac{3}{4}$). A gently humorous use of the piccolo is made in the pretty Trio, in the major key, the middle section of which is decidedly Schubertian. Our old friend *grandioso* had been applied to the last bars of the Scherzo and in the fully-written out repetition, after the Trio, with fuller scoring, is even more applicable.

Fourth Movement. *Allegro con spirito.* The grand 'travelling' tune with which the music begins, Ex. 10, announces that rare thing, a completely successful last movement; something which Dvořák never again completely achieved. The rhythmic impetus of the music never flags, and it brings to us, as does Smetana's *Vltava*, all manner of enchanting things on its broad stream. One of these, sung first by the clarinet, must be quoted, Ex. 11. We have had instances of Dvořák putting his themes into notes of quicker value, but in this movement he does the opposite with his main theme and gives it, by doubling the note values, a massive quality that is most effective, Ex. 12.

SYMPHONY NO. 7 IN D MINOR
(known as No. 2)

THIS symphony, commissioned by the Philharmonic Society, London, was first performed at the St James' Hall on 22nd April, 1885, under the composer's direction, and was an immediate success. Dvořák, on his own confession, had aimed at the stars. In a letter to a friend he wrote 'everywhere I go, I think of nothing else than my work, which must be such as to shake the world, and with God's help it will be so'. He wished convincingly to show the world at large that a Brahms and not merely a national composer could indeed come out of Bohemia, but he wished also to be true to his own country. The consequent tension gives point to the dramatic, and even tragic, emotional tone of the work.

First Movement. *Allegro Maestoso.* Above a drum-roll, a tremolo on the double basses, and a sustained note on the horns, violas and 'cellos give out the first theme of this fine and stormy movement. The earlier Symphony No. 4 in D minor had begun with a dark and gloomy theme, which lacked the epigrammatic terseness Dvořák gave to the present example. As so much use is to be made of the theme, it is worth paying special attention to the little two-note groups of semiquavers (*a*) that relentlessly clinch it, and to the three dotted quavers group (*b*) that immediately follows, Ex. 13.

After the clarinets have also given out the theme battle is joined: and one realizes what power lies in the simple outline of notes Dvořák has devised. Some use was made in the D major Symphony (*q.v.*) of an upward chordal progression in one long span. In the present movement a much more subtle use is made of the same idea presented in three successive spans instead of one. They lead rather unexpectedly to a horn solo, with a counter-melody on the oboe, that checks the outburst of emotion for a moment, but only for a moment, as a few bars later the full orchestra gives out Ex. 13 with the utmost power. A beautifully managed transition is then made to the second theme, allotted to flute and clarinet before going over, an octave higher, to the first violins, Ex. 14. In case this theme reminds you vaguely of something else it may be as well to say that it has a superficial resemblance (and is in the same key) to the 'cello solo in the slow movement of Brahms's Second Piano Concerto, but the way Dvořák shapes and continues the tune, and the lovely writing for the wood-wind up to the point where the first theme again darkly enters, are things entirely his own.

Dvořák never bothers much about any dividing line between exposition and development, and one can say that the development begins with the entry, on the 'cellos, noted above, and continues with a big orchestral outburst based on

Ex. 14 which dies down, at the double bar, to a continuing development of this second theme. The development section is very short, and reiterates, over and over again, those clinching semiquavers we noted in Ex. 13a. Wood-wind and horns carry the burden of the music until the full orchestra rises to the peak climax of the movement, which is also the actual point of recapitulation.

There is a coda which begins with furious intensity but gradually subsides to the drum-roll and sustained horn note with which the movement began, over which we hear a foreshortened version of Ex. 13 sounding more deeply tragic in this frustrated form. The movement ends with a whisper.

Second Movement. *Poco adagio.* Those who care to study the orchestration of the previous movement will discover with what deliberation Dvořák avoids the use of the warmest register of the strings, and his copious employment of wood-wind and horns. The same thing is true of the slow movement. The first half of the lovely tune, classical in purity of feeling, with which the movement begins is scored for clarinets, with oboe, bassoon, and pizzicato string accompaniment: the second half of the tune, an upwelling of romantic feeling which cries out for the violins, is given to flute and oboe, and then the whole wood-wind choir. Then, at last, first violins and 'cellos sing that sad and expressive phrase which was again to be heard in the last but one of Dvořák's string quartets, Ex. 15, and which defines the tragic mood of this symphony. When we go out into the country the horns are given a pastoral phrase, with delicate answering phrases for the violins and wood-wind. Considerable tension enters the music after this point when the full orchestra have a version of the opening theme from which all the lyrical beauty has vanished. A modulatory passage, in pattern, but not orchestration, similar to the one on the horns that introduces the coda to the first movement of Brahms's Second Symphony, leads to the 'cellos singing of the second, and romantic half, of the opening tune, the one truly lyrical passage for the strings in the movement. The deep sigh is heard again (violins), followed by one of

Dvořák's sudden orchestral outbursts, and then all is peaceful again as the oboes bring back the tune of the opening bars, held back till now, and the music reaches a quiet close.

Third Movement. *Scherzo: Vivace.* There is nothing gay or light-hearted about this Scherzo, but rather a restless energy that is hardly abated in the Trio. Two tunes and two rhythms make up the material of the Scherzo. Violins and violas have the *staccato* top tune, a broken utterance in 3/2, while 'cellos and bassoons have a legato counter-melody in 6/4, Ex. 16. It is this rhythmic individualization of the counter-tune, rather than its inherent interest, that makes it so effective. As one might expect, the tunes are reversed when repeated, the wood-wind playing the top tune, the violins (but at the same pitch as the wood-wind) the lower. The two further repetitions of these tunes are also varied at the top of their register, being very shrill and frenzied. Apart from short passages in which solo horns, trumpets, or 'cellos momentarily emerge, the Trio, conspicuously restless in tonality, is scored for wood-wind with string accompaniment.

Fourth Movement. *Allegro.* The broad song-like theme ('cellos, horns, clarinets) with which this movement begins, Ex. 17, is clearly of national origin – it is the first time in the symphony the national note has been sounded – and the brass, so sparely used before, now make a martial appearance. A phrase, strongly marked, also national in character, which comes in on the strings shortly after the trumpet calls, will be much used in the development. The next theme, a gracious tune in the major introduced by the 'cellos, then passing to wood-wind and violins, brings a glow of warmth into the music. As the music develops new themes appear, one strikingly similar to the 'Sword' motive in *The Ring,* and at one point the bold opening tune is made to sound exquisitely poetical by violins and flute. At length Dvořák gathers all his forces together for the splendid affirmation of D major, in the very last bars, which resolves tragedy into triumph.

SYMPHONY NO. 8 IN G MAJOR
(*known as No. 4*)

THE only reason that this work used to be known as the
English Symphony is that it was published by the English firm
of Novello when Dvořák was having one of his periodic
quarrels with his German publisher Simroek. It is, in fact,
the most national of all his symphonies and it bears witness,
also, to his dissatisfaction with classical symphonic form and
his attraction towards the symphonic poem. Dvořák establishes, in the opening pages of the symphony, a strong contrast between the first rather ecclesiastical sounding and
obviously Slavonic theme, placed sonorously in the bass
register in G minor, and the simple tune in G major, high
up on the flute, that immediately follows it; Ex. 18 and
Ex. 19. He is, as it were, at first in church and then in his
garden. The G minor section will be heard twice more,
once immediately before the development, in the form we
first heard it, and then, fully scored and at a heightened
pitch, immediately before the recapitulation: a masterly
constructive idea.

Before long Dvořák works together the repeated notes
(*a*) of Ex. 18 and the flute tune, and presently this last tune
is used for a big climax. The second subject, in B minor,
Ex. 20, is led into by a most charming phrase; and, always
prodigal in ideas as he is, a new *grandioso* phrase, in B
major, Ex. 21, follows, the exposition ending with the
repeated notes of Ex. 18. After the repeat of the G minor
section, Ex. 18, the flute tune, soon losing again all resemblance to the warbling of Dvořák's beloved pigeons,
becomes very vigorous indeed before giving place to the
repeated notes. These notes, now accompanied by a charming counter-melody, are eventually treated semi-fugally,
and then used as bass to the flute tune, just before the G
minor section, Ex. 18, is, for the last time, thundered out by
the full orchestra, the trumpets prominent, announcing the
recapitulation. This time the repeated notes and the phrase
used just before the second subject are omitted, and Ex. 19
is heard successively on English horn, clarinet, and flute.

This grand movement, one of Dvořák's best efforts, ends in a blaze of sound.

Second Movement. *Adagio.* This is the most original of all Dvořák's slow movements and may be looked upon as a little tone-poem of Czech village life. The touch of pathos in the opening bars, Ex. 22, which becomes pronounced later in the movement, is contrasted with the lovely bird-music (flute and oboe) that punctuates it, Ex. 23. The section ends with an exquisitely consolatory codetta on the G string of the violins. Then, in C major, follows the village-band music – cimbalon and all – which has caused at least one writer to blush, quite unnecessarily, for the composer. In order to return to the original mood of the movement Dvořák works in reverse, giving us the codetta, the bird-calls, and, last of all, the poignant phrases of the opening bars; but they are followed this time by a big climax derived from these latter phrases. The village band then takes charge again, though for a shorter time, and the closing bars, *delicato ed espressivo tranquillo,* rise to a sudden moment of drama which as quickly subsides, leaving the birds calling quietly in the garden.

Third Movement. *Allegro grazioso.* This simple movement, in G minor, is more of a dumka than a scherzo, and its first section is pleasantly melancholy. Flutes and clarinets begin the delightful waltz measures of the Trio, the coda, after the repetition of the opening section, being formed out of the same tune at about twice the speed. Brahms did the same thing in the third movement of his D major symphony.

Fourth Movement. *Allegro ma non troppo.* Trumpets announce the march tune that is to be the theme for the variations in this last movement, Ex. 24. Its opening notes are clearly derived from the flute tune of Ex. 19 in the first movement and the tune itself has, to English ears, something very Elgarian about it. The sequence of the variations is clear enough, but there are some subtleties, such as the variation for solo flute, with bassoon and trumpet outlining the theme below, and the variation in C minor begun by oboes and clarinets. At one point the trumpet calls make another appearance, and remind one that the movement closes noisily rather than impressively.

SYMPHONY NO. 9 IN E MINOR
(*From the New World, known as No.* 5)

DVOŘÁK's own words 'leave out all that nonsense about my having made use of original American National melodies', though less than the complete truth – because he obviously did include some tunes derived from the Negro music of which he spoke so highly – nevertheless expresses the correct view of this symphony. It is the work of a Czech composer, homesick for his own country, but observant of the country in which he is an exile, and full of the sympathy he felt for the oppressed coloured people. This symphony is 'genuine Bohemian music'.

First Movement. *Adagio – Allegro molto.* Darkness, light, and latent energy sum up the introduction to the first movement, 'cellos (violas and double-basses) contrasted with flutes (and oboes), then a sudden stab on the strings, responded to by wood-wind and horns. There follows the outline of the first part of the first theme (violas, 'cellos, horns), and a sudden outburst on the full orchestra which at once abates, leaving the violins quivering. The first theme, in the new quickened time (*allegro molto*) consists of two phrases, the one we have heard outlined (now on the horns) and a phrase in thirds (clarinets and bassoons) very characteristic of Czech folk music, Ex. 25. These two phrases, variously orchestrated, and in a succession of different keys, typifying the restless energy of the country in which Dvořák found himself, lead to a second theme (in G minor), which is certainly composed in the spirit of a Czech country dance, and delightfully scored for flute, with oboe and clarinet counter-tune, and a background of first violins holding a harmonic note and the second violins the same note, *tremolando*, an octave lower, Ex. 26. The drone-bass on the 'cellos which accompanies the second violins' playing of this tune, a little later, is of a kind associated with the dudelsack or bag-pipe. America, in fact, comes into the foreground only with the next tune, on the flute, which somewhat resembles *Swing Low Sweet Chariot*, Ex. 27. The development uses all this material in an obvious way, with the exception of the second tune, but the orchestration is so colourful that one hardly notices the comparative lack of spontaneity.

A nice touch, in the recapitulation, but one likely to escape the notice of many listeners, is the presentation of the second tune not in G minor, but in G sharp minor, half a tone higher. Both phrases of the first theme reach a big climax on the last page, but signify nothing much more than sound and fury.

Second Movement. *Largo*. Much more of the real Dvořák appears in this movement. A fine sequence of chords opens the movement, scored for low wood-wind (no flutes or oboes) and full brass, in E major (we have just heard a loud chord of E minor at the end of the preceding movement, and leads the music into the remote key of D flat major. Muted strings establish the background against which the English horn, silent in the symphony till now, sings the lovely tune which has made the fortune of the symphony, and, possibly, also of some wrong-headed person who arranged it as a Negro-spiritual to the words *Goin' home*. The words, however silly, do at least convey the real significance of this Czech tune, which is of a kind Dvořák had anticipated in his opera *The Jacobin*, a tune which expresses simply the home-sickness of a man who was never happy away from his family, home, and garden. It will be remembered that Dvořák used the opening bars of the introduction to the first movement of his G major Symphony twice in the course of the movement. In the present movement the chords of the opening bars punctuate the course of the tune once, high up on the wood-wind, the brass underlining the final chord, and are heard once more at the close. A single sustained horn note leads to a new tune for flute and oboe in C sharp minor: but as D flat is the same note and no further change occurs until the recapitulation of the opening tune it may be said that the whole movement is really in one key, a great contrast to the restless tonality of the preceding movement. The rapid notes for oboe, flute, and clarinet, which are one of Dvořák's

village-band effects, consist of a foreshortened version of the
cor anglais tune, Ex. 28, and the excitement they generate
ends with an eruption of the opening tune of the first movement on the trombones. It sounds as if Dvořák was reminding himself that he was in America, not Vysoka. This outburst intensifies the pathos of the return of the cor anglais
tune and its exquisite conclusion.

Third Movement. *Scherzo: Molto vivace*. Lively, humorous,
and rather interesting harmonically from the fact that the
chirrups of the flute, oboe, and clarinet are accompanied by
a reiterated chord on the strings, technically a discord, that
is never resolved. The downward-going chords for bassoons
and horns, two beats each, provide a nice touch of counter-
rhythm to the wood-wind, and later, much as in the Scherzo
of the D minor symphony (No. 2), positions are reversed.

The Trio in the major key (flute and oboe) merges without break into the repeat of the Scherzo, and, as in the slow
movement, there is again an eruption of Ex. 25*a* on the
horns.

Fourth Movement. *Allegro con fuoco*. This is the weakest
movement in all Dvořák's last five symphonies and makes
its way only by incessant repetition of its four-bar phrases.
A solo clarinet, with a background of strings tremolo, provides one moment of real beauty, Ex. 29, and there is a
naive charm in the 'three blind mice' phrases that soon
follow it. Sundry hints of phrases of the previous movements
rob the coda of its dubious novelty: which consists in the
appearance, as if taking a call, of the first tunes of the three
previous movements. But Dvořák has a surprise of real value
in store. After the playing, by the full orchestra, of the main
theme of this last movement, the brass ascends with the
opening theme of the first movement and the music suddenly
moves into an alien key, for a moment, hesitates between
two tonalities, and then settles down in E major, Ex. 30.
With that stroke of genius Dvořák bids the world of symphony farewell.

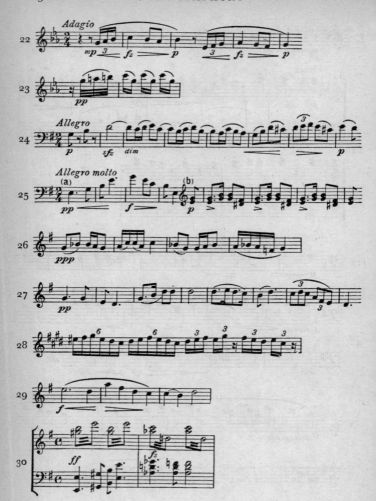

16

Gustav Mahler (1860-1911)

GEOFFREY SHARP

INTRODUCTION

MAHLER the operatic conductor is a familiar figure to everyone who has delved at all deeply into the history of music in performance. Mahler the song composer, if less familiar, is gradually finding his place in the repertoire through occasional performances of his masterpiece, *Das Lied von der Erde* (The Song of the Earth). Mahler the composer of symphonies is making less headway: like Beethoven and Bruckner he completed nine, which are very briefly summarized, with their dates, in the following table:

First Symphony (1888)
1. Adagio – comodo. 2. Con moto. 3. Moderato. 4. Tempestuoso.

Second Symphony (1894)
1. Allegro maestoso. 2. Andante moderato. 3. In ruhig fliessender Bewegung (Con moto comodo). 4. *Urlicht* ('First light') with contralto solo. 5. Scherzo, leading to *Aufersteh'n* (Thou willt rise again) for soprano, contralto, chorus and orchestra.

Third Symphony (1896)
Part I: 1. Vigoroso.
Part II: 2. Tempo di menuetto. 3. Comodo. 4. *O Mensch, gib Acht* (O Man, beware), contralto. 5. *Es sungen drei Engel* (Three angels sang), female chorus. 6. Adagio.

Fourth Symphony (1900)
1. Comodo. 2. Con moto comodo. 3. Poco adagio. 4. *Wir geniessen die himmlischen Freuden* (We taste heavenly joys), soprano.

Fifth Symphony (1902)
   Part I: 1. Marcia funebre. 2. Tempestuoso.
   Part II: 3. Scherzo. 4. Adagietto. 5. Rondo finale.

Sixth Symphony (1904)
   1. Allegro energico. 2. Scherzo. 3. Andante moderato.
4. Finale.

Seventh Symphony (1905)
   1. Adagio – Allegro con fuoco. 2. Allegro moderato. 3.
Mosso. 4. Andante amoroso. 5. Rondo finale.

Eighth Symphony (1907)
   Part I: Allegro impetuoso – *Veni Creator Spiritus*.
   Part II: Final scene from *Faust*. Poco adagio – Con moto –
Allegro. (Scored for very large orchestra with quintuple
wood-wind and other resources in proportion, also two
sopranos, two contraltos, tenor, baritone and bass, boys'
chorus and mixed double chorus.)

Ninth Symphony (1909)
   1. Andante comodo. 2. Tempo di Ländler. 3. Rondo
Burlesque – allegro assai. 4. Adagio.

Tenth Symphony (left incomplete)
   From the facsimile edition of the sketches the first movement and scherzo might possibly be performed. The rest is
too fragmentary, although a version of the Adagio, orchestrated by Ernst Křenek, has been broadcast by the B.B.C.

   You will have noticed that in the short descriptions of the
various movements I have used Italian and German terms
more or less indiscriminately. Mahler himself did likewise,
and I have used the precedent he established as my own
justification for employing Italian terms where possible as
being more readily understood by English readers. Titles
of the various vocal movements are given in German (with
an English translation in brackets) and in one case in Latin.
   None of these symphonies conform strictly to the classical

pattern, though the first, written when the composer was twenty-eight, manages to do so for three movements; even the finale is revolutionary only in the matter of its length.

The Second, Third, Fourth and Eighth symphonies all employ solo and/or choral voices which, in the first three cases, diffuse the clear outline and disrupt the homogeneity that a work must have in order to merit the term 'symphonic'. This is precisely why, in my opinion, Beethoven's *Choral* Symphony, after three magnificent movements, comes such a cropper at the end. Even Mahler, who excelled as a song-writer (as Beethoven did notably in *An die ferne Geliebte*), could not dovetail song into symphony without leaving scars and botches which become evident to the least tutored listener who is prepared to use his ears and remember what has gone before. Mahler's Eighth Symphony escapes this general condemnation because it is genuinely a choral symphony, not an instrumental work with a choral 'bit' tacked on for effect.

It is arguable that the vocal music in the Second Symphony forms the finest part of the work, a view which may be accepted without invalidating the criticism just made. In the first movement of the Third Mahler integrates the structure by using a short, trenchant melodic fragment as a kind of musical scaffolding – a remarkable example of a technique which was to mean much to Elgar a few years later. The final *Adagio* which follows the two vocal movements lifts the work to a higher plane.

The Eighth Symphony, called the *Symphony of a Thousand* on account of the enormous demands it makes in the way of personnel, is beyond the writer's powers to describe. It seems quite impossible to derive a really clear impression of the work from the score alone (though there may be some who claim to do this!) and I have yet to hear a satisfactory performance.

We come now to the remaining purely instrumental works, the Fifth, Sixth, Seventh and Tenth symphonies.

The Fifth, Sixth, and Seventh Symphonies may be considered together as they form a natural group; so do the first three, written within a period of eight years and preceding a four-year gap. This second trio of symphonies brings evidence of a change in the composer's technique. Mahler now tends to substitute combinations of similar rhythmic figures for the contrapuntal style which he may have felt he had been overworking; and yet, counterpoint is by no means to be neglected – it merely ceases to be so obviously the king-pin of the structure. The Sixth and Seventh symphonies, with their unusual harmony and strident crackling orchestration, cannot be described as being immediately attractive – they are in fact the last that we should recommend the newcomer to tackle – but the interest they have for us is increased by the great ingenuity of their scoring and orchestral layout.

The Fourth and Ninth symphonies we shall deal with in some detail in the following pages, while of the fragmentary Tenth nothing can be added to the brief details given in the foregoing table.

*

In these troubled times, when so many people speak first and think afterwards or not at all, it is the smart aleck with his snap judgement who catches the public ear and eye. Mention the word Mahler and pat comes the inevitable, irritating label, 'neo-classic', which the pert dilettante finds safe and clever because so few of us understand what it means any more than he does. Or, if he is keen enough on creating an impression to take a bigger risk, he may start to weave some verbal fantasy round the term 'Wagnerian symphonist', particularly if he is unfamiliar with Wagner's one and only early symphony. Another favourite description is 'iconoclast', which, with its obvious Greek derivation, looks suitably learned until we ask our intellectual spiv to specify the individual idols which Mahler broke.

Mahler's personality derives from too large a parcel of varied antecedents and psychological contradictions to be labelled with any clarity or point. As a composer he seldom knew where he was going, and neither can we; but it is worth while suggesting that the smaller the form in which he wrote the more convincing the result. Compare, for example,

Ich bin der Welt abhanden gekommen or the series of songs which together form *Das Lied von der Erde* (even the final 'Farewell' is not long, but only slow in time) with some of the garrulous and fragmentary pasticcios he calls upon to serve as movements of symphonies: the second movement of the Fourth Symphony and the third of the Ninth are good examples. The songs are conceived as wholes and written with an expert technique, while many of the orchestral pieces are merely expertly scored.

In view of his great experience as a conductor we shall be wise to expect Mahler's music to show a thorough knowledge of orchestration as practised by those composers whose works he was continually interpreting; but if his orchestration were nothing more than a watered synthesis of classical methods we should probably have little reason to regard him in any other light than that of a competent kapellmeister. From a purely technical standpoint, however, Mahler's music represents a considerable advance on anything written previously. This is not to suggest that 'orchestration' as such is the only really significant facet of his creative work, or even that it is the most important, and no one should close his mind on this subject without examining Mahler's re-orchestrations of the Schumann symphonies (which ought to be played and aren't) and of the Beethoven *Choral*. But it is reasonable to suppose that an artist who was primarily a conductor of genius would show such creative originality as he himself possessed above all in writing for that instrument on which he lavished such great care in his practical work.

An examination of Mahler's scores will show that this is true; they are full of minute instructions which give some clue to the profundity and exactitude of his recreative imagination, as well as containing countless examples of technical ingenuity unrivalled since Berlioz.

It is significant that the composers who have contributed most to the extension of the musical idiom and the development of musical resources as they apply to composition are precisely those whose sole aim was 'expression', of whom three of the most important are Monteverdi, Beethoven, and

Berlioz. All new directions and possibilities are invariably found to be due to such pioneers; they are never the result of tonal empiricism – the mere wanton juggling with sound for sound's own sake; an axiom first stated, as far as I know, by Cecil Gray in *The Sackbut* nearly thirty years ago.

Mahler's aim undoubtedly was 'expression', but it is doubtful whether what he wanted to express was always worth the trouble he took over it.

There remain two criticisms of Mahler's music which cannot be dismissed lightly: those two corner-stones of contemporary disparagement – pseudo-naïveté and banality. But let us have them in basic English so that we know what we are talking about: childishness (which Mahler, like some of his critics, confused with naïveté), and vulgarity or triteness. Neither charge can be refuted. Mahler's attempts to come to terms with the realms of childlike fantasy were always childishly inadequate and there is no doubt at all that he was often vulgar.

Let us try to see his personality as it were in a nutshell. Morbid childhood: mixed religious background: fanatical enthusiasm for music and boundless energy in his pursuit of it; all this fused into a barely stable amalgam by the innate complexity of the Jewish tradition. No wonder Mahler's music alternately fascinates and appals, with its peculiar kaleidoscopic confusion of the ridiculous and the sublime, often on the same page.

But, to return to our main argument, we must, I think, admit that childish platitude and vulgarity do not justify vast pains being taken in their expression, either individually or, horror of horrors, both together.

In some respects Mahler the composer is in the direct line of descent from Schubert through Schumann, Berlioz, and Bruckner. That his music has not the intrinsic value of theirs can be deduced from the foregoing argument; but he will have, and indeed is having his reward. Mahler's is very much the role of the catalyst in a chemical reaction. So many composers have had and are having their creative processes stimulated by the pioneering efforts which Mahler made, all unwittingly, on their behalf. Berg, van Dieren,

Sibelius, and Walton are four obvious examples, while Britten and Shostakovich are also apparently conscious of the Mahlerian influence, without having realized how easy it is to ape mannerisms and how little it signifies.

Mahler's greatest achievement has been the substantial enrichment of the musical idiom, and he holds a position similar to that of Berlioz as a pioneer of orchestral means of expression, without, however, rivalling the Frenchman in the matter of pungent musical invention – but who could?

Even so, his music is well worth investigating, as we hope to show in the following analyses of the Fourth and Ninth symphonies.

SYMPHONY NO. 4 IN G

IN England Mahler's Fourth Symphony is played less rarely than the others. I was about to suggest as the reason for this the fact that it is scored for small orchestra; but it is not. For the absence of trombones is more than offset by the extravagant demands for flutes, oboes, clarinets, and bassoons together with Mahler's beloved array of kitchen utensils to be beaten, banged and otherwise encouraged into articulate speech at moments of climax.

Tovey calls the work a pastoral symphony and describes the opening as 'farmyard noises' – obviously a poultry farm. But the farmyard is soon overawed by Ex. 1 (a), the most important melodic figure in the movement, and its more rhetorical 'coda', Ex. 1 (b), pounded out by the basses. Among the profusion of fragments that might be quoted, Ex. 2 has a double claim in the ingenuity of its counterpoint and also the fact that it leads to the dominant and the second subject proper, Ex. 3, whose all too obvious simplicity is really less unsubtle than it looks. The farmyard returns and again ushers in Ex. 1, whereupon the movement conforms (if this is the word) to that standby pattern of late romantic composers – the free rondo. A theme which I do not quote precedes a further visit to the poultry farm, then follows Ex. 3 in A major, ultimately sideslipping into E flat minor. Some pseudo-development leads to C major

with the top line of Ex. 2 much in evidence. Ex. 1 (a) returns, sufficiently sure of its effect not to need to begin at the
beginning. Not to be outdone, Ex. 2 and Ex. 3 follow, the
latter with some emphasis and Mahler's own special brand
of rich full tone. The farmyard serves its final purpose in
this movement by introducing the coda in which Ex. 1 and
Ex. 2 share the last word.

The second movement, scherzo, is also a free rondo: not
particularly similar to the first, but not sufficiently contrasted. This is one of Mahler's most conspicuous faults, which
we shall encounter again in the middle movements of the
Ninth Symphony. After an introduction, which I do not
quote, a solo violin, tuned up a half-tone, insists on C minor
in a tawdry, aggressive and thoroughly common tune, Ex. 4.
Mahler's instruction is 'Wie eine Fidel', suggesting the
coarse, wiry, piercing tone of the street musician: this must
be the only symphonic theme fit for such to play. Two
episodes intervene before the return of our common tune,
after which all three themes have an extensive outing in C
major. This is followed by an extensive coda.

The third movement, of which we quote the first nine
bars in Ex. 5, is a set of free variations, very free. There is
no rigid constant feature, but the nearest approach is to be
found, naturally, in the bass over which Mahler's melodic
and contrapuntal fantasies weave seemingly endless patterns. Together with the first movement this forms the hard
core of a very unequal work. Tovey, not altogether relevantly, compares the middle movement of Sibelius's Fifth
Symphony: the context is entirely different, as are the
respective composers' mental climates. After 61 bars, at
Viel langsamer, Mahler turns to E minor where an oboe
meditates pensively over a diminished version of the bass:
other instruments develop the idea with some vigour on
the way back to the tonic key. An increase of speed con-
fuses the two versions of the bass and the counterpoint
becomes more involved. The oboe theme comes back in
G minor and moves to C sharp minor, where it negotiates
a stirring climax leading to a series of four new variations,
after which the coda takes fire, surprisingly, in E major,

but the last words are spoken in G major and its dominant.

The finale consists of a setting for solo soprano and orchestra of a naive poem taken from *Des Knaben Wunder-horn*. It is quite short. The precocious small child's raptures over the joys of a tinsel and gingerbread heaven certainly take more stomaching in 1949 than they did nearly fifty years ago! Even then Mahler himself found it necessary to warn the singer to avoid any suspicion of parody! At one point the farmyard returns from the first movement and the music turns into E major towards the end, as the slow movement had done.

In view of what we have already said to the effect that the indiscriminate juxtaposition of symphony and song within one work is an artistic mistake, this seems a good opportunity to try to explain why Mahler so often intro-duced just this. We have written that Mahler's aim un-doubtedly was 'expression'. In addition, he found the old classical symphonic form overburdened with new develop-ments, embellishments, and extravagances of all kinds – a true case of too much strong new wine all but bursting the old wine-skin of previously-accepted symphonic form. Mah-ler, keener on 'expression' than on 'form', had no com-punction over adding voices and finally bursting the skin; though it seems that in his last symphony, now to be dis-cussed, he finally recognized the unsuitability of the human voice as a protagonist in symphonic music.

SYMPHONY NO. 9 IN D MAJOR

WHEREAS the Fourth Symphony can with justice be called a hotch-potch of ideas not always fully digested by the composer, the Ninth can readily be cleared of any such implication. In England Mahler's First Symphony, with its elaborate finale, is usually said to be out of proportion; now, although this criticism is not entirely undeserved, it is most unfortunate, in that it avoids the main problem of the late Romantic symphony by pretending that it does not exist. During the latter half of the last century the symphony showed a growing tendency to reserve the full force of its argument for the finale, in contrast to the classical principle by which the audience were encouraged to pay most attention to the first movement.

Mahler's First Symphony is a child of its time, not without its own attractions and interesting also as a fore-runner of the Ninth. But if the Fourth is neo-classical in the sense of pouring too much new wine into an old bottle already overstretched, Mahler's Ninth is classical neither in form nor in spirit.

For in this work Mahler reaches his own personal apotheosis in the realm of autobiography. While, as we have said, Mahler's symphonic music lacks the sheer artistry of his song-writing, this Ninth Symphony, even though it runs for seventy-five minutes, bears witness to a fining down of the composer's mental processes late in life. Here we have a warmth of harmony, and not only in the finale, which, for example, contrasts emphatically with the sour fiddling we have already described in the second movement of the Fourth.

In this last movement Mahler aspires to the summit achieved by Bruckner in the slow movement of *his* Ninth Symphony, and, incidentally, shows us, far better than mere words, why he could not achieve it.

In spite of his striving after naturalness of expression, Mahler's orchestration (he requires quadruple wood-wind and a full complement of brass and percussion), with its individual use of the E flat clarinet and double bassoon (to mention only two of his more peculiar soloists!), is far more worldly and more obviously 'calculated' than Bruck-ner's. Not that Bruckner's orchestral technique is crude or ineffective: this is merely an English superstition. But Bruckner achieved greatness as a simple soul who never tried to hide his inmost thoughts behind the curtain of sophistication – he almost certainly never knew it existed – while Mahler spent most of his composing hours behind that curtain which he so earnestly and evidently tried to penetrate. But we have no space to digress.

No comment, however brief, on Mahler's orchestration can evade drawing attention to his masterly use of the horn,

which he understood more thoroughly than any other
composer apart from Richard Strauss, and his development
of Bruckner's fanfare style of trumpet writing.

Now to examine the structure of the first movement.
This is the outstanding example of a new form created by
Mahler, and in it he almost, but not quite, subjugates his
life-long weakness for discursive digressions: no mean accomplishment in a movement lasting half an hour.

There are three main sections, the first and last employing
the same material, followed by a short ornamental cadenza
and coda. Here is a diagram with page references to the
full score (Universal Edition: Boosey & Hawkes):

A	B	A	*Cadenza*	*Coda*
Main	Interludes	Main		
Orchestral	and songlike	Orchestral		
Section	Material	Section		
	alternated			
Page 1	Page 18	Page 51	Page 56	Page 58

In the first five bars we encounter a rhythmic sequence, a
harmonic sequence reminiscent of *Das Lied von der Erde* and
an introductory thematic fragment. What we may describe
as the main theme begins in the sixth bar, a theme which
the violins continue as shown in Ex. 6. A modulation into
D minor introduces the theme we quote as Ex. 7 which,
with trumpets added, soon becomes Ex. 8. Another half-
dozen new or derivative excerpts could be quoted before
we reach our middle section, but space does not permit
such lavish use of examples and the reader must make his
own way through the score as far as page 18.

Now we have three interludes and two songlike episodes.

(1) The first interlude employs both the rhythmic and
    harmonic sequence with which the movement opened
    and also Ex. 8.

(2) The first song episode begins on page 22 with the main
    theme (from bar 6 above) on the horn. Then Ex. 7
    and Ex. 8 are heard up to page 26.

(3) The second interlude, beginning on page 36, is a mere
    two pages contrived from Ex. 7 and Ex. 8 in com-
    bination.
(4) The second song episode begins in D major with a
    decorated form of Ex. 6 played by two solo violins.
(5) The third interlude (p. 48-51) is funereal in character
    and leads back to a shortened form of the main
    orchestral section.

All but one of the chief melodies re-appear before Ex. 7
and Ex. 8, again in combination, introduce the cadenza
from which we quote the oboe and solo violin figures,
Ex. 9 (*a*) and (*b*), as being especially noteworthy. A dominant trill introduces the coda with Ex. 7, after which follow
a remarkable horn figure, Ex. 10 (*a*), and a conspicuous
and effective flute solo before the solo violin clinches the
argument, Ex. 10 (*b*).

The second movement is an enormous and often grotesque mixture of Ländler, or Schubertian country-dance,
and Scherzo. There are four sections: I. Three dances;
II. Repetition of second and third dances; III. Development of first and second dances; IV. Return to the beginning and coda. The two fragments of Ex. 11 (*a*) and (*b*)
introduce the main theme, Ex. 12, and the three form a
group often to be used in double counterpoint. The second
dance is a waltz in E major in rondo form: the theme,
Ex. 13 (page 66 of the score) is derived partially from
Ex. 11 (*b*). There are two episodes and a subsidiary theme
which we do not quote. Towards the end (page 71) Ex.
11 (*a*) and (*b*) re-appear in combination. Then the first
episode leads vigorously into the third dance which we
quote in Ex. 14, which twice appears in counterpoint with
Ex. 12. The main feature of section II is a set of six variations on Ex. 13. Then Ex. 14 ushers in the third dance
(page 85). Section III develops the first dance (page 87)
and later we have four variations on Ex. 13 leading to
Ex. 14. Section IV consists of combined fragments of all
three dances leading to an exceptionally beautiful coda of
reminiscence.

Mahler called the third movement *Rondo Burlesque*. You

may feel that as with the first two movements of the Fourth Symphony the composer has here shown an insufficient sense of contrast between consecutive movements of a large-scale orchestral work. Fundamentally this is the only 'difficult' movement of the four, but the obscurities begin to clarify once the relationship between these last two movements is understood. Here, for the last time, Mahler appears as Bombastes Furioso, caustic, cynical, ironic, intolerant and dictatorial, as he has been throughout his active career. Within the two movements he turns to resignation and passive acquiescence in his lot: that this should be accomplished with touching pathos is the major marvel of his Ninth Symphony. Let us delve a little deeper and see how it is done.

After three preliminary motives the principal subject of the rondo appears (page 102). Then follows an interlude (page 108), then a variation on the principal subject (page 110). Next we have a theme for horns (page 111), which will re-appear in the finale, followed by a second interlude. Mahler quotes his own earlier works in this rehash of a turbulent life of music-making, and, after a reference to the Pan theme of the first movement of his Third Symphony (page 129), a theme arrives which we have to quote, Ex. 15, for the important role it is to play in the finale. At page 134 a complete change of expression prepares us for the sombre finale and Ex. 16 is protracted with great feeling. Ex. 15 and Ex. 16 (pages 141-7) foreshadow a kind of recapitulation. The horn figure from page 111 returns, as does Ex. 15 (page 153). Then follows a coda in the form of a march and a stretto (page 162). After another march episode the movement is rounded off as it began.

This very brief description is deliberately devoted to those elements in the structure which are to influence the course of the finale. There are many other important features of the movement which will become apparent with a study of the score, but we have space for only the outstanding landmarks.

Mahler cast his final *Adagio* in rondo form. We are given a series of repetitions of the main theme interrupted by

short episodic fragments. The melody, Ex. 17, is derived
from Ex. 15 and Ex. 16, and it in turn gives rise to two
continuations which we show in Ex. 18 and Ex. 19. The
horn theme also returns from page 111. The main melody
returns on page 169 and again in variation form on page
171. A short episodic section leads to a reminiscence of the
finale of *Das Lied von der Erde* (page 173). There follows a
free fantasia beginning with Ex. 19, after which Ex. 17
makes two further appearances (pp. 177-9). A coda based
on Ex. 18 and Ex. 19 brings the movement to an end in a
mood similar to that of the first movement.

A passing reference to *Abide with Me* (page 177) fails to
cloy the rarified beauty of the closing pages, which are
paralleled, in the writer's experience, only by the final
section of the *Adagio* of Bruckner's Ninth Symphony; there
is sheer artistic mastery about the quiet, halting, broken
phrases with which each of these great composers bids us
farewell. At the last nothing grandiose or rhetorical remains,
but simply music distilled from widely-ranging experience.

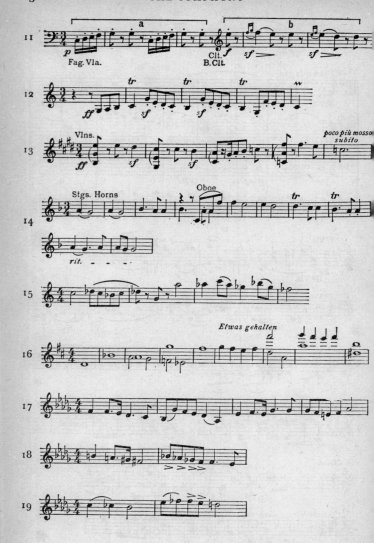

17

Edward Elgar (1857-1934)

F. BONAVIA

INTRODUCTION

A FOREIGN musician who professed to admire Elgar's music as a whole expressed the opinion that Elgar's symphonies were pleasant and interesting enough – but 'unsymphonic'. If it is possible to write a satisfactory symphony and yet be unsymphonic then the famous lines, 'Why has not man a microscopic eye? For this plain reason – man is not a fly', represent perfect reasoning.

It is possible that what the critic meant by that sweeping (and damning) statement was that Elgar's symphonies were unlike other people's symphonies – which is perfectly and, indeed, obviously true. But the same may be said of all other symphonic composers. Beethoven's are unlike Mozart's and belong not to the eighteenth but to the nineteenth century. Elgar's symphonies conform in every respect to the general conception of what a symphony in four movements should be, but the idiom is that of the early twentieth and not the early nineteenth century.

The first requisite of a symphony is that the material should be varied enough to capture and hold the interest of the listener throughout its four movements. If the composer complies with this condition the style becomes a secondary consideration; as a French critic said of other things: 'every style is permissible except a style that is boring and wearisome'. No exception can be taken in this respect to Elgar's symphonies; there was no intention to accuse the symphonies of lacking interest. But Elgar secures variety by means that differ from those of Beethoven or Brahms as much as their means differed from those of their predecessors. The eighteenth century found all the variety

it needed in contrasting two themes and in key-relation.
The dynamic genius of Beethoven was compelled to alter
materially the form they had evolved; Elgar had to go
further.

Theorists still point out the first and second subject in
all Beethoven's first movements. It is not to be denied that
Beethoven adheres in the main to the classical sonata-form,
but it is also undeniable that you have to look very closely
to discover the second subject of some Beethoven symphonies. When we speak of two subjects or themes we
naturally assume a certain degree of equality between
them. Now already in the *Eroica Symphony* (1804) the second
subject has nothing like the importance of the first. After
remarking on its beauty Sir George Grove has to admit that
'strangely little use is made of this beautiful passage in the
working-out. In fact ... it only re-appears in the due course
of the reprise.' What had happened? Simply this, that
Beethoven had so much to say, had so much new light to
throw on his main subject that he no longer needed to
elaborate the subsidiary one. It is the same with the C
minor symphony where the second subject appears in asso-
ciation with the first or with a rhythmic design derived
directly from the first. Brahms did not, Elgar could not
ignore that example.

As for the spirit which these great symphonies embody,
it is – nor could it be – other than the spirit of their time.
It may be rather fanciful to imagine Beethoven exalting
the French revolution in the finale of the C minor. It
would be even more fanciful to imagine him completely
unaffected by the passionate poems of Korner, by the
idealism of the German poets of the day. The choice of the
Ode to Joy, the prisoners' chorus of *Fidelio* show how deeply
he felt about liberty. That spirit was not that of Elgar's
day, nor was it Mozart's, and it would be absurd to
expect to find it in the work of either predecessor or
successor.

The dramatic element in Mozart expresses the individual;
in Beethoven the mass. In Elgar it is again the man who
expresses himself, but it is a man who is in touch with the

mass of his countrymen as Mozart never was, a man who could enter into other men's lives and desires nothing so much as to do something that men can take to their hearts.

The discussion of Elgar's music is also vitiated and embroiled by the composer's technique, which is now presumed to be 'old-fashioned'. Much has happened since Elgar was writing symphonies, but do we not attach too much importance to technique, and does it really matter whether technique is of to-day or of yesterday? The general public does not recognise the existence of such a problem, since apparently it enjoys an evening of Bach even more than an evening of Schönberg. Elgar's technique may be that of a period that has gone, but it does admirably fulfil its purpose in presenting the composer's thought clearly and effectively. It is not by any means the technique of a reactionary, neither is it the technique of a revolutionary. It does not ignore the fact that Wagner mobilized chromaticism, but it differs from Wagner's in other respects. It is the technique of a scrupulous and painstaking artist who accepts the gain and the loss of the system he has made his own, a system which rejects to some extent the stability of tonality and close key-relation for the greater range and variety offered by new and more elaborate innovations. Technique is with him the servant and not, as with some moderns, the master; the true and great originality of Elgar is not in his technique, but in his thought and his emotion – which is not little considering that when he began to write most of his contemporaries were wont to 'tristanise', or, even worse, to follow the method of Wagner's rival, Brahms. The theme in Elgar, as in Wagner, is often brief and poignant (both could and did write extended melodies which are not less characteristic), its eloquence being enhanced by the accompanying harmony or counterpoint with which it forms a compact whole. It is possible to analyse an Elgar symphony in respect of form and in detail as regards key-relation, but both the form and the key-relation are so much richer and more complex than in the classical symphony that the result will hardly repay the labour it implies. It is more profitable to enquire how the spirit, the essence of the music differs from that of others, and whether the accusation of being 'unsymphonic' is justified.

The individual nature of Elgar's idiom is acknowledged. The *Enigma Variations* were written when Brahms's *St Anthony Variations* were at the height of their popularity but no one has found in them a single trace of Brahmsian influence. Is there any reason why Elgar's new and admittedly attractive idiom should be unfit for the symphony? Is there not an immense variety in the idiom of the accepted symphonic composers? In Beethoven alone the type changes with each symphony. The character of the *Pastoral* is as different from the character of the Fifth as that of the Eighth differs from that of the Ninth, and one may well ask where the link is between the intimate style of Schumann and the sentimental, spectacular symphony of Tchaikovsky. A symphony is a little world in which passions clash or mingle as they do in drama. Tragedy and comedy are equally within its bounds, and the real test is not whether the material is of any one kind rather than of another, but whether it arouses and holds our interest, whether its eloquence is such as to make the listener share the thought and the emotion expressed by the composer.

There can be little doubt as to the way in which Elgar answers that test. Like most great composers he has been accused of many failings. At one time he was accused of making a show of piety; he was also accused of being commonplace – he has never been accused of being dull. There is plenty of interest and much adventure in everything he has written. All that is asked of the listener is that his mind shall be swept clear of prejudice. If you insist that every symphony must be heroic or romantic or pastoral then the Elgar symphonies will not satisfy you; if you demand strict compliance with any set of rules then again disappointment must follow. Rules have their uses; but let us not forget what has been said of the tragedies of M. d'Aubignac: 'I am glad M. d'Aubignac followed so well the rules of Aristotle,' wrote an eminent critic, 'but I am sorry the rules of Aristotle permitted M. d'Aubignac to write such an execrable tragedy.' Imagination, not pedantry, is needed to write a true symphony, and imagination is the special gift of the individual, and not common to all men. Elgar is neither epic, as Beethoven often is, nor flamboyant and erotic as Tchaikovsky invariably is, but himself, an artist who has his own message to deliver and his own way of doing it: there is the measure of his greatness.

That those who are new to his art should have some difficulty in getting to the heart of it is perhaps natural. He is the first symphonist to speak with an English voice, and there is no tradition behind him – at least no symphonic tradition – to smooth the way for the stranger. He avoids the most common sources of musical inspiration. He has left no tale of happy or unhappy lovers; he has written no amorous ditty. He has, on the other hand, given much thought to grave subjects – nature, death, the poetry of his native land – all subjects which elevate the mind; he delighted in the society of his fellow-men as in their activities.

Keats says somewhere that ''tis the eternal law That first in beauty shall be first in might,' a saying which neither the poet nor his commentators have explained satisfactorily. Taken literally it is, to say the least, obscure. But if by beauty is meant gentleness of mind, and if we can substitute force or generosity for might, we have there the two poles within which the symphonic composer lives and breathes. The gentleness that comes of strength is as characteristic of the art of Elgar as the violence that comes of a weak temperament is characteristic of Tchaikovsky. Both force and gentleness have their special moment in Elgar and play their part in the symphonies, as in everything that came from his pen.

These qualities also characterize works in which, being wedded to words, they are even more easily identified. The impulse, the desire to compose, however, does not need the stimulus of poetry to be set going. Thousands have read the *Faerie Queene* but only one man realized in reading it that he, too, had the poetic genius. Millions of men have seen a 'host of daffodils', but only Wordsworth made out of the experience charming poetry. As with the poets, so with the musicians. All creative artists know that 'fine sounds are floating wild about the earth', as Elgar himself explained to the well-meaning but foolish individual who asked him where he found the source of his music. Music and poetry are everywhere, though it is given to only a few to declare their power.

To give a detailed analysis of Elgar's symphonies is beyond the scope of the present chapter and would take us far beyond its limits. It is also permissible to question whether readers gain by the method, or by learning that, having once read in a textbook that a certain modulation was bad and unendurable, Elgar proceeded to prove it good and endurable in his symphony. It is not thus that great works are written. The process, moreover, might lead us into debatable questions of technique, for, although technicians are firm believers in the infallibility of their system, they do not all believe in the same system. It may be more profitable to consider a few characteristics as they occur in each symphony.

SYMPHONY NO. I IN A FLAT

THE form of the First Symphony is more unconventional than that of the No. 2 in E flat. Like Berlioz's *Fantastic Symphony*, it has a motto which is, however, much longer and more pregnant than that of the French work. It is stated and re-stated in a prologue or introduction (*Andante, nobilmente e semplice*) some fifty bars in length. It is quite simple, Ex. 1. Its progress is so smooth and so securely bound to the key of A flat that in the whole introduction one finds but one accidental hinting at modulation, a D natural, which in the very next bar becomes D flat again. It is otherwise with the main subject of the Allegro, Ex. 2. The change of key (from A flat to D minor) is abrupt and, although the only key consistent with the whole subject is

D minor, there are accidentals in every bar, both the tonic and dominant chords being neatly avoided. The days when the main subject was in the tonic and, after mild flirtation with related tonalities, a dash was made for the dominant have been left a very long way behind. To note all the harmonic changes in any one of Elgar's movements may profit the student as much as and even more than a text book. It does not help the average listener, since its practical value has declined. To ascertain how by respectable modulation one may pass from one key to another is not particularly illuminating, since all keys are permitted and all transitions allowed. Dissonance is not prepared now and resolved and other means are used to secure the reasonable, logical development of the musical idea such as rhythm, stress, and design which link up periods and episodes.

In the opening *Allegro* Elgar changes the time from 2–2 to 6–4, but there is no abrupt interruption in the design. Before reaching the 6–4 episode the melodic line which consisted of four stresses giving a new note or chord for each beat becomes a mixture, Ex. 3, where the four-stresses bars alternate with bars where notes change only on the first, second, and fourth beat – three stresses – and prepare the listener for the 6–4 which now will seem unexpected, as all original work must be, but none the less logical and inevitable. After a dozen bars we come to Ex. 4, which sounds new and is, in mood, quite different from anything that came before. But a glance suffices to show that it is closely related to the fifth bar of the allegro, while the bass reproduces some of the characteristics of the first bar.

The process could be continued to the end of the symphony, showing how closely knit the texture is. This ability to write long, contrasted yet connected periods is as much part of the equipment of the true symphonic composer as the invention of striking subjects and harmonies. Had the instinct been wanting in Elgar there might have been some grounds for talking about the 'unsymphonic' symphonies.

The return to the 2–2 time is similarly prepared by a design of four even notes in the preceding 6–4 section. New ideas are grafted on to the old as, for instance, at Ex. 5, where lower harmonies hint at the melody of the opening *Andante*, while chords struck on the weak beats of the bar repeat the device used when the main theme is repeated after a bridge passage in the exposition.

Extremely happy is the change shown in Ex. 6. Those chords unsupported by the bass give the impression of a garland magically suspended in the air. These and other elements, with a return of the motto theme, make up the material of a logical and completely satisfactory symphonic movement.

The second movement, an impetuous *Allegro molto* in F sharp minor, adheres to the usual scherzo form, and for all its excitement it has more of the scherzo spirit than some similar movements of Beethoven. Scherzo means jest, and the scherzo of the Ninth Symphony could be a jest only to titans and cyclops. In form Elgar's is straightforward, but in the concluding episode the semiquavers of the main theme are presented in augmentation as crotchets paving the way for an experiment which, perfectly successful with Elgar is not to be commended to less gifted artists. The scherzo melts away into the *Adagio* and its very beautiful melody is made up of the same notes which opened the scherzo. The time values are different; the emotions they express are worlds apart, Ex. 7. So great is the contrast that no one who hears the symphony for the first or the second time is likely to discover the connection between that very tender melody and the fiery, chaotic *perpetuum mobile* of the scherzo. We do not know whether the scherzo was written before the *adagio* or vice versa. Elgar returned no answer when questioned about it. It seems probable that the *adagio* came first, since it is easier to turn a well-conceived period into chaos than to evolve order out of chaos.

Other salient features of this lovely movement are a phrase that has all the freedom of an improvisation while being neatly welded to the whole and a combination of two fine melodies, Ex. 8.

The last movement opens with an Introduction in D minor (*Lento*) and it is only after three-fourths of the

movement have gone that we are taken back to the tonic
key of the first movement, A flat. During the Introduction the
motto is noted again with another theme which plays a
very important part in the development and may be a
distant – a very distant – relation of the descending notes
of the motto, Ex. 9. It will not do, however, to attach much
importance to superficial resemblances. It was pointed out
to Elgar that the concluding phrase of the *Enigma Variations*
bore a very striking resemblance to the four notes in the
motto of the First Symphony. Elgar replied that he had
never been aware of it. Notes used are of little importance
in comparison with the use that is made of them. The last
movement (*Allegro*), once begun, is like a mighty surge
forward to lead, after more adventures, to the final statement of the motto now embellished and enriched with every
device of the art of orchestration.

SYMPHONY NO. 2 IN E FLAT

THE Second Symphony was begun during the lifetime of
King Edward VII and was meant early in 1910 to be a
loyal tribute. But the King died in May of that year and
it is dedicated 'to the memory of His late Majesty, The
King'. The composer was then faced with a very unusual
problem. Most, if not all, symphonies have a character of
their own. The *Eroica* is 'heroic' in every movement, just
as the *Pastoral* is pastoral in every one of its parts. The
variety and contrast between movements is still consistent,
with a central idea more or less common to all. There is in
this no question of a programme, but of the star which
happens to be in the ascendant when the symphony is
conceived. But a symphony inspired by the glories of a
peaceful and prosperous reign was no longer consistent with
a symphony dedicated to the king's memory.

Elgar's success in solving the difficulty – the symphony is
perfectly homogeneous – gives us an insight into his mind.
The solution is satisfactory not because of some possible
juggling with the material but because this composer could
rise above personal feeling and impression. There is no

apparent inconsistency because in the description of loyalty and sorrow the artist's emotion, however deep, is not allowed to cloud reason. He does not deal lightly with the subject; he does not assert that we all owe God a death; but treats it as one would who sees a purpose in all things. We have only to compare it with Tchaikovsky's *Trio in memory of a great artist* to see the difference in the attitude of two composers. Except for a brief flirtation with a frivolous mazurka Tchaikovsky sees a world plunged in gloom. Elgar, on the other hand, however deep his sorrow at the death of a king whose kindness he had experienced, takes a much broader view. His grief is relieved by thoughts of a well-spent life and of a peaceful reign, and is no further removed from a feeling of national pride in achievement than Milton's *Il Penseroso* is from *l'Allegro*. There is hence no inconsistency in joining the parts that were written before to those that were written after the king's death.

The expression of sorrow culminates in the noble threnody that constitutes the third movement; but it only tinges slightly the remainder. The first subject (*Allegro vivace e nobilmente*) is, accordingly, confident and free from any hint of mourning. Its tonality is perfectly clear, Ex. 10. Extension and development of the design of the third bar leads to Ex. 11. The next subject to be introduced, Ex. 12, is important for two reasons.

It is described by Tovey as 'an iridescent mixture of several keys', and W.H. Reed defines the harmony as changing twice in every bar. The harmony is quite clear; the passage wavers between major and minor but the changes would satisfy the most pedantic of harmony teachers. All that happens is that Elgar avoids the dominant chord – a procedure common enough – and strikes instead the dominant of the dominant, thus avoiding the obvious.

Reed goes on to explain that the harmonic changes are necessary: the regularity of the rhythm and dynamic marks might otherwise create an impression of monotony. In spite of the restless harmony the passage is monotonous in performance if the interpreter puts his trust in dynamic marks and overlooks the natural trend of a phrase that rises and falls in so unmistakable a way that the composer did not think it worth while to call attention to it.

A third theme, Ex. 13, completes the most important material of the first movement. An unusual feature of the symphony is the change that occurs in the first and third movements, when suddenly the atmosphere seems to darken as if a bank of lowering clouds had blotted the sun out of the sky, Ex. 14. One wonders whether these two episodes formed part of the original composition or whether they were added after the death of the king; the effect is dramatic, but fully consistent with the general character of the symphony, which is grave rather than sad.

A fine dignity tempers the grey tones of the elegy (Larghetto) which forms the second movement. Some consider it 'the highest peak' attained by Elgar. It certainly expresses with fine artistry a feeling of national rather than individual mourning.

The Third Movement is a Scherzo-Rondo (*Presto*), the lightest, most graceful, and fanciful scherzo imaginable, Ex. 15. When the darkening occurs here, leading to a climax of terrific force, its effect is to scatter the elements of the first theme, which seem to go scampering like a covey of frightened birds. The movement includes a fine example of Elgarian sequences when, by a change of colour, a phrase that at first appeared as proud and masterful is turned into meek pleading. With the Fourth Movement (*Moderato e maestoso*) we return to lofty dignity, its opening subject moving with the inevitability and evenness of an ocean tide, Ex. 16.

The end is peace. The concluding coda is one of the finest things in modern music – extremely moving and extremely stately. We would have to look far to match either this part with its masterly grafting of other themes, including the main subject of the first movement, or the brilliance of the scherzo.

Unusual these symphonies may be; 'unsymphonic' they are not. Both have a unity, literal and spiritual, that is as evident and logical as any unity imposed from without. They express the thought and emotion of a musician who does not parade independence but will not let any consideration stand in the way of 'truth' – the accurate presentation of his fancies and his imaginings as he conceived them.

The learned author of the Grammar of Assent has described how passages which the schoolboy learns by heart and which seem to him purely rhetorical will later, with experience of life, reveal a new meaning and 'pierce' him. Those who have known Elgar's music for some time may have had a similar experience, for it stands the test of time uncommonly well.

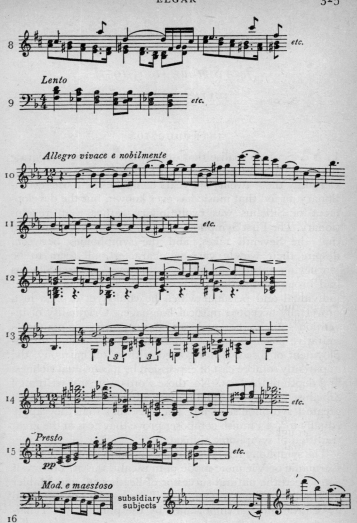

18

Jean Sibelius (1865-1957)

JULIAN HERBAGE

INTRODUCTION

It is difficult to realise that only twenty-six years separate the production of Sibelius' First and Seventh Symphonies. Certainly those twenty-six years comprise the most revolutionary period that music has ever known, but the development of Sibelius was evolutionary rather than revolutionary. The First Symphony already indicates the direction that the Seventh takes, and the symphonies between, despite their widely varying characters, all seem to be journeying towards the same goal. From the outset Sibelius had brought something new to the symphony, something individual and personal which he could yet express in a universally accepted musical language. 'Originality of invention – uncommon passages – a very energetic manner – imitative passages almost innumerable – the frequent employment of discords unresolved with a full harmony, the apparently sombre cast of expression by a continual richness and depth of the bass.' No, those words were not written of Sibelius, but by a contemporary of Beethoven about the greatest symphonist of all. The very fact that they apply equally to the Finnish composer prove that he is in the great tradition of symphonic thinkers.

The symphony has often been claimed to be an essentially Germanic or Viennese mode of musical thought. Brahms is considered the natural successor of Beethoven, and Mahler of Schubert. The symphonies of Tchaikovsky are dismissed as of little musical importance by the pundits, yet Tchaikovsky proved, after a hundred years of virtual monopoly, that the symphony was not an essentially Germanic or even Western European form of musical expression. In his colossal climaxes, often built up through the simple expedient of repetition, Tchaikovsky shows himself master of a new, dynamic and vital mode of symphonic thought. His symphonies have the essential quality of being an experience. They return to Beethoven's description which he used when writing of the *Pastoral Symphony* as 'more an expression of feeling than of painting'. They develop through inherent growth.

Sibelius was attracted towards the Slavonic school represented by Tchaikovsky, rather than the German post-romantics. The Finns are a branch of the Ugrian race, which, before their migration northwards, inhabited the banks of the Volga. When Western Europe looked towards Rome as a cultural and religious centre, the East looked towards Byzantium. It is natural, then, that Sibelius should have little in common, except superficially, with the civilized urbanity of the modern Latin peoples, and it is significant that his early reading was classical and mainly Hellenic. The clear thought and simple directness of expression of the classical Greek authors had much affinity with his own Finnish legends and sagas. Like the Greeks of antiquity, his closest companion was Nature. It was Nature and the forces of Nature which had shaped the poetry of Finland, with its forests, lakes, and the surrounding sea. Throughout the music of Sibelius one is conscious of this direct contact between Man and Nature. There is an elemental, pagan strength in all his writings, but this characteristic is tempered by his other studies – his love of mathematics and astronomy in particular. His own nation, during the period of his symphonic productivity, was often struggling against oppression, so that he became, both by instinct and conviction, the national musical poet of his race, combining the physical hardihood of its primitive tradition with the intellectual strength of its awakened nationalism.

From the outset, the music of Sibelius had its roots in his native soil, and it was natural that he should look to the Scandinavian and Slavonic countries for his models. Perhaps the chief influences discernible are those of Tchaikovsky, Grieg, and Liszt. Sibelius, like Tchaikovsky, is primarily a melodist, and his melodies often have a wide architectural span. But, like Tchaikovsky, Sibelius realised that melodies do not lend themselves to symphonic development. Like Tchaikovsky, he built up his development sections by repetition, but, unlike Tchaikovsky, by the repetition of small fragments which at their first appearance seemed to have little constructional importance. This has led to much misunderstanding about his symphonic procedure by critics who measure with the yardstick of classical usage. Cecil Gray, for instance, writes of Sibelius, in his Second Symphony 'introducing thematic fragments in the exposition, building them up into an organic whole in the development section, then dispersing and dissolving the material back into its primary constituents in a brief recapitulation.' If such a thing really happened, it would be the negation of symphonic form, for to disperse and dissolve the process of symphonic growth would be a defeatist conclusion to any piece of symphonic thought.

The symphonic method in Sibelius' seven symphonies follows a consistent line of progress. The First Symphony is already an individual work, written in his thirty-fourth year when Sibelius had fully matured in musical craftsmanship and personality. As a child Sibelius had begun to compose, even before he had received theoretical instruction. Up to his twenty-fifth year he had remained in Finland, and had decided on the career of a violin virtuoso, though he had also entered Helsinki University as a law student. It was through the influence of Busoni that the young composer was persuaded to study in Germany and Austria, at that time divided between the worship of Wagner and Brahms. Sibelius's studies at least had the negative effect of convincing him that his own path lay in the direction of neither composer, and it was not until his return to Finland that he found his own personal style. His acknowledged early compositions significantly begin with opus 6.

The Finland of the 1890's was under the heel of the Russian Government. Free speech and the right of assembly were suppressed, a sure incentive to the rise of a nationalist movement. Sibelius with nationalist zeal immersed himself

in the study of the *Kalevala* and other Finnish epics, producing his first characteristic work, *Kullervo,* a symphonic
poem in five parts, for soli, chorus, and orchestra. Shortly
after this followed *En Saga,* written at the invitation of
Kajanus, and the four *Lemminkainen* legends, of which *The
Swan of Tuonela* shows both his indebtedness to Grieg and
also the deeper and more primitively mystical quality of his
music.

SYMPHONY NO. I IN E MINOR

IT was in 1897 that Sibelius, at the age of thirty-two, received
an annual pension from the Finnish Senate. Shortly afterwards he visited Italy, and on his return to Finland set to
work on his First Symphony (1899). He was already a
mature individuality and musician, and his symphony broke
with convention, if not with tradition. The introduction, a
sombre clarinet melody over a timpani roll, though it recalls
the later symphonies of Tchaikovsky, is no less 'a profound
human document'. It recurs at the opening of the Finale,
and so provides a 'motto' to the whole symphony.

The main *Allegro energico* starts in G major with two
broad and vigorous melodies, the first begun by violins in
canon with violas and 'cellos, Ex. 1. The answering tune is
given to first violins and 'cellos in octaves. Conventionally,
we should expect to see these themes take the most important part in the development, particularly when the first
of them is restated with increased vehemence. But a
transitional passage brings a short, dancing phrase on the
flutes, Ex. 2, and it is this short phrase which we shall find is
pregnant with possibilities of development. It is as if, at
first, we have been viewing some vast panorama, and
suddenly a little breeze has distracted our attention. Our
interest switches to this slight movement of the elements,
and behind it the whole vast scene dissolves. The broad,
panoramic melody is faintly echoed in the tranquil second
subject allotted to the oboe, in canon with flutes and
clarinets in octaves, Ex. 3.

The development is carried out by that use of orchestral

figuration which, in Sibelius, seems to resemble the movements of the elements, and in which short, pregnant fragments of previous themes are tossed, as it were, by the wind.
The scene, which from our first view had been static, comes
to life, as we become aware of the forces of nature which
shape it. Gradually we regain our perspective as the second
of the broad melodies emerges into sight, its theme nobly
expanded. The thematic material at last receives its final
synthesis, through which it seems to achieve an additional
dimension. The whole movement displays a gradual growth,
a widening and deepening of perception. The grand but
impersonal vision of the opening has, in the free recapitulation, become part of our being, the development having
been an experience which has converted an exterior impression into a physical and spiritual reality. The movement is
in sonata form, but in the recapitulation the themes
reappear in another order.

In the slow movement once again a broad melody is
announced from the outset, Ex. 4. When this has been fully
established a new theme on the bassoon is taken up in canon
by the woodwind, and begins the process of breaking down
the broad melody into its constituent phrases, the chief of
which is the two-bar repeated phrase in Ex. 4. An apparently inconspicuous counter-subject on flute and clarinet, Ex.
5, will later serve an important role in the development, and
reappears also in the orchestral texture of the Finale. Soon
a variant, in inversion, of the main theme is introduced
fortissimo, and in canon, by strings and woodwind, Ex. 6.

After a brief reappearance of a fragment of the main
melody on solo 'cello, an episode, *molto tranquillo,* is provided
by the horns, against a light accompaniment from the violins and harp arpeggios. The return of the original tempo
brings back the main melody, after which there is a free
development, in which Ex. 5 and 6 appear in combination.
A powerful orchestral climax is reached before the final
return of the main melody, after which the movement fades
tranquilly into silence.

The material of the Scherzo is easily recognizable, though
the two-bar figure in quavers first heard on the flute and

echoed by the clarinet may easily escape attention, Ex. 7.

Actually it grows in importance until a fugato is reached, where it is combined with the phrase that gives rhythmic impulse to the movement. The Trio shows Sibelius as a melodist, and his use of counter-melody is again reminiscent of Tchaikovsky.

The Finale (*Quasi una Fantasia*) opens with the introductory clarinet melody from the first movement, now stated *largamente ed appassionato* in octaves on the strings. The following *Allegro molto* exploits several short phrases of a restless, turbulent character. The tempo changes to *Andante assai* for one of the broadest and most lyrically impassioned melodies that Sibelius ever wrote, and later a fugato is built up from a phrase adumbrated in the *Allegro molto,* Ex. 8.

The semiquaver figure, together with a semiquaver version of Ex. 5, provides an orchestral background over which woodwind and brass fling out the short fragments of the *Allegro molto* which dominate the final pages of the score. In conclusion three terse chords from brass and woodwind give place to two quiet pizzicato chords on the strings, an abrupt and typically Sibelian ending.

The First Symphony displays the salient features of Sibelius's style. His broad, songlike themes set the scene and provide the climax to each movement, but it is the apparently insignificant fragments of phrases which, built up into elemental strength in the orchestral texture, supply the development through which the broad melodies achieve an extra dimension on their final restatement.

SYMPHONY NO. 2 IN D MAJOR

IT often seems that a composer's Second Symphony (1901–2) causes more argument and dissension among critics than his First. Beethoven and Brahms are examples to the point, and Sibelius is no exception. Rosa Newmarch writes of Sibelius's Second Symphony that 'the structural methods are a trifle more conventional' than those of the First, yet Cecil Gray describes the internal organization, particularly of the first movement, as amounting at times to 'a veritable revolution, and to the introduction of an entirely new principle into symphonic form'. The truth of the matter is that original composers rarely advance along the lines that critics have mapped out for them. They are not, in fact, interested in 'advancing' at all, but merely in organizing their musical thought into the most pregnant form. The subject-matter of Sibelius's First Symphony, like that of Brahms's First Symphony, is romantic and tragic. Each composer's second symphony is inspired more directly by nature. Brahms, when he wrote his Second Symphony, was living by a lake in the Carinthian Alps; Sibelius composed much of his Second Symphony in the genial climate of Italy. A comparison of the opening themes of Brahms and Sibelius is quite striking, particularly since they are both in the same key. They even share a similar rise and fall, yet one notices, significantly, in Sibelius a tendency towards modal melody, a sure finger-print in his style which we may already have observed in Ex. 2 from the First Symphony (Dorian mode based on C sharp).

Actually the first movement of Sibelius's Second Symphony is in stricter sonata-form than the corresponding movement in his First Symphony, but the presentation of his material is more unorthodox. The second group of subjects conventionally enters in the dominant key of A major, but so unexpectedly that we do not realize its importance until later in the proceedings, Ex. 9. This theme has three typically Sibelian finger-prints; first, the long-sustained opening note, then the slow trill, and finally the descending interval of a fifth, which is a germinal motive throughout the symphony (cf. Ex. 10, Ex. 13, second bar, and the conclusion of the main theme of the Finale).

Two further fragments from this group of subjects need attention, first, a scurrying passage in octaves on the strings, and second, a phrase of ascending fourths and descending fifths on the woodwind, Ex. 10.

Development begins with the second subject, Ex. 9 being combined with the scurrying string passage, now in thirds on the violas. Ex. 10 is obviously destined to take an important place in the development section, and next the

opening melody, accompanied by its inversion, is treated in
canon, and later joined by a new version, Ex. 11, of the
theme originally heard, in the exposition, on violins alone.
The music rises to a climax, and this theme, announced in
full harmony and in its original form on the brass, heralds
the recapitulation, in which the second group of subjects
conventionally returns to their tonic key. There is no coda,
but the movement ends as it began with the introductory
accompaniment figure which acted as a prelude to the first
main theme.

The second movement begins in more sombre mood,
though its later happenings are highly dramatic. It opens
with a rising-falling passage on pizzicato basses, which
seems to be an adumbration of the theme finally stated on
the bassoons in octaves, Ex. 12.

As strings and horns join in, the mood gets more tense and
excited, and explosive fragments of the main theme are
thrown between wind and strings, until on the entry of the
brass a climax is reached, and the music sinks to a silent
pause. A broad melody is now given to the strings richly
divided into nine and ten parts, Ex. 13, while flutes and
bassoons provide a running accompaniment, mainly in
thirds and sixths. The alternate natural and augmented
fourth of the key is another fingerprint in Sibelius's style.
The whole material is repeated, fuller and more intense in
orchestration, after which there is a brief and highly dramatic coda, in which sombre thematic fragments are interspersed by savage trills on the woodwind and a rushing
passage on the strings.

The Scherzo, a *moto perpetuo,* moves at a breathless pace
on the strings, the woodwind interjecting from time to time
a short phrase of melody, Ex. 14. The contrasting Trio,
Lento e suave, opens with a lyrical tune on the oboe that gains
expressiveness through its nine-times-repeated opening note.
Scherzo and Trio are heard again, and a gradually mounting climax foreshadows the broad, triumphant D major
melody that dominates the Finale, Ex. 15. This magnificent
melodic paean covers a span of forty-four bars, and during
half of its course the remarkable pedal bass (D–C sharp) is

heard. A more flowing and lyrical transition leads to the contrasted second subject in F sharp minor. Its theme, heard in the woodwind over a soft drum-roll and a running scale passage on the strings, bears a resemblance to a passage in the composer's later *Night Ride and Sunrise*, and this section certainly possesses the atmosphere of some nocturnal journey. A short codetta to the exposition brings a significant phrase, of which more will be heard later, Ex. 16.

In the development, which begins in F sharp, a four-bar phrase from the principal theme, with a continuation in running crotchets, is treated fugally, and Ex. 16 suggests material for a counter-theme, the crotchet figuration being maintained throughout in the orchestral texture.

The opening minims of the principal theme build up to a climax, heralding the recapitulation, in which the principal theme is announced against a crotchet figure in the woodwind. The second subject reappears in the tonic minor, but blazes into the major to introduce the short *coda* which supplies a magnificent peroration to the whole symphony.

Sibelius, alone among modern composers, can provide an epic ending that has nothing of self-consciousness or bravado in its grandiose strength. The Finns themselves regard this movement as symbolizing the triumph of their national aspirations. Certainly the wide expressive range of this symphony, from its pastoral opening to its victorious conclusion, is one of the greatest of Sibelius's symphonic achievements.

SYMPHONY NO. 3 IN C MAJOR

A PERIOD of three years separated the First and Second Symphonies. Five years elapsed before the completion of the Third Symphony (1907). It is dedicated to Granville Bantock, who had been a pioneer in introducing Sibelius and his music to the English public. It is straightforward and direct in expression, and this fact, combined with its light-hearted opening, has caused it to be considered by some the least important of the seven symphonies. The same, superficially, could be said about Beethoven's Eighth Symphony, yet both works show equally a fundamental advance in each composer's evolution. It is illuminating to note the way in which both Beethoven and Sibelius depart from precedent in introducing their second subjects in these respective symphonies. Beethoven's symphony is in F, yet by an ingenious harmonic side-slip he first brings in his second group of themes in the unorthodox key of D major, and then by another side-slip reaches the conventional dominant key of C. Sibelius adopts completely opposite, but equally unusual tactics. His partiality for the augmented fourth, or tritone, has already been remarked upon. In the festive first group of themes the natural and augmented fourths (F and F sharp) have alternated, and a sudden transition on the brass, made on the ascending wholetone scale C, D, E, F sharp, brings the music with a Schubertian *coup-de-théâtre* into the remote key of B minor for the entry of the second group of themes, begun by a broad melody on the 'cellos, and continued by a running semiquaver figure on the strings, Ex. 17, which leads the music towards the conventional key of G major. This most individual group of themes concludes with a passage (*Tranquillo*) for strings in contrary motion, an echo of the running semiquavers on the flute, and a repeated split chord on strings and wind, based on the whole-tone scale (C sharp, F, A, D sharp, G).

In the development the running semiquaver figure provides an almost constant background, over which are heard fragments of the first group of themes, particularly the opening figure, and the phrase Ex. 18.

Ascending notes on the horns suggest the *tranquillo* string passage, and soon bassoon, clarinet, and oboe meditate in turn on the broad 'cello melody, while the running semiquaver passage is carried on by violas alone. The recapitulation is undertaken with some freedom, the broad 'cello melody being given to the strings in unison, and the *tranquillo* passage reappearing on *pizzicato* strings. A short coda both completes and contrasts the restatement of the material of the movement.

The second movement has a veiled quality. Only woodwind, horns, and timpani support the strings, which are muted throughout, and generally plucked. The pace is neither fast nor slow, and the dance-like theme introduced by the flutes, Ex. 19, is countered by the solemn, chant-like phrase interjected by clarinets and bassoons, Ex. 20. The flute theme broadens into an extended melody, built from intermittent phrases of characteristic yet subtly elusive rhythmic pattern, and finally the clarinets add a cadence-phrase which is later repeated with an oriental persistence as the strings take over the main theme. A brief episode based on Ex. 20 provides a short relief before the main theme again returns on the wood wind over a *pizzicato* accompaniment in quavers on the strings. The pace quickens slightly for a section begun by *pizzicato* strings and suggested by the three opening notes of Ex. 19. This is answered by quiet, rushing passages in thirds, alternately on flutes and oboes, and with clarinets and bassoons in contrary motion. This short section, lightly scored, yet highly charged with a luminous atmosphere, leads to a repetition of the main theme on the violins; violas, 'cellos, and basses providing a rising-falling pizzicato accompaniment, and the wood-wind again using the cadence-phrase as a counter-melody. The conclusion recalls the chant-like phrase of Ex. 20.

The Finale is the most individual movement of the symphony, and could certainly never have been imagined, much less written, by any other composer. It shows, more than any work written before it, the path that Sibelius was to take in his later symphonies. Thematic material is used, not as a continuous line, but more as the disconnected strokes of a brush or pencil in sketching. A series of rhythms of such short lines is built up, while the texture, though full of sudden tone-contrasts, is kept aery and luminous through the elimination of the unessential. The repetition and interrelation of these rhythmic patterns and phrases form an ever-growing design, and when the design reaches its full dimensions, the music is halted, often abruptly, for Sibelius is the last man to make an unnecessary peroration.

For the first forty bars of this finale, the pedal-note of C is rarely absent, though it moves imperceptibly from violas to basses, horns, and bassoons in turn. Over this note, an implicit drone-bass, lively fragments of a dancing melody are given out, apparently disconnectedly, by the woodwind. Again, in this movement, there is the alternation of the natural and augmented fourth, as in this typical thematic passage, Ex. 21. Gradually, still without changing the pedal note, the key-centre shifts to A minor, and an undulating arpeggio figure is announced by the strings in canon, and summed up by flutes and clarinets in the phrase, Ex. 22.

The undulating string arpeggios subside, but the pedal C is retained, first in the violas and later in the 'cellos, while the melodic fragments of the opening combine in a new pattern with Ex. 22. The undulating string arpeggios re-appear in F minor, and over them is heard for a moment the adumbration of a marchlike theme on the horns. The music builds to a climax, after which a free fugal passage on the strings seems to exploit the chromatic possibilities of the figure given out softly at the opening by the violins. Over this soon come recollections of Ex. 22, and finally the violas announce the march theme hinted at earlier by the horns. The time signature now changes to four-in-a-bar, and the remainder of the movement is occupied solely by the march theme, given first to the 'cellos, Ex. 23, and then stated with ever-increasing power and vigour until the whole orchestra is joined in full force in its forward-surging paean.

The feeling and character of the Third Symphony strikes a new, direct and personal note. The First Symphony had been predominantly heroic, sombre and romantic; the Second had covered a wide range from the pastoral, through the dramatic, to the epic conclusion. The Third Symphony does not cover so wide a field, either in length or in scope, but the personality of the composer emerges, strengthened and more individually mature.

SYMPHONY NO. 4 IN A MINOR

In the autumn of 1913, a year after his Fourth Symphony had been completed, Sibelius wrote, in a letter to Rosa Newmarch: 'it strikes me more particularly that musicians are still writing in the post-Wagnerian style – with the same laughable pose and the still more laughable would-be pro-fundity'. Earlier he had written of his Fourth Symphony: 'It stands out as a protest against the compositions of to-day. Nothing, *absolutely nothing*, of the circus about it'. Few would deny this latter statement, yet it is strange to find a critic refer to the mood of the Fourth Symphony as 'one of the deepest tragedy and gloom'. The clue to it, surely, is that here Sibelius is 'alone with nature's breathing things', as Rosa Newmarch put it. Basil Cameron went to Järvenpää to study the work with the composer. In the course of their conversation Sibelius pointed to a picture showing a valley, with a rainstorm on one side, and bright, cold sunshine on the other. 'I was with my brother-in-law when he painted that picture,' he said; 'I also put that incident into my Fourth Symphony,' indicating the passage in the score.

The symphony opens with a quiet phrase, on the muted lower strings and bassoons, which, in various forms, domi-nates nearly the whole of the music. The opening four notes, C, D, F sharp, and E, imply the now-familiar augmented fourth, and the subsequent slow, rocking alternation of the F sharp and E provides a bass for a theme on the solo 'cello characterized by its rising and falling intervals of a third, Ex. 24. This theme is gradually taken up by the strings in canon and in thirds, but its serene climax is shattered by forceful chords on the brass. The strings, in answer, recall the opening 'motto' notes enforcing the augmented fourth by a leap of an octave, but their sudden climax is succeeded by a tranquil *tremolando*, over which an echoed horn call is heard. A further violent phrase on the brass leads to a re-peat of Ex. 24, after which clarinet and oboe in turn give out the 'motto' notes, now with the natural, and not the augmented, fourth. The development begins with Ex. 24, which soon turns into a meandering soliloquy by solo 'cello followed by violas and violins. Out of this develops a *tremo-lando* figure in the strings which soon bases itself, in canon, on repetitions, in changing keys, of the four 'motto' notes. The atmosphere is of some sudden, light, yet gusty storm. A fragmentary ascending phrase is tossed between flute and clarinet. At the climax the 'motto' notes are heard again on oboe and 'cello, with a variant of them on clarinets, horns, and bassoons. Then suddenly the forceful brass chords return, to be followed by the tranquilly echoed horn call. There is a short recollection of Ex. 24, and the movement concludes with a variant of the 'motto' notes, rising softly on the 'cellos and dying away on the violins.

The Scherzo begins in lighthearted manner with a tune on the oboe, lightly accompanied by violas, characteristic in its long-held opening note. The violins soon join in, and the tune becomes a dialogue, containing this curious passage of repartee, Ex. 25, with again the inevitable augmented fourths. The violins complete the tune started by the oboe, the time changes to 2/4 and the upper strings introduce an episode in unison and octaves dominated by the constant rhythm of a crotchet followed by two quavers. This is cut short by a return to triple time. Sustained chords on the brass are answered by softer chords on the woodwind. Ex. 25 appears in the 'cellos and violas and works its way to the upper strings, who repeat the end of the opening section. A fresh episode follows in which the flutes, in thirds, play a variant of the oboe theme, *tranquillo*, and are answered, as in the opening, by the strings. The clarinet softly recalls the oboe tune in its original form to introduce a repetition of the opening section. The remainder of the movement is marked *doppio piu lento*, and is based on a new theme, which, however, appears to be a sinister relation to what has gone before, Ex. 26.

It is given out against a rising *tremolando* bass and is answered by an upward rising phrase in the same rhythm, which also ends with the same *sforzando* interval of an augmented fourth. The mood has changed, and even when the first violins finally echo in F sharp the opening notes of the oboe tune, it has lost its original gaiety, and they are forced down a semitone to finish on E and F, the notes which the second violins have sustained, *tremolando*, throughout this entire section, as a sinister reminder of the original key.

The third movement is marked *Il tempo largo*, and this instruction is never altered throughout. The opening dialogue between the two flutes, Ex. 27, provides the background

to the music, and the main theme, with its characteristic rises of a fifth, is faintly foreshadowed in a short
passage for horns. It begins to take further shape in a 'cello
passage which follows the repetition of Ex. 27 (played on
bassoon answered by clarinet), and the 'cellos again, accompanied by a tremolando string figure, elaborate it still
further, answered by a free inversion of its first bars on
violas and oboe in turn. A phrase suggested by the opening
of Ex. 27 is introduced by clarinet, bassoon, and then oboe,
Ex. 28, and holds attention until the main theme returns,
broadly stated by the strings in octaves over a rocking
accompaniment on the woodwind. After a brief further
development of Ex. 28, the main theme appears in full
grandeur on the strings, woodwind and brass supplying
noble harmony, Ex. 29.

A short coda follows, throughout which the violas sustain
a dominant pedal in syncopated rhythm, while bassoons and
then clarinets give out a phrase which will form the opening
of the Finale. The music gradually sinks to silence as Ex. 28
is repeated by flute and clarinet and descends the strings
from violins to pizzicato basses.

In the Finale a new instrument is added to the orchestra –
the glocken (bells). Its whole part consists of a repeated
phrase of four notes, but its appearances act as signposts in
the course of this most original movement. The opening,
on the strings, consists of the phrase already heard on
bassoons and clarinets towards the close of the slow movement. This passage does not return in the recapitulation,
so we may consider it as an introduction, and the entry of
the bells gives the signal for the arrival of the main thematic
material. This consists of a series of short phrases, of which
the following only can be quoted, Ex. 30.

The next theme, begun by 'cellos, moves mainly in rapid
quaver motion, though it is marked *affetuoso*. Taken up by
the violins it leads to a repetition of the Ex. 30 material and
then to a passage on the strings dominated by an *ostinato*
bass, in which the alteration of the notes A, G sharp seems
to carry an echo of the similar device in the Finale of the
Second Symphony. This material is developed at some

length until the alternation of the chords of A major and E flat over the bass B flat leads to a new motive. At first this is only suggested by the woodwind, over a bell-like minim figure in fifths on the strings, and before it appears in full a chromatic passage of suspensions is heard over the descending bell-like fifths. This motive finally appears in the violins in the form of Ex. 31 over alternate B, D sharp minims from the basses. The key signature changes to C major, woodwind and brass hold sustained chords, while the strings softly rush up and down the scale. There are suggestions of the viola theme from Ex. 30, and the bells soon add their four-note phrase, ushering in the free recapitulation. At its climax the bells enter for the last time with their characteristic phrase, after which the chromatic passage of suspensions provides material for the coda. The phrases get gradually more attenuated, until a series of chords in A minor bring the symphony to a quiet close.

The Fourth is claimed by some critics to be Sibelius's greatest symphony. It is certainly one of his most individual works, and displays to the full his highly personal method of dealing with symphonic structure. The thematic material all seems to have some inner relationship, so that it is often difficult to decide whether a new theme is not in reality merely a new aspect of a previous one. The first four notes of the symphony are embryonic of much that happens later, and the beginning of Ex. 27, which has a similar melodic contour, seems to be a fuller and more pregnant expression of this underlying thought. This phrase covers a span of a fifth and then drops a semitone to the augmented fourth. A close study of the score will show clearly the constructional importance of these two intervals alone. Almost every music example quoted has one or the other of them as a salient feature. In fact, the closer one examines the thematic fragments, the more one becomes conscious of a general underlying pattern. As Sibelius once said: 'There is a logic that creates an inner connexion between all the motifs of a symphony.'

The form of the Fourth Symphony is equally individual. A typical feature is the dovetailing together of the climax of the development and the start of the recapitulation, and the occasional abandonment in the recapitulation of a phrase which has exhausted itself, so to speak, in the development. Though it often takes some time at the beginning of a movement for the main thematic material to appear with clarity, the conclusions have an epigrammatic clarity and conciseness. Unlike most symphonic perorations, they often take up a disconcertingly unforeseen trend of thought. There is none of the symmetry of architecture in this music, but rather the asymmetrical growth of nature. Yet beneath this superficial waywardness can be discerned the most closely knit musical organization.

SYMPHONY NO. 5 IN E FLAT MAJOR

IN the Fourth Symphony Sibelius had withdrawn into himself; the composer was solitary with nature. Outside events were soon to make such seclusion impossible, and certainly unnatural to a man with such a deep love of country as Sibelius possessed. On this account the Fifth Symphony, (1915–19) recalls the spirit of the Second Symphony both in its pastoral opening and in its triumphant conclusion. But this retrogression is spiritual, not musical. The Fifth Symphony progresses further along the individual path of its predecessors.

In the Second and Third Symphonies Sibelius had combined his Scherzo and Finale into one movement. In the Fifth Symphony, much more subtly, he combines together a very free first movement and a Scherzo. The opening horn call sets the scene for the first group of themes. The woodwind take up its opening notes and soon add a tailpiece of semi-quavers, from which evolves in turn a semiquaver continuation in thirds. The key signature changes to G, and over an ascending *tremolando* passage on the strings, a transitional theme on the woodwind – a free, syncopated inversion of the horn call – leads the music to this new key for the second group of subjects. This begins with a broad syncopated theme for strings and woodwind, and is followed by a rocking, syncopated figure similarly scored. The opening horn notes reappear on trumpet and flute to complete the exposition. The key signature returns to E flat for what can only be described as a free repetition of the exposition, but this time both groups of subjects are in the tonic key, and are accompanied throughout by a tremolando figure on the strings derived from the wood-wind passage in thirds. A short chromatic passage which linked the first group of themes with the transition now becomes of importance. It is first heard on the horns, and afterwards, in extended form, on violins and 'cellos in octaves, Ex. 32.

With this the development proper begins, the woodwind, particularly the bassoon, interjecting fragments of this chromatic theme as the strings provide an atmospheric background derived from it. The music broadens as the transitional theme itself takes the upper hand, until a modulation to B major brings a few brief bars of recapitulation. The time signature changes from 12/8 to 3/4 and the main scherzo theme makes its appearance, Ex. 33. It is seen to have more than a passing resemblance to the woodwind first subject and the opening horn call. Gradually the figuration in the strings works back to the tonic key of E flat, and against a texture based on the opening horn call the scherzo pursues its course, until the trumpet introduces a new motive, Ex. 34, over a crotchet bass figure which alternates between E flat and D. The music modulates once more to B major, and horns and bassoon take over the new motive. Strings and woodwind provide two offshoots from it, the second, with strong syncopated accents, being introduced in canon. The drum holds a pedal G, the key signature returns for good to E flat, and the crotchet bass figure gradually mounts the scale until the violins reach a tremolando chord of F flat. Over bell-like alternations of the chords of E flat and F flat fragments of the Ex. 34 group of themes are tossed about until the syncopated motive dominates the scene and itself is broken up into short crotchet figures which are windswept over strings and woodwind, providing one of the most remarkable passages in the whole symphony. At its climax the trumpets announce the opening horn call, the main second subject is suggested by the horns and soon blazes out on the full orchestra. A short coda follows, at ever-quickening pace, in which, over a tonic pedal the trumpets fanfare on the four opening notes of the horn call, and finally the brass compresses the four notes into a series of sustained chords, to which violins, flutes and oboes provide an arpeggio in rapid crotchets.

As a respite after the eventful happenings of the double movement with which the symphony opens, the second movement has a guileless simplicity. It is constructed throughout on the repetition of a little rhythmic phrase first heard *pizzicato* on violas and cellos, and then in a snatch of tune on the flutes, Ex. 35. This little phrase is extended into a melody of some forty bars in which the flutes, upper and lower strings carry on a three-cornered conversation, using always this same rhythmic pattern, against quiet sustained chords on horns and woodwind, in which a dominant pedal is nearly continuous. Soon this dominant pedal (D) is emphasised through the note C sharp being used as a sort of long appogiatura to it, and against this background, first the upper and then the lower strings have a quaver variant of the main theme. A more flowing version of the theme is heard (*poco tranquillo*), but soon the quavers are resumed and the music quickens to its original speed. A change of key signature to three flats brings a companion variation of the *poco tranquillo* phrase, and on the return to the key of G the bass is of interest for the hint it gives of the bell-like motive, Ex. 36, on the horns, which is to dominate the Finale. The orchestration and counterpoint become more elaborate and the speed imperceptibly increases until the climax of the movement is reached. The *andante mosso* of the opening is resumed, with the drums softly rolling an alternate dominant and tonic pedal, from which the music escapes through the reiterated E's of the violins, followed by a similar passage based on repeated F's. The coda is begun by *pizzicato* violins and violas, but soon a flowing solo on the oboe is accompanied by an undulating *tremolando* on the strings, to which, as a pendant, flutes, oboes and clarinets supply the simple and unassuming concluding bars.

At the beginning of the Finale the second violins, divided

into four parts, set up a *tremolando* accompaniment and at once the violas enter with a *moto perpetuo* theme. This theme has two typically Sibelian characteristics, the long-held note with which it starts (A flat, the sub-dominant of the key), and the later alternations of A flat and A natural. The first violins take up this theme while the violas play in sixths beneath them. Woodwind and basses are added, and soon the basses, in strongly marked minims, announce the bell-like motive which is to dominate the movement. The *moto perpetuo* subsides, horns and upper strings take over the bell-like motive, while the basses give out the same motive in augmentation. Against its steady rhythm woodwind and 'cellos sing out a broad melody, Ex. 36, which lasts some eighty bars, during the latter part of which the key signature changes to C major. With a return to E flat the development begins, and concerns itself mainly with a new version of the *moto perpetuo* on the woodwind, especially oboes. After a 'false start' in F, the recapitulation suddenly arrives at the unexpected key of G flat, the bell-like motive being allotted to the upper strings, and horns being silent. The broad melody is more amply treated than before, making a harmonic excursion into E flat minor, so that, on reaching the point where it originally modulated into C, it nobly returns to the tonic key of E flat, while the trumpets take over the bell-like motive, and the bass moves in syncopated minims. The music broadens to a magnificent peroration, in which the bell-like motive gradually ascends on the trumpets, its steady rhythm clashing yet blending with the slow, syncopated pulse of the strings. There is a slight quickening toward the climax, and six widely spaced, hammered chords bring the Symphony to an end.

SYMPHONY NO. 6 IN D MINOR

WHEN Sibelius was about to sketch his Sixth Symphony (1918) he wrote that the music would be 'wild and impassioned in character. Sombre with pastoral contrasts. Probably in four movements with the end rising to a sombre roaring in the orchestra, in which the main theme is drowned.' It was five years later that the symphony was published and during that time the 'programme' was evidently greatly altered. The wild and impassioned character, the sombre roaring are conspicuous by their absence, and it is the pastoral atmosphere which the music exudes throughout. One is tempted, thinking of Beethoven's sixth, to describe this symphony as Sibelius's *Pastoral*, and certainly there is a mental serenity which pervades all four movements and suggests a summer landscape as contrasted with the more wintry scenes of the Fourth Symphony.

In many ways the Sixth Symphony is the most individual of Sibelius's works. In it he exploits to the full his power of building up an orchestral texture, an atmospheric background, from almost insignificant thematic fragments. These extended orchestral episodes, or development sections, are further linked in this symphony by a broader underlying design, the chief feature of which is the series of descending sequences on which the orchestral figuration is built. This design is apparent in all four movements, so that the whole symphony characteristically suggests four different aspects of the same basic musical idea.

Though the symphony is described (not on the score) as being in D minor, there is no key-signature to the first movement, or, indeed, to the opening of the last movement, and the frequent use of the major sixth removes the music from a sense of minor tonality, except at the brief conclusion. There is, indeed, much of a suggestion of the Dorian mode, though it is by no means deliberately or consistently employed.

The first movement opens with a polyphonic passage for strings, in which the melodic outlines suggest the basic descending figure upon which much of the development is constructed. The first hint at a theme comes from the oboes and flutes, Ex. 37.

The second group of themes, begun by flutes and oboes in thirds, exploits the descending motive once more, and soon the strings start the development with a reiterated figuration based on the flute phrase in Ex. 37. A phrase derived from the second group of themes is heard from

oboes and clarinets, and the oboe phrase from Ex. 37 is
later heard in the 'cellos. In the recapitulation the opening
polyphonic passage disappears altogether, and is replaced
by a new theme which seems prophetic of a passage in the
Seventh Symphony (Ex. 50*b*), Ex. 38. The material
of the second group reappears in reverse order, after which
the whole thematic material is kaleidoscopically reviewed
before the brief, tranquil, yet almost questioning coda.

The second movement is conceived throughout in one of
those quiet atmospheric moods that never rise above a
mezzo-forte. It begins with a series of syncopated 6/5 chords
on flutes and bassoons. The gentle rise and fall of these
chords, and their individual harmony, underlies all the
happenings of the first section. Over this background the
strings enter with two thematic motives, the characters of
which can be seen from Ex. 39 (*a* and *b*).

This material is freely repeated, with Ex. 39 (*b*) taking
an important part in the orchestral figuration. A short
development section follows, begun fugally by the strings
with a new version of Ex. 39(*b*), though later Ex. 39(*a*) in
amplified form plays an important role. This section breaks
off suddenly for a new thought, at slightly quickened pace.
The strings, playing *flautando* and in semiquavers, establish
a shimmering background of descending chords containing
the augmented fourth and the major seventh. Against this
the wood-wind interject short phrases which have the rise
and fall of the opening chords. As a coda there is the briefest
suggestion of Ex. 39 before the music closes on a plagal
cadence of G (Dorian mode).

The brief scherzo provides a characteristic example of
Sibelius's method of foreshortening symphonic form. Of the
opening group of themes, the introductory, galloping motive on the strings is most important later, Ex. 40. A rushing
semiquaver passage on the strings leads to a second subject
or transitional theme on the flutes, repeated by the oboes,
Ex. 41. There follows a lengthy elaboration of Ex. 40, the
galloping rhythm being sustained antiphonally by string
and wood-wind, while first violins, later joined by 'cellos,
career headlong onwards. There is a free recapitulation of

all the material heard up to this point, followed by a short coda, based on the theme which followed the introductory galloping motive.

As one proceeds with the Sibelius symphonies, the conventional musical analysis, consisting of an indication of the general structure, interspersed with a few thematic quotations, becomes increasingly unsatisfactory. The musical thought has become so subtilised that only copious quotations, showing the inter-relation of thematic material, can give any idea of the constructional processes (probably instinctive and not conscious) in the composer's mind. The Finale of the Sixth Symphony is a case in point. The time signature is *allegro molto*, though the introduction is a broad chorale begun by violins, wood-wind and horns and answered antiphonally by the lower strings. This introduction contains the germ of practically all the thematic material of the movement, and when the speed direction of *allegro molto* becomes perceptible, the thematic material is discovered to be related to the broad introduction. Only two examples can be quoted: the opening theme of the *allegro*, Ex. 42(*b*), is derived from the following bars from the chorale introduction, Ex. 42(*a*), while the phrase Ex. (43*b*) from the allegro is obviously related to the phrase Ex. 43(*a*) from the introduction and also to Ex. 39(*b*) from the slow movement. This exposition is repeated (without the introductory chorale) with only slight changes of orchestration, and a development section follows. In this once more we hear the familiar descending sequences which underlie each movement of the symphony. The last section consists of a development and recapitulation of the chorale themes in their original form (but at *allegro molto* pace), followed by a coda, *doppio piu lento*, in which a phrase from the chorale appears in the 'cellos, with a free mirror inversion in the violins. The final bars, too, have a subtle relation to the opening bars of the movement. Such a description is necessarily arbitrary, and the student will find many thematic relationships hardly touched on here. This movement is perhaps the quintessence of Sibelius's musical thought, and repays the most careful study.

SYMPHONY NO. 7 IN C MAJOR (1924–5)

IT seemed inevitable that Sibelius, with his instinctive sense of thematic inter-relationship, should eventually write a symphony in one movement. The last movement of the Second and Third Symphonies and the opening movement of the Fifth show that this problem had already absorbed his attention. In actual fact it appears that the one-movement form was inwardly forced on the composer in spite of his original intentions. It was not a deliberate design, as with Liszt, but the outcome of subconscious co-ordination of musical material. Writing seven years before the work was completed, Sibelius had declared 'The VII Symphony. Joy of life and vitality, with *appassionato* passages. In three movements – the last an Hellenic rondo.' But, knowing himself, he added 'All this with due reservation.'

When the symphony came to be written (1924-5) it displayed a completely individual structure, perhaps the only really coherent one-movement work ever written. It is quite impossible to dissolve it into sections, and, even as regards its general outline, the symphony is possible of analysis in various ways. The dovetailing and combination of the thematic material is even more subtle and complex than ever before, and the thematic fragments are often foreshadowed long before they achieve their final shape. Perhaps the simplest way of analysing the work is to consider the opening *adagio* in C as an introduction and first group of themes, the *Un pochett. meno adagio* as a transition, adumbrating a second group derived partly from the first. These develop into a scherzo when the key changes to three flats, and appear in new combination at the *Vivacissimo*, together with a new version of a theme from the first group. This leads to an *Adagio* development section concerned chiefly with the main theme of the symphony. The pace then quickens to *Allegro molto moderato* for a scherzo section which introduces new ideas as well as dealing with new versions of old material. The final *Adagio*, which follows a *presto* linking section, provides a recapitulation-coda concerned mainly with the opening group of themes.

The upward scale with which the symphony begins, ending unexpectedly with the chord of A flat minor, is reminiscent of Beethoven's descending scale opening to Leonora No. 3. It is followed by several half-suggested thematic motives, of which the most important can be summarized in Ex. 44. Ex. 44(b), indeed, contains the germ of the whole symphony. Its influence can be seen in Ex. 46(a) and Ex. 47(a) and it appears in inversion in Ex. 47(b). A variant of it provides Ex. 51, and the last four notes of the violins in this symphony are based, with an octave leap, on this motive. It serves the same purpose, indeed, as the descending fifth in the Second Symphony and the augmented fourth in the Fourth Symphony.

Then comes a lengthy polyphonic passage, begun by divided violas and 'cellos and later joined by violins and basses. The shape of several of its melodic phrases suggest the contour of later themes, but it is the first trombone which announces the main motive of the symphony, Ex. 45. Two final thematic phrases of this group need quoting, and for convenience they will be given as they appear together, Ex. 46. A recollection of the rising scale passage leads to a quickening of pace to *Un pochett. meno adagio,* and the introduction of a second group of themes. These are suggested in various guises, until at the change of key signature to three flats, they settle down to a lively inter-relationship. Again it is necessary, for the sake of compression, to give two pairs of themes as they occur together, rather than in the order, or even in the shape, of their original appearance in the *pochett. meno adagio* section. First comes Ex. 47, followed by a variant of Ex. 46(b), after which, at the change to *Vivacissimo,* another pair, which had earlier appeared separately, are brought together, Ex. 48, and followed by a new version of Ex. 47(b) and the variant of Ex. 46(b). The speed slackens, though the strings still keep up a running chromatic figure, and as the tempo reaches *adagio* Ex. 45 is heard on the trombone, the accompanying strings suggesting a minor tonality rather than the major of the opening. Horns, answered by wood-wind, give out a phrase related to Ex. 44(b), but which, in the light of future events, is really one of the themes of the following scherzo, after which there is a brief transitional passage, beginning with Ex. 48(*a*). At the *Allegro molto moderato* comes the scherzo section, which introduces the theme Ex. 49, suggested, possibly, by the polyphonic passage at the opening, and the more important group which begins Ex. 50, and of which the continuation contains an upward-running scale passage and a variant of the theme (horns answered by wood-wind from the end of the *adagio* section. This latter shortly gives rise to a related idea, derived from Ex. 44(*b*), Ex. 51, which, together with Ex. 48(*a*) and another thematic recollection, provides a trio section. Scherzo and trio are freely repeated (or developed would be a better word), Ex. 48(*a*) appearing in free inversion. The time changes to *Presto*, and over a string figure suggestive of Ex. 51 the horns are given an ascending scale motive which leads into the *Adagio* recapitulation-coda. Here the first group of themes enter in a new order. First comes Ex. 45, broadly on the trombone, then Ex. 46 and lastly Ex. 44(*a*). The final bars echo the opening notes of the trombone theme, reduced to their simplest form.

To describe the Seventh Symphony of Sibelius in a mere thousand words and with a restricted use of music examples is a formidable task. Many will object that the examples chosen are not fully characteristic of the thematic ideas which they represent. The themes of Sibelius are here in a continual state of growth, and any quotation of them cannot possibly show the process whereby they grow. Their relation to one another, too, can be indicated only at a particular point in their development. The symphony demands the time factor for its fulfilment, and only a close study of the music can cover the deficiencies of this analysis.

The Seventh Symphony was the last that Sibelius was to give to the world, though an eighth, and perhaps even a ninth, were said to exist. In August, 1945, the composer wrote to Basil Cameron 'Dear old Friend ... my eighth symphony has been "finished" many times, but I am not contented with it yet. When the time comes it will be a pleasure to me to give it in your hands ... Yours, Jean

Sibelius.' And if any visitor had the temerity to question Sibelius about the work which the whole world was anxiously expecting, he merely quoted an old Scandinavian proverb – 'One doesn't sell the bearskin until one has shot the bear.'

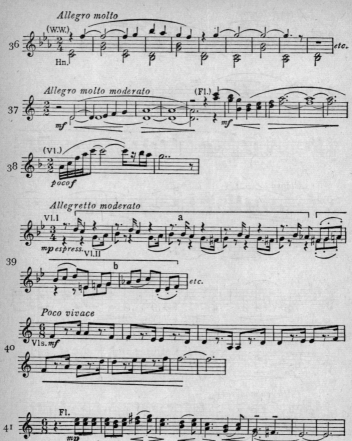

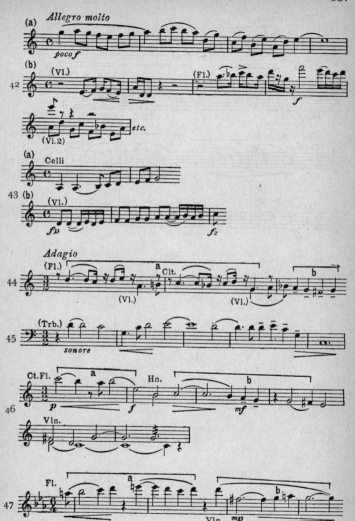

19

Ralph Vaughan Williams (1872-)

SCOTT GODDARD

INTRODUCTION

VAUGHAN WILLIAMS has published six symphonies. These stretch in point of time from his earliest work to the present day. Their appearance at comparatively regular intervals through his long career makes them a reliable form of reference and a particularly valuable type of material for the study of his music as a whole. For the symphonies contain examples of all the elements of his style and show all aspects of its development. Dates are as follows: the First (the *Sea Symphony*) finished in 1910, the Second (the *London Symphony*) finished in 1914 and revised up to 1920, the Third (the *Pastoral Symphony*) finished in 1921, the Fourth in F minor finished in 1935, the Fifth in D minor finished in 1943, and the Sixth in E minor finished in 1947.

As a type, symphony is the outcome of the most acute reasoning and the most mature thought a composer can bring to bear upon the facts presented to him by experience. In some instances the degree in which a symphony is the eventual, perhaps final, result of such experience can be apprehended. That happens when certain aspects of this reasoning and thought have already partly been dealt with in works of other types. When a symphony thereupon completes the process and for the first time brings these elements into a new logical sequence it has the effect of summing up the composer's development and opening up other perspectives. Such instances are here. In every case Vaughan Williams's symphonies are extensions of qualities and of types of thought that had already begun to appear in previous works. And to understand the relationship of the symphonies to his music as a whole it is necessary to know certain of these works preceding them. As a guide to that wider study (desired not so much by the casual concert attender as by the deeply interested listener), the following short list of related works is given: For the First Symphony, the cantata *Towards the unknown region*. For the Second, the *Fantasia on a theme of Thomas Tallis* and the opera *Hugh the Drover*. For the Third, the opera *The Shepherds of the Delectable Mountains* and *The Lark Ascending*, for solo violin and orchestra; for the Fourth, the ballet *Job;* for the Fifth, the oratorio *Sancta civitas* and the Suite *Flos Campi*; for the Sixth, the cantata *Dona nobis pacem*, the opera *Riders to the Sea* and *Job*.

Vaughan Williams's symphonies are not difficult to approach. Those who have a feeling for Tudor polyphony (church and secular) and for folk music can come close to them instantly and easily, more so than those whose sympathies are either for the nineteenth century romantics or twentieth century neo-classicists, such as Stravinsky and Prokoviev. With the exception of the *Sea Symphony* these six works by Vaughan Williams are somewhat uncouth to the more elegant minds of the day, a little rough and rather long. But though some movements are leisurely there are none of the lengthy perspectives of Bruckner or the crowded canvasses of Mahler. They are in fact within the comprehension of the normal symphonic listening patience. The listener may find himself let in for surprises. The brusqueness of the Fourth has startled those who, forgetting *Job,* settled contentedly into the more lyrical passages of the *London* and the *Pastoral*. Eight years later the piling of one soaring outline upon another in the Fifth disappointed those who had accepted the Fourth; forgetting that Vaughan Williams had presumably a mind liable to the call of Whitman's 'restless explorations', they had imagined he was for ever settled in his latest mood, that of the Fourth; and that, they had already decided, was to be his last word.

There are three rhapsodical works among those mentioned above as ancillary to the symphonies: the *Tallis*

Fantasia, the suite *Flos Campi* and *The Lark Ascending.* Rhapsody is a type of thought that Vaughan Williams has explored extensively. To the music created under that impulse he has brought much concentration of expression. It is a quality that might seem out of place among the trance-like ecstasies which are supposed to be the basis of rhapsodising. But in fact there is a point when concentration overcomes the dream and injects logic into its system. It is at that moment that rhapsody in music becomes symphony, that *The Lark Ascending* goes over into the *Pastoral Symphony* or *Flos Campi* is crystallized in the Fifth. The actual moment can hardly be defined, though the result is there, more clearly apparent than anywhere else in the slow movements where conventionally the mood should tend towards rhapsody. In the *Sea Symphony* the slow movement at first heaves ponderously, vaguely to and fro with all the indecision of rhapsodical dreaming. The opening sentence 'On the beach at night alone' places the movement at the very centre of the sphere of rhapsody. 'I think a thought of the clef of the universes and of the future' is pure rhapsody; Whitman but not Vaughan Williams follows it with one of his magnificent, sprawling episodes of rhapsody over mankind, the least apt for music in all the poem. A more significant omission by Vaughan Williams, because here the words might have submitted to music, comes later; the significance is in the fact that by this omission the texture is woven closer, and rhapsody brought within the range of symphony. And, though ecstasy remains, rhapsody vanishes as the slow movement comes to the climax 'A vast similitude spans them.' And when the music returns to its initial mood, that now has too precise a meaning to be any longer of the nature of rhapsody.

The same can be heard in all the slow movements. The symphonic writer's intensity of concentration dissipates rhapsody instantaneously in the slow movement of the Fourth, as might be expected in a work dominated by such direct statement. On the other hand the corresponding movement of the *Pastoral* keeps near to rhapsodical utterance;

it is a matter never far from the symphony as a whole, though it never takes complete charge. In the Fifth also it is strong in the slow movement; there too it almost, but never wholly, draws the music away from symphony to its own orbit of vision. This pull between the complementary and exclusive elements of rhapsody and logic is one of the strongest productive elements in symphonic creation. Inevitably rhapsody has to give way, though not to the point of absolute extinction. Slow movements allow it to live on and in Vaughan Williams's symphonies it is given unusual freedom there.

The writing of meandering rhapsodies *on* one's own or other men's ideas is an ancient form of waste. The British folk-music revival gave it new chances. Many years elapsed and much energy was spent before it was borne in upon the consciousness of musicians that rhapsodising was one of the most hazardous and difficult forms to work in intelligently. When the time comes to look at Vaughan Williams's completed work it will be noticed that he has perfected a technique in that difficult art, so as to bring shape into the dream and fulfil it logically; which is why he can well allow rhapsody the space it has in his symphonies.

It will be noticed too that there are no perorations at the end of any of these symphonies. The problem, whatever it may be, the idea, the vision is left in indefinite progression. The Fourth ends with an interrogatory clause, the question with which it began. The *London*, the *Pastoral*, the Fifth die down into the silence from which they were summoned. Only in the *Sea Symphony* is there the suggestion that a peroration of some grandeur is forthcoming; it is Vaughan Williams's last work under the influence of Parry, the inspiring teacher whose missionary zeal found expression in precisely this orator's gambit, the final, unquestionable peroration. Whitman made use of it often. Vaughan Williams ends the *Sea Symphony* with a long decrease that at last enters silence. It is the method of the exploring mind, the thinker rather than the teacher, a way of thought Vaughan Williams appears to have kept always in view.

NO. I, THE SEA SYMPHONY

FIRST Movement: 'A Song of all seas, all ships'. *Andante maestoso*. 'Behold, the sea itself', Ex. 1, are the opening words of the First Movement. They are preceded by a fanfare cast in a rhythm that is immediately recognized when heard later in the movement, heralding the line 'Flaunt out visible as ever the various flags and ship signals'. This fanfare belongs as well to the Scherzo of which it is both the first and the last sound. It is there also at the end of the last movement where it needs listening for carefully – greatly transformed, much slower, softer, and very low in register as it is by then.

With the fortissimo shout of the chorus comes another significant point, a change, Ex. 1(*a*) from the B flat minor key of the fanfare to a very distantly related major key (D major). The change on the word 'sea' is startling; not a single note in the new chord is the same as that in the one before. The voices move only a semitone away from the first chord, yet the effect is limitless. Thereupon begins the first, Ex. 2, of many large themes; this is the 'limitless heaving breast' of the sea on which are the ships 'steaming in and out of port'. And then the baritone's solo about the 'rude brief recitative of ships sailing the seas ... of dashing spray and the winds piping and blowing'. Another broad tune for 'a chant for the sailors of all nations'. The fanfare brings in 'the various flags'; one of them reserved 'especially for yourself and for the soul of man'. It is the 'token of all brave captains and of all intrepid sailors and mates'. The chorus take this to themselves, voice following voice as they sing of 'all that went down doing their duty' and so come to the 'emblem of man elate above death', Ex. 3. And now (the compressed recapitulation of this first-movement symphonic scheme) the 'pennant universal' (music of Ex. 2) and the coda 'all seas, all ships, all brave sailors'.

Second Movement. 'On the beach at night alone'. *Largo Sostenuto*. The heave and surge of the sea as it laps the shore is in the orchestral music that precedes the baritone solo 'On the beach at night alone'. The music of this movement is of two kinds. There is the orchestral introduction and all the vocal music (baritone accompanied by a semi-chorus of contraltos) as far as the words 'I think a thought of the clef of the universes and of the future'. This can be studied in Ex. 4; the chord-change in Ex. 1(a) is here and with that the slow movement begins. The second kind of music comes directly after the end of Ex. 4 with the words 'A vast similitude interlocks all'. Here the key becomes a clear and direct major, and great contrast is brought by the sturdy character of the theme that the horns first play, unlike the moody beginning of this movement and similar to the broad themes of the first movement. The idea of all these 'lives and deaths, all of the past, present, future' is so immense that the voices grope towards it one after the other. But they join to affirm the conviction that similitude 'shall compactly hold and enfold them'. It was Whitman's huge vision; the man trying to share it is left once more on the beach at night alone. His comment is a broken echo of his first words. The orchestra then is left to deal with the thoughts woken by that vision of a possible similitude; it has all the remainder of the recapitulation, playing much of what the man once had sung but now finds no voice to utter.

Third Movement. 'The Waves'. *Allegro brillante*. The rhythm of the fanfare, Ex. 1, brings in 'the sea ship ... the whistling winds ... the white-grey sails taut to their spars and ropes'. And there are 'below, a myriad waves hastening'. The movement is one of haste at first, gradually broadening as the undulating, liquid, uneven waves are reached at sea, Ex. 5, far from the beach where the dreamer lately stood. And on this 'whirling current, laughing and buoyant' there is seen 'the great ship sailing' to a great melody. The ship passes and her wake is 'Flashing and frolicsome under the sun'. The picture dissolves into 'a motley procession with many a fleck of foam and many fragments', and the music into the fragmentary processes of whole-tone scales, a shifting, keyless episode leading at once everywhere and nowhere, reaching a note of suspense over which the fanfare again sounds. The first part of this scherzo movement is now recapitulated, shortened in form as the waves 'lift up their necks, following the stately and rapid ship'. That word 'following' naturally shapes itself to the fanfare rhythm and with those combined the movement ends as suddenly as it began.

Fourth Movement. 'The Explorers'. *Grave e molto adagio*. The last movement has the most complex scheme. Whitman's *Passage to India* has been much condensed, but there still is left, even when the long lists of his visions and aspirations has been eliminated, a large expanse of poetic imagery for the music to enhance and support in its own kind of sound. In Ex. 6 (taken from a passage in the middle of the movement where themes are combined) there may be found the music of the solemn opening sentence 'O vast rondure swimming in space, covered all over with visible power and beauty, alternate nights and days and the teeming spiritual darkness'. This the chorus deals with and to it is given the next episode which tells how 'down from the gardens of Asia descending, Adam and Eve appear, then their myriad progeny after them'. Out of the teeming darkness, now peopled with this myriad progeny comes the 'restless explorations' of the soul which cries 'Whither O mocking life?' As Whitman speaks to the soul and tells it that the 'first intent remains' the music begins to clear, to become diatonic and definite in the style of the former melodies from the three other movements, such a one as has been heard for the 'emblem of man elate above death'. To that the music comes with the 'poet worthy that name, the true son of God ... singing his songs'. This is the symphony's highest point of ecstasy. (The outline of the vocal polyphony is in Ex. 6 from the third bar onwards.) The two solo voices sing, Ex. 7, 'O we can wait no longer' and the chorus at length can answer 'Boundless O soul thou journeyest forth'. That is the end of philosophising and spiritual exploration in heavenly seas. The sea of our globe is what the soul now sails forth upon for its journey through the 'deep waters only'. The music once heard with 'O we can wait no longer', Ex. 7, now sounds with 'O my brave soul, O farther sail', and gradually approaches the silence with which it imperceptibly blends.

NO. 2, THE LONDON SYMPHONY

FIRST Movement. *Lento – Allegro risoluto*. Very slowly and softly the bass strings begin the Introduction with what sounds as though it were no more than the merest fraction of a tune, Ex. 8, formed out of two rising fourths a tone apart followed by another minute fragment, a short rocking figure in which clarinets and horns join the upper strings. The whole short episode is more significant than at first appears, for both these elements are to be heard again. This symphony, although it deals with the moods rather than the scenes of London, has nevertheless a few frankly pictorial effects introduced into its fabric. One of these is heard just before the introduction ends and the first movement proper begins; it is the Westminster chimes. After that has been heard a climax rapidly approaches. There is a blank beat before the first theme of the *Allegro* crashes out, Ex. 9. For some time the music is intensely energetic; then lyrical and ecstatic. Single short themes stand out such as the one (4 bars after letter D) which suggests the whistle of a guttersnipe. The chief part of the second subject, Ex. 10, is given to the brass. For a moment it seems as though the music is going to turn towards grandeur. But that quality hardly has time to tell before it is deflated by the common sprightliness of a companion theme, Ex. 11. Out of this material there grow other related themes, which as they are developed produce remarkable variants such as the long and exquisite passage (between letters BB and FF) which is of notable ecstasy.

Second Movement. *Lento*. Over a slow repeated rising figure which someone has likened to the city turning in its sleep, the cor anglais utters the chief melody of the slow movement, Ex. 12. The full strings take this up and as it comes once more to an end the horns dovetail on to it a repetition of the last two bars which contain the rising fourth that began the symphony and henceforth is to become the significant interval of this movement. The strings now provide a background of wide stretched, soft repeated chords against which resound the horn call, the rising fourth. After a time this section quietens to silence. There is a pause and then a solo viola, at a very slightly quickened pace, brings in the second main theme, Ex. 13. All that now happens (and there is a great deal which, because of its intrinsic vitality, sounds new) is bound up with these themes. A keen ear will quickly note such passages as the piccolo tune (four bars after letter E), which is a pert version of the viola soliloquy. There is a moment of pictorial allusion, the jingle of hansom cabs. Then a return to the horn call against the background of string chords and finally the viola soliloquy ends the movement.

Third Movement. *Scherzo (Nocturne): Allegro Vivace.* The Scherzo portrays the gay licence of London's long evenings from their start to the moment when the dead of night comes on and London at least appears to sleep. Then it is that the airs of the countryside blow through her streets and across her parks and gardens while for a short space of time the petrol fumes are dissipated. The music moves quickly and lightly. The scoring is transparent, sometimes opaque. There are many scraps of tune, no really extended melody for some time. Early on the clarinets have some-thing to say (6 bars before letter A), which is capped by the full strings, Ex. 14. The section ends with a solo bassoon chattering over a bar-long figure, which is then taken over almost inaudibly on the bass strings, and suddenly taken up again by the horns as though they had discovered it for the first time. Once more what may be called a definite fact intrudes. Its entry is easily apprehended, as the bassoon begins to chatter again with the 'cellos to help it this time until it comes to rest. Then divided strings and muted horns turn themselves into a mouth organ, Ex. 15, after which the drum and fife band strike up. The Scherzo section is then repeated with alterations, night falls and the echoes of gaiety dissolve into silence.

Fourth Movement. *Andante con moto.* A short introduction, harmonically rich and heavily scored, prepares the way for the solemn march, Ex. 16, which opens the movement proper. Then the pace quickens and very soon after that there comes the short second theme, Ex. 17, strongly and loudly played by the upper strings, brass and wood-wind. By now the chief material of the movement has been displayed. The development of these themes is concise, urgent and impetuous. Out of it there grows a contest between the march and a figure which at first seems new, but eventually is found to be an echo of the first movement, Ex. 9. Suddenly all becomes quiet. Westminster chimes are heard; and now the Epilogue begins. It is formed out of the first notes of the symphony, Ex. 8, which spreads from the bass strings throughout the whole orchestra until it arrives at the highest notes of a solo violin. London turns once more in its sleep (trumpets, cornets and horns), turns back again (wood-wind *crescendo-decrescendo*) and the music sinks gradually into silence.

NO. 3, THE PASTORAL SYMPHONY

FIRST Movement. *Molto moderato*. The first movement begins with an undulating line of triads played (or, as it sounds, sung) by three flutes and a bassoon; and after three bars the bass strings and harp rise to meet this music with a design that the reader will find, as to its beginning, in the final bar of Ex. 18, which gives the violin solo coming immediately after the music for harp and strings. That has grown out of the flutes' design from the opening bars. In this natural development of one theme out of another there is a fundamental characteristic of Vaughan Williams's method in symphonic writing. It was a method already partially present in the two preceding symphonies. Here in the *Pastoral* it is the basis of the whole work, where each movement has references to another with which it is linked (See Exs. 18*a* and 19*b*). There is an important elaboration of part of the flutes' design (first four bars of Ex. 19), and a new subject, in this first group, on the cor anglais (last four bars of Ex. 19). The chief second subject group is heard soon after this on a solo 'cello, Ex. 20, as the music starts to move a little more quickly. That part of the movement in which the development of this material takes place is short and merges imperceptibly into the final section. The

themes steal back almost unnoticed, the texture is undisturbed, the atmosphere quiet and cool. The chords of Ex.
19 return, now spread over a great expanse of the orchestra,
impressive because for all the vast extent of these chords
they are still calm and distant, a mood and manner informing the whole symphony.

Second Movement. *Lento moderato.* There is another
characteristic that now appears, the simultaneous use of
opposing tonalities, i.e., the minor chord below the major
melody at the start of this movement, Ex. 21. It will be
noticed that this is sounded very softly; the effect is in
keeping with the emotional nature of the symphony, music
that compels by the most gentle insistence. In that example
there is the first main theme. From it there arise others so
nearly related to it as to have almost no intrinsically
individual quality. From two or three notes, Ex. 21*a*, in
the main theme comes a new phrase; from a part of that
there grows a fresh design. The music seems to think its
way from point to point. The texture is opaque, there is an
impression of distance and vague intermingling of lines
with no apparent contrasts. Then contrast comes; a new
and individual theme, long and like a cadenza, and with it
a new quality of tone, a natural trumpet, Ex. 22, with
extended string chords moving in similar motion, and
through keys only distantly related to it, below. Then a
short outburst from full orchestra, surprising because of its
sudden and unexpected force; on which the music recedes
again into its quietude. There is a much shortened return
of the first part. Again the cadenza theme is reached,
played now on a natural horn. And that brings in the end
where the divided violins rise in designs (similar to those in
the first bars of the first movement) to end with the small
falling interval of a third, Ex. 21*b*, with which the movement began.

Third Movement. *Moderato pesante.* In a symphony
notable for its low level of emotion and its absence of
dramatic emphasis this third movement has the function
of a release of tension. Contemplation gives place to vigour
and animated comment. In the score this movement is not

called a scherzo though it comes at an appropriate point
for such a movement. Its robust constitution is such that,
in so far as the character of music in abstract movements
can ever be defined, this might stand for humour. In Ex. 23
there is the beginning of the movement, the main subject.
(Apropos cross-reference between movements and the
general closeness of relationship between themes, see Ex.
18*c* for the earlier version of this theme.) The triplet figure
(i.e., three notes to a beat) on bass strings and bassoon
answered heavily by the same tune in duplets (two notes
to a beat) on horns suggests ponderous slow-minded con-
verse, which is indeed the mood of the movement. There
is a slight quickening when a new tune for soft trumpets
and trombones is reached, Ex. 24, and see also Ex. 18*b*.
Then a large climax (in this movement alone do any
extended passages of vigour and loud tone appear) where
the tunes of Exs. 23 and 24 combine. This passes and a
single flute with harp accompaniment begins a new melody
which alters the mood to lyricism and calm again – Ex. 25,
and see also Ex. 22*a*. The earlier tunes then combine with
this and the music moves into the major (G) of the minor
key, in which it began, for the second section, which may
be called the Trio of the Scherzo. It is an abrupt change.
The new theme, Ex. 26, is remarkably forthright and of a
strikingly simple shape; quite fresh in material and unrelated to the rest of the symphony. This section is succint
and much to the point. Then the first section begins again
but is sternly truncated, with telescoping of Exs. 24 and 25
in counterpoint of masterly skill. In no time the Trio tune,
Ex. 26, returns still more impulsively. One more outburst
of the opening, Ex. 23, restores it to the chief place before
there begins a very rapid coda through which new shapes
grow out of old material (for instance, a tune for solo flute
that sounds new and is in fact the offspring of Ex. 25).

Fourth Movement. *Lento*. Over a soft drum roll a distant
human voice (a soprano or a tenor off-stage) sings a long
chant, the music of which recalls Ex. 18*a* and parts of the
trumpet cadenza in the slow movement. A short comment by
the strings, a pause and the chief theme of the movement,

Ex. 27, is played first on the wood-wind, with brass gradually added, and then on the strings. The music now alternates between this broad type of rich melody and various references, some of them urgent and passionate, to the opening cadenza for solo voice. One of these references takes the form of a fresh statement for 'cello of the cadenza, taken over later by a solo flute. Still linked to this subject the music grows in strength. A climax comes when the cadenza theme is given with great magnificence by wood-wind and strings in bare octaves. The texture then is thickened by polyphony throughout the whole orchestra. The music subsides into the *Lento* of the beginning of the movement. There is a short passage for strings in recollection of Ex. 27 which takes the music up to the high strings. These sustain an upper octave A while below that the solo voice is heard in the distance as it was in the beginning. It finishes and the violins' held octave fades into silence.

For those interested in technicalities, one reason for the remarkably close inter-relation of themes between the movements of this symphony is that the music is preponderately pentatonic. This would inevitably lead to such similarities. More notable than these likenesses between the movements is the richness of invention that creates from pentatonic material themes that have such individuality.

SYMPHONY NO. 4 IN F MINOR

FIRST Movement. *Allegro*, This symphony starts abruptly. Already within the short space of seven bars of quick time two important and distinct moves have been made. The bare octaves of the first subject have been announced, Ex. 28, and the character of the subject (i.e., the span it makes of one semitone over the octave) has been established in the three opening bars. During the fourth and fifth bars another principle begins to shape itself, a two-bar counterpoint which, in absolute contrast to the large span of the first subject, turns within the restricted space of a couple of tones and their attendant semitones. Thus rapidly has the music been telescoped. The semitonic grind which is a subsidiary feature of the music in the opening bar has now become the main interest and opened a way for the second of the two important moves made in these few bars, the set of four notes, Ex. 28x. This is the chief unit of construction of the symphony. It is worth while spending adequate time in getting these seven bars clear; for they contain the two principles on which the whole symphony is founded, that of expansion in the leap of a ninth in bars one and two, that of contraction (the other end of the telescope) in the four notes of bars six and seven, Ex. 28x, where the music turns in upon itself. One more unit remains to be noticed and with that the basic material of the symphony has been displayed. This occurs six bars further on at Fig. 1 in the score. Its form is a succession of fourths; they start in unison, rise above and fall below simultaneously, expanding like the wings of a double door. (See Ex. 32 for what comes from this; also Ex. 34 and in the Fifth Symphony Ex. 40). The next point to pause over (Fig. 5) is the design of repeated chords (horns answered by wood-wind) and a theme above it on the strings, very expansive and impetuous, Ex. 29. The next important subject, Ex. 30, is played first (two bars after Fig. 8) on the G strings of the violins and violas. The development of this material is rich and concentrated. From the four-note unit comes a long, wandering soliloquy for a solo bassoon, and after that the unit is changed again into a loud jigging rhythm which brass, wood-wind and the strings worry in turn. The development section is short, based almost wholly on the four-note unit, with no mention of the other subjects except for the set of rising fourths which end this section and usher in the recapitulation; this is shortened and much concentrated but has the subject of Ex. 30 more slowly unfolded, a most impressive transformation from which arises the design of the short coda.

Second Movement. *Andante moderato*. This begins with the expanding design (see Exs. 32 and 34) of rising and falling fourths on the brass. Immediately there follows the main subject, Ex. 31, played smoothly on muted violins over a pizzicato bass. An oboe takes the theme, a clarinet joins in, then a bassoon; these wind instruments evolve music in which the design becomes more angular. The angularity (its steepness accentuated in sequences of oscillating fourths) leads naturally to the idea with which the movement began, the great widening of vision, and this the brass takes up once more. Between these two principles of clear statement and the slow processes of thought, the movement is developed. It ends with a remarkable passage, where muted trombones accompany a solo flute.

Third Movement. *Scherzo: Allegro molto.* The scherzo is an epitome of the terse and concentrated character of this symphony. That concentration of material, heard (Ex. 28) in the opening seven bars of the first movement, is here also, Ex. 32, where the basic four-note unit (*x*) comes immediately after the first subject, both very forcibly stated. In Ex. 33 there are two further parts of the construction heard simultaneously – before that, separately; a harsh, spasmodic utterance below, a jigging rhythm above ending in a rising third that will be recognized many times again. The Trio section is dominated by a bucolic tune, Ex. 34, of super-imposed fourths played by tuba, trombones and bassoons. The scherzo then returns, according to custom, but much concentrated. It leads to a short coda centred on the four-note unit and thus, without a break, into the finale.

Fourth Movement. *Finale con epilogo fugato: Allegro molto.* The first two bars, Ex. 35, are a stronger, brighter affirmation of the pizzicato bass at the opening of the slow movement, Ex. 31; the next two bring the music back to the thinner and more acute sounds of semitones that are the real nature of the symphony; and bars five and six start the uncouth galumphing accompaniment below the next tune, Ex. 36. The relationship between the descending semitone in the third bar and the same in the first bar of the symphony, Ex. 28, is obvious; less so is the derivation of what seems a new theme, Ex. 37, when it first is played (at Fig 6) on wood-wind and strings. But this also is an example of the near inter-relation of themes throughout this closely-woven music; here the relationship is to the bass of the last two bars of Ex. 35 and thereafter to the repeated notes of Ex. 36. From then onwards there is no fresh material. Instead there is copious reference to what has already been displayed in previous movements; a *Lento* passage similar to that in which the second subject of the first movement, Ex. 30*a*, is recapitulated (Fig. 17 of that movement), followed by an Allegro molto (Fig. 14 of the last movement), where trombones and tuba have the four-note unit; and that in turn succeeded by the rising fourths of the first movement (and of the third, for which see Ex. 32). All this re-grouping of earlier material gives the movement the character of an authoritative summing-up in closely-reasoned thinking. Lastly there is the fugal epilogue, the coda not only of the movement but of the symphony as a whole and the logical outcome of all that has gone before. This has been a symphony of terse and concentrated statements and it is right that it should be brought to a conclusion by this kind of cool reasoning. But music engenders its own heat, and the fugue, its subject the four-note unit, is high in temperature. Combined with the fugue subject are the other main elements of the movement, but the four-note unit gains the most force. It almost has the last word. But this is seized by the first theme of all, Ex. 28, from the opening bars of the work, and the work ends at once after that final, uncompromising re-statement of the initial idea. There is no more to say.

SYMPHONY NO. 5 IN D MAJOR

FIRST Movement. *Preludio. Moderato.* The symphony starts with a soft low octave held by the strings on C; above it a D major call for two horns. (Ex. 39*a* shows the repeat of this at bar 5). What key does the ear receive? These are contending elements of tonality and in the sense of hesitation between them lies one of the two main characteristics of the symphony.

The other is the assurance of the rest of the music; and that tells the more for this background of uncertainty.

The symphony seems to have been going on in some hidden region before its sound reaches our ears. In the horn-call, that at first seems little more than an echo of sounds the ear has not caught, there is an air of unreality. The music seems mysterious and withdrawn. Although its form is clear there is a pervading sense of irresolution and expectancy. Anything might happen; the music might turn away to almost any quarter. The sensation is caused probably by the deliberate foregoing of a definite key at the start and by the subsequent choice of keys through which the music moves into unforeseen regions. Especially is this felt when the first-subject matter, Ex. 38, returns in the accepted first-movement style but not in the expected tonic nor even in a closely related key, but in one very distant.

The horn call is a detail that pervades the whole movement; it will be heard again in the finale. Peculiar to this movement is the theme which begins in bar 3 as a fragment and becomes a full tune three bars later, Ex. 38b. The second subject, Ex. 39, is close to the first (see b in each). There is no mistaking it as it soars into a new key far distant from any that the music had previously reached, a glowing major key (E) rising out of a minor (C) of opaque darkness. There is a rapid development in a precipitous *Allegro* and a recapitulation which ends with the distant horn call and the held bass exactly as at the start.

Second Movement. *Scherzo: Presto.* The scherzo is rich in material; there are at least four important themes. The first of these, Ex. 40, is heard (by a keen ear) in the fourth bar; which is as much as to say that it is there from the first, for the pace is extremely rapid. Moving softly and quickly in large octaves on the strings, this theme then becomes the background to the next for solo flute and bassoon, Ex. 41, a mere hint more obtrusive. Sudden gusts on wood-wind, sudden answers on strings and a return to the opening manner but now taken over by the wood-wind. So the movement progresses, by stealth, as it seems. (Each movement of this symphony offers notable opportunities to those tempted to label abstract works.) The tune now in play, Ex. 41, becomes more acute in rhythm (played now *staccato*), also somewhat louder. Thus it prepares for the harsh croak of oboe and cor anglais in the next outstanding theme, Ex. 42. The movement continues, never loud except for short ejaculations. A new theme in what is generally the trio section of such a movement brings an aloof solemnity into the music, Ex. 43, while above this heavy texture the strings continue their rapid undulations (in figures derived from Ex. 42a). There then comes a reappearance of the opening material, much concentrated and quickly giving place to Ex. 42 changed from triple to duple time. The whole atmosphere is intensified with changes back and forth between threes and twos, the rhythms heightened with brass and percussion, the temperature raised to fortissimo. Suddenly it all quietens; the breathless pace remains, the hush of the opening returns, and so the movement ends, blown away on a whisper from the strings.

Third Movement. *Romanza: Lento*. It is said that this movement was once headed by a quotation from Bunyan's *Pilgrim's Progress*. Of that no trace remains in the printed score. Material for the movement has, as is known, been taken from previously written music to do with that book. This movement is the central point of the symphony; to the Romanza it rises, from it the music proceeds to its final ecstasy, itself a reflection of the passionate outburst here, Ex. 45. Before that great exclamation there has come the slow, eloquent music of the first part. The design of that is vast, spread chords on divided strings (as in the first five bars of Ex. 44) alone, then repeated as background to the cor anglais theme, Ex. 44a. The next noticeable theme is for flute solo with oboe and clarinet in imitation; the germ of it is in the previous movement, Ex. 40. A slight increase in speed, a greater one in dynamic intensity and gradually a new thought arises out of what has already been heard in Ex. 44c. This is what has been called the Great Exclamation, Ex. 45. It is at once the revelation of a new vision and the transformation of the familiar into the unforeseen (for which refer to Exs. 38b, 39b, 43a, and their derivatives in the preceding movements). The pace now

begins to quicken, there is more general animation as the
wood-wind take up a new tune that has grown out of
Ex. 44b and is urgently stated in a climax at Ex. 46. The
cor anglais melody, Ex. 44a, becomes a horn solo against a
background of tremolando upper strings. The trumpet
answers; and then follows a great outburst of all the brass.
Three statements of the piercing call in Ex. 46 are given by
full strings. What remains has to do with the rich polyphony
of the Great Exclamation (see Ex. 45). Thereafter the music
quietens, a solo horn pianissimo utters the theme in Ex. 44
and the movement ends as the music sinks to the lower
strings.

Fourth Movement. *Passacaglia: Moderato.* The single
quotation given here, Ex. 47, shows the material on
which the passacaglia is built, the music from which it
develops, and the relationship of that music to the rest of
the symphony. In this example the two constituent parts
of the material are displayed, the bass and the treble. The
former, as may be expected in a passacaglia, is heard not
only as a bass but as a treble and, again true to type, is
noticeably persistent. The latter is similarly adaptable; it
will change places with the basic passacaglia tune when that
rises to the upper parts. But its significance is greater even
than that of the passacaglia bass, for it has in it true elements
of the previous movement's great exclamation (see Ex. 45
and for an earlier form Ex. 38b), and from that will arise all
the more exalted music of this movement. Thus the treble
tune becomes eventually the foremost in the whole movement. In the working out of this dual problem between bass
and treble melodies, their development combined and apart
lies the substance of this movement. And since both tunes
have roots in earlier movements (for a derivation of the bass
at Ex. 47b see Ex. 38b) this movement, of which they are
the basic elements, gathers to it all the thought and the
implications of that thought from the beginning. It serves
one of the two chief functions of a finale by delivering a
final assessment. (The other function of a finale, a newer
feature, is that of carrying the symphony over into a
problematical future by leaving it indeterminate. This will

be heard in the Sixth Symphony.) At length the music reaches a point where the passacaglia bass hovers round its original first note and the next below it, the low pedal C which was the first note of the symphony (Ex. 38, the bass). And so the music of the *Preludio* returns to end the work. From it there arises Ex. 38*b*, which naturally goes over into the treble melody of the passacaglia, Ex. 47, and that in turn to the last bars of that melody which are from the Great Exclamation, Exs. 45 and 47*a*. By then the whole of the strings are playing over a huge span and the work ends. The technical terms for this would be imitation, inversion and contrary motion. But, more than motion, there is emotion here which must find other words to describe it.

SYMPHONY NO. 6 IN E MINOR

FIRST Movement. *Allegro*. This symphony is played without a break between the movements, which are linked together by a held note. There are here the two typical centres of first movement form, round which the music is grouped: each has two outstanding themes. The movement starts (*allargando fortissimo*) with an expression of curbed energy suddenly released, Ex. 48. But the music is at once made fast to a chord of E minor which persists throughout the headlong descent of the strings, a passage strongly braced with cross accents (breaking up groups of four into sets of three). Again restraint is put on the music, Ex. 48*b*, again energy is released, now the music is anchored in F minor. Out of the cross-accent design grows a theme for the brass, which in turn develops into the next main theme of the first group (score, Fig. 2). Key and time change for the chief theme of the second group, Ex. 49. Here also the accents of the melody are distributed across and against those of the bass. From this evolves the companion theme of the group, Ex. 50, which becomes the most spreading melody of the movement. Its importance increases when at the climax of the development (based until then exclusively on its companion subject, Ex. 49) it is given out by full brass. And after recapitulation of all the first group material this melody alone stands for that of the second group. First on octave strings, accompanied by harp chords, and then with gradual increase of power it is carried to a great climax that leads to a *fortissimo* re-statement of the first bar of Ex. 48 and so to the end of the movement.

Second Movement. *Moderato*. The principle of alternating major and minor, foreshadowed in the preceding movement (see the first and last chord in Ex. 49) and eventually to become the fundamental principle of the whole work, is now to be still more firmly established. The slow movement starts on what is to be a long journey: but first the music hesitates, hovering between one and the other tonality, Ex. 51*a*, in thoughtful indecision. The music increases in volume. The brass, Ex. 52, utters a new theme; but, forceful though this is, there is still no solution of the conflict of tonalities. This theme next appears *pianissimo*, enlarged to spread over a huge span of five octaves, wavering back and forth in shadowy outlines that almost but never wholly reach definition. That is reached later, Ex. 53, when the drums set up the rhythm of the first theme (see Ex. 51*a*). The drum taps reach immense dynamic force, then decrease; while above and below the rhythm of the drums the first theme (Ex. 51) starts on a long development, during which the music, growing in intensity, burgeons with fresh shapes that arise from the themes already displayed. The texture becomes heavier, the temperature more fiery. The drum rhythm becomes a trumpet call; on the strings loud, rapid, swirling designs of chords emerge from the conflict of major-minor tonalities which dominates this episode. At length the two elements are left with only the drums' rhythm for support. Still unresolved they alternate and in so doing lose height and force. An unaccompanied cor anglais breathes a lost echo of the first melody, Ex. 51, and the movement ends in a hushed discord formed from the repeated drum rhythm below a held note one semitone above.

Third Movement. *Scherzo: Allegro vivace*. Most of the material of this movement is in Ex. 54 and there, too, is displayed the manner in which it is constructed. Construction is the apt term here. The quotation shows how the music is built up from the first low B flat through a series of fourths each separated by a semitone. In bar 5 the pace at which they ascend is doubled and in bar 7 it is doubled again. In bar 8 the movement enters its next phase, a design of repeated quavers interspersed with semi-quaver passages, Ex. 54b. This material is rapidly and stridently displayed and developed. Out of its opening bars, Ex. 54a, there grows a wide spreading figure that dominates the music almost exclusively up to the point of entry of the second main theme (score, Fig. 9). Through change of key and rhythmic design this takes on the character of a completely new melody, and is in fact the only constituent of the movement that has the attributes of melody. It starts with repeated notes followed by a short descending scale passage, a design already present in Ex. 54b. But as it continues it shows individual traits, and later, when the first part of the scherzo has returned, this second related theme gains an increasing importance. One other passage should be noted, a striking inversion of the linked fourths, Ex. 54a, now in the bass (wood-wind) with bare fifths above, now in the treble with rapid rising scale passages below, all very irresolute, tenuous, portentous, and fluid.

Fourth Movement. *Epilogue: Moderato.* The epilogue now begins its unhurried thoughtful course through reminiscences of past happenings in other movements. First a long fugal contemplation, cool, somnolent, deliberate as the rise and fall of a sleeper's breath. The theme takes its first four notes, Ex. 55a, from the first of the symphony, Ex. 48, its next group of four, Ex. 55b, from the second theme of the scherzo. Thus a synthesis is created and the function of the epilogue defined; it will bring the symphony to a conclusion in time and as far as may be to one in thought also. The music continues to move searchingly through many sinuous extensions of this fugal theme, always soft in tone and light in volume. Throughout the whole movement the pace does not appreciably quicken nor does the music louden above a dim mezzo-forte. The texture is in transparent part writing, slightly thickened at times by successions of light chords. There are notable passages of octaves strings above muted horn chords, for solo oboe above muted trombone chords, Ex. 56, bars 3-5, for muted brass in octaves below tremolando string octaves, for harp harmonics (the fugue subject in augmentation) against wind and string counterpoint. There are huge sighing coupled chords for muted strings much divided (see Ex. 56, bar 2) which recalls the same design in the first movement, Ex. 48a. The tension produced by this music, so ominously reticent, never relaxes; rather it increases. The coupled chords, Ex. 56, are whispered now by muted horns. The passage of fifths, Ex. 56, bar 1, once more leads to an oboe solo, longer this time and unaccompanied. Finally, while pizzicato bass strings murmur broken clauses of the fugue, the other strings alternate between an E flat major chord and a minor chord of E. Each is an inversion (lacks, that is, its fundamental basis); and thus to the indeterminate alternation of the two is added individual elements of indecision in each. It is the E minor chord that is the least decisive. And when the music ends on that most questioning of all the chords of this final clause, the symphony is left in an infinitude of speculation.

20

Sergei Rachmaninov (1873-1943)

ROBIN HULL

INTRODUCTION

RACHMANINOV is the least-known of popular composers.
This claim is no tricky paradox; the facts speak for themselves. Of course the public are immensely familiar with
the Second and Third Piano Concertos, the *Paganini
Rhapsody*, a few preludes for piano, and a handful of songs.
But what else? Some of Rachmaninov's most important
works are seldom or never heard. These include his
symphonic poem, *The Isle of the Dead*, the *Vesper Mass*, the
four-movement cantata, *The Bells*, two published symphonies, and several large-scale compositions for piano solo.
The Fourth Concerto remains a closed book to the majority;
the 'well-known' preludes are but a fraction of the total;
and the 'familiar' songs still leave about seventy to be
explored. In short, Rachmaninov is commonly judged on
evidence that gives little clue to his range. Some of the
most persistent opinions about his music are impossible to
reconcile with evidence of any kind whatever. No study of
the symphonies can be profitable unless these miscon-
ceptions are first examined.

The prime fallacies can be summarized as follows:
'Self-pity is the keynote of Rachmaninov's music. Its
emotional substance reflects a brooding melancholy, a
will-less resignation, and unswerving concern with passivity
or death. There is no note of struggle or aspiration in his
works. Their prevailing moods are fatalistic to the point of
morbidity.' First, the question of self-pity. Such weakness
might be suspected, possibly, in the opening movement of
the first piano concerto. If it occurs elsewhere, we still
await chapter and verse for the allegation. The reason for

failure to substantiate the charge is quite clear. Two inherent qualities of Rachmaninov's style are dignity and self-command which (unlike Tchaikovsky at his weakest) he preserves even at the great climaxes. These qualities cannot and do not co-exist with self-pity. That 'keynote' seems to be deduced, not from musical evidence, but from the composer's nervous collapse after the failure of his first symphony. Yet anyone with a practical grasp of psychology must know that recovery from nervous break-down calls for a supreme exertion of will and character. And Rachmaninov did make a successful recovery, from which he never relapsed. So much for this reach-me-down theorizing about self-pity.

The Second and Third symphonies are but two of many works that refute the notion of sustained melancholy, will-less resignation, and failure to aspire. It is true that each symphony, in its different way, is influenced by a 'Fate' motto. But the purpose and effect of the motto is to pose a strictly musical problem, and in both works the composer reaches a triumphant solution. The principle of this method is identical with that employed by Beethoven for his Fifth Symphony. The nature of Rachmaninov's premises de-mands a sense of tragedy – this is stronger in the Second Symphony than the Third – yet by far the larger part of each work is serene or frankly exuberant. The main argu-ments are virile, not resigned, and the respective finales are joyous. The same can be said of the first three Piano Concertos and the *Paganini Rhapsody*. Even the sombre *Isle of the Dead* owes much of its tremendous and tragic power to the self-controlled objectivity of the composer's treatment. The justice of these comments can be proved by anyone willing to scan the printed page and accept the evidence of his own ears. The perverse refusal of Rach-maninov's critics to follow either course is explicable only as an attempt to justify their temperamental distaste for his romanticism.

Rachmaninov's Symphony, No. 1 in D minor (Op. 13), was a disaster of youthful pride. Written in 1895, and produced two years later at St Petersburg, the score was roundly condemned for bad music and worse orchestration. The composer owned that these strictures were fully deserved, and never allowed the work to be published. His next symphony, No. 2 in E minor (Op. 27), composed at Dresden in 1907, belongs to the fruitful period of the first Piano Sonata and *The Isle of the Dead*. It shows the complete maturity to be expected after the re-emergence of his creative powers in the second Piano Concerto (1901). The four movements of No. 2 in E minor are spacious and sometimes leisurely in design. Rachmaninov seems to have realised that certain passages were too prolix, if we may judge from cuts made with his sanction. The style is luxurious, often rhetorical, and as free from 'forward-looking' elements as the Elgar symphonies. Yet one can hardly find fault with the work for being true to its period. The strength of the music lies in its sustained vitality, richness of lyrical invention, and a glowing eloquence capable of rising to extraordinary power. This energy is especially notable in the Scherzo (second movement) and the tumultuous Finale. On the whole, the ideas strike one as more arresting than their discussion; the arguments of the first and final movements are rather prone to mark time, and this weakens their structure. The symphony is orthodox in pattern but extremely individual in thought. Rachmaninov's orchestration is lavish, yet finely judged to each shade of mood, and the effect of his full resources at moments of crisis can be electrifying.

Symphony No. 3 in A minor, Op. 44 (1936), reveals important points of contrast with its predecessor. The lighter and more pointed method of orchestration makes for increased clarity. The lyricism achieves a new buoyancy; the strenuous pages have a keener edge. One finds, too, a more pliant and adventurous handling of material. There is a much firmer balance between ideas and argument; rhetorical passages are few; and the design shows a tautness that gives little quarter to leisurely sentiment. Rachmaninov's pattern, though rooted in tradition, contains many a novel twist during its three movements. His slow (second) movement encloses a Scherzo – *Adagio: Allegro vivace: Adagio* – and provides the pivot on which the whole balance of the symphony depends. The main discussion in the Finale is a magnificent piece of fugal writing which springs from the opening theme. And the initial motto of the work gives unity to the entire concept in a manner whose inevitability satisfies the most stringent claims of logic and creative imagination.

SYMPHONY NO. 2 IN E MINOR

First Movement. *Largo – Allegro moderato*. The Symphony begins quietly with a slow, dark-hued Introduction (*Largo:* pp. 1–9). In the first six bars (p. 1), Rachmaninov presents the triple motto of fate which exerts a strong influence during the work. The three sections of this motto are Ex. 1 (*a*), a sombre fragment for 'cellos and basses; Ex. 1 (*b*), a fanfare-like phrase for wood-wind and horns; Ex. 1 (*c*), a poignant theme for first violins. Of these, Ex. 1 (*c*) has the most far-reaching effect.

The whole motto is repeated. Then the material of Ex. 1 (*c*) broadens out with fuller orchestration, and reaches a powerful climax in the strings (p. 7, bar 5). The tension gradually subsides until the Introduction is gently rounded off by a cor anglais solo based on Ex. 1*a* (p. 9, bar 7). A single bar for strings provides a link with the main body of the movement (*Allegro moderato*). The *Allegro moderato*, bringing a more restless mood, follows the normal sonata-pattern of exposition (p. 9), development (p. 22), re-statement (p. 41), and coda (p. 57). There are two main themes. The first comes after four preliminary bars. This is an urgent, richly expressive melody for first and second violins (p. 10, bar 2). Ex. 2. After its immediate repetition the melodic line of Ex. 2 merges into a broad, subsidiary tune which acts as a pendant (p. 11, bar 13). It soon leads to a spirited bridge-passage (p. 13, bar 1) whose triplet rhythm foreshadows the second main theme. The latter is closely heralded by a clarinet solo (p. 16, bar 4). The theme itself (*Moderato*: G major) starts as a lyrical dialogue between wood-wind and strings (p. 16, bar 6) (Ex. 3). The theme of Ex. 3 is repeated, with triplet elaboration in the accompaniment, and its influence remains until the subdued close of the exposition. Rachmaninov marks a repeat for the entire *Allegro moderato*, but few conductors respond to this optimism.

The beginning of the development (p. 22, bar 1: E minor) strikes a note of restrained passion. Its radical elements are a chromatic, descending phrase for violas (p. 22, bar 1), derived from Ex. 1*a*, and a rhapsodic version of Ex. 1*c* given to solo violin (p. 22, bar 3). These ideas are interwoven with the initial notes of Ex. 2 (cor anglais: p. 22, bar 12), and their taut argument results in a climax (p. 27, bar 6). A vivid recall of Ex. 1*b* by the brass (*Meno mosso:* p. 30, bar 1) prepares the way for fairly extensive discussion of Ex. 2 (violas: p. 32, bar 5) whose subject-matter is worked up to a great crisis (pp. 36–38). Dramatic outbursts on full brass close the development (pp 38–40), and lead into the re-statement of Exs. 2 and 3. Here Ex. 2 is handled in an intense and concentrated style carrying the movement towards its fiercest climax (p. 45, bar 2). The melody of Ex. 3, omitted from the development, is now given a generous innings (pp. 48–56), and a strongly rhythmic handling of Ex. 1*c* provides the foundation for an eloquent and impassioned coda (pp. 57–66).

Second Movement. *Allegro molto.* The second movement, a Scherzo in A minor, is much simpler in design. Two bars of well-marked rhythm preface the vigorous first theme for horns and strings (p. 67, bar 3) (Ex. 4). This is repeated and extended till the music works up to brilliant fanfares for brass (pp. 72–74) founded on the basic rhythm. Then the ferocious mood gradually subsides in preparation for a lyrical, second tune given to the strings (*Moderato:* p. 77, bar 1). But this tranquillity is soon dispelled by a return of the Scherzo-rhythm (*Con moto:* p. 80, bar 1), and the full-length recall of Ex. 4 (p. 83, bar 1), whose vehemence ebbs away to a mere skeleton of the rhythm and ends in a general pause (p. 87, bar 17). The middle section of the Scherzo, founded on Ex. 4, is vividly contrapuntal (*Meno mosso:* p. 88, bar 1). The opening material is then re-stated (*Tempo I:*

p. 100, bar 1). Towards the close, Ex. 4 identifies itself
with the baleful character of Ex. 1*b* (*Meno mosso:* p. 121,
bar 8), and this ominous influence prevails to the end.

Third Movement. *Adagio*. The slow movement (A major)
is lyrical and rhapsodic. It has two main themes. The first
appears as an introductory figure on the strings, but claims
the importance of a true 'subject' (p. 124, bar 1), Ex. 5.
It is followed at once by the second chief tune, an idyllic
melody for solo clarinet (p. 125, bar 2), Ex. 6. This forms
the substance of a lengthy sentence rounded off by Ex. 5
(p. 128, bar 3). The atmosphere of idyllic calm is ruffled
when semi-quaver figures for strings recall the dark mood
and material of Ex. 1*c* (*Poco più mosso:* p. 129, bar 3). But
the rhythm of Ex. 1*c* itself becomes peacefully transformed
into an oboe solo (p. 131, bar 7) upon which the principal
climax is built (pp. 136–138). A general pause precedes the
return of Tempo I (p. 140, bar 4) where Ex. 5 is heard as
a horn solo, dovetailed with Ex. 1*c* on solo clarinet, and
followed by Ex. 6 on the strings (p. 141, bar 8). The subtle
combination of these elements, Exs. 1*c*, 5 and 6, is sustained
until the close of the movement.

Fourth Movement. *Allegro vivace*. The Finale in E major
is triumphant. Its basic rhythm is boldly established in six
bars of introduction, and then the first main theme blazes
out with tremendous vigour (p. 151, bar 1), Ex. 7. The
virile impulse of Ex. 7 is kept up at full strength (pp. 151–
156). This feeling of tautness does not slacken when the
basic rhythm is used as background for a tense, march-like
interlude (p. 158, bar 1) before the lengthy repetition of
Ex. 7 (p. 161, bar 2). A broad *Con moto* passage (p. 168, bar
3) heralds the second main theme, a tune of glowing eloquence, presented in D major (p. 170, bar 1), Ex. 8.

The eloquence of this tune is poured out for eleven
luxurious pages, and is stemmed only by a brief echo of
Ex. 1*c* (*Adagio:* p. 182, bar 1) before the original tempo is
restored for the development (p. 182, bar 7). The composer's
argument is based on the material of Ex. 1*c* and the rhythm
of Ex. 7. He builds up an atmosphere of ever-increasing
excitement by weaving descending scales into the texture

(pp. 183–193) rather on the lines of Variation 22 in the *Paganini Rhapsody*. This prepares the requisite mood of triumph for his ample re-statement (p. 194, bar 1). The subject matter of Ex. 7, the march-like interlude, and Ex. 8 (omitted from the development) is reviewed in full. When Ex. 8 has been carried to a broad and passionate climax (pp. 225–227), a swift coda in the rhythm of Ex. 7 brings the symphony to its resplendent conclusion.

SYMPHONY NO. 3 IN A MINOR

First Movement. *Lento – Allegro moderato*. The first movement combines strong individuality of thought with a traditional pattern – introduction (p. 1), exposition (p. 3), development (p. 18), re-statement (p. 48) and coda (p. 59). The introduction is restricted to eleven bars. In the *Lento* section (bars 1–4), the motto of fate which recurs throughout the symphony is at once heard on clarinets, horns and solo 'cello, Ex. 9. After a general pause, the tempo changes to *Allegro moderato* (bar 5), but the introduction continues with a flourish for full orchestra. The second violins then bring in an accompanying figure, and this serves as background to the first of two principal themes in the main body of the movement (p. 2, bar 5), Ex. 10.

A more cheerful version of this tune is given to first and second violins (p. 3, bar 9). It is followed by a bridge-passage of triplet figures which soon makes way for the warm and lyrical second theme on the 'cellos (p. 8, bar 1), Ex. 11. The subject-matter of Ex. 11, repeated and elaborated by the strings (p. 9, bar 5), is brought to a climax for brass in an *Allegro* section (p. 14, bar 1), and dominates the exposition until its close (p. 17, bar 7). A repeat is marked for the exposition (pp. 3–17).

The development re-establishes the tempo of *Allegro moderato*, and quickly sets to work with a treatment of Ex. 10. This starts on the bassoons (p. 18, bar 3), accompanied by triplets for violas (*vide* bridge-passage of exposition). A new, subsidiary motif is added to the discussion by solo oboe, and the influence of the triplet figures steadily increases, though the importance of Ex. 10 is asserted boldly by horns and trombones (pp. 31-33). An outburst for full orchestra, whose rather freakish scoring includes the xylophone (pp. 41-43), is cut short by the ominous motto (trombones: p. 44, bar 1). An echo of the motto on solo horn ends the development. The re-statement (p. 48, bar 6) deals briefly with Ex. 10, but is generous to Ex. 11, for which the development found no place. This lyrical tune also forms the basis of the coda (*Allegro:* p. 59, bar 2), towards whose close the motto is again heard.

Second Movement. *Adagio – Allegro vivace – Adagio.* The second movement, with its home-key in C sharp major, begins quietly with an inverted version of the motto on the horns (*Adagio ma non troppo:* p. 67, bar 1). In the tenth bar the first chief melody appears as a tranquil solo for violin, Ex. 12. This tune forms a lengthy sentence which ends in an important semi-quaver figure (p. 69, bar 7). The latter will reappear as a structural link with the *Allegro vivace* (p. 86), and again for the resumption of the *Adagio* (p. 123), Ex. 13. The second main theme, serene and flowing, follows almost at once as a flute solo with harp accompaniment (p 70, bar 2), Ex. 14.

The flute melody is repeated on solo bass clarinet against the shadowy background of the motto (muted brass: p. 72, bar 1). Richer treatment of this tune reaches a climax in the strings (p. 75, bar 2), after which Ex. 12 is briefly recalled by solo flute (p. 76, bar 3). The remaining pages of the *Adagio* (pp. 77–84) are devoted to an elaboration of Ex. 14 with very full scoring. The semi-quaver figure, Ex. 13, then reappears to herald the *Allegro vivace* (p. 86, bar 2). This section (pp. 86–119) takes the place of a Scherzo. Its purpose is to develop the rhythms of Exs. 12 and 14 separately and in conjunction. At first this process is confined to the skeleton outline of the rhythms (pp. 86–92), but the pattern of Ex. 12 is soon transformed into a vigorous theme for strings (p. 92, bar 2). The rhythm and material of the new theme assert their influence throughout the middle of the Scherzo (pp. 92–106), and the composer then treats the rhythms of Exs. 12 and 14 with continued intensity. The Scherzo's headlong pace is halted by three transitional pages (*Alla breve:* pp. 120–122), the semi-quaver figure, Ex. 13, now returns, and the original tempo of *Adagio* is restored (p. 123, bar 1). Here the re-statement is much condensed. The two main themes appear in reverse order: Ex. 14 on the strings (p. 123, bar 5), and Ex. 12 on oboe and strings (p. 124, bar 4). An echo of the inverted motto brings the movement to a subdued close.

Third Movement. *Allegro*. A brilliant flourish for full orchestra opens the Finale in A major (p. 129, bar 1). The ruling idea, a theme of immense energy, is presented by the strings in the second bar, Ex. 15. The rhythmical impulse of this theme spreads to every department of the orchestra, and maintains its virile course for thirteen pages. Then comes a lyrical episode in C sharp minor (*Meno mosso:* p. 142, bar 1) whose theme of sweeping arpeggios has the appearance but not the significance of a true 'subject'. In any case, its duration is short-lived, for the material of Ex. 15 reasserts itself (*Allegro:* p. 146, bar 1) in what proves to be a false start to fugal development. The check comes from a thunderous statement of the motto (p. 147), though the setback is exceedingly brief. After a general pause the fugal development finally breaks loose with a splendid transformation of Ex. 15 (*Allegro vivace:* p. 149, bar 1), Ex. 16.

The working-out of Ex. 16 is orthodox in method but highly resourceful in invention and detail. Rachmaninov sustains the tremendous impetus while submitting his material to every conceivable variety of treatment, and even finding a place for the second theme from his slow movement, Ex. 14, within this elaborate texture. The course of the *Allegro vivace* is, maybe, overmuch prolonged, for the re-statement of Ex. 15 – similar to Ex. 16 in mood – still lies ahead. This return to Ex. 15 is reached by a 'false start' like that employed to herald the fugal development, extending over five pages, and reaching a tumultuous climax (pp. 178–9). The re-statement itself (p. 180, bar 1) is on ample lines that do not wholly avoid an undue effect of twice-trod ground. The coda begins light-heartedly with

a gay tune for flutes accompanied by a completely benevo-
lent version of the motto in the strings (*Allegretto:* p. 195,
bar 1). But this suggestion of flippancy proves deceptive.
The composer builds up an overwhelming climax by artfully contrived stages – *Poco a poco accelerando* (p. 199, bar 2),
Allegro (p. 201, bar 3), *Allegro vivace* (p. 204, bar 1). This
titanic crisis loses some of its tension in an unaccountably
bad piece of scoring just before the close (pp. 207–8), but
the final bars match the movement as a whole in their
proclamation of victory.

21

Sir Arnold Bax (1883-   )

H. G. SEAR

INTRODUCTION

WHEN Sir Arnold Bax produced his First Symphony, in 1922, he had already established a reputation with such frankly romantic works as *The Garden of Fand, Tintagel,* and *November Woods.* The vogue for programme music had reached its peak; it was to become a bone of contention. But symphonies by British composers were few, performances were sparse and recognition was small, though it is on record that Elgar's First Symphony, which appeared in 1908, had won a hundred hearings by the end of its year. Within the first two decades of the century symphonies of Franck, Mahler, Bruckner, and Sibelius had been heard here; Strauss's *Domestic,* Harty's *Irish,* Scriabin's *Poem of Ecstasy,* Vaughan Williams's *London* and *Sea* Symphonies, and Elgar's Second Symphony.

Bax has seven to his credit. The fact that no one now is overcome by surprise when an Englishman composes a symphony is probably due to his labours and those of Vaughan Williams. Now while seven symphonies do not necessarily entitle a man to a place in a nation's music, work of Bax's consistent quality does; but it is still necessary to see it against its native background. We may wonder that a composer so given to work of a literary character (for that is what, so far, his music was) should decide to couch his conceptions in symphonic form; and we may enquire how well he succeeded. For symphony imposes a strict discipline; and if a man thinks to infuse it with poetical ideas which all shall read, he must first be well versed in past traditions, since, in the final reckoning, it is his music *qua* music which counts, and not its literary connotations.

Bax himself would be the last to deny a strong leaning towards Celtic subject-matter, though this, in his case, is surely as much acquired as instinctive. Yet there is that in his face which seems to indicate an exceedingly sharp-cut vision; and it can be said at once that one of the most notable features of his music is the beautiful clarity of his line. The tag 'Celtic twilight', then, has been applied too often and too easily. Another fact is the driving force of emotion, though this too, must make for clarity. Complex Bax's music undoubtedly is, but transparently complex on the whole. And we may be allowed to believe that when he turned to symphonic composition, he recognized the demands of discipline, and that, however elaborate his apparatus, he saw to it that it should work smoothly and clearly. His first three symphonies, in fact, are fraught with conflict between his imagination and his intellect.

His complexity demands concentrated listening and in this regard he is his own enemy. The orchestral forces he employs are so great that the opportunity for hearing his major works cannot be provided frequently, and Bax has subjected himself to charges of a forbidding intricacy and over-orchestration.

Bax has a highly individual feeling for melody, but it is not always one that makes instantaneous appeal. Mental power is present, measuring, curbing, enhancing. His treatment of his melodies has a greater significance than the tunes themselves. He cannot bear literally to repeat them. He must clothe them afresh; and the new array implies a new attitude and approach.

His thematic material tends towards several distinct types. A marked feature is the repetition of a single note before the full curve is plotted; one of these notes is liable to be flattened. An example of this can be discovered in most of the symphonies. Another is a melody of from eight to twelve bars, kept approximately within the range of an octave, which is, in fact, a shuffling of the chromatic scale. The opening theme of the Third Symphony, Ex. 1, may be cited here. Then Bax shows a liking for a short motive which leaps upwards in fifths, falling back a brief step at the end. The First Symphony makes great play with one of these for 'cellos and basses; the Second for tuba; the Third, also for tuba, Ex. 2; the Fifth for 'cellos. In great contrast with these is the sweep of sustained melody, often given to violins, which is one of the most lovable features of his genius, Ex. 4. The dynamic drive at the back of his mind leads him in all the symphonies to introduce at least one theme which implies a whole series of rhythmic patterns, and which, whether as accompaniment, or internally, keeps the work in constant motion.

Bax's rhythms are extremely varied, ranging from the sharply defined patterns which tempt the thoughtful listener to count them out in all their detail, to a flexuous tune obtained by altering the time signature from bar to bar. The latter is one of the commonest features of Bax's symphonic style. In the First Symphony he prescribes a restless rhythm, alternating two-four with common time and then bidding the performer steal a fraction of a beat (*poco rubato*) to secure the actual rhythm his imagination has glimpsed. The reader should note these alternations in Ex. 1; and it may be hazarded that the single bar of one-eight that occurs a little later is the only example in modern music.

His harmony follows no acclaimed system, new or old; it is his own. That is, he moves steadily forward, following a perfectly natural bent, with a discerning ear for variability and a firm hand to control it. The label that fits best is 'chromaticism'; he confesses to an early enthusiasm for Wagner and later for Elgar. Yet he is like neither. His orchestral tissue reveals strongly-defined strands in its polyphonic flow, and as this flow more and more becomes second nature to him it tends to diminish harmonic luxuriance for its own sake. Only two of the symphonies follow declared tonality, the first and second, and these are respectively described as being in E flat, and in E minor and C. Yet none of his critics has accused Bax of vagueness.

He uses a large orchestra with much delicacy. He may require such extras as the heckelphone, sarrusophone, tenor tuba, and a versatile battery of percussion plus a piano and organ, but they are employed for timbre more than for volume. He affects a tricoloured ribbon of melody produced, shall we say, by cor anglais, trumpet, and 'cello or other such combination. Generally speaking he seems to avoid giving a melody to a single instrument. His three trumpets are apt to move in parallel sixths, his trombones in octaval progressions. When he calls for two harps the parts are differentiated. He likes to impose a sudden quiet in lower brass while flutes, say, and horns are loudly and strongly marked. Brass that has been kept muted will be suddenly opened. Half his strings may be muted, half plucked, played below the bridge or with the wood of the bow; he rarely divides his strings as Sibelius does (except perhaps in the Fifth Symphony, dedicated to Sibelius), but he often deploys them in small groups. His chiaroscuro is precious to him and bears the mark of careful retouching. In a note of his own, Bax says of the introduction of the Third Symphony that 'the basic idea of the music is adumbrated as through a dark haze', and later 'the sombre mists ... again flood the landscape'. Yet he is careful to pick out such melody with a sufficient sharpness.

Three movements are enough for his purpose; save in the instance of the sixth, the scherzo is absent. But humour is not his strong point, his *Picaresque Overture* notwithstanding. Repose seems to be a deep need of his nature and this he seeks not only in his lyrical middle movements but even in quiet episodes in the often fierce outer movements. He sums up the whole work in a contemplative epilogue.

His themes are swiftly marshalled and they reflect a kinship which in itself gives a surprising unity. This seems to be instinctive; yet he attains formal unity by carrying a main theme, Ex. 1, into all three movements. His resourcefulness is perhaps seen at its best in the ingenuity with which he develops these themes in their proper place or illuminates with an altogether new light in movements of a different character, Exs. 8 and 9.

For one influence to which an earlier composer was subjected his modern descendant is exposed to a hundred.

Bax has confessed to that of Wagner, Strauss, and Elgar. Here and there in the symphonies there are reminiscent phrases, Delius, Borodin and, by reason of his chromatic progressions, even Franck; yet most of them appear to be unconscious influences. It is a very personal music, yielding less to analysis than to sympathy and intuition. Bax says himself that it is 'often difficult to understand at first hearing, even to experienced musicians'.

With all this in mind one may go on to a more detailed examination of the Third Symphony, not only because it is more accessible in its nature, but because gramophone records are available.

SYMPHONY NO. 3

First Movement. *Lento moderato – Allegro moderato.* Its first theme, not supremely interesting in itself, immediately appears three times: first as an unaccompanied solo for bassoon, Ex. 1, then, overlapping it, on a clarinet whose partner introduces one of those embellishments so dear to Bax's soul; and finally on the flutes. This is fertile material. Through the dark mist in which it envelopes itself, the seed of a typical Bax leap is thrown up by 'cellos and basses; and over a string bass which emerges from Ex. 1, what Bax calls a liturgical theme may be caught, first from wind and then from strings.

This string bass has already suggested a strong six-eight rhythm, now, *allegro moderato,* firmly asserted by full wood-wind. It is the signal for a broadening of Ex. 1 and a new adumbration of Ex. 2. The marked rhythm and the flexuous melody are deftly combined and set forth in Bax's 'sensuous beauty of orchestral sound'. The pace is ferocious and Ex. 2 makes its first proper entry on an open tuba.

So far we have an excellent example of Bax's rapid dialectic, with swift response to every idea propounded. But now with the most delicious harmonization of Ex. 1 for five solo violins, Bax's passion for delicate beauty is disclosed and with it his need for relaxation.

A *lento moderato* introduces a new theme, Ex. 3, sustained

and tranquil, for strings. Bax can hardly dwell upon it fondly enough. There enters a rhythmic motive for horns which may be noted as yet another of the composer's basic musical thoughts; and Ex. 3 will presently be seen to own kinship with the main theme of the next movement.

But Ex. 1 is due for return, this time on violas, joined by violins in careful order. Recapitulation is now in full flight and its onrush is fierce and unrelenting. All Bax's art of instrumentation is brought to bear on the setting forth of themes that are now familiar. He provides an extraordinary sensation which seems at first to disguise his real musical purpose; but with attentive listening the essential thought bodies forth in clear definition.

Second Movement. *Lento*. In the second movement we are again permitted to see the composer's initial idea in embryo. It is stated barely, as a horn solo. At once, through a haze of muted strings, a deeply moving figure that is fundamental to the whole section is heard as a viola solo. Then over a mesh of harp tone a trumpet enunciates a new version of the initial theme. A celesta introduces a faery strain and the viola figure, tinted now by a harp and bass clarinet, is heard once more. Still as a trumpet solo comes the principal theme proper, Ex. 4, followed by a statement, in character, of Ex. 1 for violins and cor anglais, Ex. 8. Now Ex. 4 is seen in many aspects as through a dream, and the pulsating viola figure assumes a strange robustness suggesting an inexorable march in an unsubstantial world of reverie. There is a moment of rare loveliness when a solo horn enters with a curiously remote melody over the faint tinkle of harp and celesta and a diaphanous tissue of tone contributed by three soloists in each line of strings.

Finale. *Moderato*. Epilogue: *Poco lento*. The utter tranquillity of the *lento* is dispelled in a flash by the first note of the finale, delivered by bassoons, horns, and gong. The air has become vigorous; the period of respose is over. The first sturdy string figure should be held in mind; it is of great importance. But the real theme is announced by clarinets and violas, Ex. 5, over a rattle of tenor drum. It is

jocose and sets the prevalent mood, inclining every fresh
thought and feeling to willing sympathy. Mark well the
rhythmic impetus Bax loves to win for a repeated bass
figure over which Ex. 5 raps out for the second time. Mark
too how closely every successive thought is related to what
has preceded it, for the argument is fast as well as concentrated.

So fast, in fact, that Bax has again to seek one of his
moments of repose. This occurs as a brief cor anglais solo,
Ex. 6, one of those themes of his that rises typically from
a group of reiterated notes. Although vigour has not
departed from the movement it would appear that with
this motive a glimpse of final serenity has been caught.
The jollity has not evaporated, however; the melodic and
rhythmic game is energetically prosecuted to the very
threshold of the Epilogue.

A most singular feeling for unity has been demonstrated.
A relationship with the opening of the finale and even
with the viola figure of the second movement is maintained
in the first two pages of the epilogue: a choral accompaniment is laid down over which floats, from oboes and
clarinets, the simplest of melodies, Ex. 7. Its beauty is
incomparable, and throughout the whole of this passage
there is the subtlest feeling for cadence. Soon wood-wind
sets up a soft swinging motion, followed by strings, and the
three muted trumpets voice the last transformation of Ex. 1
in parallel sixths, Ex. 9. It is like the ghost of the past.
Horns glide gently downwards; a solo violin wafts a refrain
to the heights. Another wisp of melody is sung by a horn
over the accompanimental figure with which the epilogue
started and the symphony dies away into silence.

One is left with the impression that this music, individual
to the last degree as it is, is born not out of experiment but
of experience.

By sanction of the composer the first three symphonies
have been bracketed together. They embrace a period of
struggle and only in the epilogue of the third is this
resolved. The frequent use of the direction *feroce* is symp-
tomatic of Bax's state of mind. But in the fourth the music

is no longer embattled. The tendency to profuse ornamentation, too, is less pronounced. The themes themselves emerge more definitely but just as rapidly. The general mood is extrovert and the epilogue, an astounding outburst, takes the form of a triumphal march. It is as though, looking back, Bax has found a still more urgent need to throw his vision outwards.

The full effect of this shines forth in the Fifth Symphony. The total conception of the work must have been present in the composer's mind long before setting pen to paper, so closely bonded in unity is the whole composition. Here Bax feels no need for cyclic themes; and yet once the symphony becomes familiar the last bars of the superb epilogue are visible in the opening tune for wood-wind, bass strings, and percussion. And by this time one begins to get measure of the fact that it is difficult almost to impossibility in Bax's music to withdraw this motive or that effect from the context without partially destroying it, so finely integrated is the substance, so quintessential the smallest detail.

SYMPHONY NO. 6

ALTHOUGH it may now be said that Bax has disposed of his internal problems, the difficulties of the Sixth are not really diminished. Bax has won a still greater power of concentration. He has modified his form; or rather, internal necessities have modified it for him: his finale takes the shape of an Introduction, Scherzo, and Epilogue, the last being even more carefully wrought *within* the movement. The word Introduction takes on a special importance because, although the three sections are not thematically connected, the opening passages always contain the true germ of the matter.

First Movement. *Moderato – Allegro con fuoco.* Thus the somewhat acridly scored theme given forth by horns and wood-wind presages the principal subject of the first movement; and the *ostinato* figure, Ex. 12, held over a pedal for many bars, is promoted to some height in the course of development.

The dramatic atmosphere once charged, the ostinato Ex. 12 is given new shape and serves as accompaniment to the principal subject, Ex. 10, of the *allegro con fuoco*, proclaimed by wood-wind and trumpets. The horns drive the theme onwards, inciting the whole orchestra to tempestuousness. Careful examination of the treatment even so far is richly rewarded: every phrase, however small, retains a close relationship.

After the storm the serenity of the second subject, Ex. 11, sweetly sung by flutes, is delightful indeed. The counterpoint of the horns should not be missed; a new phrase of the ostinato for strings cannot be.

A third, ancillary, tune follows at once, in high strings related in mood to Ex. 11. (It might in fact be said to be the natural offspring of Exs. 10 and 11.) This is one of Bax's momentary pauses in which he prepares himself for strenuous discharge.

Development begins with a new version of the ostinato Ex. 12*b*, the prelude to an intensive discussion of Ex. 10. The composer's habitual respite has served him well. At this moment his mind is clearer than ever it was in preceding symphonies. The subject-matter is wonderfully disposed and spaced, the ostinato declaring its kinship with Ex. 10 in various unexpected positions, the whole structure steadily building up to a great climax, led brilliantly by trumpets.

Bax's faculty for reducing thematic stuff involving rhythmic variation, orchestral display, and careful argument to its pith is well demonstrated in the brief recapitulation. It is neatly done. Ex. 10 appears in violins and clarinets; a trombone smoothly chants Ex. 11 and a coda move forcefully and inevitably to an abrupt close.

Second Movement. *Lento, molto espressivo.* In the second movement the six introductory bars have their usual importance. They contain a germ which will expand and divide. The violins set out in an extended melody of high lyrical beauty, Ex. 13, wonderfully borne, not by a formal accompaniment, but by a dream-like orchestral tissue whose range of tint seems inexhaustible. The melody passes to cor anglais, to oboe, to viola with bassoons, oboes and clarinets, on and on, each time varied yet always itself.

A change is brought by trumpets which introduce a livelier motion, Ex. 14, not without suggestion of a 'Scotch snap'. It, too, is handed to oboes and then horns. And then once more serenity prevails in a new melody for three clarinets richly decorated by strings, and, if anything quite so formal is to be found in Bax, looking very like a free inversion of Ex. 13. That lovely tune and Ex. 5 return, garbed anew, and the rapt meditation is complete.

Finale. Introduction: *Lento moderato*. Scherzo: *Allegro vivace*. Trio: *Andante semplice*. Epilogue: *Lento*. The finale commands the most watchful interest. The theme which dominates the whole movement, aptly changing its character as it goes, is first heard in the introduction on a clarinet directed to be played as sweetly as possible. Much as is the case of the bare opening theme of the Third Symphony, the other two clarinets provide decorative tendrils, the harmonies being enriched meanwhile by horns and harp. Strings then possess themselves of Ex. 15, striving to infuse it with calm.

A new subject, Ex. 16, and Bax's word for it would be 'liturgical', so rich in suggestion are its shape and harmony, is given out by wood-wind and then, almost as if in re-action, the pace quickens, becomes a little livelier, and the Scherzo is launched, *allegro vivace*. A six-eight rhythm is set; a bassoon responds to it with a hint of Ex. 15. Yet even this is mere preludial matter to the real *scherzando*, led by violins, which establish the inner nature of Ex. 15, but oddly in contention with the liturgical theme, Ex. 16. It looks as if the latter will darken the whole movement, but Bax shifts to a Trio to gain poise.

This trio is exquisitely simple, its subject first given to a solo harp over divided strings, then to cor anglais and violins, Ex. 17. It is submitted to a many-coloured play of orchestral finesse until at last the scherzo theme, Ex. 15, returns, stronger now.

Rhythm must be rigidly enforced. The scherzo rushes forward in all its fierce strength, charged with dramatic impulse. The heavy brass roars forth, Ex. 15, pushing forward until there is an overwhelming appearance of the liturgical theme, flutes and piccolo whirling away in the heights. It is a stupendous achievement, and, as it proves, a catharsis. In the Epilogue the strings are finely divided and through this magical web of tone Ex. 15 sounds on horns. The sense of peace attained is almost as ecstatic as the crisis we have just undergone. It is one of Bax's sublimest inspirations.

Then, as horns and violas chant distantly the first phrase of Ex. 15, then clarinets, then strings, four horns whisper Ex. 16 for the last time and all is hushed. Resignation, at length? No, a sense of sanctuary secured. Bax seeks haven in a remote world of supernal beauty.

That is the atmosphere breathed in the seventh symphony. The work is simpler in texture, mellower in expression than its forebears. If the first movement expresses struggle, the lyrical slow movement indicates flight to a realm of legend. A land of music, possibly, for, in the finale, Bax finds leisure to state a theme, to work out a set of formal variations, and once more to discover the tranquillity of absolute peace in an epilogue.

These seven works have occupied a span of seventeen years of the composer's life. Changes of outlook and of method were to be expected. From the conflict of the first trilogy to the more serene atmosphere of the last symphony is a normal human process, and Bax does not seem to have been greatly stirred by the events of the times in which he lives. Apart from his nostalgia for regions not quite real, his problems would appear to be purely musical problems.

His social position has enabled him to be independent of public office, teaching, and the many bugbears which beset creative artists. His symphonic works leave the impression of a keen intellect and a subtle feeling for beauty which is well-nigh tyranny. He has been called a musician's composer. The term is not without reproach: it implies a close study of effects to be recognized only by a select order. Yet who can imagine an orchestra of his dimensions playing to an audience of theirs? Would that satisfy Bax? Can it be true that having completed these most significant works he is content? That the work done, he cares no more?

The scores themselves almost suggest this to be the case. There are the main themes, individual and characteristic. There is the elaborate development, resourceful and absorbing. And there is the passion for decoration, mostly restrained in the symphonies, but present. Intrinsically their value stands high; extrinsically the stark age in which they were conceived may deduct from their current value a swift depreciation. But time and social development will vindicate their quality.

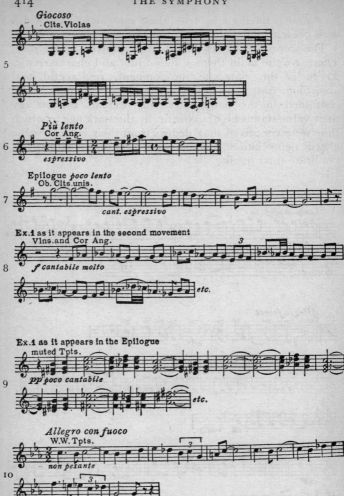

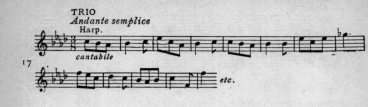